VICTORY IN
AUSTRALIA

Brian Statham, left, and Frank Tyson lead the England players off the
Sydney Cricket Ground after a devastating display of fast bowling had
secured a thrilling 38-run victory.

VICTORY IN AUSTRALIA

THE REMARKABLE STORY OF ENGLAND'S GREATEST ASHES TRIUMPH 1954–55

RICHARD WHITEHEAD

BLOOMSBURY SPORT

LONDON · OXFORD · NEW YORK · NEW DELHI · SYDNEY

BLOOMSBURY SPORT
Bloomsbury Publishing Plc
50 Bedford Square, London, WC1B 3DP, UK
Bloomsbury Publishing Ireland Limited
29 Earlsfort Terrace, Dublin 2, D02 AY28, Ireland

BLOOMSBURY, BLOOMSBURY SPORT and the Diana logo are trademarks of
Bloomsbury Publishing Plc

First published in Great Britain 2025

A catalogue record for this book is available from the British Library

Library of Congress Cataloguing-in-Publication data has been applied for

ISBN: HB: 978-1-3994-1502-6; eBook: 978-1-3994-1503-3

6 8 10 9 7 5

Typeset in Bembo Std by Deanta Global Publishing Services, Chennai, India
Printed and bound in Great Britain by Clays Ltd, Elcograf S.p.A.

MIX
Paper | Supporting
responsible forestry
FSC
www.fsc.org   FSC® C018072

To find out more about our authors and books visit www.bloomsbury.com
and sign up for our newsletters

For product safety related questions contact productsafety@bloomsbury.com

For John Woodcock

1926–2021

The Sage of Longparish

CONTENTS

The MCC squad line up for the camera soon after arrival in Australia. Back row, left to right: Harold Dalton (masseur), Colin Cowdrey, Johnny Wardle, Brian Statham, Tom Graveney, Bob Appleyard, Vic Wilson, Jim McConnon, Frank Tyson, Peter Loader, Keith Andrew, George Duckworth (baggage-master/scorer). Front row: Reg Simpson, Godfrey Evans, Peter May, Len Hutton (captain), Geoffrey Howard (manager), Alec Bedser, Bill Edrich, Trevor Bailey.

INTRODUCTION

The Ashes series of 1954–55 was the high watermark of English cricket in the 30 years after the Second World War. It arrived in the middle of an exhilarating period in which the England team did not lose a Test series for seven and a half years. In contrast to their modern-day counterparts, the players enjoyed fame far beyond the confines of their sport. The captain Len Hutton, the flamboyant batsman Denis Compton, the deadly medium-pacer Alec Bedser, the ebullient wicketkeeper Godfrey Evans, the theatrical fast bowler Fred Trueman, the stylish batsman Peter May and several others were not just elite cricketers, they were household names.

Yet the task of winning an Ashes series in Australia remained formidably hard. As Hutton prepared to lead his players on a six-month assignment in the autumn of 1954, he had no illusions about the extent of the challenge that lay ahead: 'The grounds are hard, the ball is hard, the men are hard – you need to be harder than they are to beat them.'

This would be Hutton's third Ashes tour, and he had absorbed the lessons of thumping defeats in 1946–47 and 1950–51. 'Cricket in Australia demands quicker reflexes simply because everything, by which I principally mean the pace of the ball from hand to batsman or from bat to fieldsman, happens so much more swiftly than in England,' he said. Although he had masterminded a 1–0 victory in the closely fought Coronation series of 1953 – England regaining the

Ashes for the first time in 20 years – it did not necessarily mean his team were favourites to repeat the success away from home.

Winning in England was one thing, achieving victory in Australia represented a task of a quite different order. Hutton understood from bitter experience that a potent pace attack held the key to success. 'These people use Tommy guns and we use water pistols,' he complained to his opening partner Cyril Washbrook during one doomed Ashes assignment. This time, however, he felt he had the weapons in his armoury to match the home team in this key battleground. In the shape of Brian Statham and the untried but extremely quick Frank Tyson, Hutton believed he had the ammunition to counter the threat of the Australian new-ball pair Ray Lindwall and Keith Miller.

But before he could walk up the gangway of the SS *Orsova* for the 10,000-mile voyage to defend the Ashes, Hutton had to overcome a determined effort to remove him from the captaincy by some of the most influential figures in the sport. Although a private members club, the Marylebone Cricket Club (MCC) acted as the governing body of English cricket. Deeply conservative and isolated from the social revolution that was beginning to reshape society, they had only reluctantly appointed Hutton in 1952 as England's first professional captain.

There were senior figures within MCC's headquarters at Lord's who were desperate to restore an amateur – a cricketer of independent means who did not rely on the game for his livelihood – to the leadership before the team left for Australia. In the summer of 1954, this led to an unedifying plot to remove Hutton, causing deep personal distress to a sensitive man who bore the weight of one of the most high-profile jobs in the country with immense dedication and seriousness. Fortunately for England's chances in Australia, the coup failed, and his triumph over the doubters was a historic moment in the development of the English game.

This was the background against which the storied series of 1954–55 began. When it was over, it was clear that England's victory was a landmark achievement which would resonate down the decades. Such a decisive triumph on Australian soil is vanishingly rare and to appreciate its significance it is necessary to delve briefly into historic statistics.

England's 1954–55 win was their solitary success in Australia between 1933 and 1971, and there has been only one since 1987. But to win in Australia after losing the first Test has only one parallel and that was as far back as 1911–12. England's lamentable recent record in Australia only adds lustre to the achievement: in six 21st-century tours, England have won a solitary series and only four Tests. Included in that harrowing casualty list are two 5–0 humiliations and two series surrendered 4–0. All this teetering pile of statistical evidence explains why the triumph of 1954–55 can justifiably be claimed to be the pinnacle of victories in the near 150-year history of the England team.

Hutton was 38 by the time he set out on the assignment that was the culmination of his career ambitions. The mid-1950s marked a tipping point in cricket history when an older generation, who had served in the Second World War and carried English cricket in the difficult years that followed – Hutton, Compton, Bedser, Evans and Bill Edrich – began to fade from the scene to be replaced by an exciting new generation of talent – May, Colin Cowdrey and Tom Graveney, as well as Tyson and Statham.

The nature of the tour makes it an almost unrecognisable enterprise from the one undertaken under the captaincy of another Yorkshireman, Joe Root, in 2017–18 (the Ashes tour of 2021–22 was played under Covid restrictions and is not a valid comparison). With long-haul air travel in its infancy, Hutton's team travelled by sea, taking 23 days to reach Australia. Once there, they did not leave for the next five months. With two Test matches in New Zealand tacked on to the end, the entire tour lasted nearly six months. Hutton opted for a recuperative sea journey back to the UK, extending his total absence from home to eight months.

His team were in Australia for 50 days before the first Test, playing seven matches to become attuned to climate and conditions. The Ashes series began in Brisbane on 26 November and finished on 3 March. During that time, the players travelled thousands of miles across a vast country. Flying was still a new and sometimes unnerving experience, and more often they packed into hot, uncomfortable trains, sometimes travelling overnight. It was a tour in the genuine sense of the word. As well as the major cricket centres of Brisbane, Sydney, Melbourne and Adelaide, MCC played matches at Bunbury,

Rockhampton, Newcastle, Launceston and Yallourn. These up-country fixtures were designed to fly the flag, tighten the bonds between two nations and give the locals a glimpse of glamorous sportsmen, long before television made their faces ubiquitous.

Root's players experienced Australia rather differently. They flew in around three weeks before the series began and played three warm-up games before the first Test. Once the series had begun there was only one match for out-of-form or fringe players to refocus or establish claims to a place. The Ashes were concluded in six-and-a-half weeks, five high-pressure Test matches having been shoehorned into that time. Apart from a warm-up game at Townsville, they did not set foot outside the leading cities. For those players not involved in the subsequent one-day series, the tour lasted a little over two months.

Hutton's party undertook their long and arduous tour with a back-up team of three – manager, baggage-master/scorer and masseur – whereas Root's Test squad contained 16 support staff, including coaches for fast bowling, spin bowling and fielding, a specialist in strength and conditioning, a security manager and a performance psychologist.

Yet it is misleading to view the Test series of 1954–55 entirely through a rose-tinted lens. The contests were as keenly fought as any of the modern era. 'Hutton's was a side that didn't kiss and hug and mob each other when they won. That would never have done,' John Woodcock, the distinguished cricket correspondent of *The Times*, wrote in 2009. 'They shook hands and patted backs and left it at that. But they cared just as much, and if they were nothing like as fit and muscled as their counterparts today, they made up for that with their craftsmanship.'

It was John who inspired this book. To spend a few hours in his home in the picturesque Test Valley village of Longparish was to be led on a journey through the corridors of cricket history in the company of an expert guide. As *The Times'* cricket correspondent between 1954 and 1987, he witnessed some of the game's greatest moments and counted as close friends some of its leading players. John loved to talk about the tours he had made to cover the England team's winter assignments overseas – to the West Indies, Pakistan, India, New Zealand, South Africa and, in his view best of all, Australia. And it was the 1954–55 series, which began just a few weeks after his appointment by *The Times,* to which his reminiscences regularly returned.

It was the shining light in John's eyes when he talked about the gripping battles and this charismatic group of players that made me want to revisit the series, to study the progress of those Tests in minute detail, and try to recreate the drama for the modern reader. This was sporting theatre of the highest order – a tale that deserves to be retold. I also wanted to capture the characters at the centre of the action – many of whom are among the greatest names in cricket history – and a sense of what it was like to tour Australia more than 70 years ago, when two generations of England cricketers came together in an alliance that gripped the country back home, a nation for whom cricket was still part of everyday life. This is the story of that triumph.

DRAMATIS PERSONAE

England

Len Hutton

The England captain since 1952 and the No.1-ranked batsman in the world since 1950 was feeling the strain of high office and the burden of a nation's expectations. Physically frail and a born worrier, he was drained by the turmoil of the 1953–54 tour of the West Indies. As the first professional to lead England in the 20th century, he felt a keen responsibility to his fellow players.

Bob Appleyard

Able to operate effectively in two styles – brisk off-spin or medium pace – Bradford-born Appleyard had rewritten the record books by taking 200 wickets in his first full season. But he was then struck down by tuberculosis, a threat to more than just his career. His return to action in 1954 was remarkable.

Trevor Bailey

An all-rounder of equal value as batsman, bowler, loyal vice-captain and cussed opponent. No one did more to facilitate England's 1953 recapture of the Ashes, even if it meant resorting to blatant gamesmanship. His dedication to winning – or at least not losing – was regarded with suspicion by senior figures at MCC.

Alec Bedser

A record-breaking wicket haul in the 1953 Ashes, plus his propensity for bowling unplayable deliveries, made the Surrey seamer the bowler most feared by the Australians. He was rested in the winter of 1953–54 to conserve his energy for the Ashes assignment.

Denis Compton

Still the most naturally gifted batsman in England, even if his persistent knee problems – a national obsession – often left him hobbling. He had a great tour of Australia in 1946–47 and a wretched one four years later. Oozing Hollywood charisma, he enjoyed a hectic social life on tour.

Colin Cowdrey

Just 21 in 1954, he was in his final year at Oxford University, where he was the captain. His elegant strokeplay, allied to a rock-solid technique, offered hope to all those who craved a revival in classical amateur batsmanship.

Bill Edrich

At 38 and after a period in exile caused by wild off-the-field excess, his Test career was widely assumed to be over. But Hutton valued the gutsy qualities Edrich had shown in abundance during RAF combat missions in the Second World War, for which he was awarded a Distinguished Flying Cross.

Godfrey Evans

The best wicketkeeper in the world was pure box office and the heartbeat of the England side in the field. For that, and his gift for the spectacular moment that could turn a match, Hutton tolerated his late nights and love of a party.

Jim Laker

Although his first-class debut was delayed by the war – where he honed his off-breaks on matting wickets in Egypt – he quickly became a feared opponent. 'He makes you think,' said Hutton. Yet his regular impressive hauls for Surrey failed to convince the England captain that he had the stomach for Test combat.

Tony Lock

A match-winner in the Oval victory that wrested the Ashes from Australia in 1953, there were nevertheless mutterings about the kink in his action, not least from the Australians, especially when he bowled his lethal quicker ball.

Peter May

Technically accomplished Surrey batsman who, at 24, should have been approaching his peak. But he had been targeted by the Australians in 1953 and had played in just two of the Tests. A century on a Port-of-Spain featherbed on the 1953–54 tour had not entirely satisfied the doubters. Widely considered to be future captaincy material.

David Sheppard

The establishment's top choice to replace Hutton was a fine batsman as well as a public school- and Cambridge-educated amateur. But his future in the game was complicated by his decision to play only when his studies to join the Church allowed.

Brian Statham

Fast as well as accurate, he impressed his captain with his uncomplaining day-in-day-out application as well as his wicket-taking in the West Indies. Neville Cardus thought his fellow Lancastrian looked 'as if he had escaped from a Lowry canvas.'

Fred Trueman

The tearaway Yorkshire fast bowler, around whom myths and legends were already beginning to coalesce, was probably too young and raw – on and off the field – to be selected for the West Indies tour, and he had done his future prospects no good at all.

Frank Tyson

A rival for Trueman in pace, but otherwise poles apart, he was reading English Literature at Durham University and was known to recite Wordsworth while walking back to his mark. While a handful of games for Northamptonshire had revealed potential, it amounted to little more than that.

Australia

Ian Johnson
One of three candidates for the vacant Australian captaincy, Johnson, a purveyor of slow off-spin, had not been selected for the 1953 Ashes tour and seemed to be drifting out of the game until given a pep talk at a party by outgoing captain Lindsay Hassett.

Ray Lindwall
The best fast bowler in the world, the mere mention of his name struck fear into English hearts. In naming him a Cricketer of the Year in 1949, *Wisden* praised his 'superb control of length and direction, his change of pace and general skill, the like of which in a slower bowler could be classed as cunning.'

Keith Miller
Alongside his great pal, and fellow party animal Compton the tousle-haired Miller was the most charismatic cricketer in the world. A dangerous fast bowler and a batsman capable of match-turning innings, his smart captaincy of New South Wales was winning admirers.

Arthur Morris
The third captaincy contender was the solid left-handed opener from New South Wales who had hit three hundreds in the 1948 series. Despite being just 5 ft 9 in, he had a presence that intimidated some bowlers.

MCC

Ronny Aird
'Lord's was never a happier place than during his secretaryship,' said one tribute on his retirement. With his staff, Aird undertook the huge logistical task of organising the tour of Australia, although he was not above internal MCC politics.

Gubby Allen
Shaping up to be the most powerful figure in the committee rooms at Lord's as his mentor Sir Pelham Warner (80) began to take a back

seat, he was captain of England before and after the war, steeped in the amateur ethos and remained wary of Hutton.

Harry Altham

In 1954, Altham became chairman of the home selection panel and of the group choosing the squad for Australia. He had been awarded the DSO and the Military Cross in the First World War, and was Treasurer of MCC and a distinguished cricket historian. Despite being as much of an Establishment figure as the rest of the Lord's cabal, he was a staunch supporter of Hutton.

Walter Robins

An arch intriguer who was at the root of the plot to unseat Hutton, Robins, an attacking leg-spinner, had captained England against New Zealand in 1937 (Hutton's debut series) and was an advocate of 'brighter cricket'. He could be temperamental and was once thrown off a golf course by Enid Blyton.

Three great wicketkeepers: George Duckworth, MCC's baggage-master
and scorer, hands the gloves to Keith Andrew (centre) with the approval
of Godfrey Evans (right).

Original Publication: Picture Post – Book of the Tests 1954–5 – Denzil Batchelor

The moment of truth at the Gabba: Len Hutton watches Ian Johnson toss the coin before the first Test.

I

DEBACLE IN BRISBANE

'A gamble more fitted for Monte Carlo than Brisbane'
Australian journalist R.S. Whitington on
England's decision to put Australia
in after winning the toss

*'Alec Bedser's bowling may ultimately be the chief factor in deciding
the destination of the Ashes'*
Former Australian captain Lindsay Hassett
before the series began

*'When we take our catches – and when we have just a modicum of
luck – we can beat this Aussie side'*
Frank Tyson remains optimistic
after England's defeat

DRAMA AT THE TOSS

Ian Johnson waited … and waited. The newly appointed captain of Australia, resplendent in his green and gold-trimmed blazer, paused with a coin in his hand and looked across at his opposite number Len Hutton. But the England captain, also immaculate with a navy blue MCC touring blazer worn over his whites, did not meet his eyes, his mind clearly distracted and elsewhere. As Hutton prevaricated, a small posse of photographers was also being kept waiting. It was 11.05 a.m. on Friday 26 November, 1954, and the group were gathered in the middle of the Brisbane Cricket Ground. Johnson and Hutton were about to toss up before the first match of a five-Test Ashes series: custom and practice was that the home captain would flip the coin, the other would call, and the winner of that first preliminary duel would declare an intention to bat or bowl.

Only this time it didn't happen like that. Instead, Johnson stood by while Hutton conducted an intensive examination of the pitch. Earlier Hutton had completed a thorough inspection with a coterie of his senior players. Now, he kept Johnson hanging around while he fussed over the surface again, walking up and down the 22-yard strip three times, rubbing and prodding the parched earth like a cautious second-hand car buyer examining the bodywork of a prospective purchase.

Finally, Hutton signalled he was ready and Johnson flipped the coin. The photographers snapped away before rushing off to the pictogram machines that would transport their pictures 10,000 miles back to England, providing a whiff of exoticism for millions of newspaper readers as they coped with a devastating blast of high winds, torrential rain and flooding. Hutton called 'heads' and the coin came down in his favour, the first time he had won the toss in what was his sixth Test as captain against Australia. But he would not be rushed into giving his decision: there were no broadcasters clamouring to know his intentions, no interview to relay the news to thousands of TV viewers, no big screens to announce the tidings to the spectators filing into the ground. Instead, Hutton began to head back towards the pavilion with a quizzical Johnson at his side. 'We walked off and he still hadn't said a word,' Johnson recalled. 'We

were almost at the gate when he said, "You can take first strike, Ian."
I said, "Thanks Len."'

It was a moment of huge significance for both men. Despite not
having played Test cricket for two years, Johnson, soon to celebrate
his 37th birthday, had been named a week earlier to lead Australia's
mission to win back the Ashes surrendered in England in 1953. He
was all too aware that there were many among his countrymen,
and some among his teammates, who believed that the luminescent
all-rounder Keith Miller or the dutifully diligent vice-captain Arthur
Morris would have been better appointments. Outside Johnson's
native Victoria, there was a widely voiced view that he owed his
promotion to a long friendship with former teammate Sir Donald
Bradman, now the chairman of selectors – or at least to Bradman's
antipathy to Miller.

For Hutton, 38, the occasion was even more portentous. The end
of his Test career was drawing near – his fragile constitution would
not stand the strains of international sport for much longer – but
he considered it the culmination of his life's work to become the
first professional England captain to win a Test series in Australia.
He had returned earlier in the year from a stormy tour of the West
Indies mentally and physically exhausted, and had spent much of the
summer of 1954 laid low by fatigue and back trouble. He played in
only two of England's four Tests against Pakistan, scraping 19 runs,
and had been burdened by the additional strain of a plot to unseat
him from the captaincy.

Ahead of Hutton, Johnson and their players lay five Test matches
spread over the next three months – Brisbane, Sydney, Melbourne
and Adelaide, then Sydney again in late February. They knew the
contests would be followed with rapt attention in countries separated
by thousands of miles and whose differences at first sight appeared to
be greater than their commonalities.

England was small, cold, damp, only now emerging from the
aftershocks of victory in the greatest war mankind had known,
constantly invoking its great history while becoming increasingly
shackled by it. Australia was a sun-kissed land of vast empty spaces,
endless skies and boundless optimism, increasingly prosperous
and forging its own identity and culture. Yet the presence of the
cricket captains of the two nations in Brisbane that morning was

testimony to how much the nations still shared. Australia's bonds to what many of its citizens still called 'the Mother Country' had been demonstrated just a few months earlier when Queen Elizabeth II's visit had brought vast enraptured crowds out on to its streets.

To play in an Ashes series represented the pinnacle of an English and Australian cricketer's life, a chance to establish a name and reputation that would remain carved in sporting folklore. Yet the reverse was also true: failure in this most forensically examined competition could ruin a hard-won reputation and sabotage a career. The stakes were high, the pressure to perform enormous. Hutton knew this better than anyone; he carried the mental scars from four post-war Ashes series in which he had been constantly in the crosshairs of Australia's fastest bowlers Ray Lindwall and Keith Miller.

But the two captains also knew that the unfolding narrative of the coming weeks would be just part of the stories of their lives. Like many of the men who played under them, they had been grateful to be able to resume careers interrupted by the Second World War. In March 1941, Hutton slipped on a mat in an army gymnasium, fracturing his left forearm and suffering a dislocation of the ulna at the base of the wrist. It was a career-threatening injury which required three operations to correct. As a result, his left arm was almost two inches shorter than his right. 'It took so long to become sound that I began to wonder if I ever would play again,' he said in the late 1980s. He had to remodel his technique and was never again able to play free of pain. Johnson had his own war stories after serving in a Beaufighter squadron in the Royal Australian Air Force, where he reached the rank of flight-lieutenant and saw action in the south Pacific.

The sun shone from a blue Queensland sky as the temperature inched towards its zenith. With an early-afternoon peak of 25°C (78°F), this was not a hot day by Brisbane's standards, nor was there the level of subtropical humidity which can make the city one of the most challenging places in the world to play cricket. But for the England players who had recently endured one of the dampest home summers in memory, the Australian climate was one more formidable obstacle to overcome if they were to retain the Ashes.

Hutton's decision to put Australia in, now conveyed to the crowd via the PA system, was a sensation. In most team sports, the toss of a coin before the action begins is of little significance, but in cricket it dictates the terms on which the battle is fought. The statistics suggesting Hutton had made a serious miscalculation were piled high, like the watertight evidence of a lawyer about to open an unlosable case.

In this the 391st Test match, it was only the 35th occasion that a captain winning the toss had asked the opposition to bat first (there had been only seven instances in Australia). Just eight of those 35 had resulted in victories for the side who had taken the bold option, while 14 times the move had ended in defeat. In 163 previous England-Australia contests, the captain winning the toss had put in the opposition only 10 times. England had not taken such a gamble in the Ashes since the Headingley Test of 1926, when Arthur Carr had then been forced into a rearguard action to save the match after following on. No England captain in Australia had put the home team in since Johnny Douglas at Melbourne in February 1912. Douglas's team had won by an innings, but that was in the fourth Test with England already 2–1 ahead – a knockout punch designed to floor a tottering opponent. It was the only occasion – home or away – on which England had won after putting Australia in: Hutton was going against orthodoxy in the opening match of a series that was, pundits and bookmakers agreed, too close to call.

'A gamble more fitted for Monte Carlo than Brisbane,' wrote the Australian journalist R.S. Whitington. John Arlott recalled 'little bonfires of argument' around the ground as the news was digested. 'It is not the kind of gamble I care for,' sniffed Alan Ross of the *Observer*. MCC tour manager Geoffrey Howard had been delayed by administrative duties at the team hotel, but when he eased into his seat a few minutes after play began at 11.30 he was surprised to see Alec Bedser running in to bowl and Australia openers Arthur Morris and Les Favell at the crease.

However, Hutton's intentions should he win the toss had been predicted since, two days earlier, he had emerged from a meeting of the tour selection panel – Hutton, Howard, vice-captain Peter May, wicketkeeper Godfrey Evans and batsman Bill Edrich, with input from former England wicketkeeper George Duckworth, the tour party's scorer and baggage-master – to name a team nervously bolstered by the inclusion of six batsmen, but with just four bowlers, all of them seamers. Bedser, Brian Statham, Frank Tyson and Trevor Bailey were being asked to shoulder an enormous burden, more especially since in Australia first-class matches featured eight-ball overs.[1]

As the majority of English journalists concluded, the one-dimensional attack left Hutton little alternative but to try to exploit any early assistance from the pitch if the toss gave him the opportunity. 'Obviously Hutton will be guided finally by the look and feel of the wicket on Friday morning, but the strong likelihood is that he will take the plunge,' E. W. Swanton told his readers in the *Daily Telegraph*. 'Indeed the shape of the attack makes doing so almost imperative.'

There was less understanding about the absence of a spinner in the XI. 'It's enough to make the diehards of the past eat their beards in fury,' spluttered the *Daily Herald*'s Charles Bray. 'It's not even three fast bowlers and a spinner – heaven help their poor feet by the end of this Test.' Swanton calculated that in 314 Tests, England had only once not selected a spinner. That had been at Melbourne on the Bodyline tour 22 years earlier and had resulted in their only defeat of the series. He summed up the mood in Brisbane: 'There is thunder in the sky and thunder in the cricket community.'

Perhaps the press pack were miffed because the unexpectedly early team announcement upset their early-evening plans. 'We were going off to a cocktail party at Government House with the Governor of Queensland,' John Woodcock of *The Times* recalled. Drinks and polite conversation had to be delayed while stories were hastily filed. Woodcock voiced what everyone was thinking. 'Who is going to bowl spin?' he asked Hutton. The England captain said that Edrich, who rarely bowled his off-breaks for Middlesex, would provide any overs of slow bowling that might be

---

[1] Eight-ball overs continued in Australian cricket until the 1979–80 season, when they were reduced to six, as standard in the rest of the world.

needed.[2] That led to more scepticism from the correspondents and reinforced a theme they had all been pursuing during the build-up matches – why on earth had Denis Compton, who had bowled just one over on tour, not been given a chance to sharpen his left-arm wrist-spin?

This was the team, in batting order, that Hutton would lead at the start of the defence of the Ashes:

	County	Age	Tests
★L. Hutton	Yorkshire	38	72
R.T. Simpson	Nottinghamshire	34	24
P.B.H. May	Surrey	24	17
M.C. Cowdrey	Kent	21	0
D.C.S. Compton	Middlesex	36	63
W.J. Edrich	Middlesex	38	35
T.E. Bailey	Essex	30	27
†T.G. Evans	Kent	34	57
F.H. Tyson	Northamptonshire	24	1
A.V. Bedser	Surrey	36	49
J.B. Statham	Lancashire	24	17

12th man: J.V. Wilson (Yorkshire)

When the team news reached the UK, Yorkshire captain Norman Yardley, vice-captain on the first post-war Ashes tour in 1946–47, was about to address the annual dinner of the Wensleydale Cricket League. Gravely, he said the line-up represented 'a bit of a gamble'. His views were reported on the front page of the *Yorkshire Post*, while inside cricket correspondent J.M. Kilburn, Hutton's staunchest ally among the travelling journalists, wrote, 'The selection seems to offer alarming hostages to fortune.'

So why did Hutton abandon his native caution for what seemed such a high-risk strategy? Several factors were at work. First, and above all, was his belief that if the Ashes were to be won it would be by pace. 'We have two fast bowlers, something we have not had

---

[2]Edrich had once been one of the fastest bowlers in England – at Lord's in 1938 he broke Hutton's finger ruling him out for a month. Hutton returned just before his record-breaking innings of 364 against Australia at The Oval, but by 1954, Edrich was bowling largely innocuous off-breaks.

for a good many years,' he told BBC Television's recently launched programme *Sportsview* in the build-up to the Test. Tyson and Statham were Hutton's shock troops, but he also had the leading Test wicket-taker in the world in Bedser – the scourge of Australia in four series since the war – and the lively fast-medium of all-rounder Bailey. These four were inked in to play before the MCC party landed in Fremantle, but other unforeseen complications had emerged in the six weeks since.

One was the lack of wicket-taking penetration shown by the trio of spinners in the party, Bob Appleyard, Johnny Wardle and Jim McConnon. Between them they had collected just 19 wickets in the six first-class tour matches, with only Appleyard's second-innings five for 46 against South Australia offering a suggestion of match-winning potential. Still troubled by a rib injury he had picked up in a collision with a spectator during the stop-over match in Ceylon (now Sri Lanka), Appleyard had struggled to adapt to conditions that were entirely alien. For Yorkshire, he switched between conventional seam and swing with the new ball or medium-pace off-spin when the ball got older or conditions were helpful. Neither seemed to work in Australia. 'The ground was very hard, and coming in to bowl was like running on concrete, which I found very difficult,' he explained. 'The ball didn't turn as much as it did in England and it didn't swing either.'

McConnon, controversially chosen ahead of Jim Laker to fill the off-spinning role, was out of the running anyway, hospitalised after being hit an excruciating blow in the groin while fielding at short leg in the tour match against Queensland. In the same game, Wardle, who bowled left-arm wrist-spin and orthodox slow left-arm, had seen his chances of making the Test XI hit when he was on the receiving end of some heavy punishment from Queensland's tailenders.

Hutton's mind may have been finally made up by an open-wicket practice session held on the same pitch the day after the conclusion of the state match. On a worn surface offering them some assistance, neither Appleyard nor Wardle made a compelling case for inclusion. Nevertheless, the absence of a recognised slow bowler reignited the debate that had raged after the prolific Surrey pair Tony Lock and Jim Laker were left out of the tour party in July. 'Wright or Lock, one feels, would have been sure of a place tomorrow,' wrote Woodcock, dragging Kent leg-spinner Doug Wright into the argument, even though he hadn't played a Test for four years and had taken just 11 Test wickets in Australia in 1950–51.

The *Daily Mail* was more shrill, calling for Lock to be summoned from his fireside. 'Hutton must wire home Send Lock' ran the headline. 'Lock is in a class of his own,' wrote correspondent Alex Bannister, insisting Lock could be ready to play in the third Test at Melbourne on New Year's Eve if he flew out now. Bannister then rather shot down his own story – or at least the headline cooked up by the sports desk in London – by adding, 'It is up to Hutton, and I think he would be most reluctant to add to his already overburdened party.' Bannister did reveal, however, that an unnamed Australian batsman had been distinctly unimpressed after facing Appleyard in a tour match. 'Surely Appleyard was hiding something from me because he never once turned the ball,' Bannister had been told.

In naming six batsmen plus Bailey, the tour selectors were influenced by the fragility of MCC's top order in the build-up matches. Those who could be said to be in decent form were only Hutton, with hundreds against Western Australia and New South Wales, and 98 against South Australia; Denis Compton, with centuries against South Australia and Queensland; and Colin Cowdrey, with a hundred in each innings against New South Wales. Edrich was a renowned Test-match scrapper, but he went into the match with a tour average of nine.

The England players greeted the team announcement with scarcely more enthusiasm than the press. On emerging from the selection meeting Evans relayed the news to Bailey. 'Good God, I must have a double Scotch straight away,' Bailey said. 'Fancy picking a side like that. The last time this was done, Jardine did it and it didn't work then.' The quotes may have owed something to the inventiveness of Evans's ghostwriter, but the subsequent bar-room chat left a lasting impression on the wicketkeeper. 'I have always felt that if Trevor hadn't taken that gloomy view of our prospects we might have done better,' he wrote in his autobiography. 'It spread to the side and I am quite certain that it reacted badly on almost everyone. Despondency is infectious.' Tyson, meanwhile, recalled, 'It looks as if we want to bowl first hoping to exploit what early life there is in the pitch.

Quite a gamble when you consider that the weather forecast is set fine and hot for the next few days.'

The Australian selection, made 24 hours before the announcement of Johnson's captaincy, caused less controversy but was not greeted with unanimous approval either. By naming a squad of 12 with an average age of 28½ and 251 caps, the selectors – Bradman, Jack Ryder and Dudley Seddon[3] – were treading warily. Les Favell, the 25-year-old opener from South Australia, was the only new face. 'Not a very inspiring team at all. England have little cause to worry much about their prospects now. Nor have our selectors given us much to boost our confidence,' growled former Australia leg-spinner Bill O'Reilly, a long-time Bradman adversary.

Bradman flew into Brisbane from Adelaide the day before the Test, passing time on the flight by reading Hutton's autobiography *Cricket is My Life*. He was joined on the plane by umpire Mel McInnes, an official in the South Australia Mines Department, who would be standing in his eighth Test, but his first at Brisbane.

With the captaincy still to be rubber-stamped, this was the Australian XII:

	State	Age	Tests
L.E. Favell	South Australia	25	0
A.R. Morris	New South Wales	32	38
K.R. Miller	New South Wales	34	40
R.N. Harvey	Victoria	26	29
G.B. Hole	South Australia	23	15
R. Benaud	New South Wales	24	8
R.G. Archer	Queensland	21	4
R.R. Lindwall	Queensland	33	38
†G.R.A. Langley	South Australia	35	14
I.W. Johnson	Victoria	36	28
W.A. Johnston	Victoria	32	24
A.K. Davidson	New South Wales	25	5

[3] Jack Ryder had played in 20 Tests in the 1920s and captained Australia in the 1928–29 Ashes series, when Bradman made his debut. He was a selector from 1946 to 1970. Dudley Seddon did not play Test cricket, but was a selector between 1954 and 1967.

As it turned out, England's early announcement was no guarantee against the scuppering of their best-laid plans. When Hutton led his team out, Evans was missing from the group. His indisposition was variously described as a chill, flu or heat stroke, the result of an over-energetic game of squash two days earlier. Masseur Harold Dalton recorded in his diary that the wicketkeeper had a temperature of 101°. 'Doctored him up,' Dalton wrote. Remembering the misery of sitting in his hotel room recovering from septic boils on his foot and wrist during the Trinidad Test the previous winter, Evans was desperate to play. A doctor left the decision to him after a final examination two hours before the start, but he had spent a wretched sleepless night and Evans knew it would be taking too much of a risk.

Instead, after just one full season in county cricket with Northamptonshire, Keith Andrew, 24, would make his Test debut. He had never even seen a Test match. Andrew, married less than two weeks before England's departure in September and destined not to be reunited with his wife, Joyce, for another five months, heard of Evans's illness on the radio in his hotel room. He spent a twitchy, sleep-deprived night. No one knocked on his door to prepare or reassure him. 'You'll be all right, lad,' Duckworth, who had been England's wicketkeeper in the 1928–29 series, said – but that was the extent of his pre-match briefing.

The loss of Evans was incalculable. His habitual sloppiness in county matches may have infuriated his Kent colleagues, but under the arc lights of Test cricket he was generally recognised as the best wicketkeeper in the world, certainly since the retirement of the silky Australian Don Tallon the previous year. His worth to the side was not just measured in his glovework, but can be judged in the words his teammates used to describe him: 'the fulcrum of inspiration', 'the chief whip', 'the shop steward'. Andrew, who had not previously observed Evans at close quarters, noted, 'His effervescent personality brought the whole day to life and very often part of the night.'

Andrew had been named as Evans's deputy for the cool unobtrusive excellence of his wicketkeeping. 'He takes Tyson's thunderbolts as a butler might accept a calling card, with no notice at all,' wrote Alan Ross. 'He would not, I think, get near some of the things Evans catches: but greatness and great competence are rarely akin.' However, all agreed, a player who had made his County Championship debut only six months earlier could not be expected to slot seamlessly into the role of the team's chief cheerleader.

DUEL UNDER THE SUN

Keith Andrew was put to the test immediately. From the Vulture Street End with the pavilion behind him, Alec Bedser marked out his six-stride run-up and loosened his huge frame. His imposing physique – 6 foot 3 and 15 stone – was not the reason Bedser struck cold fear into the hearts of Australians. After a Test debut delayed by the war, Bedser, now 36, had taken 103 Ashes wickets at an average of 26. No one had taken more in an England-Australia series than his 39 in 1953.[4]

As the cricket historian David Frith wrote, 'Most of the world's top batsmen in the late 1940s and early 1950s attributed to Bedser the finest ball bowled to them.' In the build-up, the Australian newspapers conveyed the sense of awe with which he was viewed. 'Alec Bedser's bowling may ultimately be the chief factor in deciding the destination of the Ashes,' wrote Lindsay Hassett, Australia's captain in 1953, in a syndicated column in the *Brisbane Courier-Mail*. In the same newspaper later in the week, the caption on a picture of Bedser and twin brother Eric playing bowls began 'Cricket's greatest bowler.' It was a neat sub-editor's pun, but the respect was obvious.

Bedser's mastery was not achieved by high pace: he bowled at around 75-80 mph, well below the speeds generated by Ray Lindwall and Keith Miller or Frank Tyson and Brian Statham. His stock delivery moved into the right-handed batsman, and he utilised his shovel-like hands to spin rather than cut his leg-break. He rarely deployed the outswinger, fearing it would scramble his radar-like accuracy, though his natural delivery moved away from the left-hander, a noteworthy point given that Australia's two key batsmen, Arthur Morris and Neil Harvey, batted left-handed.

[4]This total has been surpassed five times since, and is led by Jim Laker's 46 wickets in 1956.

The challenge to Andrew's reflexes did not come from speed: instead it was that Bedser insisted on having his wicketkeeper standing up to the stumps. With Arthur McIntyre at Surrey and Evans with England, he had established a telepathic understanding, but Andrew had kept to Bedser only once, in the tour match that had finished earlier that week. By common agreement, he had done a fine job, but now he had been thrust into the pressure-cooker environment of an Ashes Test. What he did not know was that Bedser was harbouring his own doubts. On arrival in Australia two months earlier he had contracted shingles, a painful viral condition that left a rash over his right shoulder. He had missed the first three first-class games and despite getting through 31 overs (and taking two wickets) against Queensland, privately he was not entirely sure his recovery was complete.

'I wanted to play and Hutton wanted me – but the plain fact was I was not fit enough,' Bedser recalled. 'None of the doctors were able to forecast how long it would take for me to recover my strength.' His readiness had been the subject of considerable debate among the tour selectors. In the end, as Evans revealed, 'It was generally felt that Alec should play because of the psychological effect on the opposition.'

There was enough breeze to ruffle Bedser's shirt as he set a field of two slips, Edrich and May, a gully, and three close-to-the-wicket fielders on the leg side – Compton, Cowdrey and Hutton, the captain positioning himself at leg slip. The cinematic grandeur of the occasion, the vital importance of the opening exchanges, and the knowledge that two well-matched sides were about to lock horns sent a palpable frisson of excitement around the ground. It even cut through the seen-it-all world weariness of the press box. 'One was conscious of how many miles had been travelled, how many weeks spent in preparation, for just this,' wrote Alan Ross. 'Bedser loped up under sierras of high cloud, Favell took a good-length ball high up on the pad and the hollow in the pit of the stomach stirred.' For the debutant Les Favell, the moment was terrifying. 'What am I doing out here?' he remembered thinking. There was another dot ball before Favell pushed Bedser's third delivery down to mid-off for the first run of the series.

That brought the resumption of one of Test cricket's epic rivalries. Bedser was Morris's nemesis, dismissing him 18 times in Tests. No bowler in Test history had achieved such mastery over an opponent.[5] In 1953, Bedser had taken Morris's wicket in the first innings of each of the five matches. But it was not an entirely lopsided contest. Morris had scored 696 Test runs at 87 in England in 1948, and by the end of his career had an average of more than 50 against England. On the field, their rivalry was intense, but off it the pair were the warmest of friends. After Bedser dismissed Morris four times in five innings in 1950–51, the England seamer handed him a copy of Hassett's book *Better Cricket* with the sections on batting helpfully underlined. When Morris hit a double-century in the next match at Adelaide, he handed the book back, with the bowling tips highlighted.

But there must have been anxiety in Morris's mind as Bedser ran in. A tendency to shuffle across his crease had regularly been his undoing in 1953, and his determination to correct that technical fault and to ignore the temptation presented by balls pitched on his leg stump came at the expense of fluency. He survived these early examinations but little more. At the Railway End, Hutton handed the new ball to Statham, calculating that he would have a better chance of extracting any early movement than the express pace of Tyson. With Bedser added to the slip cordon, Statham introduced Favell to the unforgiving intensity of Test cricket with a textbook maiden. 'Favell did his best to find the ball with the bat's edge and failed, and then was so nearly bowled that the stumps still standing looked ashamed of themselves,' wrote J.M. Kilburn.

It was in Bedser's second over that an incident occurred that echoed down the decades and might have changed the course of the match, and the careers of the bowler and England's tyro wicketkeeper. To the fourth delivery, Morris got an inside edge and the ball deflected sharply to Andrew's right: it was a fractional chance at best – there was no run, the over was another maiden and, in the absence of any reaction on the field, none of the journalists made anything of it. 'It

[5] The record is now held by Australia's Glenn McGrath, who dismissed England opener Mike Atherton 19 times, but Bedser–Morris is still second on the list.

was not known to us at the time that Morris was dropped before scoring,' wrote E.M. Wellings of the *Evening News* in his tour book *The Ashes Retained*. 'Evans might have made the catch, but there can be no certainty about that.'

In his close-of-play report, syndicated to daily newspapers around the UK, Norman Preston praised Andrew's 'quiet efficient wicketkeeping. He could feel well satisfied with his first day as a Test player. Certainly he has not let down the side.' Andrew remembered the crucial moment vividly in Stephen Chalke's biography, *Guess My Story*, explaining that it was a thick inside edge and when you're standing up to medium-pace you can only take the line of the ball, so you don't have time to adjust to edges. 'I didn't keep that well,' he said, 'but, as God is my judge, I never got my hands anywhere near that ball. When I went into lunch, I never felt that I'd missed a catch.'

Yet over the next few days the narrative began to shift. In his second-day report for Sunday's *News of the World*, Harry Ditton wrote, 'Though young Keith Andrew, as understudy to Godfrey Evans, kept passably well the fact is that he missed Morris off Bedser before he had scored.' Andrew was also upbraided by Alf Gover in the *Sunday Pictorial*, and Ross's *Observer* piece mentioned it too. Not all saw it as an opportunity spurned. 'He who holds the mistake against Andrew is indeed a capricious critic,' thought Wellings. The Australian journalist and former Test player Alan Fairfax, writing for the English Sunday title the *People*, believed Andrew had been 'magnificent'.

For writers who had not even been aware of the edge – Andrew was standing at the far end from the press box, which looked over mid-off – suddenly to bring it to the attention of their readers indicates there may have been some hotel-bar muttering from the players on the evening of the first day. In a change of tack, *Wisden* editor Preston highlighted it in his match report for the 1956 Almanack. Bedser's biographer, Alan Hill, bemoaned Andrew's 'lapse' on his subject's behalf. The choice of word brought an indignant response from tour manager Geoffrey Howard. 'No, no, no. That's most unfair,' he told Chalke. 'It was off the inside edge. Alec always made the ball hit the ground hard, it bounced a lot, and he got late swing. An edge like that, any wicketkeeper would be lucky to take it.' Tyson, Andrew's friend and county colleague, reflected, 'It was hardly a chance, but substitutes for Godfrey Evans must expect comparisons.'

Reprieved or not, Morris and Favell batted on. While the England bowlers toiled to extract any help from the pitch or the atmospheric conditions, they remained admirably disciplined. It was not until the seventh over that Morris got off the mark and it was the eighth before Australia inched into double figures. When drinks were taken after three-quarters of an hour, Australia had crawled to 19. Hutton deployed his attack in three-over bursts – Bedser gave way to Tyson and Statham to Bailey, before Bedser and Statham returned at opposite ends. This was partly to conserve their strength, and partly as a deliberate tactic to slow down the over-rate, a key element of Hutton's strategic thinking.

The eagerly anticipated introduction of Tyson to Australian audiences did not disappoint, his first ball producing 'gasps of astonishment' from the crowd, even if Morris played it comfortably enough to mid-on. Soon after, Morris lost his cap as he evaded a Tyson bouncer. His pace may have impressed, but not his appearance. '"Fearsome Frank" turns out to be a mild and studious-looking young man with a receding hairline,' wrote Arthur Richards of the *Brisbane Courier-Mail*. It quickly became clear, however, that even Tyson's speed was not going to provide the breakthrough that England craved. 'The pitch was, by contrast with its companion lying alongside, a blatant imposter,' said Ian Peebles, the former England leg-spinner, now working for *The Sunday Times*. In shuffling his pack, Hutton had revealed his full hand to Australia in the first 40 minutes.

Disaster, though, was stalking England. When Morris flashed Tyson recklessly over point, Compton ran round from third man in a vain effort to stop the ball going for four. In common with other Australian grounds, the fence marked the boundary, not a rope several feet inside the playing area as is now commonplace. At Brisbane the fence was a wooden construction of the kind usually seen enclosing suburban gardens. Compton put his left hand out to check the momentum of his dash, and caught the third and fourth fingers between the palings. His colleagues gathered around while he ruefully assessed the damage, but he carried on fielding for a few minutes until replaced by 12th man Vic Wilson.

At lunch Compton went to hospital for an x-ray which revealed he had broken the metacarpal bone of his fourth finger. The news plunged the England dressing-room into gloom. At tea, Howard issued a press statement saying that Compton would not field for the remainder of the match and would bat only in an emergency. Already it seemed certain he would miss the second Test. 'Compton breaks finger' was the front-page headline in that night's London *Evening Standard*, bringing the bad news to Compton's home city.

In Brisbane, the disappointment extended to the crowd at the Gabba. 'When an announcement was made over the public address system telling what had happened, there followed one of the most extraordinary silences I think I have ever heard,' wrote Howard in a letter to MCC assistant secretary Billy Griffith. 'I know that one cannot hear a silence, but you will know what I mean.' R.S. Whitington pointed out that the accident had happened on the same part of the ground where, eight years earlier, Compton had endeared himself to the Australian crowd by accepting a drink from a spectator. 'Nobody but Compton would have kept trying to save that boundary,' he wrote. 'But what would cricket be without Comptons?'

It was a sliver of compensation, but 10 minutes before lunch, and just after Australia had reached 50, England at last made a breakthrough. Favell had looked thoroughly at home in Test cricket in making 23 off 62 balls, but now he miscued an attempted hook off Statham and the ball flew from his glove to short square leg where Cowdrey took a smart low catch. By then Morris was beginning to get ominously into his stride, hoisting a Bedser no-ball for a straight six which landed, Ross noted, 'between two alarmed ladies with parasols, patently at that moment discussing other things'.

It would have done Hutton's growing sense of foreboding no good at all to see Keith Miller striding out into the middle. Only Compton could equal Miller for scene-stealing charisma, and he made his usual theatrical entrance, marching out of the players' gate, head erect, 'arriving at the batting crease as if to imply that everything which had gone before was just an entrée and now we were going to receive the meat of the matter,' wrote Margaret Hughes, an English writer and the lone woman in the press corps, one of a seven-strong team from Sydney's *Daily Telegraph*.

Hutton was right to be worried. After the interval, Miller went on the offensive. He was not a batsman to drag his heels in any circumstances, but now he must have been bristling from the captaincy snub. He took 12 from Bedser's seventh over, the second of a gruelling spell of seven in a row from the Railway End, including a no-ball that disappeared for six over long-on, dispatched with the long, languid swing of a professional golfer: the mighty blow, wrote Woodcock, would have 'cleared the spire of Salisbury Cathedral'. There was also a late-cut for four off Tyson 'like a beau flicking snuff from his fingertips,' according to Denzil Batchelor in the *Picture Post Book of the Tests*. But when he tried to repeat the stroke against Bailey, he dragged the ball on to his stumps and was gone, one short of his fifty. 'The joy went out of the play when he left,' observed Arthur Gilligan, England's captain in Australia 30 years earlier.

That left Australia 123 for two with tea approaching and Neil Harvey joining Morris in an alliance of the two greatest left-handed batsmen in the world. Undercooked and out of form, Harvey had reached double figures just once in four first-class innings that summer, failing three times against MCC in tour matches. Now 26 and a senior member of the team, he was no longer the fresh-faced teenager who had been one of Don Bradman's Invincibles in 1948. His arrival in Brisbane earlier that week with his South African wife Iris had been deemed worthy of a front-page picture in the *Courier-Mail,* but fame was no guarantee of form. 'Harvey started like a man playing from a memory which he had lost,' wrote the Australian writer and broadcaster A.G. Moyes. Both batsmen played and missed outside off stump, Morris preferring to take blows on the body and collect the bruises rather than succumb to temptation when England pitched short.

In the third over after tea, Morris, on 55, hoisted Bedser down to Bailey coming in off the boundary at fine leg, but a routine catch was spilled, the fielder sinking to his knees as he made a despairing grab at the ball.'The taking of that catch would probably have meant the dismissal of Australia for 250,' thought Wellings. The sense of calamity was increased by the fact that Bailey would not normally have been fielding in the deep. Against Queensland he had damaged two fingers of his right hand in the slips – permission for him to bowl with the fingers strapped had to be sought from Johnson – and it was impossible not to conclude he had been protecting the damaged hand when he attempted to complete the catch.

Morris then edged Tyson through the slips for four while Harvey got in a tangle trying to hook the same bowler and the ball flew over Andrew's head to the boundary. England's outcricket may have been sloppy, but the marginal moments were going against them. Not long before stumps, Harvey might have been run out by a direct hit from Simpson, but the ball whistled past the stumps and went for four overthrows. By the close at 5.30, Australia were 208 for two, with Morris 82 and Harvey 41. England had bowled just 58 eight-ball overs in the day (a rate of 11.6 an hour), which would have been a little over 77 six-ball overs in a home Test, well below, Swanton pointed out, the 20 overs per hour regarded as normal by an English crowd. It was a busy evening for medic Harold Dalton. 'Pace bowlers tired out at the end of the day,' he wrote. Tyson had a touch of sunstroke, Bailey complained of sore feet, Statham needed a late-night massage.

Close of play: Australia 208–2 (Morris 82★, Harvey 41★).

Hutton was inconsolable. 'What's the matter with you, Len?' asked Bedser. 'There's no bloody bombs dropping you know.' Reflecting on the decision more than 30 years later, Hutton regretted not changing his plans when Evans was ruled out. 'When Godfrey was unavailable I should have cancelled my idea of putting them in to bat had we won the toss. That was mistake number one and I don't think we ever really recovered.' This was less a comment on Andrew's wicketkeeping than Evans's role as the team's heartbeat.

There was a further reason why he had made a grave miscalculation. On the first morning, Lindwall was still recovering from what reporters had been told was flu, but in reality was hepatitis that had prevented him from bowling in the second innings of MCC's match against Queensland. His face, reported Whitington, was 'as pallid as an opium addict's'. By the time he was needed to bowl, Lindwall had completed a further three days' convalescence.

The tone of the morning newspaper reports in England was as funereal as the over-rate. 'Upon Hutton, I suppose, will fall the odium for an unsuccessful gamble,' wrote a glum Swanton. 'Misfortune has followed England here today,' said Woodcock, 'thrusting them on to the defensive and ravaging their ranks, and their position at the close of play is unpromising indeed.' 'A black day for England,' said the *Manchester Guardian*'s Denys Rowbotham (the paper did not drop the 'Manchester' from its masthead until 1959).

Hundreds of hand-wringing words were devoted to Hutton's decision at the toss, though most English correspondents believed the team selection made inserting Australia the only option. They felt the England captain had been swayed by Brisbane's reputation rather than the blameless appearance of the wicket when he conducted his morning examinations. Although it would undoubtedly still be hot with high humidity, the nagging worry about having to bat on a drying pitch had been removed by the new regulation which meant the strip was covered once the game began. The key change in the playing conditions had been made at the instigation of Bradman and was, as he explained in a letter to Swanton, to safeguard against a potential loss in income if bad weather drastically reduced playing time. Brisbane's steamy climate and the ever-present threat of rain (no Brisbane Test had been completed without at least one weather interruption) meant that the ground had staged some chaotic Tests.

On their first post-war tour in 1946–47, England lost by an innings after they had to bat twice when violent storms had saturated the wicket. The following year, India were dismissed for 58 and 98 on a wet pitch, and in 1950 England were involved in a bizarre contest in which both captains declared to ensure their opponents had the worst of the gluepot: 20 wickets fell for 102 runs after lunch on the third day. Hutton had played one of the greatest innings of his career in this match, making an unbeaten 62 off 102 balls in conditions lesser mortals found impossible. The downpours meant £A7000 was lost in gate money, a key reason for Bradman's initiative in changing the regulations on covering. The new rules undoubtedly influenced England's selection of a spinner-less line-up and Hutton's conviction that the early exchanges offered his bowlers the best chance of some assistance.

Hutton did not need to consult *Wisden* to be reminded that the Brisbane surface could be capricious. In the opening exchanges of the previous weekend's state match, his team had been reduced to 18 for three when Lindwall and Ron Archer exploited early life in the pitch. The England captain, who was not playing, studied the action intently from a chair placed on the boundary edge. Andy Fisher, the Australian scorer who claimed to have seen every first-class game at the ground since 1911, said he had never seen a faster Gabba wicket. 'If the curator prepares a similar pitch for the Test we are in for some fun and games,' thought Tyson. Another influence on Hutton may have been that asking the opposition to bat had briefly become fashionable. In MCC's six first-class warm-up matches, the captain winning the toss had opted to field four times. Discussing Hutton's decision with the writer Daniel Lightman years later, Queensland captain Ken Archer speculated that his decision in the state match might have influenced Hutton.

TURF WAR

In the days leading up to the Test, Jack McAndrew the Brisbane curator (as groundsmen are known in Australia) had become a minor celebrity, his views on the likely behaviour of his pitch being sought regularly. It had been his policy to prepare wickets with more moisture, which led to them being lively for the early sessions before the heat and rolling crushed any growth of new grass. The promise of helpful surfaces was one of the reasons Ray Lindwall had recently relocated from New South Wales. But the Test strip lay under a tarpaulin, cheek-by-jowl with the wicket for the state match, meaning McAndrew was unable to water the Test pitch until that game was concluded.

None of which had stopped him talking up his wicket's potential for mayhem. Press reports that the pitch would be under an overnight armed guard by 16-stone, 6 foot 3 in Brisbane policeman Sergeant W. Huey added to the sense of menace. 'The pitch will be the fastest Queensland has had because it has more grass than before,' McAndrew told journalists. 'But by Monday or Tuesday it should become suitable for spin bowlers, of whom England is lacking.' Ian Johnson was clear that he would have batted anyway and saw no demons in the wicket. When he walked back into the Australian dressing-room after receiving Len Hutton's belated invitation to bat he was sporting a wide grin. 'Fellas, he's put us in,' he said. 'But it's a beauty and I think he's made a blue.'

Decades later, *The Times*'s John Woodcock speculated that after England's early team announcement McAndrew had taken his mower and shaved off the grass. Geoffrey Howard, however, gave that idea short shrift. It seemed obvious that Hutton had made up his mind, though his agony of indecision at the toss betrayed his conflicted thoughts. 'The way he walked up and down the pitch showed that he didn't want to put us in, but the way the pitch had behaved the previous week preyed on him,' remembered Johnson. 'The fact that it took him so long to decide indicates his reluctance.' Alan Ross wrote, 'Hutton turned a blind Nelsonian eye to the wicket's evident lack of moisture, hoping, doubtless with hand on heart, that pace at the pinch might compensate for nature. It did not.' In the *Daily Mail*, Alex Bannister judged the pitch 'as docile and tame as a pussycat'. Batchelor thought it 'as devoid of vice as the quilt on your maiden aunt's bed'.

The popular papers in England cast around for a scapegoat and found one in McAndrew, an amiable-looking figure in a waistcoat and bush hat who had briefly played for Queensland 30 years earlier. The *Daily Mirror*'s Ross Hall raged, 'Len did not know how inaccurate McAndrew's forecast of the wicket was. A visiting skipper places a lot of faith in what he is told by the local groundsman. After today Hutton is going to be very, very careful in Australia.'

Charles Bray in the *Daily Herald* was similarly scathing. 'In putting Australia in he [Hutton] fell for what must go down in history as the biggest bluff of all time. McAndrew publicly proclaimed the Test wicket would be faster than any ever prepared on the ground and had more grass on it than usual. He must have Irish ancestors. It was pure blarney.' The story gained such credence that Hutton had to publicly deny he had been gulled by the groundsman. The only question he asked McAndrew, he said, had been about watering.

England awoke on the second morning, a Saturday, to find themselves the subject of ridicule. On the front page of Brisbane's *Courier-Mail*, Hutton was depicted as Father Christmas, with white beard and bobble hat (long before Photoshop, the sub-editors' scissors and gluepot must have been deployed) under the headline, 'Hutton ... he's Santa Claus to us.' Writer Arthur Richards gloated, 'England's captain Len Hutton may well be considering a change of costume … Hutton acted the part of Father Christmas to Australia in this Test. He might just as well look the part.'

Like a shipwrecked man thinking he spies land on the far horizon, England clung to the faint hope of dismissing Australia for under 400. The new ball was due immediately – though Hutton did not take it until the fifth over of the morning – but it did not take long for their ambitions to founder on the rocks of their own incompetence in the field. In the second over, Morris, on 89, edged Bedser to second slip, where the diving Peter May could not hold a difficult chance. 'It would have been a brilliant catch had he brought it off, but Test match fielders being judged by the highest standards, it could be reckoned a chance,' said Ian Peebles.

Let off for the third time, Morris completed his 10th Test hundred with an on-drive for four off Bedser. It had taken him 247 balls, with 12 fours and a six, and was his first since his double-century at Adelaide on England's last Ashes tour. It may not have been his most attractive innings, but it was made under conditions of extreme stress. The Australian tax authorities had just delivered a demand for £A718 they calculated Morris owed on his meagre cricket earnings. Newly married to Valerie Hudson, an English showgirl he had met on the 1953 tour, Morris must have been anxious about the wrangle.[6]

With the total on 249, it was Harvey's turn to be given a life when he flicked Bailey off his legs low to Bedser at leg slip, but the ball slipped miserably from his grasp. 'The big fellow went to earth wholeheartedly, but the jerk of the tumble tipped the ball from his hands,' wrote Bruce Harris in the *Evening Standard*. 'Bedser needs them these days at least knee-high,' noted Ross. Hutton then invited scorn in the press box when he gave Edrich his first bowl of the day with the ball still hard and Tyson as yet unused. Morris took seven off Edrich's first over and 14 off his second, and the experiment was rapidly terminated. A good morning for Australia was made even better shortly before lunch when Keith Andrew dived to reach a

---

[6]Hudson was diagnosed with breast cancer in 1955. She came to England for treatment – funded by the West End impresario Vivian Van Damm – during the Ashes series in 1956, when Morris wrote a book on the tour. She died, aged 34, in January 1957.

rapid edge from Morris off Tyson, but could not cling on to the opportunity.

England had not taken a wicket since the middle session on the previous day, but a breakthrough came at last in the sixth over of the afternoon when Morris, who had just nudged past 150 and the partnership beyond 200, edged Bailey to first slip where Cowdrey gratefully hugged the ball to his midriff. Morris's exit did not, however, stem the flow of runs or of spurned chances. Harvey brought up his hundred (199 balls, eight fours) with a boundary through square leg off Bedser. He now looked much more like his old self and it emerged there had been good reason for his lack of fluency on the opening day: after batting through Friday with a grumbling stomach, he had been violently ill on returning to the hotel.

In the same over he reached three figures, Harvey offered a sharp return catch to Bedser, which the bowler could not hold. The new batsman, Graeme Hole, was initially content to give his well-set partner the strike, but as tea approached and England wilted on a sweltering afternoon (Tyson cut down his run to husband his resources), both batsmen inflicted some heavy punishment. After a cooler-than-expected opening day, the England fielders were now feeling the full force of Queensland's climate. 'It was a horrible Brisbane day, stuffy and humid with never a breath of wind,' Tyson recalled. 'Exertion brought a breathlessness which in itself was an effort not unlike sucking in damp cotton wool.'

Soon after tea, however, Hutton entrusted Tyson and Bedser with the third new ball: it brought a wicket, but not in the way intended. Going for a second run, Hole was run out by Tyson's magnificent flat throw from fine leg. It can't have improved Bedser's mood much: earlier in the over Statham had dropped Harvey at mid-off, a tricky low chance to which he made a gallant attempt, but it was still the fifth missed chance off Bedser. In his previous over, his runs-conceded tally had slipped into three figures.

On 463, Harvey's long and frequently unconvincing innings ended when Bailey, belatedly atoning for the previous day's horrific miss, took a brilliant low catch at fine leg, tumbling sideways to cling on to the ball a few inches from the turf. The over, which began at 4.40 p.m., was the first maiden England had bowled all day. For a man who had made 162, Harvey earned precious little praise. 'I do not exaggerate when I say I have never seen a luckier innings in Test cricket,' wrote Harry Ditton in the *News of the World*. 'Harvey must have collected 50 of his first 100 runs off the edge of the bat.'

After waiting so long for one wicket, England had found that, like Brisbane trams, several came at once: Archer steered Statham to Bedser at gully without scoring, but after three rapid departures there were no more successes. Given licence by the mounting total, Richie Benaud and Ray Lindwall took advantage of a perspiring attack to add 39 before the close. When Lindwall brought up the 500 with a boundary off Bailey in the final over of the day, it was greeted with thunderous applause by those who had lingered until the end. Lindwall remembered that his batting efforts were a cause for concern for his captain. 'I still wasn't too well. Ian Johnson was telling me to get out so I'd be OK to bowl.'

J.M. Kilburn applauded a scoring rate for the day of around 60 runs an hour, but the over-rate was less impressive: England had bowled 114 eight-ball overs in two days. 'With English conditions and hours of play the same number of balls would have been bowled by a normally varied attack by about one o'clock on the second day,' Swanton said. Hutton's weary players were grateful for the rest day, but with so much time left in the game they must have known that there would be more foot-slogging on Monday morning before Johnson put them out of their misery.

Close of play: Australia 503–6 (Benaud 14*, Lindwall 27*)

GROUND FOR COMPLAINT

Queensland Cricket Association (QCA) officials were counting the record receipts from a second-day attendance of 30,329. Australia's newest Test venue was staging just its ninth international fixture – there had been two Tests at the city's Exhibition Ground before the Brisbane Cricket Ground staged its first Test against South Africa in 1931. It was situated in the Woolloongabba suburb of Brisbane, just a mile and a half from Lennons Hotel where the England squad was staying (they made the short trip each morning in a fleet of Holden saloon cars). Woolloongabba, an Aboriginal word meaning whirling waters, was usually shortened to 'Gabba', although it was some years before it became just 'the Gabba' and 'Brisbane Cricket Ground' disappeared into antiquity.

Its facilities were distinctly unimpressive. 'Australia's ugly duckling ground', wrote Arthur Gilligan. When England arrived for the state match they quickly decided the nets were unsuitable and relocated to a nearby private school. Nor was the accommodation for players any more prepossessing. 'The pavilion is an antique,' wrote Frank Tyson. 'Two wooden dressing-rooms cobbled together with bathrooms at the rear, a dining-room to one side and a viewing facility on a veranda in front.' Alan Ross thought the pavilion had 'roughly the dignity of a lavatory'.

Tyson may have been kind in using the term 'dining-room'. The former Australian batsman Sam Loxton told the writer Gideon Haigh about an earlier Brisbane Test. 'Just before we went out this little chap would come in and sweep everything off the table, unroll a big sheet of butchers' paper – which I guess was table cloth – and put down 12 plates. On each plate he'd stand a leaf of lettuce and lay a piece of corned beef then throw a mosquito net over the top of it.' When the ice cream came around later, the attendant often had his thumb in the tub. Each dressing-room had a trestle table for kit and 12 six-inch nails hammered into the wall as pegs. 'The dressing-rooms do not even have a fridge,' Tyson noted, 'just a large galvanised iron bathtub filled with drinks kept cool by ice blocks placed on top of them.'

All of which helps to explain correspondence between MCC and the Australian Board of Control when the tour itinerary was still being thrashed out. In November 1953, MCC submitted a schedule which omitted a Brisbane Test 'mainly, though not entirely, with a view to improving its [the tour's] financial results'. Later communications suggest the Queensland climate as well as the Gabba's reputation for lower attendances was a factor in the club's campaign.

Billy Griffith, MCC's assistant secretary, asked the *Evening News* journalist E.M. Wellings to gather some data. Wellings reported that Brisbane's most recent Test against South Africa in 1952 had produced an aggregate attendance of 23,500 and receipts of £A4800. 'Even in 1946, after a period of 10 years without Test cricket, the full attendance for a six-day match between England and Australia (Bradman and Hammond still playing) was only 77,344 and the takings £14,515,' Wellings reported. He was typically waspish about the ground. 'None [sic] who knows the Brisbane ground can be surprised that attendances are so small. Four out of five spectators in the 25,000 crowd would either be grilled black by the sun or drenched by a sudden semi-tropical storm and perhaps stunned by an outsize hailstone.' In Australia, they were having none of it. An official response landed at Lord's: 'After full reconsideration the board is of the opinion that in the interests of Australian Cricket as a whole, a Test Match should be played at Brisbane in the 1954–55 MCC Tour.'

In common with Sydney and Adelaide, the ground had a 'hill', a steep grass bank where the more vocal spectators gathered, and a large informative scoreboard (though Tyson felt the smallness of the typeface made it less useful than its counterpart at the Sydney Cricket Ground), but the majority of the crowd sat in the open – 'simmering spectators packed themselves shirtsleeve to shirtsleeve upon the slopes,' wrote John Woodcock – exposed to the pitiless sun, unless it was possible to gain some shade from a ring of Moreton Bay fig trees.

'There were some people who forgot their hats and who turned gradually pink and then red with sunburn as the day wore on,' reported Arthur Richards of the *Courier-Mail*. Few had any cover, though next to the pavilion was the Members' Stand, the largest structure on the ground. Its red corrugated tin roof at least offered some shelter, but it was still uncomfortable and unwelcoming. A concrete wall topped with broken bottles kept out the rest of the crowd and barbed wire separated the members' seating from the public grandstand. Alan Ross thought it all created a 'prisoner-of-war atmosphere'.

Things were little better for the media. 'The press box is the dirtiest I have been in,' wrote Margaret Hughes. 'Because of the heat and the dirt I have felt uncomfortable from the start and should not have been surprised to see all sorts of animals making their way up the steps of the press box.' These privations did not stop QCA president Jack Hutcheon, a 72-year-old Brisbane solicitor, viewing the scene with lordly disdain from a private box high in the Members' Stand, which bore Hutcheon's name in large letters.

Here existed a mindset that MCC officials would have recognised, with a rigidly enforced dress code and a string of petty regulations. In one of his early games at the ground, the Queensland batsman Ken Mackay earned an official reprimand for chewing gum too vigorously during an innings. Jack Fingleton, the Australia opening batsman-turned-journalist, wrote with disdain about the 'social flap doodle' around a Brisbane Test. 'In no other cricketing city I know does "society" attach itself so closely to cricket as in Brisbane.'

His view was borne out on the women's pages of the *Courier-Mail*, which breathlessly conveyed each day's fashion news from Hutcheon's eyrie. When Queensland governor Lieutenant General Sir John Lavarack[7] attended with his wife on the third day, the paper's writers almost passed out with excitement. Joined by Bradman, the Lavaracks had lunch in the ground's executive room – the food, presumably, was an improvement on that dished up for the players. Ted Williams, the QCA secretary, was consigned to a table by himself in the corner of the room.

It was all a chimera. 'The Gabba itself resembled a concentration camp,' wrote Ian Diehm in his history of Queensland cricket. 'A decaying white picket fence surrounded the playing area but, on top of the picket fence, was a wire fence topped with strands of barbed wire.' Hutcheon thought this necessary to corral the 'animals' who used the ground in winter, a reference to rugby league players and fans.

The Gabba was not just spartan, it was shambolic. On the first day, thousands missed the opening overs after insufficient turnstiles were opened. As the clock ticked towards the 11.30 a.m. start, an agitated crowd threatened to smash down an outer gate. They called for Hutcheon and Williams to appear and explain the cock-up. The only response was for Williams to tell the press that more turnstiles would be open on the second morning. A spectator who was in the crush wrote angrily of his experience to the local press: 'Now I

---

[7]Sir John Lavarack was governor of Queensland from 1946 to 1957. He fought in two world wars and was only the second Australian to be appointed a state governor. The roles were still usually filled by Britons.

know how a sheep or cow feels when pushed and prodded through the dip,' he said. Once inside, his 'reserved seat' was no more than a plank, shared with five others and open to the elements.

When fans turned up on Monday morning for the third day, they found the accumulated rubbish left by Saturday's crowds still littering the area. Two-day-old prawn heads, empty beer bottles, banana skins and bread crusts covered the ground. Williams said it had been 'too dark' to clean up properly on Saturday evening and that a team of 10 cleaners starting at 7 a.m. that morning had made only slow progress. *Courier-Mail* columnist Jim Vine was among the spectators: 'The area immediately in front of the public section of the main stand was a shocking mess, a litter of rubbish left where it had been dropped on Saturday.'

After a gruelling day in the field, the England players spent the rest day quietly recuperating. Colin Cowdrey read the lesson at a special 'Test Match' service at the City Congregational Church. It is unlikely that any of the team found much excitement. In comparison with Australia's other Test-match centres, Brisbane felt like a backwater. 'The boredom is crushing,' Tyson remembered thinking after a few days in Queensland. 'Even that veteran networker, Alec Bedser, knows no one here.'[8] Arlott was also unimpressed. 'Certain aspects of Sydney and Melbourne are cosmopolitan but Brisbane is almost truculently Australian,' he said. The position in the match hardly served to lighten the mood. 'It now seems like a nightmare,' wrote Geoffrey Howard in a letter home.

The English media's attacks on Jack McAndrew had now been wired to Australia and conveyed gleefully back to the home public. Outside the Gabba on Monday morning, the newspaper billboards read 'Squealers at it again'. Inside, Ray Lindwall and Richie Benaud picked up where they had left off on Saturday. Brian Statham had been England's best bowler, but now he found himself hoisted for six by Benaud and driven imperiously through the covers by Lindwall in the same humbling over. There was one thrilling moment when, in his follow-through, Frank Tyson picked up a firm Benaud drive one-handed and, in the same movement, hurled the ball back down

---

[8] Tyson later settled in Queensland, on the Gold Coast, and died there in 2015, aged 85.

the pitch, shattering Benaud's stumps. The moment was greeted rapturously by the crowd, but the square-leg umpire ruled Benaud had jumped back into his crease in time.

There were also some fun and games between Tyson and Lindwall when the Australian played what Tyson considered some 'cheeky and disrespectful strokes' and the England bowler breached an unwritten code that fast bowlers did not deliver bumpers to their brethren by making Lindwall duck under a bouncer. Finally, with the first ball of his 28th over, Tyson earned his first Ashes wicket; Benaud caught at deep extra cover by May off a miscue. Tyson's confidence was not shaken. 'I'm convinced that I deserved better figures,' he said.

Any thoughts of a declaration before the interval ended when Ian Johnson strode out to join Lindwall after Trevor Bailey had bowled Gil Langley. Exhausted as well as depressed, England's fielding became increasingly ragged. At 563, Statham, leaping high at mid-on, dropped Lindwall off Bailey. Johnson was then the beneficiary of three misses in his jaunty innings of 24. He was put down by Simpson on the boundary – 'probably because he was running round unpleasantly close to the pickets,' thought Swanton – by Cowdrey in the gully, and, finally, by Cowdrey again after he and Simpson failed to agree which of them should go for a steepling hit over mid-on.

Thinking Cowdrey had taken the catch, Johnson began to head off, only to be summoned back by Hutton. After that reprieve, Johnson played out the remainder of the over from Bedser before the interval and over lunch informed Hutton that he had declared. The England players were wilting in the heat. 'The sweat was pouring from my brow, I could taste the salt in it,' Andrew recalled. 'My concentration was in tatters. I think I'd got a touch of the sun.'

A total of 601 for eight declared represented a grotesque failure of Hutton's gamble. In 11 and a half hours and over seven sessions, Australia had compiled the highest Test score made by a side being put in to bat.[9] Despite their yeoman efforts, each of England's four

[9]This record has subsequently been surpassed nine times – the highest score in a Test by a side after being put in is now 735 for six declared by Australia against Zimbabwe at Perth in 2003–04.

seamers had conceded more than 100 runs – 'The English bowling figures made a study in higher mathematics,' said Wellings. Bedser, the attack leader, finished with 37–4–131–1, while Tyson, the secret weapon, suffered even greater damage, 29–1–160–1. Only Statham, with 34–2–123–2, escaped criticism. 'It is not easy to bring to mind a better fast-bowling exhibition than this,' wrote Bill O'Reilly of the Lancashire bowler.

Worse than their ineffectual attack was England's shambolic fielding. Most journalists agreed there had been 12 dropped catches, though there were several other half-chances. Woodcock calculated fielding errors had cost England 260 runs. Denzil Batchelor reckoned that no Test had seen more dropped catches since England v South Africa at Headingley in 1907, a match played between heavy showers. In addition, there had been much ponderous work in the field and countless sloppy returns.

FIELDING QUESTIONS

England's malaise was not wholly surprising. Godfrey Evans's absence brought the average age of the XI down, but there was little chance of them earning high marks for athleticism. It was taken as read among the English press that Australia would be slicker movers, better throwers and safer catchers. Yet some wondered whether Hutton's team had focused sufficiently on closing the gap. During the final Test of the summer of 1954 against Pakistan at The Oval, Crawford White of the *News Chronicle* lamented the standard of England's fielding and offered Hutton his solution. 'He must hold special practice sessions to try to improve our appalling close-to-the-wicket catching.' Before the shambles unfolded in Brisbane, the *Daily Telegraph*'s E.W. Swanton had taken up the theme. 'Has everything possible been done since our landing in Australia to minimise the points of weakness in the MCC side which were recognised when it was picked?' he asked in his Test preview. 'Will it go on to the field in the best possible fettle?'

Swanton was not alone in citing the example of the South Africa team which had toured Australia two years earlier. Written off and unregarded, they drew the series 2–2 thanks to consistently brilliant fielding and a ferocious work ethic instilled by Jack Cheetham, the captain. 'Cheetham established a curfew and all sorts of rigid rules and the curriculum included regular physical training,' said Swanton. 'To have visited such a system suddenly on this much more sophisticated team of Hutton's would hardly have worked. Still one feels that some sort of compromise involving, among other things, more rigorous practice would, in certain directions, have had good results. The throwing-in for instance could have been improved and surely, too, the lower batting.'

Brisbane Butterfingers – England's Missed Chances

Total	Batsman	Bowler	Description	Runs cost
1–0	Morris (0)	Bedser	Andrew fails to lay glove on thick inside edge	153
147–1	Morris (55)	Bedser	Bailey puts down sitter at fine leg	—
215–2	Morris (89)	Bedser	Diving May fails to hold edge at slip	—
249–2	Harvey (58)	Bailey	At leg slip, Bedser drops the ball on impact with ground	104
293–2	Morris (136)	Tyson	A fourth life for Morris after Andrew fails to reach edge	—
343–3	Harvey (103)	Bedser	Bowler drops sharp caught-and-bowled opportunity	—
448–3	Harvey (153)	Bedser	Statham grasses low chance at mid-off	—
493–6	Lindwall (20)	Bailey	Lindwall dropped at leg slip by Cowdrey as 500 nears	44
563–7	Lindwall (52)	Bailey	Statham, now at mid-on, leaps but fails to hold on	
593–8	Johnson (16)	Bedser	Simpson can't reach high hit running around boundary	8
595–8	Johnson (18)	Bedser	The usually reliable Cowdrey drops chance in the gully	—
599–8	Johnson (22)	Bedser	Another skyer falls between Simpson and Cowdrey	—
Total runs cost: **309**				

The pre-Test game against Queensland had exposed the team's Achilles heel. Ross Hall of the *Daily Mirror* noted that the youthful

Colin Cowdrey had been moved close to the bat after two catches had been dropped off Statham. 'Cowdrey's competence in the slips drew attention to the poorness of our fielding.' In *The Times*, John Woodcock described Compton and Bedser 'reacting in the slips like old men'. When it emerged that Hutton might put Australia in if he won the toss, Ross crossed his fingers: 'We shall have to catch all our catches.' Instead, the opposite happened. After the second day's play, Hutton addressed the issue in front of the press, making the point that sound tactics and good bowling were useless if fielders did not hold catches. Nevertheless, his attitude to fielding was demonstrated years later when he remarked to Mike Brearley, who as England captain in Australia in 1978–79 commanded a magnificent fielding side, that his idea of practice was to 'knock a few balls in the air and see if anyone caught them'.

Trevor Bailey was more succinct, calling England's fielding 'an absolute shambles'. J.M. Kilburn explained, 'A missed chance in Australia is more important than in England because the next one tends to be so far removed in time and toil.' In his final autobiography, Hutton recalled, 'England also sowed the seeds of their own destruction by dropping catch after catch in the worst exhibition of outcricket I was obliged to endure in my time in office.'

He may not have dropped any catches, but Hutton was not immune to criticism. Ditton attacked his deployment of England's meagre resources. The 12th man Vic Wilson, one of the best close-to-the-wicket catchers in England, spent most of his time on the boundary. Simpson, a fine cover point, was also frequently out in the deep while Tyson and Statham were given too much extra work to do as boundary riders. 'Bedser found himself as England's cover point, which must make Jack Hobbs and Cyril Washbrook think a bit,' wrote Charles Bray in the *Daily Herald*. 'Hutton fussed with his field like an amateur chess player who is always touching his pieces, half moving only to hesitate and dither,' said Neville Cardus. 'Even Edrich was sent to third man. Nobody at Lord's has seen Edrich fielding near the boundary.'

Alan Ross thought Hutton 'a lonely figure struck down by as many disasters as any overworked heroes in Greek mythology' as he emerged from the pavilion with Reg Simpson to begin the mountainous task of saving the Test. All knew a phase of play was beginning that could determine the outcome of the match. 'The air was charged with excitement,' said the *Courier-Mail*'s Arthur Richards. 'Through luncheon one had awaited England's innings with a cold feeling in the pit of the stomach,' wrote Woodcock. It was 1.40 p.m. on a blazing hot Brisbane day when Lindwall paced out his run at the Vulture Street End and Hutton marked his guard: the best fast bowler in the world against the game's greatest opening batsman – here was the ultimate in Test cricket.

Lindwall's first exploratory ball outside off stump was met confidently by Hutton, who sent it racing past gully to the boundary. The England captain played the next five deliveries defensively, but groped for the seventh outside off stump as it moved fractionally away and got the thinnest of edges through to wicketkeeper Gil Langley. Australia's delight was unrestrained – 'dancing jigs and prancing around like children,' said Woodcock – but Hutton waited for umpire Col Hoy to confirm the bad news. To complete a seismic opening over, Bill Edrich then guided his first ball past gully for four.

The sight of Miller taking the new ball at the Railway End confirmed there would be no respite for England. Simpson ran two for an edge that eluded the slips but then, feet rooted in his crease, was yorked by Miller's fifth delivery. Peter May's first Test innings in Australia lasted seven balls before he was bowled off his pads in Lindwall's second over. Three England wickets had fallen in 13 calamitous minutes. 'It was one of those days that make you feel you can never get enough of big cricket,' wrote Richards.

Colin Cowdrey, 21 and in his first Test, walked out with England reeling at 11 for three. Edrich seemed intent on counter-punching, hooking Ron Archer – who replaced Miller after his initial three-over burst – for successive fours. But with the first ball of his second over, Archer had Edrich caught behind for 15 and England were 25 for four, effectively five with Compton unlikely to bat. From outside the ground, two cheerful blasts were heard from the whistle of one of Brisbane's suburban steam locomotives.

It was not lost on anyone that the Australian bowlers instantly located a fuller, more threatening length than their English counterparts. 'The early Australian bowling was right up to the bat so that the ball was being given the maximum chance of doing something in the air,' said Swanton. At least Cowdrey now had for company the redoubtable Bailey. Less than an hour earlier, Bailey had been on the veranda filming Hutton and Simpson as they walked out – now, yet again in a career defined by rearguard actions, he had the job of restoring England's dignity. They made a contrasting pair but, helped by the withdrawal of Lindwall and Miller from the front line, Cowdrey and Bailey set about the rebuilding operation. Cowdrey discovered that the Test arena was not necessarily devoid of chivalry. 'I pushed one away to get off the mark and Keith Miller patted me on the back and said something like, "You might get a few more."'

Cowdrey was cautious. He played out two maidens from Lindwall and one from Miller, but when he began to find the boundary regularly – 28 of his first 33 runs came in fours – his quality shone through. 'There was no doubt from the start of his innings about the true class of his batsmanship nor, as his innings progressed, of his extraordinary mature judgment and ideal temperament,' wrote *The Sunday Times*'s Ian Peebles.

Cowdrey was merely confirming the good impression he had made on and off the field. 'What a grand lad the young Colin Cowdrey is – in every way,' Geoffrey Howard said in a letter home. 'So modest, shy and pleasantly spoken. And what a fine choice he has been: the most criticised choice of all too!!' Despite the 14-year disparity in their ages, Cowdrey had become fast friends with Margaret Hughes. During the match, he sent her a note suggesting a trip to see a local production of *The Mikado*. The gap between press-box and dressing-room was 15 yards, but she had to use one of the ground's post offices to respond by telegram.

More unexpected than Cowdrey's elegance were the three fours Bailey hit in an over from Benaud, followed by an overthrown five during the next from left-armer seamer Bill Johnston. 'The funeral march had turned into a gallop, rather as if some irreverent urchin had put a squib behind the coffin,' said Ross. Their alliance had reached 82 when, off the first delivery of the final over of the day, Cowdrey played a ball from Johnston via his foot to Graeme Hole at first slip. Certain he had not touched it, Cowdrey stood his ground but umpire McInnes gave him out. The modern-day official has the benefit of a third umpire and TV reruns from every angle – a

21st-century Cowdrey would have asked for a review – but in the 1950s he had to rely on the speed of his eye and judgment.

Photographic evidence of the aftermath suggests the Australians were equally unsure it was out. There was enough doubt for the official scorers, George Duckworth and Andy Fisher, to seek clarification as to whether Cowdrey had been leg-before. They found the umpires had already left the ground. 'The ball which dismissed him was a replica of the ones which earlier he punched through the covers,' wrote Lindsay Hassett, blaming caution caused by the approaching close for Cowdrey's departure for 40.

Close of play: England 107–5 (Bailey 38*, Tyson 0*), trail Australia by 494 runs with five first-innings wickets in hand.

Freddie Brown, England's captain on the previous Ashes tour, who was in Australia for the *Daily Mail* and providing syndicated columns for Australian newspapers, thought the wicket 'the final nail in England's coffin', which was not a particularly insightful piece of punditry: at 107 for five, England were 344 short of the follow-on with five fit batsmen.

The fourth day – 30 November – was prime minister Sir Winston Churchill's 80th birthday. Geoffrey Howard cabled Downing Street from Brisbane, 'We could do with your 80 not out today, sir!' The *Daily Express* imaginatively linked England's struggles to the celebrations. '80 not out: howzatt Hutton' was its banner headline running right across the broadsheet front page above one story detailing how Sir Winston would spend the day and another, from cricket correspondent Frank Rostron at the Gabba, reporting on the opening session.

Churchill's landmark was a welcome distraction from the bad news from Australia. The prime minister was the subject of gushing newspaper supplements and even the left-wing *Daily Mirror* joined in the good wishes. 'The old man is 80 today,' its front page said. 'Let us forget politics for the occasion and give him a mighty cheer.'

Given less prominence was a four-paragraph story on the front of Brisbane's *Courier-Mail*, reporting the offer of £100 from local businessman C.J. Coles Smith to the batsman who hit the first six of the day. Coles Smith had attended his first Test match the previous day and had relished the sixes hit by Benaud and Johnson: now he wanted to incentivise more big hitting. The reward was claimed off the second ball of the 11th over of the morning, when the arch-stonewaller Bailey lofted Johnson between long-on and midwicket. 'It was though a puritan had turned gangster,' wrote A.G. Moyes. Bailey claimed – with a straight face – he had no idea of Coles Smith's offer, though later he vaguely recalled some dressing-room discussion before the start of play. 'What made me feel there might be some substance to the story had been the reaction of the Australians on the field,' Bailey recalled in his autobiography. 'They had appeared rather more aggrieved than usual when the umpire had put his arms aloft and I thought I had caught something close to "lucky lugger".' At the close, Bailey rushed back to the hotel and made a phone call to confirm the story. Coles Smith arrived later to make good his offer, with the handover solemnly recorded for radio.

'I only hope offers like this go on for the next two or three months,' joked Hutton, but it was a passing moment of frivolity: by the time Bailey received his cheque, England were just about beaten. The day had begun in searing heat. 'This morning's air was like an oven and the outline of distant Mount Gravatt was shrouded in cloud,' wrote Swanton. 'The signs, we were told, portended thunderstorms. But how many? How severe? And, above all, when?' Bailey reached his fifty off 198 balls, but Tyson, Bedser and Andrew failed to get into double figures, and although Statham hit two fours and batted for 37 minutes, he gifted Ian Johnson his third wicket of the morning. 'Statham swung three times wildly at Johnson and was rightly bowled. It was the kind of irresponsible cricket for which a small boy would have his ears boxed,' wrote an outraged Ross. 'Attention to detail has long ceased to be the mark of the English county cricketer, who knows it all without having bothered to learn. A bowler rarely troubles to bat or a batsman to bowl. Thus do we lose Test matches.'

Statham's carelessness was compounded by the fact that it was only five minutes until lunch and meant Compton now came out to bat one-handed – he would not have batted if Bailey had been out. He emerged to a sustained standing ovation. 'Claps and beaming smiles from the ladies and whistles of greetings from the boys,' wrote Swanton. 'There was never such an uproar since Bradman retired.'

He had to face just one ball before the interval, sportingly bowled wide of the crease by Johnson, but contrived to survive another 14, and somehow make two one-handed runs, in the afternoon while Bailey tried to hit out. Bailey had made 88 off 283 balls in four hours, 24 minutes when he was bowled by Bill Johnston: it was his highest score against Australia (and remained so), and had occupied 26 minutes longer than his epic act of defiance at Lord's in 1953 that had done so much to secure the Ashes. England were all out for 190, still 411 behind with two days and two sessions to go.

THE LAST RITES

Enforcing the follow-on was a formality for Ian Johnson, and a few minutes after two o'clock Len Hutton and Reg Simpson again walked out to face the full fury of Ray Lindwall and Keith Miller. With so many runs still in the bank, Johnson and Lindwall could afford to set a field of immense hostility – three slips, two gullies and two short legs; only mid-on and mid-off were not in close-catching positions.

As in the first innings, Hutton hit Lindwall's first ball for four – this time off his legs through square leg. When Hutton played the second delivery in the same direction, there was no run, but it prompted Johnson to move up to short mid-on. Off the fifth, Hutton survived a confident lbw shout. To the seventh, Lindwall's inswinger, the England captain edged the ball into his pads from where it looped in the direction of Bill Johnston at short square leg. Back on his heels, the fielder could not reach it. 'Davidson would probably have just about got there,' thought Swanton. When Hutton left a fast final ball outside his off stump it concluded an opening exchange of theatrical intensity that had reduced the ground to a hushed silence.

The England openers had survived for 40 minutes and scraped together 22 when they were parted in a manner that was entirely avoidable. Hutton edged Lindwall between Hole and Archer at first and second slip, but neither could grasp a difficult chance: as the ball dropped behind them, Simpson foolishly called Hutton through for a single and was run out when Favell, dashing back alertly from third slip, retrieved the ball and hit the stumps with his throw. Scenting blood, Miller – switching to the Vulture Street End for a second spell – redoubled his efforts to Hutton. He got his man off the penultimate ball of his second over, the England captain trapped leg-before to a well-concealed slower ball. 'Keith Miller bowled three overs as good as any I have ever seen,' wrote Charles Bray in the *Daily Herald*. 'They were superb in their fire and their hostility.'

Hutton's departure made an Australian victory almost inevitable, but there was an air of disappointment around the ground. 'The world's greatest batsman, here once in four years – and then the crowd gets just a glimpse of action before he walks back again to the pavilion,' lamented Arthur Richards. As the applause for Compton's appearance had shown earlier, the Gabba provided an even-handed audience. 'I have not played before a crowd that gave the visiting team more support or watched the game more closely,' Hutton said after the match. This cannot have been PR schmoozing as the team were not returning to Brisbane and there was no prospect of him being back in four years' time.

At 23 for two and after that shattering blow, England might have subsided lamely. But this was the landmark birthday of Britain's great wartime leader, and the occasion demanded a show of fight-them-on-the-beaches defiance. Edrich, who had a distinguished war record, was joined by vice-captain Peter May in a partnership that demonstrated that the battering England had taken over the past four days had not impacted on the resolve of the party. He may have been inspired by the derision which had greeted his selection, but Edrich – after being dropped off Miller before he had scored – prospered and, either side of tea, began to play some attractive attacking shots. 'His timing improved to match his indisputable determination,' wrote J.M. Kilburn.

For Swanton it evoked memories of Edrich's seven-hour 219 in the timeless Test against South Africa at Durban in 1939, when his presence in the team had also been widely questioned. May, meanwhile, after initially struggling to pierce a predatory ring of Australian fielders, began to play with a fluency that brought sighs of contentment from the contingent of former Australia Test players in the press box. On 26, Edrich was dropped by Hole off Johnson, but he responded by hitting a no-ball from the same bowler over long-on for six. At the close – despite a further reprieve when Johnston put down a caught-and-bowled chance offered by May – the partnership was worth 107, with Edrich 68 and May 39. They looked, said Swanton, 'astonishingly comfortable'.

Close of play: England 130–2 (Edrich 68★, May 39★), trail Australia by 281 runs with eight second-innings wickets in hand.

A weather forecast that included the threat of showers may have troubled the sleep of the Australians slightly, but not for too long. Not many agreed with Freddie Brown that England had a chance of a 'miraculous escape'. After the intense interest at the start of the match, there were fewer than 5000 people inside the Gabba for its conclusion. 'So deserted were the green slopes under the impressive premises of the Bengal Chutney Company that a solitary squatting gentleman was able to strip to the waist, turn his trousers up and enjoy a leisurely sun-bath with no one a cricket's pitch length either side of him,' wrote Ross.

Edrich and May were largely untroubled until Lindwall brought one back to May that kept a shade low and an innings rich in promise ended at 44. 'It was notable that he put the bat against the ball with a sharp rap of the wrist even when playing purely defensively, as indeed do most of the great,' noted Peebles. Edrich batted on but just before lunch was bowled while having an ugly heave at Johnston for 88, matching Bailey's first-innings score. To add to Edrich's frustration, it then rained – 'a steady and fairly heavy fall by English standards, but not by any means torrential as sub-tropical Queensland understands the term,' wrote Arlott – but the stoppage was a mere half-hour and, on a cooler afternoon, Australia methodically completed the victory that most had predicted since the opening session.

Colin Cowdrey attracted criticism for crawling to 10 off 83 balls, suppressing his natural instincts and ceding control to the bowlers. Bailey used up more than an hour and a half for his 23, and against the spinners was surrounded by so many close fielders that he disappeared from view, but he was brilliantly caught by a diving Gil

Langley off Lindwall. In his past nine innings against Australia, Bailey had spent more than 22 hours at the crease and scored 333 runs. After that, only Tyson of the tailend batsmen provided any resistance, but he returned to the dressing-room in a furious mood after getting out. Compton had been talking up his chances of scoring runs with one hand, claiming he had been honing a new technique in the nets, but there was still surprise when he walked out at No. 10.

The press felt the risk of making his injury worse far outweighed any other considerations – 'A regrettable error of judgment on the part of all concerned,' wrote Peebles. But, as Geoffrey Howard said in a letter to Lord's, 'The atmosphere in the dressing-room is so different from that in the press box, and Denis simply could not bear the thought of the ship going down whilst he stood by in a lifeboat.' Compton lasted three balls before being caught behind off Richie Benaud. Finally, at 4.11 p.m., Neil Harvey took a brilliant running catch on the boundary – holding the ball at eye-level like a baseball catcher as if to give the England fielders a lesson in technique – to remove Brian Statham off Benaud and the first Test of the 1954–55 Ashes series was over. England were all out for 257 and, with more than a day to spare, Australia had won by the crushing margin of an innings and 154 runs. It remains Australia's fourth-biggest innings victory over England.

It was a notable triumph for Ian Johnson in his first Test as captain – not that it seemed that way. 'He left the field in silence,' said the *Courier-Mail*. 'Nobody clapped him, nobody cheered as he made his way unobtrusively between spectators who had jumped to the field when play ended. He entered the pavilion almost unnoticed – after a victory that will go down into cricket's history books.' The few spectators who drifted on to the outfield seemed more interested in examining the pitch. 'It might have been the end of a drawn grade game,' said Ross. The England players were invited to share their opponents' champagne. The inevitable inquests began immediately. At the end of the fourth day, the *Daily Mail*'s Alex Bannister had written, 'Outside Brisbane's gasworks tonight is a notice which reads "Ashes given away." I am assured it was not meant to refer to catch-dropping fielders or to batting collapses.'

Generally, England's mood remained upbeat. 'When we take our catches – and when we have just a modicum of luck – we can beat this Aussie side,' thought Tyson. Geoffrey Howard agreed. 'I will not fear to say now that this Aussie side is not a great one by any means,' he wrote home. Back at Lennons Hotel, Hutton reinforced the message by inviting the seam-bowling quartet to his room and uncorking a bottle of champagne, a thank you for their unstinting efforts. It had fallen to Howard to go into the Australian dressing-room to congratulate the victors. He found Johnson cocksure and a little patronising. 'I just hope I don't have to do that again,' he said to Hutton on his return. England's undented confidence sprang from the feeling that everything that could go wrong had done – misguided selection, wrong-headed thinking at the toss, Evans's absence, Compton's injury, wretched fielding – and that they had to put only some of those things right to stand a chance of getting back into the series at Sydney in two weeks' time.

Publicly at least, Hutton had the ability to smile at his misfortune. In a good-luck message to his football counterpart Billy Wright, due to lead his team against world champions West Germany at Wembley hours after his own team's defeat, Hutton wrote, 'MCC wish best of luck to you and your team. Hope you score as many goals as Australia scored runs, and if you win the toss make sure you don't put 'em in – kick with the wind.' England won 3–1 with a stellar performance by right-winger Stanley Matthews, at 39 a year older than Hutton. It gave Fleet Street sports editors a chance to shift the focus of their pages away from the debacle in Brisbane.

Bailey, whose 31st birthday was two days after the end of the Test, had invested his generous bequest from the local businessman in as many bottles of champagne as £A100 could buy. In the air-conditioned comfort of Lennons Hotel, the squad held a party more akin to those usually enjoyed by teams who have won a Test match. 'Players and friends wandered from room to room, surprisingly happy and optimistic about the future,' said Tyson. 'But we kept our socialising and our optimism to ourselves, away from the public eye and the press.' Hutton exuded quiet confidence about the destiny of the Ashes. Later, things got more rowdy. 'It was a good night but I sometimes wondered what the other residents thought,' wrote Bailey, 'Especially at around 5 a.m. when one of my colleagues – it had to be Peter Loader – decided to knock over one of the bottles, which stretched in what appeared to be an unending chain down the whole corridor, and they all toppled over.' 'Lennons has probably never forgotten it,' said Loader.

Two days later, Howard had to settle the bill for a 16-day stay by a party of 21: it came to £A1400. 'Awful isn't it: I don't know how we can expect to see a large profit out of the tour with expenses so high unless we get really phenomenal gates,' he wrote. One by one, the players were called into the manager's room to settle their individual expenses. Johnny Wardle, who was keen to ensure he saved as much money to send home as possible, owed less than a pound, but he still disputed each item. 'I didn't have this bottle of milk, someone must have forged my signature,' he argued. In comparison, Bill Edrich had amassed a debt of £A45, mostly in telephone calls to a woman he had met on the voyage to Australia. He didn't quibble. Howard recalled, 'He said "Oh, if you say so." He signed W.J. Edrich and walked out.'

As professional sportsmen must, the England players moved on and began to focus on the enormous challenge of getting back into the series at Sydney. But for Keith Andrew, the wicketkeeper thrust into the team at the eleventh hour, the perception that he had missed a key chance so early in the match proved impossible to shake. Dennis Brookes, the Northamptonshire captain, recalled a conversation with Crawford White of the *News Chronicle*. 'He was still talking about that catch two or three summers later. The reporters all damned Keith for it.' Andrew himself reflected, 'It's funny isn't it, how often that match in Brisbane comes up in cricketing talk.' For the next decade some sound judges reckoned him to be the best wicketkeeper in the world, but he did not become first-choice when Godfrey Evans's Test career ended in the summer of 1959. In fact, Andrew played in just one more Test, against West Indies in 1963.

At the Centenary Test at Lord's in 1980 he shared a coach journey with Arthur Morris. The talk turned to the Brisbane Test 26 years earlier and that fateful inside edge. Morris dismissed it as a chance, but followed up with an extraordinary revelation: 'I nicked one before that, and you didn't appeal.'

FIRST TEST

Brisbane Cricket Ground　　　26, 27, 29, 30 November and 1 December, 1954

AUSTRALIA FIRST INNINGS

			Balls	Minutes	4s	6s	Out at
L.E. Favell	c Cowdrey b Statham	23	62	80	3	—	1/51
A.R. Morris	c Cowdrey b Bailey	153	326	419	18	2	3/325
K.R. Miller	b Bailey	49	84	86	4	1	2/123
R.N. Harvey	c Bailey b Bedser	162	279	380	17	—	5/463
G.B. Hole	run out	57	89	120	4	—	4/456
R. Benaud	c May b Tyson	34	51	93	1	1	7/545
R.G. Archer	c Bedser b Statham	0	8	5	—	—	6/464
R.R. Lindwall	not out	64	95	131	11	—	
†G.R.A. Langley	b Bailey	16	21	29	2	—	8/572
*I.W. Johnson	not out	24	23	20	2	1	
Extras	b 11, lb 7, nb 1	19					
8 wkts dec (129 overs, 690 mins)		**601**					

Did not bat: W.A. Johnston

ENGLAND BOWLING

Bedser	37	4	131	1
Statham	34	2	123	2
Tyson	29	1	160	1
Bailey	26	1	140	3
Edrich	3	0	28	0

DEBACLE IN BRISBANE

England won the toss and decided to field   Hours of play: 11.30 a.m.–5.30 p.m.
Umpires: C. Hoy (Queensland), M.J. McInnes (South Australia)

ENGLAND FIRST INNINGS

			Balls	Minutes	4s	6s	Out at
*L. Hutton	c Langley b Lindwall	4	7	4	1	—	1/4
R.T. Simpson	b Miller	2	5	10	—	—	2/10
W.J. Edrich	c Langley b Archer	15	28	42	3	—	4/25
P.B.H. May	b Lindwall	1	7	5	—	—	3/11
M.C. Cowdrey	c Hole b Johnston	40	183	190	7	—	5/107
T.E. Bailey	b Johnston	88	283	264	11	1	10/190
F.H. Tyson	b Johnson	7	23	23	—	—	6/132
A.V. Bedser	b Johnson	5	10	8	1	—	7/141
†K.V. Andrew	b Lindwall	6	15	13	—	—	8/156
J.B. Statham	b Johnson	11	33	37	2	—	9/181
D.C.S. Compton	not out	2	15	15	—	—	
Extras	3 b, 6 lb	9					
All out (76.1 overs, 314 mins)		**190**					

ENGLAND SECOND INNINGS (following on)

			Balls	Minutes	4s	6s	Out at
*L. Hutton	lbw b Miller	13	61	60	2	—	2/23
R.T. Simpson	run out	9	27	40	—	—	1/22
W.J. Edrich	b Johnston	88	212	193	13	1	4/163
P.B.H. May	lbw b Lindwall	44	126	145	6	—	3/147
M.C. Cowdrey	b Benaud	10	83	68	2	—	5/181
T.E. Bailey	c Langley b Lindwall	23	89	95	4	—	6/220
F.H. Tyson	not out	37	83	85	1	—	
A.V. Bedser	c Archer b Johnson	5	13	19	—	—	7/231
†K.V. Andrew	b Johnson	5	12	7	1	—	8/242
D.C.S. Compton	c Langley b Benaud	0	3	2	—	—	9/243
J.B. Statham	c Harvey b Benaud	14	13	6	2	—	10/257
Extras	7 b, 2 lb	9					
All out (90.1 overs, 374 mins)		**257**					

AUSTRALIA BOWLING

Lindwall	14	4	27	3	17	3	50	2
Miller	11	5	19	1	12	2	30	1
Archer	4	1	14	1	15	4	28	0
Johnson	17	5	38	2	21	8	59	1
Benaud	8.1	1	43	3	17	5	38	2
Johnston	21	8	59	1	8.1	1	43	3

AUSTRALIA WON BY AN INNINGS AND 154 RUNS

The match was scheduled for six days but completed in five

Attendances

First day: 16,500. Second day: 30,329. Third day: 16,142. Fourth day: 9,237. Fifth day: 4,800

Total: 77,008.

Debuts: L.E. Favell (Australia); M.C. Cowdrey, K.V. Andrew (England).

Twelfth men: A.K. Davidson (Australia), J.V. Wilson (England).

Sources: Barry Valentine, Charles Davis (sportsstats.com.au), cricketarchive.com, Richard Cashman

David Sheppard runs back on to the field at Hove after being named England captain for the second Test against Pakistan at Trent Bridge.

II

PLOTS, COUPS AND THE ENGLISH CLASS SYSTEM

'Here is a piece of what I should regard as direct service to the wider interests of the Kingdom of God which you can render'
Archbishop of Canterbury Geoffrey Fisher encourages
David Sheppard to take the England captaincy

'I suspected that someone, somewhere, was trying to get me out of the captaincy – for what reason I did not know'
Len Hutton, his job under threat

'I am relieved to know that the selectors have thought I am the right type of fellow and I shall be proud and happy to lead an England side in Australia'
Len Hutton, after being reappointed as
England captain

A HOMECOMING

Evening had fallen by the time the SS *Ariguani*, a banana boat operating between Kingston and Bristol, eased into Avonmouth harbour. For the 16 cricketers on board, 20 April, 1954 marked the end of a tour that had begun more than four months earlier when they were photographed on the steps of a BOAC Stratocruiser at London airport, raincoats buttoned up against the winter squalls. Now they returned from the West Indies at the end of a sunny early-spring Tuesday that followed a warm Easter weekend.

The two-week journey across the Atlantic had been uneventful, though there had been rough seas in the early days of the voyage. How rough depended on who you asked. 'A bit choppy at first,' said captain Len Hutton in his customarily dry, understated manner. Tom Graveney disagreed: 'There were times when the boat seemed to be standing on one end.' Yorkshire fast bowler Fred Trueman and Surrey left-arm spinner Tony Lock would have sided with Graveney: the pair, inseparable on the way home as they had been throughout the tour, had not emerged from their cabin for days.

Gradually, as the *Ariguani* steamed farther away from Jamaica, the mood had lightened. Charles Palmer, the embattled tour manager, said, 'I remember as the journey progressed thinking, "We're not far from home now," and we perked up a bit.' Three players had their wives for company. Dorothy Hutton, Jean Evans, wife of wicketkeeper Godfrey, and Valerie Compton, the South African heiress who had married England's star batsman, Denis, three years earlier, had flown out to join their husbands for the tour's final stages.

By the time the ship reached home, the county season was a week away, so the players might have been grateful for the chance to relax on the journey. But, as vice-captain Trevor Bailey pointed out, the travel arrangements were the wrong way around. Becoming the first MCC squad to fly out on a Test tour may have conveyed a thrilling touch of modernity, but the players needed an outgoing sea voyage to bond and formulate battle plans. Once the series was over, most wanted to be home as swiftly as possible. Perhaps especially after this tour.

It was too late to head home once the *Ariguani*[10] had docked, but exception was made for Graveney. Met by his wife Jackie and brother Ken, he was driven the three miles to his home in Bristol to meet his six-week-old daughter Becky for the first time. Jean Evans had brought a photograph of the new arrival out to the West Indies, but that had been Graveney's sole contact with his expanded family. It is a story that reflects the strains imposed on an international cricketer's domestic life by long winter absences. 'Modern Test cricket is a non-stop merry-go-round of hard work and travel,' Graveney noted in his autobiography. Five years later, when her father returned from a six-month tour of Australia clutching a toy koala bear, Becky Graveney locked herself in the bathroom to hide from 'this strange man'. Not that MCC were completely oblivious to the issues: off-spinner Jim Laker had been allowed to fly home because his wife Lilly was pregnant.

The following morning, the remaining players collected their luggage and filed down the gangway before embarking on the final leg of their trips. Trueman was laden with gifts for his family at home in south Yorkshire, including a large bunch of bananas. Alan Moss, the Middlesex fast bowler, had also taken advantage of the ship's cargo: with the end of wartime rationing still two months away, bananas remained a prized commodity. For Hutton, there was one more press conference alongside Palmer before he and Dorothy could head for Pudsey. Hutton must have been drafting his tour report for MCC during the fortnight's journey. Journalists were among his grumbles. 'I was approached far more often than I anticipated due possibly to the fact that the press were always conveniently situated in the same hotel,' he wrote.

Nevertheless, the notebooks and questions had to be faced once more. Knowing the diplomatic tip-toeing expected of them – and the presence on the quayside of MCC assistant secretary Billy Griffith can hardly have helped to loosen their tongues – Hutton and Palmer offered emollient words in dealing with the trip's many controversies. But the captain was less reticent in addressing the progress of the

---

[10]The *Ariguani* had also brought an MCC team home from the Caribbean in 1926, before the West Indies had been granted Test status.

Test series, the standard of umpiring and the challenges presented by febrile Caribbean crowds. 'We should have won in the West Indies,' he said. 'The brilliant light and fast wickets – like baked clay – and the continual noise affected our younger batsmen. It was like an English cup tie. I could not make myself heard in the field. There is no cricket like it in the world.'

He praised some players: Brian Statham was 'as good as any English fast bowler since the war', and gave qualified backing to others: Trueman still had quite a lot to learn and had 'his good and bad spells'. Palmer, meanwhile, heaped the credit on the captain for England's fightback from 2–0 down to draw the series. Hutton had scored 677 runs at an average of 96.71 in the Tests, including a monumental double-century to set up victory in the final match. Palmer said, 'He played a great part technically and the measure of his contribution is seen when it is realised how much he had to contend with outside the cricket field.'

Surprisingly, given his dislike of the hype that had preceded the series against West Indies, Hutton was not shy in discussing the challenges of retaining the Ashes in Australia the following winter. He thought the younger England players would have gained immeasurably from the pressurised atmosphere experienced on the tour. 'We must have a very good chance in Australia,' he said, underlining that the exposure to hostile crowds would prove beneficial. 'There's nothing like a West Indian crowd: certainly they are far tougher than even the crowd at Sydney.' On the dockside were the wives of Bailey, Palmer, Lock and Willie Watson. As the players said their farewells, they were leaving behind what *The Times* later dubbed 'the second most controversial tour in cricket history'.

CARIBBEAN CAULDRON

No Test series has created a legacy to match MCC's tour of Australia in 1932–33. In an attempt to curb the phenomenal run-scoring feats of Don Bradman, the England captain Douglas Jardine conceived a plan which involved his pace attack – spearheaded by the Nottinghamshire duo Harold Larwood and Bill Voce – bowling deliberately at the bodies of Australia's batsmen (hence the term

'Bodyline') with a packed close field on the leg side. Intent on self-preservation, the Australians offered easy catches as they fended the ball off. Jardine's shock tactics were startlingly effective: Bradman's average was reduced to a mere 56 – it had been 139 in England in 1930 – as England won the series 4–1 and regained the Ashes. The result, though, took second place to the furore it sparked, fracturing relations between the teams and demolishing Australian notions of English fair play.

While the MCC tour of West Indies in 1953–54 did not generate the same level of outrage, it proceeded against a background of seething sporting and political tension. The trip was significant from the outset because Len Hutton was the first professional captain to lead England overseas. After steering his team, in 1953, to a first Ashes series victory since the Second World War, his appointment for the follow-up assignment in the Caribbean might have been expected to be a formality, yet it was far from a matter of rubber-stamping his captaincy. At Lord's, from where MCC had been overseeing the national team's foreign expeditions since 1903, there were grave doubts whether a professional cricketer, by definition a man plucked from the ranks, could cope with the sporting, diplomatic and social demands of a challenging tour.

As Hutton and his men returned home, senior figures in English cricket administration felt events in the West Indies had confirmed their worst fears. Not that MCC were free from blame over how the trip unfolded. 'It was incredibly badly organised,' Trevor Bailey recalled in 2009. 'To pick a manager who had never managed a side before, a captain who had never captained overseas before and a vice-captain who had never done the job before ... it was bound to be a bit shambolic.' On the eve of departure, Sir Walter Monckton,[11] minister for labour in Sir Winston Churchill's Tory government, had warned the players in general terms of some of the political pitfalls awaiting them, but that was the extent of the briefings.

---

[11]As a schoolboy, Walter Monckton played for Harrow in a famous 1910 game against Eton at Lord's. It became known as 'Fowler's match' after Eton's Robert Fowler scored 64 in Eton's second innings follow-on, then took eight for 23 as Harrow were bowled out for 45. Eton won by nine runs.

The trouble began during their stopover in Bermuda, where they found a colour bar in operation in tourist hotels, and continued in Jamaica where almost immediately the cricketers were exposed to the competing tensions of the region. While the black population were increasingly agitating for an end to British colonial rule, the expat whites were growing fearful that their idyllic existences were under threat. The players quickly became tired of being buttonholed at cocktail parties and told, as one recalled, 'You must beat these people or else our lives won't be worth living.' Those residents most obsessed with class were affronted that MCC had sent an England team under the command of a state-educated professional captain after the previous tour had been led by the Old Etonian Gubby Allen. They missed the fact that Allen's team had been soundly beaten.

On and off the field, the incidents piled up like a charge sheet against Hutton: bad behaviour in hotels and at social functions, dissent on the field, a bowler no-balled for throwing, an umpire called a 'black bastard'. The young Fred Trueman was often at the centre of complaints, though on at least two occasions the culprit may well have been somebody else.

Coming off the field on 205 not out at tea on the third day of the final Test in Jamaica, Hutton brushed past a man apparently trying to congratulate him. Unfortunately, it was Alexander Bustamante, chief minister of Jamaica. Hutton, wrapped in concentration during an epic innings, did not recognise the politician. The unintended snub, smoothed over after intense diplomacy, caused the most public of all the rows on the tour. There were other troubling incidents unconnected with the behaviour of the England players, but indicative of regional tensions. During the third Test in Guyana a riot broke out in the crowd after local hero Cliff McWatt was run out. And an arson attack destroyed the main stand at Trinidad's Queen's Park Oval in the build-up to the fourth Test.

If Hutton wondered what awaited him when he reported back to Lord's, the contents of a telegram delivered to the team hotel in Kingston on the eve of the final Test gave a broad hint. The MCC missive read simply, 'Stressing importance no resentment shown to umpires decisions under any circumstances in fifth Test and no comment made to press.' As he opened the envelope, perhaps he expected a good luck message. Instead there was just a warning that the reputation of the club – and English cricket – took precedence over the result.

To an extent, the England captain and his team had been caught between the often confused and contradictory aims of MCC tours. As the club's head of heritage and collections Neil Robinson said at a symposium at Lord's in 2023, 'Cricket tours from their very early origin were about a lot more than just playing cricket in far-flung places. They were part of the social glue that held English-speaking communities together right across the globe.' But while he dutifully attended the plethora of official and semi-official functions (later urging MCC that in future they should be drastically cut back), Hutton was more interested in winning than diplomatic missions.

If the 2–0 defeat under Allen in 1947–48 had not been warning enough, a comprehensive 3–1 reverse in England in 1950 had underscored that the West Indies side were now a major force in international cricket. 'The days of missionary work and Caribbean semi-holidays were over,' said Surrey batsman Peter May. Hutton, whose approach to the game had been shaped in the unforgiving environment of the Yorkshire dressing-room of the 1930s, would always have put results ahead of goodwill. In four Ashes series since the war, he had simultaneously admired and endured the hard-nosed approach of the Australians, with a growing conviction that this was the way that Test series were won. But after a few days at home – not enough time to recover either physically or mentally – the England captain knew the inquest would begin. What he might not have anticipated was a fight to hang on to his job.

AN INQUEST AND A PLOT

Nine days after stepping off the *Ariguani*, Len Hutton and Charles Palmer reported to Lord's. It was the evening before the traditional season-opening fixture between MCC and Yorkshire. Towards the end of a cold and cheerless first day during which, eight miles away, West Bromwich Albion defeated Preston North End in the FA Cup final, Hutton emerged to open the Yorkshire innings and was applauded to the crease by a crowd appreciative of his herculean efforts in the Caribbean. He nudged a single to get off the mark, but then edged a wide delivery from Surrey captain Stuart Surridge on to his off stump. In a precursor to the miserable summer ahead, the rest of the match was washed out.

Hutton's initial debrief alongside Palmer – at which he may have handed in his tour report – was with Lord Rosebery, the former captain of Surrey, son of a Liberal prime minister and incumbent MCC president; Harry Altham, the treasurer and newly elected chairman of the home selectors; and Ronny Aird, the secretary. The next evening, Palmer faced MCC's main committee on his own. Two days later, after the match had been abandoned, Hutton had a meeting with the selectors. Palmer recalled his own encounter. 'There were one or two people who made you feel that you had your head on the chopping block and they just wanted to see how the axe was going to be wielded.' He must have performed well because in the following days two letters dropped through his letterbox.

Altham wrote to say, 'How admirable I thought you were when you came to Lord's for the difficult committee meeting.' The second letter, from Gubby Allen, began, 'Just a line to congratulate you on a fine performance yesterday. You had to take on a section of the committee which was, and I know what I am talking about, very hostile to the events of last winter and were looking for any slip on your part which would help their case. You were so very clear and forthright in your answers that they got absolutely nowhere.' Allen then tackled what was surely his main reason for writing: 'Looking to the future now, I would like your opinion. Do you think a manager on a rather higher level is a solution and indeed a worthwhile proposition, especially if Len is to captain?'

This was a transparent attempt by Allen to push his claims for the role of manager on the forthcoming Ashes tour. As Hutton was shortly to discover, there was no limit to the politicking and plotting that went on in the Lord's pavilion. Much of this emanated from a powerful inner cabal consisting of Allen, Sir Pelham Warner and Walter Robins.

The octogenarian Warner wielded less power within MCC than had once been the case, but although Allen was emerging as his anointed successor, he retained an influential voice. Warner had chaired the selection committee for the West Indies tour and naturally took an interest in the post-mortem. He was able to exert his influence, too, through his editorship of *The Cricketer*, the magazine he had founded in 1921 and where he contributed often anonymous op-eds. Allen, 51, had seen his career advanced by Warner's patronage, particularly in his appointment as captain for the fence-mending post-Bodyline Ashes tour of 1936–37. As one of Douglas Jardine's pace attack four years earlier, he had refused to participate in the captain's tactics. He was already one of the most influential voices in the game, a veteran administrator and a canny, calculating committee man. Robins, 47, completed a triumvirate of former Middlesex captains, leading the county as recently as 1950, and had been Allen's vice-captain in Australia. He was another vocal advocate of what was usually called 'brighter cricket' – in essence a more attacking approach to the game.

Hutton was clear about the trio's influence, calling them 'the "inner circle" who direct the policy of the game'. Their doubts about Hutton were not only because he was the son of a builder who unapologetically earned his living from cricket. He was viewed as an exemplar of a dour professionalism which was threatening public interest in the game. They were not alone in questioning Hutton's tactical acumen: after defeat in the second Test in the West Indies left England in danger of losing the series, a group of senior players had confronted the captain and demanded that his safety-first approach be abandoned.

At Lord's, there were also concerns about Hutton's personality. 'I do not feel Hutton is a leader,' Warner had said in a letter to Australian prime minister Robert Menzies after the tour. Warner's *Cricketer* magazine carried a number of pointed articles about captaincy in the spring of 1954. Warner, Allen and Robins now formed an alliance with Errol Holmes, an MCC committee member and former captain of Surrey, who was to play a key role in the intrigue that now threatened Hutton's tenure, although they got Aird to do much of the dirty work.

The first hint to the outside world that a major story was about to break came in an exclusive by Charles Bray in the *Daily Herald* on 10 May. Under the headline 'Lifting the load from Len Hutton,' Bray outlined the distinct possibility of 'a drastic change in the responsibilities and duties of captain and manager for the Australian tour'. He made it clear that Hutton would probably continue as captain, but many off-field responsibilities would be off-loaded to a 'big boss' who would probably be 'an influential member of the MCC committee, or even the MCC secretary [Aird] himself'. Bray added, 'It is designed primarily to relieve the captain of the 101 awkward decisions he has to make outside the actual playing. It is a sensible plan. One that should have been adopted years ago.'

The idea floated at the end of Allen's letter to Palmer clearly points to Bray's source. His story continued, 'It will work provided the right man is found. G.O. Allen comes to mind. He has taken a side to Australia, is a member of the MCC committee and, significantly, will help to choose the team this winter.' It is not hard to imagine Allen and Bray being friends, and the journalist would certainly have regarded Allen as a contact to be cultivated. Bray had played for Essex as an amateur, sometimes acting as captain, before the war and would have fitted in easily at Lord's. 'His personal style was such that he was frequently presumed to be the gentleman from *The Times*,' said his *Wisden* obituary in 1994. But the source could have been the notoriously indiscreet Robins, who would also have encountered Bray in Middlesex-Essex matches.

There were certainly solid arguments for tweaking the role of tour manager after Palmer's unhappy experience in the West Indies. Rather unkindly, Bailey described the bespectacled Palmer as 'a natural for the role of a hen-pecked bank clerk in a farce'. Palmer admitted, 'It got to the stage where I didn't know where the next arrow was coming from – all I knew was that it was coming.' He was just 34, three years younger than Hutton, and, as the amateur captain of Leicestershire, had been selected as player-manager, primarily as a means of trimming costs. One of the key recommendations of his report was that no manager should again have to combine the two roles.

A week after his 'big boss' exclusive, Bray had an even bigger scoop. Elbowing the England football team's pre-World Cup defeat by Yugoslavia out of the back page lead slot was the revelation that David Sheppard, presumed lost to international cricket as he studied at Cambridge for a career in the church, was being considered to lead England's defence of the Ashes. 'Supporters of the campaign – and they include some very influential members of the MCC – want the man who led Sussex so brilliantly last season to be captain of England in Australia this coming winter,' Bray wrote. The words 'include some very influential members of the MCC' must have made Hutton choke on his toast and marmalade: until this revelation, they were the only people who knew anything about the idea.

Sheppard was a compelling candidate for MCC. First, and most importantly, he was an amateur. He was also charismatic, good-looking and blessed with an easy charm. At Cambridge University, he had outperformed even the prodigy Peter May. In 1950, Sheppard had scored 227 against the touring West Indians. The following summer, including appearances for Sussex at the end of the university term, he passed 2000 runs for the season, and in 1952 was top of the national averages with 2262 at 64. His 1581 runs for Cambridge that summer are frozen in time as a record after university cricket was stripped of first-class status in 2019.

He was elevated to the Sussex captaincy at 24 in 1953 and lifted them from 13th to second in the Championship, narrowly missing out on the county's first title. 'We always said he was the best captain we ever had,' said the all-rounder Alan Oakman. 'He led by example and he supported everyone – and he didn't swear at us either.' But Sheppard became convinced that his future lay with the church and he began a two-year programme of studies at Ridley Hall, Cambridge. He was planning to play for Sussex in the summer holidays, but was fully committed to returning to his course in the winter: going to Australia had not entered his mind.

Now he found himself dragged unwillingly into the planning of a coup d'état. Sheppard was invited to visit Aird at his home – the plotters were careful not to have their preferred candidate spotted inside Lord's. Aird informed Sheppard in advance that his front door would be unlocked. 'You can come straight in without too much chance of recognition,' Sheppard remembered being told. 'We went to conspiratorial lengths to prevent anyone knowing that we were discussing anything.' Yet he was dismayed when Bray's story made the plot public and suspected Holmes, who had 'made much of the running' and was 'a natural backstairs intriguer', as the source of the leak.

Sheppard was in a quandary, not least because Hutton was a friend. 'Was it right to break my training for the ministry for two terms?' he wrote. 'Was it right to offer myself as a rival as captain to Len

Hutton? As I thought about the first question and discussed it with older friends, it seemed that, if I were to captain the side, this was an altogether different contribution to make to cricket than simply going as a member of the team. Rightly or wrongly I decided that it would only be right to break my training if it was a question of the captaincy.'

Sheppard was undoubtedly sincere and his decision to pause his studies if offered the captaincy was supported when, at the end of June, he received a letter from the Archbishop of Canterbury, Geoffrey Fisher. The two men had never met, but Fisher had received a letter from Sheppard's Cambridge college principal Cyril Bowles, in whom Sheppard had confided after the first approach from Aird. 'One can quite understand it was a difficult decision for you to make,' Fisher wrote. 'I would like merely to say that, as far as I can judge, I entirely approve of your decision. Here is a piece of what I should regard as direct service to the wider interests of the Kingdom of God which you can render: and, as I understand, there really is a crying need for someone to bring back into the higher ranks of English cricket a sort of moral decisiveness which has been slipping.' Hutton, it can be assumed, would have been unimpressed to learn that he had been lacking 'moral decisiveness'.

Sheppard had made up his mind after consulting Norman Sykes, Dixie Professor of Ecclesiastical History at Cambridge. Born at Liversedge in the West Riding, Sykes would, said his *Times* obituary, 'excuse himself from other obligations if Yorkshire were playing cricket in the neighbourhood'. Sheppard had introduced Sykes to Hutton a few years earlier: Sykes had been thrilled to meet one of his heroes, while Hutton came away impressed by Sykes's knowledge of the Moravian religion, a branch of Protestantism under whose strict principles Hutton had been brought up.

As the story gathered momentum, Hutton kept his counsel. 'I tried not to say or do anything that might be misconstrued,' he wrote in his end-of-career memoir. 'For all the consideration about my welfare that was implied I suspected that someone, somewhere, was trying to get me out of the captaincy – for what reason I did not know.' When Sheppard asked Sykes how he thought Hutton might react if he were to replace him, Sykes, who had recently been in contact with Hutton, said he thought part of him might be relieved to shed the burden of leadership.

Trying to establish exactly what – if anything – passed between the two leading characters in the story is hard to deduce because of Sheppard's conflicting accounts. 'Perhaps the simplest thing would have been to ask Len himself, but the opportunity did not present itself,' he recalled in his autobiography in 1964. But Hutton was in Cambridge from 19 to 21 May for Yorkshire's match against the University, ample time for contact to be made, assuming Sheppard was in the city.

Interviewed by Michael Marshall in the mid–1980s, Sheppard allowed himself to be 'rather more indiscreet'. In his second version, he recounted a conversation when the issue was at its peak in which Hutton said, 'I think they are going to ask you to captain England in Australia. I very much hope you will agree and we'll tell you what to do.' More confusingly, a slightly different version of this conversation appeared in Sheppard's book, placing it in 1952 when it could have had nothing to do with their competing claims to lead the defence of the Ashes. Sheppard's biographer, Andrew Bradstock, also believed the conversation had been in 1952.

The question of whether Sheppard was good enough to open the innings in Australia doesn't seem to have been widely debated. On the back of his exploits for Cambridge and Sussex in 1950, he had been chosen for the Ashes tour of 1950–51. This was less of a selectorial gamble than it might now appear. The standard of university cricket was high and the players had, after all, also proved themselves in the Championship. But Sheppard struggled with the pace of Australian pitches – bowlers quickly noted, and exploited, his high backlift – and while, with Hutton's help, he made technical adjustments, he came home with a top score of 41 in three Test innings in Australia.

He had also played in two home Tests, both against a weak Indian attack in 1952, scoring 119 and sharing in an opening stand of 143 with Hutton at The Oval. Nevertheless, his domestic form was good: while captaining Sussex in 1953 he had made 2270 runs at 45 with seven hundreds. And the quality and elegance of his strokeplay was not in question – 'He was a magnificent batsman, technically one of the best,' said Fred Trueman, not normally free with compliments to amateurs.

AMATEUR HOUR

The roots of why MCC were so keen to return to an amateur captain lay buried deep in the history of the game and the English class system. We may now view the 1950s as a time of growing prosperity and increased social mobility as the reforms of the post-war Labour government began to chip away at class barriers. In reality progress was glacial. As the historian David Kynaston pointed out in his book *Family Britain 1951–57*, some 90 per cent of respondents to a survey by the *People* newspaper in 1950–51 placed themselves into a tightly defined social class.

From cricket's earliest days as a codified and organised sport, there had been two types of player – the professional, for whom the sport was his livelihood, and the amateur, a man with a secure income outside the game who played as a leisure pursuit. The difference was enshrined in the Gentlemen v Players fixture, first contested at Lord's in 1806 and in the mid-1950s still played twice a season. This was no hit-and-giggle affair: outside of the Test matches, Gents v Players was the blue-riband event of the summer. The match at Lord's was often viewed as a Test and tour trial, with both teams chosen by the home selection panel.

It was axiomatic that a county or England captain would be an amateur. In 1954, only five of 17 county captains were professionals, a measure of the ingrained belief that the gentleman amateur possessed leadership qualities and commanded a respect that the professional could not match. In county committee rooms as well as among the hierarchy at MCC, it was thought that a professional captain whose living was at stake would be less likely to take risks in pursuit of victory. This specious argument was demolished in 1951 when Warwickshire captain Tom Dollery, the first professional to lead a county on a full-time basis, guided his team, all of whom were also professionals, to the Championship. They did it with a brand of dynamic, enterprising cricket in stark contrast to the grey conformity of many of their rivals. 'Dollery showed that the paid player can become a captain in the real sense of the word,' wrote *Wisden*'s Norman Preston in his 1952 Editor's Notes. 'Dollery has raised the status of the professional.'

County Captains in 1954

County		Appointed	Status
Derbyshire	Guy Willatt	1951	Amateur
Essex	Doug Insole	1950	Amateur
Glamorgan	Wilf Wooller	1947	Amateur
Gloucestershire	Jack Crapp	1953	Professional
Hampshire	Desmond Eagar	1946	Amateur
Kent	Doug Wright	1954	Professional
Lancashire	Cyril Washbrook	1954	Professional
Leicestershire	Charles Palmer	1950	Amateur
Middlesex	Bill Edrich	1953*+	Amateur
Northamptonshire	Dennis Brookes	1954	Professional
Nottinghamshire	Reg Simpson	1951+	Amateur
Somerset	Ben Brocklehurst	1953	Amateur
Surrey	Stuart Surridge	1952	Amateur
Sussex	Hubert Doggart	1954	Amateur
Warwickshire	Tom Dollery	1949†	Professional
Worcestershire	Ronnie Bird	1952	Amateur
Yorkshire	Norman Yardley	1948	Amateur

*Edrich had been joint captain with Denis Compton in 1951 and 1952.
†Dollery had been joint captain with Ronald Maudsley in 1948.
+Edrich and Simpson had given up their professional status in order to be appointed captain.

In the minds of professionals, attitudes remained hard to shift. During the fourth Ashes Test at Old Trafford in 1926, the England captain Arthur Carr was struck down by tonsillitis. The selectors went to the dressing-room to ask Jack Hobbs, England's greatest cricketer, to take over. Hobbs, 43, who had just become the highest run-scorer in Ashes history, was playing in his 47th Test,[12] but he was also a professional and was, as his biographer Leo McKinstry observed, 'immersed in the tradition of amateur leadership'. Hobbs's first reaction was not to accept the honour, but to consider the claims of a teammate: 'But Mr Stevens is in the XI,' he said. Greville Stevens, the Middlesex

[12]Hobbs's final total of 3636 runs in Ashes matches is still second on the all-time list. Don Bradman (5028) has the most.

leg-spinner, was 25 and making just his second Test appearance, yet Hobbs's instinct was that the Oxford-educated amateur should take over the team. Hobbs was talked round and thus became the first professional to lead England in a home Test, albeit as a stand-in. The Kent amateur, Percy Chapman, was drafted in as captain for the series decider at The Oval.

Hobbs's use of 'Mr' when referring to Stevens was also revealing. Amateurs were normally addressed in this way, while professionals, especially when spoken to by their captains or in correspondence from their employers, would usually be called by their surnames. Tom Graveney found himself in trouble for breaching protocol in 1950. 'Well played, David,' he said to Sheppard after he had reached a century for Cambridge University against Gloucestershire. Basil Allen, the martinet amateur captain of Gloucestershire, was furious. 'He's Mr Sheppard to you,' he snapped. Later, Allen sought out Sheppard in the Cambridge dressing-room. 'I must apologise for Graveney's impertinence,' he said, 'I think you'll find it won't happen again.'

On scorecards and in the pages of *Wisden*, the initials of amateurs were given before their Christian names, while professionals' initials came after. So when Hutton and Sheppard shared their Oval opening stand against India in 1952, the scorecard would have read 'Hutton L.' followed by 'D.S. Sheppard'. The divisions ran deep. Some professionals found later careers as coaches at private schools, where they would be expected to be deferential to their young charges. 'Come on, Sir, get your feet to the ball,' Bert Robinson, formerly of Northamptonshire, called to the teenage Ted Dexter at Radley College in the early 1950s.

On many grounds, amateurs still changed in different dressing-rooms and entered the field via different gates. The Nottinghamshire batsman John Clay remembered playing under the amateur England opener Reg Simpson. 'We'd go down to London to play at Lord's, we'd be standing up in the third class and he'd be sitting down in the first.' While the Notts professionals eked out their five-shillings meal allowance, Simpson ordered smoked salmon. At The Oval, Surrey's post-war professionals were not allowed to drink in the members' bar. 'The eyes of the world are on you,' captain Errol Holmes told them. 'You can't afford to be seen drinking with the members.' This form of sporting and social apartheid was still in operation when the merits of Hutton and Sheppard as England captains were being debated in 1954, and neither man apparently chafed at the iniquity: it was an accepted part of the sport.

The amateurs were not, however, a homogenous group. Their abilities varied widely: Simpson was considered the bravest and one of the best players of fast bowling in the country; Bob Barber of Warwickshire scored one of the great Ashes hundreds at Sydney in 1966; Peter May still ranks high among England's greatest post-war batsmen. Nor was appointing an amateur a guarantee that the game would proceed along Corinthian lines: Douglas Jardine's amateur status did not prevent him becoming the most ruthless Test captain the game had seen.

The MCC panjandrums pushing for Sheppard to take England to Australia might have overlooked an incident the previous summer at Cheltenham when, with Gloucestershire pursuing a small target on the last afternoon, the Sussex captain ordered his bowlers to fire the ball wide down the leg side to stem the scoring (the so-called leg theory despised by Gubby Allen). The match was drawn, but Sheppard was ashamed of his tactics. When the teams met again a fortnight later, he sought out Gloucestershire captain Jack Crapp to apologise.

Some amateurs, however, were hopeless and only earned their place in a county side through family connections or influence on the cricket committee. 'An amateur is a chap who says "I am available on that day and I will be playing." Not, "If you pick me..."' said Percy Fender, captain of Surrey in the 1920s. Often they led a team of hardened experienced pros, who ended up making the key decisions anyway. The anachronisms continued: at the end of 1957, the professional Dennis Brookes, having just led an unfancied Northamptonshire to second place in the Championship, had to make way for the amateur Raman Subba Row, while in 1960 Graveney was removed from the captaincy of Gloucestershire in favour of Tom Pugh, a colourful Old Etonian who finished his career with an average of 18. Pugh at least had the compensation of making the shortlist for the screen role of James Bond, missing out to Sean Connery.[13]

---

[13] Pugh later married Kitty Green, who had a role in the Bond film *Thunderball*. He was once arrested on suspicion of running a brothel on the King's Road, but not convicted.

It was against this stultifying background that in 1952 Hutton became England's first full-time professional captain. The number of amateurs among the country's leading players had been dwindling since the war, a harbinger of changing times. But there had still been a reluctance behind Hutton's promotion. 'His gravest fault was being a professional and the selectors (Yardley, Brown, Bob Wyatt and Leslie Ames) came in for grave criticism, especially Yardley, who, as Yorkshire captain, was thought doubly treacherous to the cause,' wrote Derek Birley in *A Social History of English Cricket*.

The most famous quote on the subject of amateur captaincy had been made in 1925 by Lord Hawke, the president and former captain of Yorkshire. 'Pray God no professional shall ever captain England,' he said at the county's winter dinner. 'I love and admire them all, but we have always had an amateur skipper and when the day comes when we shall have no more amateurs captaining England it will be a thousand pities.' Hawke's remarks were made in response to an article written by the maverick Lancashire spinner Cec Parkin in the *Weekly Dispatch*, suggesting that Hobbs was the obvious appointment as England's next captain. Sir Pelham Warner, later part of the cabal keen to oust Hutton as captain, attempted to explain what Hawke had intended: 'What no doubt Lord Hawke meant was that it will be a bad day for England when no amateur is fit to play for England.' However, when denigrating Hutton in a letter to Robert Menzies, Warner wrote, 'Was Lord Hawke right?'

The first indication that times might be changing came on the Ashes tour of 1950–51 when Denis Compton, a professional from a north London state school, was appointed vice-captain to Freddie Brown. Compton's promotion ahead of him roused Hutton to fury and his journalist friend Jim Kilburn had to talk him out of refusing to join the tour. In the event, Compton's performance in Australia provided an unexpected boost to Hutton's CV. The Middlesex batsman's charisma did not translate to the work-a-day realities of captaincy. Compton did not cut back on his customary hectic social life on tour, struggled with the bat (his Test average was 7.57), and watched as Brown frequently consulted Hutton on tactical matters. Hutton's behaviour, meanwhile, was unimpeachable and he scored 533 runs at 88.83 in the Tests.

Still MCC squirmed over his elevation. Hutton was aware of the talk of change – the subject must have occupied hours of downtime in county dressing-rooms – but recognised that deeply conservative forces were at work. 'I knew that in a country such as England, where tradition governs so many things, almost a revolution in our way of thinking would be needed to bring about such a change,' he wrote. When asked about the captaincy on his return from Australia in 1951, he had insisted he would accept the job only if he could do so as a professional.

That did not prevent MCC making a late effort to persuade him to change his mind and turn amateur, as Hutton's idol Walter Hammond had done in 1938. There would have been no shortage of businessmen ready to offer Hutton a sinecure, but he would have none of it. 'I felt that an opportunity had been given to me to serve cricket and the professional cricketer as had been given to few men,' he said. By the time he was announced as England's new captain on 26 May, 1952, it was not unexpected, yet it still made most front pages the next morning.

The news was generally welcomed, if cautiously in some quarters. Geoffrey Green, the cricket correspondent of *The Times*, contributed some of the most cogent words, as befitting someone known for covering the vastly more egalitarian world of football. 'Though there are many who will look back with anxious eyes and with sorrow at the passing of an age, there are yet those who will welcome the ending of an anachronism,' Green wrote. 'The amateur, in the older meaning of the word, no longer truly exists. He has largely been destroyed by the economic circumstances of the mid-twentieth century. Further, to find such a man, both with the character to lead and also the quality indisputably to hold a place in an England team, has progressively become more difficult. In this age of so-called equal opportunity for all the professional player has at last attained his fullest stature.'

In the *Daily Express*, Pat Marshall saw it as a step towards the battles to come with Australia. 'Now England can get down to business – the business of putting herself back in her rightful place – ON TOP,' he wrote. 'Yes, they fear Len in Australia for his ruthless efficiency as much as they do any man. They know how much he drives himself: they fear he might be able to drive others as relentlessly.' Crawford

White of the *News Chronicle* spoke for the majority when he wrote, 'This will be widely popular, because the public likes the idea of the best man for the job getting it.' Even the *Daily Telegraph*'s arch-Establishment man, E. W. Swanton, offered a polite nod of qualified approval. 'It is always a pleasure when distinction comes to a man great in his own sphere, who wears his honours as modestly as a Hutton.'

A comfortable 3–0 win over a struggling Indian team did not prove the point either way, and there was no winter tour in 1952–53. But recapturing the Ashes in 1953 and inspiring a fightback in the West Indies should have given Hutton some security of tenure. Instead, he found himself clinging to office.

BACK IN CHARGE

The opening weeks of the summer of 1954 were among the most miserable of Len Hutton's career. Dealing with back pain, jaded in the aftermath of his troubled winter in the Caribbean, facing an unsubtle and suddenly very public attempt to remove him from the England captaincy, he became, in his own words, 'run down and rather dispirited'. He recalled, 'When a cricketer is not 100 per cent fit, every degree of physical stress is felt more keenly than the last and, at the same time, his mental anxiety increases.' News of MCC reaching out to David Sheppard must have sent his stress levels soaring. As David Woodhouse wrote in his book on the West Indies tour, Hutton's low mood 'was attributable more to his sense of having his neck measured up than the fact that his back was playing up.'

On Sunday 2 May, the rest day of the MCC–Yorkshire fixture, Hutton was at Waterloo Station to meet the 16 players who made up the first Test tour party from Pakistan. The team's arrival at Southampton had been delayed by a gale battering the south coast. 'I'm sorry about this weather of ours,' Hutton told their captain Abdul Hafeez Kardar as he stepped off the train. Hutton's sentiments would become all too familiar to the visiting cricketers during a summer of unrelenting gloom.

Later in the week, Hutton was confirmed as captain for the first Test, starting at Lord's on 10 June. Although it was customary to name the captain for one match at a time, at least early in the season, the decision was attacked by Crawford White in the *News Chronicle*. 'Their caution could mean that they are by no means sure that Hutton will retain the captaincy for the Australian tour and they are giving themselves and the tour selectors room for manoeuvre,' he wrote. 'There may be some wisdom in that but I would warn our selectors that they will face one of the biggest public outcries in sport if they attempt to bypass Hutton at this time.' White's words, while hinting that he may have known about the misgivings over Hutton at Lord's, require further explanation.

Teams for home Test matches were named by a home selection panel under the aegis of the Board of Control, whereas MCC appointed a selection sub-committee for tours. There was considerable overlap. In 1954, both groups were chaired by Harry Altham, the MCC treasurer who had played for Surrey and Hampshire, but had no international experience. He was in his first and only year as chairman. 'Why Harry was asked to be chairman in '54 I have no idea,' said his grandson Robin Brodhurst in 2022. 'He agreed to do it purely for the one year.' Altham, a housemaster at Winchester College, was an irreproachable servant of the game and the author of one of the standard historical texts, *A History of Cricket*, a part-work first published in book form in 1926.

Both selection panels included Walter Robins, Norman Yardley, the Yorkshire captain, and Les Ames, the former Kent and England wicketkeeper, who, two years earlier, had been the first former professional to become a selector. The group choosing the tour party was supplemented by Gubby Allen and Charles Palmer. It was at least a more cohesive group than the 11-man committee which had chosen the 1950–51 squad. The overmanning in the selection process led to MCC sending out what Neville Cardus called 'the weakest conglomeration of cricketers which has ever represented this country at cricket against Australia.'

Hutton's appointment may have improved his humour, but it did little for his scratchy form. He had a top score of 63 from eight innings by the time he missed a couple of Championship games to undergo mud-bath treatment on his troublesome back in the Yorkshire spa town of Harrogate. Clearly, it was time for a break.

'Specialists confirmed what I had long suspected, that the trouble had been building up for six or seven years,' he said.

There were other reasons for his gloom. On 10 May, it was announced that George Hirst had died at 82. The great Yorkshire and England all-rounder (36,356 first-class runs, 2742 wickets), had been Hutton's first coach when he arrived as a new boy at Headingley. 'He did more for me than any other cricketer,' Hutton said. A front-page editorial in the *Daily Mail* was a sign of Hirst's stature. 'He was good humoured and obstinate, cheerful and stubborn, a traditionalist and an innovator,' the paper said. 'He loved cricket – and cricket loved him.' Affection for Hirst was one area at least where Hutton and Allen spoke in unison. 'The nicest, kindest man in the world,' said Allen of the man who had been his coach at Eton.

A fortnight after the revelation that Sheppard was under consideration to take over the captaincy, the MCC committee formally debated the issue for the first time. The minutes note, 'After considerable discussion in which Mr C.H. Palmer and Mr R.W.V. Robins, members of the MCC selection sub-committee, were invited to join, it was decided that no special instructions should be given to the MCC selection sub-committee concerning the captaincy for the tour to Australia, 1954–55. It was agreed that the sub-committee should be given a free hand to recommend the captain considered by them to be best fitted for the position and that should they recommend L. Hutton his selection would be approved by the MCC committee.' At first reading, this might seem to be an endorsement of Hutton, albeit a lukewarm one. But the very fact that it was debated at all, and merited 'considerable discussion', indicates that Hutton's future as captain was in serious doubt.

A measure of the England captain's mounting anxiety was that he now chose to write to E.W. Swanton, hardly a natural ally. Hutton was aware that the man from the *Telegraph* was formidably well connected at Lord's and would have had a good sense of the mood of the committee. Hutton's letter has not been preserved, but Swanton's response read, 'You say you hope those in authority have still "a little faith" in me,' he wrote. 'From all I know they have a great deal. I believe there may be some who wonder whether it is asking too much for you to get half the runs in Australia and run the whole show as well. I should say your captaincy in England is automatic until '56 inclusive. As for the Australian Tour, there is perhaps a case for and against. There is a great deal of heart-searching on the subject – and, I think, it is now realised belatedly by everyone that a great mistake was made in not sending to West Indies a strong manager who could have really helped you.' Swanton went on to say he could see 'the many points on both sides'.

Meanwhile, Hutton returned to cricket in time to lead England in the first Test against Pakistan, although the continuing wretched weather meant he had just two innings to recalibrate. He made one against Sussex at Hull, before hitting 44 on the first day of a rain-ruined Whitsun weekend Roses match at Headingley. The Test was similarly soggy. 'We want to see the sun,' Kardar grumbled in the build-up, but he waited in vain: play did not begin until 3.45 p.m. on the fourth day. Pakistan were hustled out for 87, but when England responded just before lunch on the final day, Hutton was yorked for a 13-ball duck by Khan Mohammad. When England were 30 ahead with nine wickets down, Hutton declared in the hope of exploiting the fragile confidence of Pakistan's frontline batsmen. They lost a wicket in the second over, but recovered to secure the expected draw.

The long hours waiting for a break in the weather enabled Hutton to have some important conversations. He was left in no doubt that talk of replacing him for the Ashes tour was not solely newspaper speculation. 'A former England captain made it clear to me that I was not everybody's choice as captain,' he wrote. His confidant may have been R.E.S. Wyatt, recently removed from the home selection panel or, intriguingly, Douglas Jardine. The architect of Bodyline was an admirer of Hutton and a member of a committee handling the logistics of the forthcoming tour.

Four days after the end of the Test, Hutton was back at Lord's for Yorkshire's Championship match against Middlesex. More agitated than ever, he had a meeting with Ronny Aird after the first day and set out his position. Aird assured him the speculation had not emanated from Lord's – a politician's half-truth at best – and suggested Hutton explain his position in a letter to the committee. Hutton recalled, 'I told them briefly that if MCC wanted me to captain England in Australia, I would be most happy to accept the responsibility, as I felt I could do the job successfully. On the other hand I said that if they preferred to consider my selection only as a player, I would be equally pleased to go and give my fullest support to whoever else was elected captain.'

Hutton's decision was not necessarily clear cut. The financial implications were considerable. By travelling as a player, Hutton would be paid the regular tour fee of £850 (around £19,500 in 2025). However, as he told Aird, newspapers were already offering him contracts worth £10,000 (now more than £230,000) to cover the series. 'But it was not as a *journalist* that I wanted to go,' Hutton said. He must have written his letter immediately, because the MCC committee discussed the matter two days after the Hutton-Aird meeting. It was agreed to hand Aird's report on his conversation with Hutton to Altham, who would relay its contents to the selection sub-committee. 'The secretary was asked to emphasise the confidential nature of the matter,' record the minutes, presumably a reference to earlier leaks.

Having made his views plain to Aird, Hutton's stress levels may have dropped a little. But there was an insight into the extent of his turmoil in a conversation between Kilburn and Yardley as the Yorkshire party made its way to face Essex at Romford after the Middlesex game. 'Look, are you going to make Leonard captain for Australia?' Kilburn asked. 'Yes, I think so. No question about it,' Yardley replied. 'For God's sake tell him or you'll have him in a mental home,' Kilburn shot back. 'Put the chap out of his uncertainty.'

After two more failures against Middlesex, Hutton could go on no longer. On 23 June, his 38th birthday, it was announced by MCC that he was taking a three-week break on medical advice. He had been suffering from neuritis in his neck and back, 'produced by overstrain', said the statement, and after an examination by Bill Tucker, the 'sportsman's surgeon' who had operated on Compton's knee, he was advised to take another break. 'A good rest will put Len on his feet,' Dorothy Hutton reassured journalists calling the family home.

Kilburn used his front-page report in the *Yorkshire Post* to reinforce the point he had made to Yardley. 'If the Board of Control selection committee and the MCC selection committee, which are different bodies though containing members common to both, are resolved upon Hutton retaining the England captaincy, they might be doing a service by saying so without delay,' he wrote. 'A mind at rest helps a body in convalescence.'

Naturally, Hutton's withdrawal sparked immediate speculation about the captain for the second Test, due to begin at Trent Bridge on 1 July. Given that more than a month had passed since Bray's story about MCC's clandestine approach to Sheppard, it was odd that few saw what was coming when the home selectors entered emergency session the day after Hutton's withdrawal. In the *Daily Mail*, Alex Bannister reported that Hutton's deputy, Trevor Bailey, was 'almost certain' to be asked to take over. Bannister acknowledged 'gossip' about Sheppard, but added, 'I can see little sense in such a temporary move.' Even Bray backed Bailey's promotion, while mentioning Sheppard as a candidate to open the innings. In the *Daily Express*, Pat Marshall thought Bailey was 'odds on'. Denys Rowbotham of the *Manchester Guardian* pushed the claims of Lancashire captain Cyril Washbrook, Hutton's old opening partner, who hadn't played a Test since 1951, while dropping Sheppard's name into the mix. One writer was in the know: in the *News Chronicle*, White had a front-page story declaring Sheppard as the 'No. 1 favourite' to take over.

With exquisite timing, in both senses, Sheppard had recorded his first hundred of the season against Gloucestershire at Hove on the day Hutton's rest cure was announced. When Gloucestershire batted the following day, Sheppard left the field to take a phone call from Lord's, not returning to his place in the slips for 45 minutes. He said nothing to his teammates, but soon the PA system crackled into life to tell the crowd that he had been appointed as England's stand-in captain.

A photograph of a jubilant Sheppard appeared on the front page of the *Daily Mail* and inevitably there was speculation that he might be more than a locum. 'When questioned about the possibility of his being available for Australia, Sheppard shrugged his shoulders and refused to comment,' Bannister wrote. He did reveal, however, that MCC had asked him to play all summer and that his tutors at Cambridge had agreed. White told his readers that Hutton remained favourite to lead the Ashes tour and predicted that Sheppard would now face a level of scrutiny he had not previously experienced.

In the *Express* Marshall thought the matter had already been decided. 'David Sheppard, of Sussex, a 25-year-old divinity student, will almost certainly captain the MCC side to Australia next winter, and therein lies the story of The Struggle,' he wrote. Marshall talked of 'bitter, behind-the-scenes cricket politics' and thought 'the anti-Hutton brigade rejoiced' at news of the incumbent captain's health issues. In addition, he revealed that Bailey's candidature had been fatally damaged by a row with MCC over a newspaper serialisation of his new book. The resolutely pro-Hutton *Daily Mirror* also feared the worst: 'It's the first nail in Len's coffin' was their headline over the news of Sheppard's promotion. 'No wonder Len Hutton is now a sick man,' wrote Ross Hall. 'For months a whispering campaign has been knifing him.'

At Nottingham – where England's top three, Sheppard, Simpson and May, were all amateurs, the first such instance since 1902 – Sheppard led England capably as they eased to victory by an innings and 129 runs. The dreadful weather meant Pakistan were still woefully short of match practice. Sheppard made 37 in his only innings, but the highlight was an enchanting 278 by Denis Compton on the second day. Such was the quality of the strokeplay that his teammates were torn between enjoying his innings or following the Wimbledon men's singles final between Jaroslav Drobny and Ken Rosewall on the dressing-room television. They resolved the dilemma by watching the cricket when Compton was batting, but turning to the tennis when Bailey was on strike. In his close-of-play summary for BBC radio, Swanton praised Sheppard for signalling to Compton from the balcony to concentrate and keep going. In fact, Sheppard had been providing updates from Centre Court.

On the rest day, selector Charles Palmer was at home in Leicester when there was a knock at his front door: it was Crawford White, who 'just happened to be passing'. 'He was a bit of a smoothie,' Palmer recalled. He made the journalist a cup of tea then spent half an hour gently repelling his questions. 'It was obvious that all he wanted was to find out from me – is it Sheppard or Hutton?' By that time, the argument was beginning to swing back in Hutton's favour.

Even as Sheppard celebrated victory at Trent Bridge, he discovered his chances of leading the team in Australia were fading. During the match, Robins visited his hotel room. 'I feel we've been unfair to Len,' he said. 'He was in a very difficult position in the West Indies.' Here was one of the instigators of the plot openly backtracking, perhaps because he sensed a growing lack of enthusiasm for a change among fellow members of the selection sub-committee. Sheppard later realised that MCC had been using him to advance its plot against Hutton and re-establish amateur captaincy. Or perhaps it was merely that now even Robins was beginning to understand the levels of stress the subterfuge had inflicted on Hutton. He may also have begun to appreciate the strength of public opinion: in a 'postcard ballot' conducted by the *News Chronicle* six out of seven respondents preferred Hutton. A similar poll in the *Express* found that overall 90.7 per cent of its readers favoured Hutton. When divided geographically, 80.6 per cent endorsed Hutton in the south, shooting up to 93.7 in the north.

The matter was finally settled in mid-July. First, Sheppard was confirmed as captain for the still-recuperating Hutton for the third Test at Old Trafford. Before that, there was another examination of his leadership skills and batting credentials in the Gentlemen v Players match at Lord's. In a low-scoring game, won by the Players by 49 runs, he failed twice with the bat, each time falling to pace. In the second innings, with just a few minutes to survive to the close in mellow evening sunshine, he was dismissed by the lively Surrey seamer Peter Loader for a duck, 'comprehensively bowled by a beautiful ball,' according to *The Times*.

Perhaps more perturbing for those watching from the committee room was the failure of his captaincy. 'When Hutton's illness made Sheppard a possible alternative captain for Australia, it was obvious that, should responsibility fall upon him, much would be lost of technical knowledge, tactical subtlety and the insight which can only come from experience,' wrote Rowbotham. 'But one assumed that Sheppard's tactics would not fall below certain standards of cricket logic. One assumed also that he would not lose his grip of a game when that grip was scarcely challenged. Yesterday both assumptions were proved false.' Swanton, meanwhile, dealt with Sheppard's failures by not mentioning him at all in his final-day report.

By then, momentum had turned decisively against Sheppard's candidature. The selection sub-committee had met at the East India Club in St James's Square on the first day of the match and voted to recommend to the main committee that Hutton be reappointed for the winter tour, subject to a successful medical examination. Altham had already visited Hutton and his doctor in Sheffield and been reassured that he was returning to full fitness. How the selectors voted has long been disputed. In his 1955 Notes, *Wisden* editor Norman Preston said the decision in Hutton's favour had been by 'only a single vote', but the following year he was asked by MCC to publish a correction saying the voting had been unanimous.

Author David Woodhouse speculated that Les Ames, Norman Yardley and Charles Palmer would have remained staunch Hutton loyalists. Brodhurst had no doubt about his grandfather's allegiance. 'Harry was absolutely convinced that Len was the right man to captain the tour,' he said. That would have left Gubby Allen and Robins as Sheppard supporters. Even then, the possibility remains that Allen and Robins sensed the mood of the meeting and also backed Hutton. Palmer, who did not remember there being a vote, certainly had no doubts. 'I went for Hutton for the simple reason that I'd lived with him through thick and thin in the West Indies. As far as I was concerned David Sheppard was a budding archbishop.'

Andrew Bradstock, who published a biography of Sheppard in 2019, wrote, 'Sheppard had reason to feel badly treated by the cricketing authorities. He had not wanted to be cast in the role of a rival to Hutton, a man he counted as a friend. The selectors who were opposed to Hutton had misjudged the popular mood and Sheppard had been caught in the crossfire.' In a letter to Stanley Thompson, one of his masters at Sherborne, Sheppard said, 'In some ways I'm disappointed about Australia, but personally I think rather glad to be out of it.'

Hutton returned to duty on the day after the conclusion of the Gentlemen v Players match. Walking out to bat on the second day of the Championship match against Nottinghamshire at Trent Bridge, he was given a warm reception by the home crowd. Hutton batted for two hours in making 32. He could have been forgiven for being distracted by events 120 miles away in St John's Wood, where the full MCC committee met to discuss the recommendations of the selection sub-committee. An hour after his dismissal, Hutton received a call from Lord's with the news he had been awaiting with such anxiety. A statement was issued to the media: 'Having received a reassuring medical report, the MCC committee have appointed L. Hutton captain of the MCC team to tour Australasia this winter. He will, in common with all other players, be subject to a final medical examination before sailing.'

In Australia the story had been followed with wry amusement and perhaps some hopes that Hutton, a cricketer they feared and admired, might be sacrificed as a sop to the English class system. The respected writer Ray Robinson believed that Australians regarded Hutton's reappointment as a 'policeman's knock on the door'. Lindsay Hassett, captain in the 1953 Ashes, said, 'I think England will be a tougher proposition under Hutton than any other captain. He is the only reasonable choice.' All-rounder Keith Miller, Hutton's new-ball adversary, added, 'All along I could not credit that the captaincy would go to any other man than the one who has restored English cricket to its pedestal.'

The near nine-week saga was over – with a resolution that was generally welcomed. 'No such cricket issue has caused such public indignation and fierce discussion since the Larwood Bodyline controversy,' wrote Bray, the journalist who had first broken the story. 'Probably the selectors were never in doubt, provided Hutton was fit,' speculated Geoffrey Green in *The Times*. 'I believe that with the right support, Hutton may now reach his peak as a captain on this tour,' said Swanton. Hutton was also endorsed by Sheppard. 'I would like to wish Len all the very best of luck and success in his task of bringing back the Ashes,' he said. 'I have confidence that he will do it.'

Mischief-makers might have spotted a note of asperity in Hutton's public acceptance. 'I am relieved to know that the selectors have thought I am the right type of fellow and I shall be proud and happy to lead an England side in Australia,' he said. 'Physically I know I can stand up to it. Our chances should be bright. We are much better equipped than when we last went there in 1950.'

He made 38 in the second innings at Trent Bridge, but, captaining Yorkshire the following day against the Combined Services at Harrogate, relieved the frustrations of the previous weeks with an uncharacteristically belligerent 163, including 29 fours. At a time of compulsory National Service, there were no easy pickings in this fixture. The Services attack was led by Leicestershire's Terry Spencer, rated by Hutton as one of the brightest new-ball prospects in the country, and also contained the Hampshire slow left-armer Peter

Sainsbury. They couldn't stop Hutton. 'In 25 minutes he increased his score by 50, the bowling being as near annihilation as makes no matter,' wrote Eric Stanger in the *Yorkshire Post*.

Sheppard's period as stand-in ended in the third Test at Old Trafford, another soggy draw with three days completely washed out. Sheppard went back to playing for Sussex and resumed his studies. He did not play for England again until 1956. He eventually did get to go on another Ashes tour – when Robins engaged in a further bout of intriguing about the captaincy – when he was selected for the 1962–63 series under Ted Dexter, making a match-winning Test hundred at Melbourne.[14]

Photo by Central Press/Hulton Archive/Getty Images

Pakistan opening batsman Hanif Mohammad hits England spinner Johnny Wardle over the top during the rain-ruined third Test at Old Trafford. Stand-in captain David Sheppard is fielding in the gully.

[14]Sheppard was Bishop of Liverpool between 1975 and 1997, and became a significant public figure. He campaigned against poverty in the inner cities and was a staunch critic of the government of Margaret Thatcher.

Just back from the Caribbean, Tom Graveney meets his six-week-old daughter Becky for the first time.

Hutton welcomes his two rookie fast bowlers Frank Tyson, centre, and Peter Loader before their Test debuts against Pakistan at The Oval.

III

CHOOSING HUTTON'S MEN

'This bloke's going to be a thorn in our flesh in 54–55'
Australia's Alan Davidson after watching
Colin Cowdrey bat in 1953

'It was agreed to inform the selection sub-committee that Mr T.E. Bailey be excluded from consideration as a possible vice-captain for the MCC Touring Team to Australia, 1954–55'
The MCC committee sack
Trevor Bailey as England's vice-captain

'Not many first-class bowlers in 1950 could hit me on the pad before I could get my bat down and that one ball caused me to pay the young bowler more than usual attention'
Len Hutton notes the potential of Frank Tyson

THE RIGHT MAN TO MANAGE

The 1954 English cricket season began at 11.30 a.m. on Wednesday, 28 April at Fenner's, home of Cambridge University Cricket Club since 1848. After Cambridge had won the toss and decided to bat, proceedings were begun by Jack Bannister, the 23-year-old Warwickshire seamer, who delivered the first ball to the Cambridge captain Mike Bushby, a history undergraduate who had played a thrilling cameo against Australia's Ray Lindwall on the same ground a year earlier.

It might appear at first glance that a contest between a university XI and a county on a chilly April morning in England had little to do with the conduct of a Test match 10,000 miles and seven months away in sub-tropical Brisbane. Yet they were joined by a thread. From the moment the season began, the start of England's defence of the Ashes was at the forefront of the minds of everyone connected to the game, overshadowing England's inaugural Test series against Pakistan and Surrey's pursuit of a Championship hat-trick.

It went beyond the saga of the captaincy. With no central contracts for international players and a deep talent pool in county cricket, between 30 and 40 cricketers began the summer as potential candidates for the MCC squad. Bannister and Bushby may not have been among them, but there was huge interest and intense debate about the make-up of the touring party.

First, however, was the key matter of appointing a manager. After the strains imposed on the inexperienced Charles Palmer in the West Indies, there was a recognition that this was a critical decision. At Lord's, a sub-committee was formed to identify the right man: its members were MCC president, Viscount Cobham, a former captain of Worcestershire; Sir William Worsley, who had led Yorkshire in the late 1920s; Maurice Allom, an MCC tourist in 1929–30 and 1930–31; George Shelmerdine, a Lancashire textile manufacturer who had played for the county immediately after the First World War; and George Mann, scion of a brewing family, who had captained England in seven Tests in 1948 and 1949.

Billy Griffith, MCC's assistant secretary, was the sub-committee's preferred candidate, an appointment that would undoubtedly have been welcomed by Len Hutton. The England captain had unhesitatingly named 'the Colonel' as his first choice to accompany him to the Caribbean. Hutton's nickname for Griffith was only partly in jest. Griffith had been a D-Day glider pilot, later fighting in the Battle of Arnhem, and had been awarded the Distinguished Flying Cross. He had been prevented from managing MCC in the West Indies, however, by secretary Ronny Aird's insistence that he could not manage the workload at Lord's without his deputy.

It soon emerged that the weight of winter admin ruled out Griffith – still sprightly enough at 40 to turn out twice for Sussex in 1954 – for an even longer tour of Australia. Another name touted by the press was John Nash, the secretary of Yorkshire, who had done a sound job alongside Brigadier Michael Green on the previous Ashes tour of 1950–51. Nash, 48, lived near Hutton in Pudsey and was a respected administrator as well as an accomplished church organist.

But instead, MCC looked across the Pennines to the sub-committee's second choice and on 21 July, a week before the squad was announced, named Geoffrey Howard, the 45-year-old secretary of Lancashire. Howard had played three times for Middlesex in 1930 while on leave from his job in banking. During the war he had served in the RAF, finishing his service with the rank of acting squadron leader. He sailed to France as part of the vast Allied armada on D-Day where he was involved in the construction of the Mulberry Harbour (a temporary portable harbour) at Arromanches that played a vital role in maintaining supplies to the advancing Allied forces.

Howard's grandfather, Ebenezer, a stenographer who recorded parliamentary proceedings for *Hansard*, was the influential pioneer of the garden city movement that led to a revolution in urban planning. After the excitement of his wartime service, Howard was bored behind his desk at the bank and joined Surrey as assistant to secretary Brian Castor in 1947. Two years later, he moved north to Old Trafford. Tall, well dressed and debonair, with a Clark Gable moustache, Howard cut a striking figure.

He was also very good at his job, and it did not take long for his administrative and organisational talents to be recognised. He was chosen to manage the MCC tour of India, Pakistan and Ceylon (now Sri Lanka) in 1951–52. During an arduous five-month trip, Howard proved adept at maintaining morale. On internal flights, he sometimes took the controls of the twin-engine Dakota transporting the team around the subcontinent. Thanks to the contacts he made on the tour, he played an organisational role in the tours of the UK by India in 1952 and Pakistan two years later.

The appointment, for a fee of £850, was only cautiously welcomed in some quarters. While acknowledging Howard's administrative skills, E. W. Swanton thought MCC had blundered in departing from the usual practice of naming an assistant manager. 'They have chosen someone who does not know Australia, and one whose weight, through lack of experience, cannot count for a great deal in cricket problems,' Swanton harrumphed. 'In other words, they have thrown a great deal back on Hutton's shoulders. I believe MCC are asking an undue amount of their nominee and at the same time taking an unnecessary risk.'

ORDERING THE BATSMEN

The task of choosing the players was infinitely more demanding. Some, barring injury or catastrophic loss of form, were certain selections, their pedigree making it unthinkable the Ashes could be retained without them. They numbered perhaps eight. Whether as captain or not, Hutton would be the bulwark of the batting, but apart from him few places were nailed down. Denis Compton, the usual concerns about his right knee notwithstanding, was sure to go, as was the 24-year-old Surrey amateur Peter May. Without entirely convincing Hutton, Tom Graveney had played in 18 consecutive Tests and felt he was 'in possession'. Trevor Bailey, Hutton's deputy and a cricketer with an undisguised relish for the intensity of Ashes battle, was an automatic selection as the team-balancing all-rounder, as was first-choice wicketkeeper Godfrey Evans. Among the bowlers, Alec Bedser, who had missed the West Indies tour to husband his resources for Australia, and Brian Statham, steadfast and greatly admired by Hutton, were certainties. But no spinner had presented an unarguable case, meaning that around half the tour places were open for any players enjoying a fruitful summer.

The first problem for the selectors was the vexed question of Hutton's opening partner. The issue would have been resolved had David Sheppard been appointed captain, but when that possibility faded it remained a nagging concern. Since Cyril Washbrook's last appearance, in New Zealand at the fag end of the previous Ashes tour, Hutton had opened the batting with eight different players without acquiring the reassuring air of solidity he and his former partner had enjoyed. 'The gift they bestowed on English cricket was the confidence they gave to every other man in the side,' wrote their joint biographer A.A. Thomson. Although he would have celebrated his 40th birthday just before the second Test in Sydney, Hutton still believed his old compadre was the man best suited for the job of blunting the threat of Ray Lindwall and Keith Miller. Washbrook, however, had irritated the MCC hierarchy by imposing conditions on his participation four years earlier, effectively calling time on his international career.[15]

Reg Simpson, a lordly strokemaker who loved the physical and technical challenges presented by facing the new ball, should have been an automatic selection after a glorious century in the fifth Test at Melbourne in 1951. 'In the second part of that innings, when he gave the Australian attack its biggest thrashing of the series, Reg looked every inch a great batsman,' wrote Compton admiringly. The performance helped set up England's first Test win against Australia since the war. But Hutton was no fan of Simpson. 'This is a Test match, you know,' Hutton admonished him after Simpson advanced down the pitch to loft South Africa off-spinner Athol Rowan for four in 1951. The captain also thought Simpson's permanent suntan was evidence of a louche lifestyle. 'He used to sit out in the crowd in the sun, which annoyed Len,' May remembered.

If he could not have Washbrook, then Hutton's preference would surely have been for the combative qualities of Bill Edrich, with whom he had opened in three of the 1953 Ashes Tests. Though now batting at No.3 for Middlesex, Edrich's technique and courage meant he could be relied upon to open if required. It was not on the field but off it that his inclusion presented a problem. 'I've enough on my plate without taking him,' captain Freddie Brown had said when Edrich's selection had been discussed four years earlier.

---

[15]Washbrook made an unlikely comeback, aged 41, in 1956, playing in three Tests against Australia.

The matter was beyond Brown's influence anyway: Edrich was serving an unofficial ban after attending an all-night party during the Old Trafford Test against West Indies in 1950. He might have got away with his noisy progress down the hotel corridor on the arm of the night porter had the chairman of selectors Bob Wyatt not been in the next-door room. Edrich's exile ended only when his resolve was needed in the national cause in 1953, but he was not selected for Hutton's Caribbean assignment in 1953–54, and if he was to go to Australia – especially in the company of his favoured co-carousers, Compton and Evans – it would be at the risk of discipline and cohesion.

Edrich had provided a reminder that he could be a magnet for trouble when he appeared in court on a drink-driving offence after an accident on his journey home during the first Test against Pakistan at Lord's. After a retrial, he was found guilty of dangerous driving and fined 10 guineas, but not guilty of driving when drunk.

An alternative to Edrich was the 30-year-old Worcestershire opener, Don Kenyon. In the rain-blighted summer of 1954, Kenyon was the most prolific batsman in the country, somehow finding enough time at the crease to amass 2636 runs at an average of 51. Yet when given the chance in the first two Tests in 1953, he had looked unconvincing against high pace, falling three times to Ray Lindwall and only once scraping into double figures. He retained influential supporters, however. 'Don Kenyon is the type of player who should do well in Australia,' wrote Brown, until recently the chairman of selectors. But touring was more than a matter of technique. On the 1951–52 tour of the subcontinent, Kenyon had suffered from homesickness and made little contribution to maintaining a happy atmosphere. This could count against a player as much as talent and temperament: too many long faces could drag down the mood of the whole group.

The established middle-order batsmen performed reassuringly well in 1954. Compton led the averages with 1524 runs at 58, despite his customary absences while he managed his knee problems. As usual, his running between the wickets produced equal measures of amusement and despair. During Middlesex's Whitsun weekend fixture against Sussex at Lord's, Compton contrived to run out his brother Leslie, the crime compounded by the fact it was Leslie's benefit match.[16] Compton also ran out Fred Titmus and Alan Moss, but his brilliant unbeaten 72 on a treacherous drying surface saved the follow-on. Both sides of Compton's contrary genius were on show in one innings.

Graveney, despite taking a break when diagnosed with fatigue in late May, averaged 57, just behind Compton, and hit six centuries. His easy, languid grace continued to convey the idea to some that he lacked the appetite for Test combat. The *Daily Mirror*'s Ross Hall left him out of his predicted tour party, telling his readers, 'Despite the delight he has given me on so many occasions, the Gloucestershire man has failed too often on the big occasions.' Peter May also recorded six hundreds, and in a bravura spell in May and June scored more than 1100 runs in 16 innings. His 169 against Northamptonshire at The Oval in May was 'the innings of the season', according to the watching selector Les Ames.

The trio's good form meant the selectors were looking to fill only one or two batting slots, one if Simpson and Edrich were both selected. There was a ripple around the county circuit about the 22-year-old Compton clone Jim Parks. He was given a Test debut against Pakistan at Old Trafford, but made just 15 in his only innings of a rain-ruined match. He also fluffed his audition when selected for Gentlemen v Players at Lord's. Another fresh face was Surrey's Micky Stewart, 21. 'There were whispers around, no more than that,' he recalled in 2023. Two hundreds in his first three matches, including one against the touring Pakistanis, suggested a significant new talent was emerging.

Yorkshire's Willie Watson, one of the heroes of the 1953 Ashes, who had played in all five Tests in the West Indies, was considered a strong contender by many journalists, but there were echoes of attitudes of Graveney in Hutton's unease about Watson's languid talent. 'It's too easy for him; he doesn't take it seriously enough,' Hutton grumbled, ignoring Watson's backs-to-the-wall partnership with Bailey against Australia at Lord's in 1953. A

---

[16]Cricketers with 10 years' service were usually granted a benefit year to raise money for their retirement. One of the perks was to keep the gate receipts from a nominated fixture.

Yorkshire batsman more favourably regarded by Hutton was Vic Wilson. Watson and Wilson could be relied upon to boost the athleticism of the team's fielding.

More substantial claims were made by the Oxford University captain, Colin Cowdrey, a player apparently predestined for greatness since his father had blessed him with the initials 'M.C.C.'. He had enjoyed a startlingly successful summer in 1953, scoring a hundred in the Varsity match and a pair of fifties for the Gentlemen of England against the Australians. Watching him from the dressing-room balcony at Lord's, Alan Davidson, the Australian all-rounder, predicted, 'This bloke's going to be a thorn in our flesh in 54–55.' Most importantly, Hutton was a confirmed admirer, discerning echoes of Walter Hammond in Cowdrey's sumptuous cover drives. 'I had seen how straight was his bat and how much time he had for his shots, and told him he was a disciple of my methods,' said Hutton.

Yet Cowdrey was not quite so prolific in 1954, his aggregate and his average both falling. Perhaps it was the pressure applied by *Wisden*'s Norman Preston, who offered his support when he speculated about candidates for Australia in his Editor's Notes. The selectors resisted the temptation to blood him in the series against Pakistan. Chairman of the panel Harry Altham and fellow selector Walter Robins took a trip to the Parks in Oxford in May to see him make 94 against Lancashire, but Cowdrey believed a mixed run of scores around the time the tour party was announced in July had cost him any chance. 'I would not have picked myself if I had been a selector,' he reflected later.

OFF THE BOIL

If Colin Cowdrey remained an outsider, Trevor Bailey was a certainty. With 222 runs at 31 and eight wickets at 48, his statistical contribution to the Ashes triumph of 1953 was not compelling. Yet England would not have edged the series without his contributions. On the final day of the second Test at Lord's, with defeat seemingly inevitable, he mounted an heroic rearguard action with Willie Watson, occupying the crease for four hours for his 71. Then, in the fourth match at Headingley, when an Australian victory would have meant the Ashes were lost, he made 38 in more than four hours in the second innings, adding blatant time-wasting tactics to his trademark forward defensive, before hobbling Australia's last-afternoon run-chase by bowling deliberately wide down the leg side. The Australians were furious, former opening batsman Sid Barnes calling him a 'petulant schoolboy' in a newspaper column. Grudgingly, he was respected, though. 'Trevor was so often such a pain if you were playing for Australia against him – a damned nuisance in fact,' wrote Keith Miller.

There were other all-rounders, including Allan Watkins of Glamorgan, 'a man who does everything well,' said Norman Preston, and Yorkshire's Brian Close, still only 23 and finally recovering his teenage *joie de vivre* after a harrowing tour of Australia in 1950–51. But Bailey's stock had risen even higher in the West Indies. In the fifth Test in Jamaica, with England needing to win to square the series, he bowled into the wind in fierce heat on the opening day to take seven for 34, then, before the close, defied West Indies' new-ball salvoes as Hutton's emergency opening partner. 'I could not have wished for a better man,' wrote Hutton in his tour report. 'He is the type of man with whom I get on extremely well, because he is prepared to fight … a great asset in every way.' Though approaching his 31st birthday, Bailey, affectionately nicknamed 'the Boil', [17] seemed to the public to be Hutton's natural heir.

The reality was rather different. At Lord's, Bailey's willingness to bend the laws in pursuit of victory – or least to avoid defeat – was a source of disquiet. Gubby Allen, in particular, loathed leg theory, the negative leg-side bowling which Bailey had deployed at Leeds. Some detected shades of the ruthlessness of Douglas Jardine. Although an amateur – he had been educated at Dulwich College before reading history at Cambridge and joining Essex – Bailey was from a lower middle-class background, the son of a civil servant at the Admiralty, and was as hard-nosed as any professional. And he was also unsubtle in his pursuit of commercial opportunities to earn income from the game, even if he could not be paid for playing.

---

[17] The nickname derived from a mispronunciation by an announcer at a Swiss football stadium when Bailey was on tour with the Cambridge University team. He was an accomplished footballer.

It was one such money-making venture that landed him in trouble with MCC and handed them an opportunity to clip his wings. On tour, his typewriter was as much a part of his luggage as his bat and pads: teammates called his bedroom 'the office'. While in the Caribbean, he put the finishing touches to a book called *Playing to Win*, published soon after the squad's return. The title alone was guaranteed to raise hackles at Lord's, but it was a series of columns to promote it he wrote in the Sunday newspaper the *People* that brought the row to the surface.

The majority of the book's contents were innocent enough, offering Bailey's reflections on the previous summer's recapture of the Ashes. But in order to give the manuscript a more up-to-date feel, he added a short chapter titled 'Cricket in the West Indies'. He was in effect banned from writing about the controversies of the recently concluded tour – there was an understanding that amateurs were bound by the same contractual terms as professionals and could not write about a series for a stipulated period – but this chapter was clearly an attempt to tiptoe through the regulations. Not that Bailey had been underhand about it. In December 1953, the MCC committee considered a request from him to add a chapter discussing cricket in the Caribbean. The minutes record that, 'Permission was granted provided it was in general terms and that he submitted it to the treasurer and the secretary before publication.'

There was little that could be called inflammatory in the content, though that may not have spared him an official red pencil. Among Bailey's observations were that Caribbean cricket fans were the most fanatical in the world; lucrative contracts with northern English league clubs could threaten the availability of their players; neutral officials were the answer to poor standards of umpiring; the 'colour question' (as it was usually called at the time) needed to be resolved, with Frank Worrell a worthy candidate to become West Indies' first Black captain.

On 16 May, six days before Bailey was due at Lord's to captain MCC against the Pakistanis, the *People* ran the first of his columns, based on that chapter. It was quite different to the text of the book. Paragraphs relating to the tour were liberally inserted, using far less conciliatory language. There was no mention of the book, nor was the piece presented as an extract. Instead, the *People* billed it as a shoot-from-the-hip column by one of England's leading players. The reaction of MCC was not hard to predict. While at Lord's for the match against the touring team, Bailey wrote a long letter to Aird setting out his version of what had happened. He explained that his piece, titled 'The Australians in the West Indies', had been a general discussion about what Australia could expect on their Caribbean tour in the spring of 1955.

That Bailey wrote a fresh piece rather than the newspaper extracting a section of the book indicates that this was not a conventional serialisation agreement. While the publicity would do sales no harm, the headline 'Drama on the cricket field by the iron man of the Test matches' followed by the sub-heading 'Black eyes, bottles and such excitement!' was a far cry from 'The Australians in the West Indies', which sounded like a line from the austere pages of *Wisden*. Bailey was thrown into a panic when his literary agent Rupert Crew read him the proofs of the article on the Friday evening before publication. The next day, the first of a Championship match between Essex and Derbyshire, fortunately in Bailey's home town of Westcliff-on-Sea, frantic efforts were made to persuade the *People* sports desk to change the piece.

Horace Clark, the Essex secretary, and chairman Hubert Ashton, Conservative MP for Chelmsford and a former Essex player, were dragged into the discussions.[18] From Lord's, Billy Griffith suggested involving the General Council, the press regulatory body. It was typical of Bailey's ability to blank out distractions that amid all this he scored 48 against Les Jackson and Cliff Gladwin, one of the best new-ball pairs in the country.

In a final desperate measure, Bailey attempted to veto publication unless the *People* agreed to tone down the article. They did not have to comply and, predictably, they did not, thus triggering a disciplinary process that rumbled on for several weeks. In case he thought he might get away with it, secretary Ronny Aird assured Bailey that MCC took 'the gravest view' of his transgression. Bailey

---

[18]Ashton made his mark on cricket history in 1921 as a member of a hastily assembled all-amateur England XI that defeated the Australians at Eastbourne in August 1921. Until then, it seemed the touring team would remain unbeaten.

could not provide a copy of his original article – his agent had destroyed it, he said.

It was years before Bailey admitted that, at the *People*'s request, he had asked his brother Basil, a journalist, to 'hot up' the piece. In an effort to mitigate his brother's punishment, Basil Bailey wrote to the MCC committee taking the blame for not showing them the original chapter in the book, as they had requested when giving their agreement. He blamed 'deadline pressures' and added, 'I apologise and hope that as Trevor's comments were about cricket conditions in the West Indies and not an account of play on that tour that no great harm has been done by my forgetfulness.'

When Bailey met Sir Pelham Warner and Harry Altham, with Aird in attendance, at Lord's during the first Test against Pakistan in June, he left the meeting feeling the matter had been resolved. 'I am most upset at the whole business, but my own conscience is completely clear,' he had said in a letter. This was bluster and no one was convinced. Even in Essex Bailey had few allies. There was an exasperated tone in a letter from Ashton to Lord's. 'We found it difficult to get into Trevor Bailey's mind that he had given a categorical undertaking in two places to show what he wrote about the West Indies Tour before publication … even if there had been no reference to cricket but only to bathing beauties he had this obligation.'

On 21 June, while Bailey was involved in a Championship match against Northamptonshire at Romford and, in the course of it, passing the milestone of 10,000 first-class runs, an MCC committee instructed Aird to write to him in terms full of foreboding. In short, they did not accept his explanation and in any case his principal offence was to have ignored the terms of his agreement: 'You will I am sure realise that there is no point laying down conditions for those who accept invitations to tour with MCC teams abroad unless those conditions are carried out and unless some action is taken if and when the conditions are not carried out.'

Bailey received Aird's letter on the same day that David Sheppard was named as stand-in captain for Len Hutton in the second Test at Nottingham, a bitter double blow. He had a furious row with Ashton, refusing to sign off on an apology the MP had drafted on his behalf. Teammate Jack Bailey – no relation, but later his namesake's biographer – recalled Bailey's anger. 'It was as big a slap in the teeth as could be imagined for somebody at the peak of their career,' Jack Bailey wrote. A clearly hurt Bailey absented himself from Essex's next match and took his wife, Greta, to Paris for a few days, returning in time to play a typically selfless role in England's victory over Pakistan at Trent Bridge. It was around this time that the *News Chronicle* reported that an unnamed county had offered him £1500 a year to turn professional and join them as captain. It is hard not to wonder whether, amid the turmoil, he gave the idea serious thought.

Aird wanted to exclude him from consideration for the Gentlemen v Players match, which perhaps indicates, as David Woodhouse speculated in his book on the 1953–54 Caribbean tour *Who Only Cricket Know*, that the MCC hierarchy were motivated by animus against Bailey as much as a desire to enforce the regulations. They may have settled on the chapter about the West Indies, but it would not have escaped their attention that he also used the book to criticise the running of tours. Ashton, meanwhile, continued to express his annoyance. 'He doesn't seem to improve a great deal as he gets older,' he wrote to Aird. The secretary agreed: 'Trevor Bailey has so far proved a difficult man to work with.' Ashton also asked to be kept apprised of the process of choosing a vice-captain for Australia – presumably not because he wanted to endorse Bailey's candidature.

He need not have worried. At the meeting of the main committee on 19 July, the following was minuted: 'It was agreed to inform the selection sub-committee that Mr T.E. Bailey be excluded from consideration as a possible vice-captain for the MCC Touring Team to Australia, 1954–55, and to ask the sub-committee when considering this appointment to bear in mind the claims of youth and future requirements.' Another minute at the same meeting added: 'It was decided that should Mr Bailey be invited to tour Australasia with the MCC Team, he and all the other amateurs in the team be asked to sign an agreement similar to that signed by the professional players.'

After that, given the use of the words 'youth' and 'future requirements' it was inevitable that the selection sub-committee would alight on Peter May as Hutton's deputy. The captain was disappointed to lose the services of a cricketer of whom he had written just a few weeks earlier, 'As vice-captain I could not have wished for a better man,' especially over what he saw as an essentially trivial matter. 'It was a real pity Bailey dropped out in this way, for he would have been a strong leader with many ideas,' he later wrote.

Bailey was clearly angry and upset. When Billy Griffith sent him the standard letter of availability in early July, he refused to commit to the tour 'for business and domestic reasons'. It took him until after the announcement of the squad to write a brief apology to Aird. He was sorry 'for any trouble which my actions have occasioned' and spoke of his disappointment at losing the vice-captaincy. That was putting it mildly. He was still piqued a month later when Horace Clark wrote to Lord's on his behalf asking if he could delay his departure for Australia for a month to continue his work as assistant secretary of Essex. The request was refused.

SPARE PAIR OF GLOVES

It was unthinkable that England would take the field in a Test match without Godfrey Evans as wicketkeeper. He was, as his *Wisden* obituary said in 2000, 'The man who made the game's least obtrusive specialism a spectator sport in itself.' Evans, 34, had already toured Australia twice. On his first trip in 1946–47, Bill O'Reilly, the Australian leg-spinner-turned-journalist, wrote that wicketkeeping was the only department in which the teams were equal. At Melbourne on the 1950–51 tour, standing up to Alec Bedser, he somehow snared a genuine leg glance by Neil Harvey: a catch that left those who saw it groping for superlatives. Evans contributed crucial runs, too, and had scored two Test hundreds. His presence was considered so vital that Len Hutton was prepared to overlook his hectic social life on tour.

But he needed a deputy. Paul Gibb, 41 but still first choice for Essex, had been the second string in 1946–47, while Surrey's Arthur McIntyre, 36, filled the role four years later. He lacked Evans's flamboyance, but many thought McIntyre the most consistently excellent wicketkeeper in the game. On the 1953–54 West Indies tour, the spot had been taken by Dick Spooner of Warwickshire, who played in the fourth Test in Trinidad. Other names were discussed. Crawford White of the *News Chronicle* liked the look of Leicestershire's Jack Firth after seeing him in action at The Oval. Harold Stephenson of Somerset, blessed with a tap-dancer's footwork, also had his supporters, and the bespectacled Hampshire wicketkeeper Leo Harrison was mentioned by some writers.

But as the summer wore on, the name of Northamptonshire's Keith Andrew appeared more frequently. Before the start of the 1954 season, the 24-year-old Lancastrian, who had trained as a mechanical engineer, had made just five first-class appearances, two of them for Combined Services during his National Service. Yet after the *Daily Mail* correspondent Alex Bannister saw him in action against Worcestershire early in June, he wrote, 'He is the essence of soundness and must stand an excellent chance of going to Australia as Evans's deputy. Everything he does is without fuss and bears the stamp of class.'

Andrew had enjoyed a brief moment in the spotlight the previous summer while completing his residential qualification for Northamptonshire. The regulations allowed him to appear in non-Championship matches and he had played in the game against the touring Australians. On the first morning, Andrew completed two slick stumpings, the second of which showcased such rapid glovework that most of the crowd thought the batsman had been bowled. The dismissal was off the bowling of the former England captain Freddie Brown, then in his final year as chairman of selectors.

In his retirement memoir, *Cricket Musketeer*, Brown speculated about the Ashes tour party and named Andrew in his putative squad. 'A lot of cricketers may never have heard of Keith Andrew. They will,' he wrote. 'When he kept wicket for the county against the Australians, he impressed several of them with his efficiency.' Dennis Brookes, his captain, was also a fan. 'I never thought of Keith as learning his trade,' he said. 'He was a top-class keeper from the outset.'

It must have been via Brown's influence that Andrew was included in the MCC team for the early-season game against Yorkshire at Lord's. It was a sure sign that he was being auditioned for the role of Evans's No.2. For now, Andrew did not give a moment's thought to the idea of spending a winter in Australia. He was due to marry his fiancée Joyce Lancaster in October and the couple's plans for the big day were well advanced.

SPINNER'S TURN

One of the best-known and most frequently quoted anecdotes from English cricket's mid-fifties golden era concerns a conversation that took place in a hotel bar during the tour of the West Indies in 1953–54. The participants were England captain Len Hutton, fast bowler Brian Statham, batsman Tom Graveney – who later polished the raw material into a well-honed after-dinner routine – and off-spinner Jim Laker.

Perhaps the first published version came from Laker in his 1957 autobiography *Spinning Round the World*. Hutton began the exchanges. '"Now Brian, how would you like to go to Australia?" Brian looked surprised at the directness of the question, and did not know whether the skipper was joking or not. He decided to take the question seriously and answered, "Not 'arf! [a favourite expression among MCC players on tour] I want to go again." Turning to Graveney, Hutton said, "And what about you, Tom?" "I'd love it," replied Tom enthusiastically, "There's nothing I'd like better than an Aussie trip." A noticeable pause followed before Len looked up in my direction and inquired: "Like another drink, Jim?"' Unsurprisingly, this offered Laker a broad hint that he would not be required in the defence of the Ashes.

Even if embellished, the conversation does not throw a good light on Hutton's man-management skills and demonstrates a flagrant lack of respect for one of the country's leading bowlers. It also demonstrates a long-held belief that the wiles of English finger-spinners, even those as talented as Laker, were largely neutered by Australian conditions. Not since the 1928–29 tour under Percy Chapman had MCC sailed to Australia with a specialist off-spinner in the party. It did not offer a promising precedent: Nottinghamshire's Sam Staples suffered serious rheumatic pains on the voyage and returned home without playing a match. Laker felt the idea that his craft was surplus to requirements in Australia was wrong-headed. 'As we have so rarely sent a decent off-spinner to

Australia, anyway,' he wrote, 'it seems to me that the policy came first and the legend followed after.'

Hutton delivered an unflattering assessment of Laker in his Caribbean tour report. While admitting he was 'an extremely fine bowler' and a 'charming type of fellow', he also said he had an 'inferiority complex' and a tendency to wilt in the heat of battle. 'I feel that Laker should be considered in committee before future selection for overseas tours,' he wrote. Laker's figures had not been particularly eye-catching – 14 wickets at 33.50 in the Tests – but in the series-squaring fifth match at Sabina Park he bowled a marathon 50 overs to take four for 71. Those wickets were collected in fierce heat with a sore spinning finger and a plaster over his eye after being hit by a bouncer in the fourth Test at Trinidad.

If Laker's participation in the defence of the Ashes was doubtful, what were the chances of the left-armer Tony Lock, his Surrey teammate and spin-bowling partner? Lock had made his Test debut against India in 1952 and his first significant contribution to the national cause could hardly have been better timed: five for 45 in Australia's second innings in the Oval victory that secured the Ashes. Lock, 25, had first played for Surrey soon after the Second World War, but there was little indication that a future match-winning international bowler was emerging.

That began to change when he spent a winter coaching at an indoor school at Croydon. He used his free time to work on his bowling, but was hampered by a low ceiling beam. In consequence, he subconsciously dropped his arm a little. It was the start of a long debate about the legality of Lock's action. A week after his England debut, umpire Fred Price called him for throwing in the Indians' tour match at The Oval. Help came when the owner of the indoor nets ordered the offending beam to be raised by 35 cm (14 inches) so that Lock could spend the winter undertaking remedial work on his action. It worked – or at least it worked enough for most to give Lock a clean bill of health. 'Lock not only returned to his previous tidy action, but his spin was as vicious as ever,' wrote *Wisden* editor Norman Preston in naming him one of the Almanack's Cricketers of the Year in 1954.

Len Hutton saw plenty of reasons to doubt Lock's legality, but none not to select him. Asked if his action was not 'a little strange', the England captain responded, 'It is – but I think I will beat the Aussies next year with him.' The problem was Lock's quicker ball – delivered at a pace that most called medium-fast – with which he took many wickets. Laker explained, 'Lockie was never an out-and-out thrower, but there were many occasions when he contravened the Laws. His arm was certainly bent and generally remained bent through the delivery, which was acceptable. It was when he straightened it to jerk the ball out with greater pace that he broke the law.' Privately, Laker used less sympathetic language. 'Lockie's throwing it this year,' he told David Sheppard shortly after Lock had changed his action.

The Australians were certainly in no doubt. 'We all reckoned he threw his express delivery,' Neil Harvey told Gideon Haigh. 'It was like a 90 m.p.h. yorker and he used to knock the county blokes over left, right and centre.' Doubts or not, Lock was selected to tour the West Indies in 1953–54. The decision rebounded when he was no-balled for throwing in the first Test at Kingston, not long after he had bowled George Headley with what Clyde Walcott called 'the most flagrantly obvious throw I have ever seen'. In the *Daily Telegraph* E.W. Swanton described umpire Perry Burke's decision to no-ball Lock as 'a regrettable happening but not, I think, to be classed absolutely as a surprise'.

For the rest of the tour, Lock removed the quicker ball from his armoury, thereby reducing his match-winning potential. 'A slow bowler with a fast bowler's temperament,' was Hutton's view of Lock in his tour report. Others made similar observations. 'There has never been a more aggressive spin bowler,' wrote the historian David Frith. 'If Lockie appealed at The Oval, someone was given out at Lord's,' a teammate had said. Whether or not it was the fall-out from his being no-balled or not, Lock was left out of the four Tests against Pakistan in 1954, an ominous portent. The tour selection committee knew that Australian umpires would be primed and were desperate to avoid any diplomatic flare-ups.

England's third spinner in the Caribbean had been Hutton's Yorkshire teammate Johnny Wardle. They were county colleagues, but it did not make them friends. 'The crowds liked him and everywhere it was remarked "How good this chap Wardle is," but from the inside point of view of the team spirit and relationship with the players

Wardle showed jealousy, bitterness and envy at times,' wrote Hutton at the end of the tour. 'Wardle's case should, I feel, be discussed in committee before selection is made for future tours.' Godfrey Evans would have agreed. 'Not many people on tour have got on well with Johnny,' he remarked.

As left-armers, Lock and Wardle were vying for one place in the England team – they played together just three times – and superficially there were similarities in their personalities. But whereas Lock took his aggression on to the field, Wardle could be awkward off it: 'Undemonstrative almost to the point of surliness,' said Frith. Footage of Wardle shows his bowling arm emerging from behind his bottom and the ball curling towards the batsman in a mesmerising loop. His classical approach made him contemptuous of Lock's kinked action. In a stinging put-down, Wardle said Lock 'never had to resort to flight to get anyone out'.

But Wardle had something that made it tempting to overlook his poor contribution to esprit de corps: the element of mystery that might be vital to dismissing Australian batsmen on their own pitches. Without any discernible change in his action, Wardle could switch from bowling orthodox slow left-arm to wrist-spin, deploying a left-armer's googly, then usually called a 'Chinaman'. 'When he bowled Chinamen and googlies he was a world-class wrist-spinner,' said Trevor Bailey. In English conditions, and especially at home in Yorkshire, Wardle had to carry the burden of being the heir to Wilfred Rhodes and Hedley Verity, left-arm classicists who never felt the need to dabble in the dark arts of wrist-spin. Overseas, however, Wardle's versatility was potentially a potent addition to Hutton's arsenal.

A point of difference could also be found in the bowling of another Yorkshireman, Bob Appleyard. He could deliver conventional seam and swing with the new ball, then switch to off-breaks when it lost its shine. But even his spinners were delivered at an unusually brisk pace, while his height and high arm meant he extracted more bounce than a normal off-spinner. 'You might have said that sometimes he bowled like Alec Bedser and sometimes like Jim Laker, and you hardly realised the difference until you were out,' said Wardle. Appleyard was not thought to be in contention for a tour place in the weeks building up to the 1954 season for the good reason that he spent them in a sanatorium in the Swiss ski resort of Arosa, completing the final stages of recovery from the potentially life-threatening disease, tuberculosis.

Appleyard's story was remarkable. In 1951, in his first full season in county cricket, he had taken 200 wickets, a feat unparalleled in the history of the game. 'As close to being unplayable as any bowler I ever faced,' Bailey remembered. But Yorkshire worked him into the ground: in all, he bowled 1323 overs and, at the end of the summer, was exhausted. He spent the winter months trying to improve his stamina, but felt more tired than ever. Appleyard did not complete the first match of the 1952 season. Within days, he was in hospital in Leeds, feeling desperately ill. TB was diagnosed. Later that year, he underwent surgery to remove the top of his left lung. The recovery and rehabilitation process was long and arduous: his muscles were so wasted by months of bed rest that he had to learn to walk again. But he was inspired by the words of his surgeon Geoffrey Wooler: 'You will play again, Mr Appleyard. In fact I shall come to Headingley to watch you bowl.'[19]

It seemed fantastical that anyone could play elite-level professional sport after such an illness, but Appleyard was not just an exceptional bowler, he was an extraordinary man. On 1 May, 1954, he returned to first-class cricket in Yorkshire's game against MCC at Lord's. In just his fourth match back he took seven for 35 against Hampshire on his home ground at Bradford after being given a prolonged and emotional ovation. By the end of the month he was top of the bowling averages and after a medical examination he was cleared to carry on playing. 'Bob has shown he is up to the strain of cricket,' said Yorkshire captain Norman Yardley. Crawford White of the *News Chronicle* called for Appleyard to be included in the team for the first Test against Pakistan at Lord's. 'His courage, as well as his cricket, has a message of cheer for everybody,' he wrote. 'The selectors should give it the final storybook touch it merits.'

They resisted the temptation then, but on his 30th birthday Appleyard was called up for the second Test at Trent Bridge. He took a wicket

[19]Wooler was a surgeon of considerable eminence, who, later in the 1950s, became one of the pioneers of open-heart surgery.

with his second ball – at one point he had four wickets for just six runs – and ended his first day as an international cricketer with figures of five for 51. 'As thoughtfully varied a piece of bowling as one has seen from a bowler of his pace since O'Reilly,' thought Denys Rowbotham of the *Manchester Guardian*. He added two more wickets in the second innings, but was not retained for the subsequent two Tests. That may have perplexed some, but White thought he knew what it meant: 'Bob Appleyard's ticket for Australia can be made out now.'

In a summer of wet pitches, other spinners made strong claims for consideration. Glamorgan's Jim McConnon, 32, was a converted seamer who used his height to flight the ball cunningly, while also utilising his long fingers to extract sharp turn. A good athlete, he had been on Aston Villa's books during the war and was also a fine gully fielder. He passed 100 wickets in 1951 and had another productive summer in 1954. Against Surrey at The Oval, three weeks before the selectors finalised the MCC squad, he took seven for 23 in just 71 balls, outbowling Laker as Glamorgan recorded a sensational victory over the champions. 'Only Peter May showed the slightest idea how to play McConnon,' wrote Basil Easterbrook in the *Western Mail*.

Among the other successful spinners that summer, Warwickshire's Eric Hollies and Doug Wright of Kent were too long in the tooth for such a demanding overseas assignment. Much younger was the Sussex amateur Robin Marlar, 23, whose eight wickets in the Gentlemen v Players match must have been noted approvingly in the Lord's pavilion. Sir Pelham Warner had already urged his inclusion in the West Indies tour party. Like Appleyard, Roy Tattersall of Lancashire bowled at a faster pace than most off-spinners and retained some of the weapons from his early career as a seamer. Tattersall had played in two Tests on the previous Ashes tour after being flown out as an emergency replacement for Wright, but the feeling persisted that he was a wet-wicket bowler and that new regulations on pitch-covering in Australia would nullify his threat. Fred Titmus, the 21-year-old Middlesex off-spinner, had received a letter of availability about the tour, indicating that his claims were taken seriously. White speculated that his time could have come: 'Young Titmus might easily be one of the young men to catch that boat to Australia in September.'

Two of the most prolific spinners in English cricket were certain not to be measured for an MCC touring blazer. The leading wicket-taker in the country in 1954 was the Nottinghamshire leg-spinner Bruce Dooland, who collected 196 victims at 15.48. In fourth place in the listings – after Wardle (155) and Appleyard (154) – was Northamptonshire's voluble left-arm wrist-spinner George Tribe, who took 149 wickets at 19.79. Both were Australians who, after six Tests between them for their homeland, had thrown in their lot with English counties, effectively ruling themselves out of future consideration.

RICH SEAMS

The leading bowler in world cricket spent the winter of 1953–54 mixing concrete, hauling wheelbarrows laden with bricks and digging trenches: no one could ever accuse Alec Bedser of being work-shy. Alongside him every day as he toiled was his identical twin and Surrey teammate, Eric. With their father, Arthur, laying the bricks, they built a new family home on the edge of Woking, the Surrey town where they had been brought up. The twins lived in the house for the rest of their lives.

But why did Bedser turn builder's labourer when, across the Atlantic, England were engaged in a Test series that would establish which team could claim to be the best in the world? The reason had much to do with the primacy of Ashes cricket, even as West Indies became an emerging power. As it had been every summer since the war, when he had become England's principal strike weapon, Bedser's 1953 workload was staggering. He bowled more than 1250 overs for his 162 wickets at 16.67, a tally which included a record 39 in the Ashes triumph and 84 in Surrey's second successive County Championship. He also managed his benefit, which raised a county record £12,866 (around £300,000 today), a handy sum with a major building project in the offing, though he also shrewdly invested some of the money in setting up an office equipment company. He found time to become one of the faces of a campaign run by the Popular Television Association, a pressure group set up to persuade the government to allow commercial television. All in all, Bedser needed a rest if he was to be ready to do battle with the Australians again in the winter of 1954–55.

Len Hutton gave different accounts of his reaction to not having Bedser in his team in the Caribbean. In his final autobiography, *Fifty Years in Cricket,* published in 1984, he claimed that Bedser's absence meant that Fred Trueman was selected for his first tour before he was ready. Earlier, Hutton had written that he had welcomed the opportunity to try out Trueman and Brian Statham in harness against West Indies without having to worry about bruising Bedser's ego.

He also suggested that he had an inkling that Bedser, if not quite over the hill, was perhaps cresting the brow of one. There are scraps of evidence to support this theory. Bedser took fewer wickets in 1954 than in any summer since 1949, but was still the 12th-highest wicket-taker in the country. He also had fitness issues, missing the Lord's Test with fibrositis, a rheumatic condition, in his left hip and the fourth match at The Oval when the selectors decided to make experimental changes in the bowling attack. At other points in the season journalists dared to voice the thought that he was lacking in his customary wicket-taking nip and penetration.

But there was no question that he would lead Hutton's attack in 1954–55. Which seamers would form the supporting cast was, with one notable exception, less clear. At 24, Brian Statham of Lancashire was approaching his peak. Hutton was a fan. 'He is a very good tourist and a great trier on and off the field,' he said in his West Indies tour report. Despite missing the final Test, he had been England's leading wicket-taker in the Caribbean with 16 at 28.75. Back home in 1954, he took 92 wickets at 14.13, earning him recognition as one of *Wisden*'s five Cricketers of the Year. He had progressed rapidly since arriving at Old Trafford in the spring of 1950 with his kit in a canvas bag and his bowling boots in a brown paper parcel. Nor was he completely new to Australian conditions, having been flown out as an emergency replacement four years earlier.

There was no shortage of seam-bowling candidates, it was a home-grown skill which could be found flourishing in abundance around the shires. The perpetually overlooked Derbyshire duo of Cliff Gladwin and Les Jackson were high in the 1954 wicket-taking lists. Gladwin was the only seamer in the top five, while Jackson's reputation was such that Fred Trueman once called him 'the most underrated fast bowler that ever played cricket'. 'Bedser thinks well of Jackson, of Derbyshire, as a possible substitute for himself. What do you say?' Sir Pelham Warner asked Hutton in a letter. He must have said no, because Alan Moss of Middlesex was selected instead. Moss did not let himself down and in his tour report Hutton had just one grumble: 'He suffers from a fault which is common in young cricketers today in that he talks a little too much for a young man of 23.'

Surrey's Peter Loader also had plenty to say for himself, but he reserved much of it for opposing batsmen. A former trainee dental mechanic, Loader, 25, made great progress in 1953 and had toured India with a Commonwealth XI in the winter of 1953–54. On generally unresponsive pitches, he finished as leading wicket-taker with 47. Bedser, a county colleague, thought he was not strong enough to bowl long spells in the West Indies, but he returned from India in fine fettle and began to collect wickets regularly. In July, Bedser agreed to be left out of the Players team so that the selectors could take a closer look at Loader. He did not disappoint. In the Gentlemen's first innings he took seven for 37, his victims including a quartet of the highest pedigree: David Sheppard, Bill Edrich, Peter May and Colin Cowdrey. In the second, he removed Sheppard's off stump, had Edrich dropped twice by Godfrey Evans, and forced Reg Simpson to retire with a damaged finger: 'Five overs of forked lightning,' said the *News Chronicle*.

Loader was not express pace – generally slower than Trueman, Moss and Northamptonshire's Frank Tyson – but he moved the ball skilfully, deployed a well-disguised slower ball and had a snarling fast bowler's temperament. Plenty of county batsmen thought he threw his bouncer and the Australian spinner Jack Iverson, a teammate on the Commonwealth tour, thought him perfectly capable of bowling the occasional beamer.

Few England teams in history had been lacking in seam-bowling talent, but Hutton wanted something else: when England had last won in Australia in the Bodyline series in 1932–33, they had been able to employ a twin spearhead of high pace in Harold Larwood and Bill Voce. Hutton was convinced that it was not the traditional virtues of line and length that would help him to cling on to the Ashes, but something more explosive. It was just a matter of who would detonate the dynamite.

FRED OR FRANK?

In pre-motorway Britain, the 170-mile journey from Bristol to Stainton took several hours. After four months away from home in the West Indies, Fred Trueman must have wished the miles away. Eventually, he reached the family's tiny terraced house in the south Yorkshire mining village to find his mother, father and siblings forming a small but excited welcoming party. His sister Flo recreated the scene for Trueman's biographer, Chris Waters. 'He came back loaded with all manner of presents. There were pearls, nylon stockings and silk scarves for the girls and various bits and pieces for the boys.'

Trueman's father, Dick, sat impassively through the excitement, but eventually the question he was burning to ask could wait no longer. As Flo recalled, he said, '"There's only one thing I want to know, son. All this trouble, were you behind it?" Freddie looked him straight in the eye and said, "No Dad, honestly. I was made a scapegoat. I wouldn't dare do anything to upset you." Dad sat quiet for a moment and nodded his head. "That's good enough for me, son, that's good enough for me."'

The many controversies of England's Caribbean tour may not all have found their way into print, but no one who read the sports pages would have been unaware that it had been a stormy trip. In this, it differed from the Bodyline tour, many of the details of which remained obscured from a British audience. Anyone wanting to know more about Len Hutton's travails could soon find them on the shelves of their local bookshop. *Cricket Cauldron* by the *Daily Mail's* Alex Bannister was published in mid-May, while E. W. Swanton's *West Indian Adventure* was launched during the Lord's Test in June. Trueman had an unwanted starring role in both.

Trueman had played in the first, fourth and fifth Tests, taking nine wickets at the distinctly unimpressive average of 46.66. Overall on tour, he had 27 at 33.66. Those figures may have been respectable for a 22-year-old touring greenhorn who had previously played just five Tests, but such was the excitement around Trueman's match-winning potential that they represented a let-down. 'No captain could wish to have a better trier than Trueman. He is very keen and wanted to do well,' wrote Hutton in his tour report. The rest of his lengthy passage on his county teammate was less complimentary.

'Trueman gave me much concern and until a big improvement is made in his general conduct and cricket manners I do not think he is suitable for MCC Tours, particularly a tour such as the one to the West Indies.'

At the debrief with Lord Rosebery, Harry Altham and Ronny Aird on 30 April, Hutton and manager Charles Palmer recommended that Trueman be docked his £50 good-conduct bonus. Trueman was furious, writing to Lord's for an explanation. He was told the matter was closed, although the issue was sensitive enough for the official record to be doctored later. In addition, Hutton's incendiary report is absent from the MCC archive, although he kept a copy, which was inherited by his son, Richard. A redacted version was published in *The Cricketer* in January 1996.

It's clear that MCC were making an example of Trueman while simultaneously Hutton was offering him up as a sacrifice to deflect attention from concerns about his leadership and failure to impose discipline on the tour party. Several players must have been candidates for the same sanction but none was punished. 'There were quite a few scoundrels on that tour – Godfrey, Denis and all that lot,' Graveney said. Graveney himself had been embroiled in a diplomatic incident after a cocktail party and had been guilty of flagrant dissent towards an umpire in the fourth Test.

There was also an incident in a lift at the Marine Hotel in Bridgetown when the wife of an MCC member complained about two well-refreshed players pushing a food trolley down a corridor before jostling her and filling the air with colourful language. The next morning Trueman and Tony Lock were called to a kangaroo court in which Hutton and Palmer met the injured party and her friend. Oddly, E. W. Swanton was also present, though the captain and manager must have been sure the proceedings would not find their way into the pages of the *Daily Telegraph*. At the end of the meeting, Hutton said to Trueman, 'I thought you took that pretty well.' 'So did I, since it weren't us,' Trueman snapped back. 'I think they got blamed for a few things that other people did,' Graveney admitted. Lock later wrote, 'It transpired that the culprits were Denis Compton and Godfrey Evans.'

At the root of the problem was that nothing in Trueman's life had prepared him for the disparate demands of a long MCC tour. The cricket was one thing, but the round of receptions, cocktail parties, meetings with colonial officials and wealthy white expats quite another. He was far from the first working-class cricketer plucked from a mining village and thrust into a milieu that might as well have been from a different planet, but he was particularly ill-equipped. Even in Stainton, the Truemans were regarded as beyond the pale. 'They were a bit grubby in appearance and rough round the edges,' one resident recalled. 'Fred was different to the other kids at school: scruffy is putting it mildly.'

'It was not really his fault,' Palmer said. 'He was catapulted into a society of which he had no experience whatsoever; and he was unable to adapt to different customs, different accents and whatever.' Graveney thought that at this stage of his life Trueman was 'as rough as bag of nails'. Bannister remembered, 'He was a bit of a nuisance because he never stopped talking, but there was nothing malicious in him.' Compton revealed that the senior players had been briefed by Hutton that he would keep the young fast bowler in check. 'We were to leave him to Len, Yorkshireman to Yorkshireman,' he said. Compton quickly realised that approach wasn't working. 'I never got the impression Len had the faintest notion how to handle him.'

When standing in for Hutton in one of the tour matches, Compton disciplined Trueman himself, threatening to 'send him home on the next boat' if he did not moderate his language. Trevor Bailey, Hutton's deputy, agreed with Compton and identified a key flaw in the idea that Hutton could deal with Trueman because they shared a county dressing-room. 'Len was essentially a pre-war Yorkshire cricketer and pre-war Yorkshire cricketers would not have been like Fred Trueman,' he said. 'They were chalk and cheese.'

Once the party arrived in the West Indies, Trueman was paired with Surrey's Tony Lock, who was given vague instructions by Hutton to keep an eye on him. They became fast friends. 'I did not raise any objection to being paired with Freddie because I admired his cricket and liked him as a person,' Lock said. But Lock was also on his first tour and unversed in the polite niceties of an MCC overseas mission. Lock got on famously with Trueman but he was not the only one thinking that leaving them to fend for themselves was an odd management decision. 'Here were two youngsters of somewhat turbulent character on their first trip away from England,

and they were allowed to go their own way,' Jim Laker wrote. 'What a managerial blunder that was. Each of them should have been paired with a senior member.' For Lock, the guilt by association lasted years: he regularly had to deny stories that his good-conduct bonus had also been docked.

There was nothing new in the disquiet about Trueman at Lord's. In 1952, the summer in which he had become an overnight star with 29 wickets in his debut series against India, he was still completing his National Service in the RAF. A rather more mundane meeting with the touring team came at Gillingham in late June when Trueman opened the bowling for the Combined Services. Some of the Indians were appalled by Trueman's language and their management lodged an official complaint. To the squirming embarrassment of Colonel R.S. Rait Kerr, Aird's predecessor as MCC secretary, the issue was raised by Vice-Admiral Charles Norris, chairman of the Combined Services Cricket Association, at a lunch attended by several high-ranking Navy and RAF officers. Rait Kerr wrote to the Yorkshire captain Norman Yardley and Clifford Hesketh, a member of the county committee. Trueman was hauled in for a dressing-down, but later Rait Kerr sent a follow-up letter striking a more conciliatory tone. 'The boy,' he said 'might not have been conscious of any undesirable adornment he might be giving to his conversation.'

Does this explain the reluctance of the selectors to unleash Trueman on the Australians a year later? True, he was still in the RAF, meaning he was not always available for Yorkshire, and he had suffered an ankle injury in May, which meant his first appearance of the summer did not come until the end of the month. He was still named for the Rest against England in the Test Trial at Edgbaston, although he finished wicketless. The fact that he was selected for the Rest rather than the established England XI perhaps revealed something about his Test prospects.

The Coronation Ashes series continued without Trueman's involvement (though he was named in the 12 for the third Test at Old Trafford), until he took a clutch of wickets in July, including six for 109 in the Roses match at Bramall Lane, and MCC applied to the Air Ministry for release from his military duties. With the series still 0–0, England were in urgent need of a win to fulfil feverish national expectations of the return of the Ashes. They got their wish, England winning by eight wickets at The Oval with Trueman taking four for 86 in the first innings. 'We were all very surprised England didn't play Freddie in the first four Tests,' Neil Harvey told Chris Waters. 'We had the greatest respect for him in our side.' The final selection meeting for the West Indies tour took place on the second evening of the Test, making Trueman's dynamic intervention perfectly timed. With his National Service completed a few weeks later, they could hardly ignore him now.

But by the start of the summer of 1954 they were ignoring him again – only this time, he made it immensely more difficult. Trueman was in action at Lord's the day after Hutton and Palmer had recommended the withholding of his bonus, taking the new ball for Yorkshire against MCC. Very soon county batsmen began to feel the force of his fury at missing out on his £50 bonus. At the Parks on 6 May he had the extraordinary figures of 10–7–8–5 as Oxford University were bowled out for 58, his victims including the tour prospect Colin Cowdrey for a duck. At the end of Trueman's first over, the students had lost three wickets without registering a run.

There was no time for any of the players to scramble out of their whites at the close and make the mile-and-a-half journey across the city to the Iffley Road athletics track, but they were aware something momentous could be about to happen, and Bob Appleyard and Frank Lowson tuned into a car radio. Roger Bannister, 25, until recently a medical student at the university, produced one of the storied moments in sporting history by becoming the first man to run a mile in under four minutes. The race began at 6 p.m., the start time having been put back until the wind that had buffeted the cricketers all day had died down. Bannister's feat was the cause of huge patriotic celebration, instantly co-opted as a sign of Britain's continued global prestige, but it was missed by Walter Robins, one of MCC's tour selectors, who had been at the Parks all day and passed the athletics stadium as he left the city. He got out of his car, peered over the fence for a few moments as runners circled the track and decided it wasn't worth going in. 'Fifteen minutes later I'd missed the sporting thrill of a lifetime,' he shamefacedly admitted.

Trueman continued to collect wickets – by the beginning of June he was second to Appleyard in the averages – but when the team for the first Test against Pakistan was announced on 6 June, he was a notable absentee. 'There need be no quarrel with his omission this time, but it will be surprising indeed if he has made his last appearance for England,' wrote J.M. Kilburn in the *Yorkshire Post*. A journalist as well connected as Kilburn may have known that at their meeting a week earlier, the MCC committee had decided to seek reports from Sir William Worsley and Norman Yardley about Trueman's behaviour during the season before considering him for selection. Although he was no-balled regularly during the top-of-the-table match against Middlesex at Lord's in mid-June, then missed a couple of games with a back injury, there was no let-up in Trueman's wicket-taking, yet he continued to be exiled from the Test series.

On 18 July, shortly before the third Test at Old Trafford, a Sunday newspaper reported that Trueman would definitely not be going to Australia and had, in effect, been excluded from the England team as a punishment for his disciplinary lapses in the West Indies. More remarkable was an allegation that some players had said they would not tour if Trueman was included in the MCC squad. Harry Altham, the chairman of selectors, issued a hasty rebuttal. 'Quite obviously Trueman must and will be considered when we get down to the difficult task of picking the side to go to Australia,' he said. 'So far we have banned no one and picked no one.'

At home, Trueman said, 'Naturally, I want to go to Australia, but if I'm not picked why worry? Off the field I'm friendly with anyone, but when I'm bowling I *hate* the batsman I'm trying to get out.' In the *Daily Express*, Frank Rostron speculated that Trueman's fate lay in Hutton's hands: if the captain – whose reappointment was announced that day – insisted he wanted him in Australia he would probably get his way.

It seems obvious that events were conspiring against Trueman. There was confusion around whether or not he was one of 30 players sent letters of availability by MCC. The letters were a standard part of tour selection practice and were intended to establish whether or not a candidate had a prior professional engagement or personal reasons for not touring. The letters were a throwback to a time when there were more amateurs under consideration who may not have been able to arrange lengthy leaves of absence from their business commitments. 'I can assure you that Freddie Trueman is not one of the players who has received a letter,' Alan Fairfax told readers of the *People*.

It was true that his name was not among the first group of players to receive letters, but on 22 July, the first day of the Third Test, Altham wrote to Billy Griffith from Old Trafford asking for an availability letter to be sent to Yorkshire 'in view of the fact that we know Len Hutton would wish Trueman to be considered for Australia.' Griffith duly wrote to the Yorkshire secretary John Nash posing the question, but the letter from Lord's is dated 26 July, the day after the selectors had reached their decisions on the squad and the day before the announcement. Altham's letter adds credence to Hutton's later protestations that he had wanted Trueman to be selected.

The truth, surely, was that after the events of the winter and without the unqualified support of Hutton, Trueman was never going to go to Australia, no matter how many wickets he took in 1954. As long ago as the beginning of May, when Gubby Allen wrote to Charles Palmer wondering if 'a manager on a rather higher level is a solution' he had added, 'I am convinced that had Trueman not been a member of the team, that had you been given a different brief and more power, and that had Len been persuaded that a bloody battle did not necessarily involve a lack of courtesy, much of the trouble would not have occurred.' In his tour book, E. W. Swanton took the same view: 'I would not be happy to see his [Trueman's] name again in a touring team.'

Or perhaps the selectors were content to leave Trueman stewing because they had another bowler able to fulfil Hutton's desire to give the Australians a taste of their own medicine. His name may have been largely unknown at the start of the summer, but it soon began to feature regularly in the press. By the time the tour party announcement was due, everyone who followed cricket knew about the 24-year-old former English literature student from Durham University who was in the habit of quoting Wordsworth as he walked back to his mark – Frank Holmes Tyson.

Tyson's rise to fame shared a key characteristic with his bowling – both were extremely rapid. Brought up in the Lancashire mill town of Middleton, he had a successful exploratory trial at Old Trafford at 17, after which he was taken to one side by the county coach Harry Makepeace. 'If you come to Old Trafford I think I can make you an England bowler,' Makepeace told him. Thrilled, the teenager made his way home only to be told by his father that he would not be allowed to waste his academic potential on an uncertain career in professional sport. Tyson's next chance came when he was picked for a Lancashire second XI fixture during his National Service. Hampered by a rail strike, Tyson arrived late then hobbled off with a strained back muscle. In 1951, he wrote to the county enquiring about the possibility of appearing for the seconds, but was told by secretary Geoffrey Howard that all places were taken for the remainder of the season. He never heard from Lancashire again.

Then fate intervened. A year earlier, while at Durham, Tyson was invited to play for Redcar against a Yorkshire XI. Opening the batting for the county was Hutton. In their respective memoirs, the players remembered the fixture differently: Tyson thought it was a one-day, pre-season warm-up; Hutton remembered it as a match in his benefit season. 'The second ball Tyson bowled me was a full pitch which hit me with considerable force on the pad,' Hutton later wrote. 'I was so surprised by its pace that I had time only to move my bat about 12 inches when – thump! The ball struck me on the leg and how it hurt. Not many first-class bowlers in 1950 could hit me on the pad before I could get my bat down and that one ball caused me to pay the young bowler more than usual attention.' In his own account, Hutton noted Tyson's contact details and asked Allen, who liked to monitor the development of young fast bowlers, to see if he could use his influence to get the youngster more opportunities.

Hutton's missive to Lord's doesn't seem to have had much impact. There is no evidence that Tyson was on Allen's or MCC's radar. Instead, he became a professional for Knypersley in the North Staffordshire League. In 1951, the club arranged an exhibition match against a Commonwealth XI, recently returned from a tour of the subcontinent under the management of the former England wicketkeeper George Duckworth. Against a line-up that included the West Indies batsman Frank Worrell and the Australian all-rounder George Tribe, Tyson made a strong impression. Afterwards, another

Australian, Jock Livingston, approached him. 'We're not supposed to poach for players, but if you want to play county cricket there's a place for you at Northampton,' Livingston told him. Tyson was not worried about poaching – Lancashire had forgotten about him anyway – so he began a two-year residential qualification for Northamptonshire.

During that period he appeared in two matches against touring teams. Facing the Indians in 1952 he took the wicket of the opening batsman Pankaj Roy with his sixth delivery in first-class cricket. That was his only success, but Freddie Brown, the Northamptonshire captain, never forgot the sight of his nervous slip cordon edging five yards further back at the start of Tyson's second over. Later he would say that Tyson was the fastest English bowler he had seen since Harold Larwood. Against the Australians a year later, Tyson took two top-order wickets, trapping opener Colin McDonald lbw second ball and clean-bowling Graeme Hole with his next. Tyson played in 11 Championship games in the remainder of the summer without significant success – but whispers about his extreme pace spread like a bush fire around the county circuit.

At the beginning of June, the *News Chronicle*'s Crawford White checked out both of England's potential Ashes spearheads in one day. He saw Tyson taking the new ball against Worcestershire at Northampton, before driving 35 miles to the Courtaulds Ground at Coventry to watch Fred Trueman in action against Warwickshire. He concluded that Trueman was still faster – the day before White's visit he had taken seven for 67 – but added, 'Mind you, Tyson is fast.' Selector Les Ames was at Northampton on what White called 'Operation Australia'. The journalist was in no doubt whom he would choose. 'The tough Yorkshireman has the better action and the stronger frame, and on present indications I cannot see him being left out of the Australian tour.'

In early July there was an opportunity to see them in direct competition, when Yorkshire visited Northampton. They each took four wickets, but Northamptonshire wicketkeeper, Keith Andrew, missing the match with injury, thought he knew the answer to what was becoming an increasingly burning question. 'Frank bowls faster than any man I know in cricket now: faster than Freddie Trueman and faster than Brian Statham,' he said. 'I know because I kept to

Freddie playing for the Combined Services in 1952. I have talked to batsmen too this season. They agree, Frank is faster. It's going to be a dangerous day for me when Frank does get a flying wicket.' For his part, Tyson would only say, 'I really can't tell you how fast I am. I don't think any fast bowler can be sure about his pace. But a fast bowler needs encouragement from the pitch to bowl his fastest. Of course I would like to go to Australia, but I have to get my Arts degree at Durham University.' Tyson had failed his finals and was now facing a retake.

Tyson's returns were unspectacular, and many remained sceptical of his match-winning potential. The BBC statistician, Roy Webber, produced figures that showed that Trueman took a far higher percentage of top-order wickets. While impressed with his pace, Ralph Hadley of the *People* thought Tyson bowled too straight and did not move the ball off the pitch or in the air: 'Result: Tyson's wickets still cost too much for the pace he can work up.'

The match that turned Tyson from contender to genuine tour prospect came at Lord's in mid-July, nine days before the squad announcement. Towards the end of Saturday's play, when he had already made an impressive 60 with the bat, Tyson laid out Middlesex No. 3 Bill Edrich on the turf after he edged a ball that was only just short of a length into his face. A bloodied and clearly shaken Edrich eventually got to his feet and was helped off by the bowler: liberal quantities of sawdust were scattered around to cover the bloodstains. At hospital, Edrich was found to have a fractured cheekbone. 'I heard two members discussing whether Tyson was really fast,' wrote Charles Bray in the *Daily Herald*. 'If they have any doubts they had better ask Edrich.' Typically pugnacious, Edrich waved away the protestations of his teammates and resumed his innings on Monday morning with his face swollen and his head bandaged: Tyson's first ball was a bouncer that hit him on the body.

No less venerable a figure than C.B. Fry stood at the window of the writing room in the pavilion and pronounced favourably on Tyson's pace. Alf Gover, the former Surrey and England bowler-turned-coach, said he was the fastest English bowler since the war. Patsy Hendren, the great England batsman of the inter-war years, now the Middlesex scorer, recalled facing the great Australians

Tibby Cotter, Jack Gregory and Ted McDonald: 'Tyson equals all of them in pace and is the fastest English bowler I've seen since Larwood.'

On Sunday 25 July during the rain-ruined Old Trafford Test against Pakistan and with David Sheppard still at the helm, the members of MCC's tour selection committee were joined by Hutton at Lymm in Cheshire. There was one item on the agenda – to pick the 17 men who would defend the Ashes in Australia that winter. Edrich or Kenyon, Laker or McConnon, Lock or Wardle, Trueman or Tyson: those were the names that reverberated around the room. Their decisions would be revealed on Tuesday evening. After a summer of inquests into the disciplinary record of the players in the West Indies, controversies about the captaincy, and discussions about the character and talent of the cricketers under discussion, it had come down to this.

Bob Appleyard's recovery from life-threatening tuberculosis made his story one of the most remarkable in sport.

Ship mates: the players say their final farewells to MCC officials on the deck of the *Orsova* before their departure.

Denis Compton boards his plane at Heathrow for his four-day journey to Australia.

IV

THE LONG ROAD TO BRISBANE

'May you parentless swine go to blazes'
                    Unsigned letter to the MCC selectors

'This is the fourth time I have seen my husband off on one of these tours but I still do not feel any happier about it'
                    Jean Simpson, wife of opening batsman, Reg

'This is the best team we have sent to Australia since 1932'
                    England captain Len Hutton on the day of departure

'HERE IS THE NEWS'

At just before 6 p.m. on Tuesday 27 July, 1954, millions of Britons turned on their radios, shifted the dial to find the BBC Home Service and waited for the evening news bulletin. The broadcast does not survive in the corporation's archive, but the following morning's newspaper front pages offer broad hints about the likely content. An outline agreement had been reached with Egypt for the withdrawal of British troops from the Suez Canal zone; two Chinese aircraft had been shot down by US fighters, ratcheting up tension between the two countries; Sir Winston Churchill was set to delay his retirement as prime minister indefinitely after a slew of resignations by senior Tories; and the wretched summer weather, which had just claimed the Old Trafford Test match, now threatened to wipe out the hay harvest.

For many, foreign policy shifts, international sabre-rattling, a crisis in the cabinet and impending agricultural calamity took second place to what followed at 6.15 – the evening sports desk. It was then that the 17 players who would form the MCC party for the winter tour to Australia were to be announced. Up to this moment, with the obvious exception of captain Len Hutton, not even the cricketers themselves knew who was in and who was out: careers were about to be made, others left in tatters.

These were the names the presenter read out: Len Hutton (captain), Peter May (vice-captain), Bob Appleyard, Keith Andrew, Trevor Bailey, Alec Bedser, Denis Compton, Colin Cowdrey, Bill Edrich, Godfrey Evans, Tom Graveney, Peter Loader, Jim McConnon, Reg Simpson, Brian Statham, Frank Tyson and Johnny Wardle.

Despite the importance of the announcement, there was little time for comment or analysis. The sports news lasted five minutes, then it was straight into the evening programming with a 25-minute performance by Rawicz and Landauer, the popular Austro-Polish piano duo. Commendably, there had been no leaks of the names in the squad – despite it being finalised 48 hours earlier – though a few people were in the know. Chairman Harry Altham travelled back from the selectors' meeting in Cheshire to his home in Winchester and was met at the station by his son-in-law, Arthur 'Podge' Brodhurst, a housemaster at Winchester College.[20] Brodhurst's son, Robin, who was on the back seat, loved to recount the family legend around what happened next. 'Dad picked him up from Winchester station and as they stopped at the traffic lights at the bottom of the hill, Harry leant over and said, "I thought you might like to look at this? Particularly the two names at the bottom." And the two names at the bottom were F.H. Tyson and M.C. Cowdrey. I like to think that dad stalled the car, but I don't think so.'

The shock selections received the news differently. Frank Tyson was at the County Ground in Northampton where a Championship match against Middlesex had just finished in a tense draw. The resumption of his battle with Bill Edrich, which had brought bloodshed at Lord's a week earlier, had finished honours even: Tyson took five for 78 but the Middlesex captain hit 102.

In the home dressing-room, a Vidor portable radio was tuned to the Home Service. When it was announced that not only Tyson but also his teammate Keith Andrew had become the first Northamptonshire professionals to be chosen for an Ashes tour, there was an explosion of cheers, followed by choruses of 'For they are jolly good fellows.' The duo were carried shoulder-high in front of the delighted home supporters and waiting press photographers. The front page of the next morning's *Daily Herald* carried the picture of the celebrations and a photograph of Andrew's bride-to-be, Joyce. Their October wedding plans were now in need of urgent revision.

There was rather less euphoria a hundred miles south, at Rectory Field, Blackheath, the ground that provided the customary venue for the Kent-Surrey fixture. As at Northampton, the second day had been lost to rain, but there was a headline-making performance on the final day from the Surrey left-arm spinner Tony Lock, who took seven for 83.

---

[20]Brodhurst played first-class cricket for Cambridge University and Gloucestershire. He commanded anti-aircraft units in North Africa, and at the siege of Tobruk was seen carrying a cricket bag and asking if anyone wanted a net.

In Colin Cowdrey's later account, in part ghostwritten by the distinguished sportswriter Ian Wooldridge and published in 1976, he claimed to have heard the news that there were some surprises in the tour party before the full list was announced, then had to walk through the Surrey dressing-room where Laker and Lock were digesting the bombshell of their exclusion. 'The atmosphere could have been cut into cubes and sold as solid fuel,' Cowdrey remembered. It was only minutes later that, to his considerable surprise, he heard he was in the squad himself.

In an earlier memoir, however, he recalled hearing the news when Kent supporters with car radios began sounding their horns and calling out, 'You're in, Colin.' Whichever version is more accurate, he quickly put his cricket bag in the boot of his car and drove off to Northampton for the start of the following day's game. 'I was thoroughly embarrassed and did not relish the thought of having to justify my selection in the eyes of both the public and the cricket profession,' he said.

Lock also left Blackheath hurriedly, driving home in a fury, though he later claimed that he was not completely shocked. 'My conduct on and off the field was allegedly under a cloud,' he said, a reference to the backlash from the West Indies tour and the continuing concerns about his bowling action. Micky Stewart, the Surrey batsman, remembered that Laker was the more distressed of the pair.

The chilly atmosphere in south-east London was matched in the front parlour of the Trueman home in south Yorkshire. The last name of the 17 had barely left the BBC announcer's mouth before Fred Trueman's mother, Ethel, angrily snapped off the radio. 'It's daft. Worse, it's unfair,' she told the first reporter at the door a few minutes later. Fred's father, Dick, also had his say. 'How long is Tyson really fast for? Has he got Freddie's stamina or accuracy?' he demanded to know. His son was more diplomatic. 'Naturally, I'm disappointed I'm not going to Australia, but my best wishes to the lads selected, and I hope they'll bring back the Ashes which I helped to win last season,' he said, leaving in a slight barb.

Privately, he was furious, and the anger simmered for the rest of his life. 'It was a terrible blow,' he recalled more than 20 years later. 'It has been reported that I swore I would never play for England again, if asked. That wasn't strictly true – I said it made me feel like I would never play again. I'll never be able to forgive either Len or MCC for that.' Hutton always insisted he had wanted Trueman in the squad, but evidence suggests that is unlikely. 'I was told by a couple of the selectors that I had equal votes with everybody else and it was left to the captain and he went for Peter Loader,' Trueman said in the early 1990s. 'That surprises me a bit because I always thought Leonard was a great friend of mine.'

Elsewhere, there was more joy. Jim McConnon, the Glamorgan off-spinner selected ahead of Laker, had been travelling south from Manchester, where he had just made his Test debut, to Southampton, and was on a train when the squad was announced. On reaching his hotel, he called his wife, Pauline, at home in Newport. She told him their two young children had been allowed to stay up to see daddy's picture on television. For Andrew the euphoric mood was dimmed by an evening visit to patients at Manfield Orthopaedic Hospital in Northampton. 'To see all those men in hospital, severely disabled, it was awful,' he told his biographer, Stephen Chalke. 'So many of them had had motorbike accidents, and their lives were ruined.' Later that night he realised he had some rearranging to do: not just his wedding but a fortnight's training with the Northamptonshire Yeomanry in which he was still a reservist.

Press reaction to the squad was generally favourable. 'It accords pretty well with the more intelligent forecasts,' wrote E. W. Swanton in the *Daily Telegraph*. 'A good workmanlike side, with a good, even chance of retaining the Ashes,' thought Bruce Harris of the *Evening Standard*. 'Perhaps it is not at first sight a great side in the sense of those of 1928 or 1932,' said Geoffrey Green of *The Times* before adding 'One has great confidence in its ability to retain the Ashes.' His *Manchester Guardian* counterpart Denys Rowbotham agreed. 'Once again MCC has confounded its critics,' he wrote. 'Its selectors have chosen not merely what should prove an extremely good touring party but, against all the irrelevant predictions of recent weeks, a party every member of which justifies his inclusion on his cricketing ability.'

The omission of Trueman could not be ignored. The *Daily Herald*'s Charles Bray thought Tyson 'a very lucky young man'. He added, 'Trueman is a much better bowler and nobody is going to tell me he is not.' The paper's sympathies were revealed in a front-page headline, 'Trueman is out: how's that?' Swanton thought early success had gone to Trueman's head. 'Two or three years ago he was lauded and boosted beyond his true worth. The effect was unfortunate and for Trueman's career subsequently modern publicity has much to answer for.' Harris called Altham. 'I have nothing to say beyond the fact that Trueman was considered on the same basis as everyone else,' the chairman said. Anyone expecting unchecked outrage in Yorkshire might have been surprised by the measured response of *Yorkshire Post* cricket correspondent J.M. Kilburn. 'A philosophic silence from now on will probably serve him best, for his cricket career lies mainly ahead,' he wrote. 'He will come into his kingdom and soon, if he allows performances to speak for themselves.'

In Australia, there was disappointment mixed with relief that home crowds would not witness the spectacle of Trueman's thrilling new-ball bursts. 'The Australians will, above all, miss "bad man" fast bowler Fred Trueman,' wrote Ray Robinson of *The Sun* in Sydney. Former Australian batsman Sid Barnes wrote in the *Daily Express*, 'It is the biggest blunder in the long history of MCC blunders. They are sending a team without a personality.' Percy Millard of the *Melbourne Herald* sniffed, 'Hardly England's best without Trueman and Lock.' The former Australia wicketkeeper Bert Oldfield felt Appleyard and Wardle could emerge as England's match-winners, a point picked up by former captain Lindsay Hassett in a column in London's *Evening Standard*. 'I believe England have hopes for Appleyard to turn up their trump card. No Australian has batted against him,' he said. His mind was occupied by a more familiar foe. 'Everybody knows everything about Bedser except how to play him – we must look upon him as an ever-present menace.'

MCC Squad – Tour of Australia and New Zealand 1954-55

	Birthplace	Age	County	Tests	Bat/bowl
Len Hutton (captain)	Fulneck, Yorkshire	38	Yorkshire	72	RHB/LB
Peter May (vice-captain)	Reading, Berkshire	24	Surrey	17	RHB
Bob Appleyard	Bradford	30	Yorkshire	1	RHB/OB/RM
Keith Andrew	Oldham	24	Northamptonshire	0	RHB/WK
Trevor Bailey	Westcliff-on-Sea, Essex	30	Essex	27	RHB/RFM
Alec Bedser	Reading	36	Surrey	49	RHB/RM
Denis Compton	Hendon	36	Middlesex	63	RHB/SLW
Colin Cowdrey	Bangalore, Mysore	21	Kent	0	RHB
Bill Edrich	Lingwood, Norfolk	38	Middlesex	35	RHB/OB
Godfrey Evans	Finchley	33	Kent	57	RHB/WK
Tom Graveney	Riding Mill, Northumberland	27	Gloucestershire	22	RHB/LB
Peter Loader	Wallington, Surrey	24	Surrey	1	RHB/RF
Jim McConnon	Burnopfield, Co. Durham	32	Glamorgan	2	RHB/OB
Reg Simpson	Sherwood, Nottinghamshire	34	Nottinghamshire	24	RHB
Brian Statham	Manchester	24	Lancashire	17	LHB/RF
Frank Tyson	Bolton	24	Northamptonshire	1	RHB/RF
Johnny Wardle	Ardsley, Yorkshire	31	Yorkshire	13	LHB/SLA/SLW

J.V. Wilson (Scampston, Yorkshire, 33, Yorkshire, 0, LHB) was added to the squad in August
Manager: C.G. Howard. *Baggage-master/scorer:* G. Duckworth. *Masseur:* H. Dalton

It was a harsh reality of the remorseless county fixture list that there was little time for the players to celebrate. In a delicious twist, Northamptonshire were hosting Kent at Northampton, bringing together Tyson, Andrew and Cowdrey in the same fixture. The home pair were given the honour of leading the team out, but Tyson then bowled two wides and a no-ball in his first over. When his radar was adjusted, he took two cheap wickets, including Cowdrey, bowled for 18. At Southampton, McConnon took the only four Hampshire wickets to fall on a rain-shortened day.

Perhaps predictably, the headlines were stolen by Trueman, who was cheered to the echo at Headingley then took three wickets in his first five overs against Derbyshire, finishing the day with six for 109. The next morning, Hutton's unhappy summer continued when he was hit on the hand by a ball from Les Jackson, ruling him out for the rest of the match.

In the remaining County Championship programme, Laker and Lock gave the selectors cause to reflect on their decisions. On the day the squad was announced, champions Surrey lay eighth in the table, 48 points behind long-time leaders Yorkshire. But in the final month of the season, Laker took 54 wickets while Lock collected 51. Boosted by their ability to win games swiftly between the showers while their rivals were often kept off the field, Surrey won nine of their remaining 10 games to surge through the pack and complete a hat-trick of titles.

Meanwhile, the men who *were* going to Australia fared less well. After resisting calls to experiment all summer, the home selectors handed debuts to Loader and Tyson in the final Test against Pakistan at The Oval. Cowdrey was named as 12th man to gain a flavour of the big occasion, but found the experience so uncomfortable that he was relieved to be invalided home with a temperature caused by an adverse reaction to his pre-Australia inoculations.

A rapid ball from Tyson broke Reg Simpson's favourite bat in the nets, then he took four wickets in Pakistan's first innings, but from there it was downhill. Chasing 168 to win, England wilted in the face of a seam-bowling masterclass from Fazal Mahmood and lost by 24 runs. 'This defeat was the smack across the face our smug Australia-bound players needed,' wrote Crawford White in the *News Chronicle*. Hutton took it on the chin. 'My optimism for Australia is not affected by this result,' he said. 'You must remember that if we had not wished to give Test experience to some of our bowlers going to Australia we should have included Alec Bedser, who would have enjoyed himself on this Oval wicket.'

'YOU PARENTLESS SWINE'

No sooner had she turned off the radio than Ethel Trueman made an ominous prediction: 'The MCC will hear a rocket going off in their ears tomorrow.' She was right. In the days following the announcement of the tour party, postmen in the St John's Wood area of north London were delivering sacksful of invective through the Grace Gates for the urgent attention of the Lord's secretarial staff. Much of it concerned the omission of Mrs Trueman's son.

'What are we looking for to retain the Ashes? Nice little gentlemen with polished manners and Oxford accents, or men who get the wickets and make the runs even if they are a bit "rugged"?' asked M.W. Whiteley of Warrington, Lancashire. 'You can hardly blame people for wondering how far snobbery has entered into the omission of Trueman. As for the pace attack chosen – it's pathetic with Bedser out of form and past his prime, and Loader and Tyson completely untried. I wonder when you'll realise that we who support the game with our shillings and our interest have a right to see the best men chosen even if a few people's susceptibilities are offended.'

It was a common theme. Four members of staff from Westminster Airways in Gosport, Hampshire, also took up cudgels in the class war. 'Surely the old school tie does not come before national pride, or were the Ashes only loaned to us for Coronation year?' The quartet threatened to withdraw their support from county cricket and instead watch local club games 'where members are played on their merits and not on their social standing'. A Mr Grace from Fulwood in Preston added, 'It is obvious that because Trueman was a miner your snobbishness prevailed.'

Others could barely contain their rage. 'May you parentless swine go to blazes,' concluded one unsigned letter, which also described the selectors as 'misbegotten creatures'. 'I feel like striking you, so bitter is my resentment,' wrote Eric Godley, musical director of the

Harrogate Guild of Singers, an organisation presumably not easily driven to violence. The north-south divide was also raised. 'I suppose if Trueman had come from Surrey or Middlesex he would have been the first name on the list, but he is a Yorkshireman, born and bred, and he doesn't talk good enough for you,' wrote a correspondent from Rotherham, the heart of Trueman country. 'I think you have made the biggest blunder in cricket history,' the writer added. W.J. Crawley from nearby Sheffield weighed in, 'It is well recognised in Yorkshire that it is difficult to obtain a place in an English side if one, for example, eats peas with a knife, but surely that is a lesser offence than some that have been committed by some of the players chosen!'

That was presumably a reference to Bill Edrich's recent well-publicised drink-driving case, which was mentioned in other letters, alongside the alleged moral failings of some members of the squad. 'If Trueman is to be left out on account of some character defect, I must indicate that neither Edrich or Compton can be classified as angels,' said V.E. Birkett of Billericay, Essex. 'I should like to know how long the MCC has been the arbiter of a person's morals or social caste, and it would seem that one of the qualifications for selection is to be found drunk in charge of a motor car,' said a Mr Aldersley of Kendal in Westmorland. Another letter criticised the selection of 'Two alcohol-sodden adulterers. I needn't name the swine.'

Other selections warranted barely a mention in the correspondence preserved in the MCC archive, but Cowdrey's inclusion raised the ire of some writers. 'Colin Cowdrey. Words fail me. When batsmen of Kenyon, Watkins, Watson, Lowson, Washbrook etc etc are left at home and that idiot is taken. Well!' There were calls to include Don Kenyon in favour of Cowdrey, call up Essex captain Doug Insole instead of his county teammate Trevor Bailey and replace Edrich with Brian Close.

Most surprising of all, perhaps, were the number of correspondents withdrawing their backing for the team. 'I am one of the many hundreds in this district whose support stays at home this winter and does not go with you to Australia,' said M. Wood. 'As my son of nine says "We deserve to lose the Ashes,"' wrote Mrs B. O'Neill of St Ives in Cornwall. 'I hope that England are well and truly humbled in Australia,' said another letter.

Happily, not all the surviving tour correspondence is similarly embittered. Most of it relates to the huge volume of administrative work it took to organise an enterprise that involved sending 20 men to the other side of the world for more than six months. This was a time, of course, before mobile telephones, WhatsApp groups, satellite communications or email. Telegrams could be used for brief communications and would arrive on the day of despatch. Apart from that it was mostly a matter of sending letters and waiting for a response. In dealing with Australia, this could take weeks, especially if it was a matter of negotiating details of the itinerary. One key letter about the tour arrangements was incinerated in a plane crash in Singapore. For MCC secretary Ronny Aird, his deputy Billy Griffith and assistant secretary Jim Dunbar, the workload was formidable.

An internal MCC list of the selected squad shows that most had a telephone at home. This was not to be taken for granted: in mid-1950s Britain owning a telephone was still a luxury. During the 1956 Ashes series, when Sussex all-rounder Alan Oakman was needed to replace the injured Tom Graveney in the Old Trafford Test, the selectors were dismayed to find he was uncontactable. Chairman Gubby Allen called Oakman's local police station and a member of Hastings constabulary was sent round to tell him to pack his kit and leave for Manchester.

There was much to organise with the players, once they had formally accepted the invitation to tour and their county had granted permission. Inoculations against tuberculosis, smallpox and typhoid had to be given, and a medical certificate supplied to Lord's. Reports that some players had suffered a reaction to their injections prompted a letter to MCC from the National Anti-Vaccination League claiming it was 'extremely foolish' for the team to be inoculated before their outward journey: it received a brusque response from Aird.

Money mattered, too. The tour fee for professionals was raised to £850 (around £19,000 in 2024), a £350 increase on the amount earned by the players in the West Indies the previous winter. Superficially, this seems a generous figure, but other sports were already offering more lucrative employment. In June 1954, the British golfer Peter Alliss won his first big tournament at Little Aston in Staffordshire. The 23-year-old pocketed a £400 first prize thus, in four days, earning almost half what the MCC cricketers would in six months. The five amateurs in the MCC squad – Bailey, Cowdrey,

Edrich, May and Simpson – were paid an allowance for the entire tour of £325, designed to cover the cost of drinks, cigarettes and taxis. Hutton was given an extra £100 for expenses incurred when buying drinks and meals for guests.

Both groups of players had to sign a contract, although its terms might have been hard to enforce on the amateurs. After the problems in the West Indies, a new clause was inserted covering discipline. This asserted the right of the manager and captain to send a player home for any serious breaches, and gave them discretionary powers to hand out punishments for poor contributions to 'team spirit on and off the field'. Hutton and Howard were also in charge of deciding who might be docked the end-of-tour bonus.

Kit had to be arranged: each player had to visit the Modernist splendour of Simpsons of Piccadilly, the largest menswear store in England,[21] to be measured for an MCC touring blazer, navy blue with lapels trimmed with MCC red and yellow, and a George and dragon motif on the pocket. They were given two sleeveless and one long-sleeved MCC sweater, two caps, and two or three pairs of shirts and flannels.

'This visit to the tailor was an awe-inspiring experience for someone like me who had never before moved in Savile Row circles,' remembered Frank Tyson. The Jaeger menswear company also provided sweaters for each player, on the understanding that a team photograph would be taken for them to use in promotional material. Other companies provided two pairs of trousers and shirts. Sportswear suppliers sent additional shirts, pairs of socks, pads and gloves. Early in the sea voyage, each player was given a pair of sunglasses. Stuart Surridge, the bat-making company owned by the family of the Surrey captain, gave every player two new bats. Perhaps the commercial gift most appreciated by the team came when they arrived in Australia and found the Benson & Hedges tobacco company would be delivering 2500 cigarettes a week to their hotels.

A month after the selection sub-committee had apparently completed its work, it reconvened in emergency session at the Sports

---

[21]Designed by the architect Joseph Emberton and opened in 1936, it is a Grade 1 listed building, now housing the flagship branch of the Waterstones book chain.

Club in London. Hutton was also in attendance. The problem was that regular topic of anguished national debate – Denis Compton's knee. There were concerns that he might not be fit enough to take part in the tour. Crawford White of the *News Chronicle* recalled that Compton, 'could hardly limp up the gangplank' four years earlier. Compton was more sanguine. 'My knee has swelled like this before,' he said. 'After treatment it goes down and I can play on it again.' Nevertheless, it was decided that he would not sail with the rest of the squad but remain in London for treatment by the sports surgeon Bill Tucker and fly out later. This involved four trips a week to Charing Cross Hospital for heat treatment, and further appointments at Tucker's clinic with exercises designed to build up the strength in his thigh muscles.

In case Compton was ruled out, the Yorkshire batsman Vic Wilson was added to the party. Wilson, a 33-year-old left-hander, normally batted at No.3 for his county, but it was not purely in that role that he was called up. The sub-committee considered a medical report that Compton's knee issues were likely to be aggravated by the quick movements involved in fielding in close positions. The minutes noted, 'If an additional member of the team was to go it should be a man capable of fielding close to the wicket.'

Wilson had a reputation as one of the best close catchers in the country, pushing him higher up the list than more prolific run-scorers (his friendship with Hutton cannot have done his chances any harm either). He had been expecting to spend the winter on the 64-acre family farm near Malton, in the North Riding. 'This is a great moment,' Wilson said. 'I had intended to be dealing with my farm during the winter, but my father is near at hand and he will be able to deal with any tricky matters that arise.' Godfrey Evans would later express 'considerable bewilderment' that an opportunity had been missed to call up Willie Watson.

As MCC worked through the planning of the tour, there was concern about the likely profits from the trip and how much money would be available to distribute among the counties. Cricket's finances can appear perpetually precarious and the financial viability of county cricket was as much of a concern in the mid-1950s as it is in the 21st century. The dreadful weather in 1954 – a survey of 20th-century summers by the meteorological historian Philip Eden in the 2000 edition of *Wisden* calculated it was the coldest, gloomiest and third-wettest – made the situation more acute.

The 17 counties were addressing a combined loss in the region of £75,000, with almost all of them reporting falls in attendances and receipts. In the modern era, broadcasting and commercial revenue dwarf the money taken through the turnstiles. In 1954, sources of income other than gate receipts were minuscule. The BBC paid £2000 per Test (around £46,000 today) for the right to show a maximum of 13 hours of each match on television. Radio bulletins – ball-by-ball commentary was still three years away – cost the corporation 250 guineas per Test.

Geoffrey Howard spent time poring over the financial data of recent tours. He noted that the Australian tourists in 1953 had enjoyed a bonanza, bringing in £55,486 before expenses from the five Tests alone, without factoring in the receipts from often packed county grounds for tour matches. That contrasted with income of £24,967 for MCC's previous Ashes tour in 1950–51, which left a negligible profit, none of which found its way to hard-up county treasurers. Howard noted that the Brisbane Test, which had lost one day to rain and ended two days early, produced receipts of £A1,961, less than he had recently handed over to the Pakistan management for an Old Trafford Test in which three days had been completely rained off. As the man expected to gather up the gate receipts as he travelled around Australia, Howard took a close interest in the bottom line.

On Hutton's tour of the Caribbean, the West Indies Cricket Board of Control had paid all expenses, leaving MCC with no profit at all, despite frequently packed grounds. In Australia, it had become customary for the touring team to receive 50 per cent of the money taken at the turnstiles. The problem with the arrangement was that admission charges in Australia were low. Aird had made this point in a letter to the soon-to-retire secretary of the Australian Board of Control Bill Jeanes. His plea was successful in getting the standard ground admission charge for the 1954–55 series raised from three to four shillings. Only later did Aird discover that this was in Australian shillings and therefore worth less to MCC. A plea for a further increase was refused.

Jeanes pointed out that there were key differences in cricket-watching habits in Australia. 'Our position in Australia is, as I have mentioned in previous correspondence, very different to yours in that with our big grounds and relatively small populations we have to be very careful to keep admission charges at a level which will not create public hostility.' MCC were further concerned that members at each ground were effectively watching the Tests without payment and that admission charges for children were extremely low. At some grounds, members were allowed to take in two female guests with no extra charge.

'I think it is fair to say that Australia can only afford to make these sweeping gestures to their public because of the large sums of money they are taking home as a result of tours in other countries,' wrote an exasperated Howard. Frustrated by their inability to extract the concessions they wanted, MCC issued a pre-emptive strike, explicitly threatening to cut the gate-receipt percentage Australia would take home on their next tour in 1956.

THE BACKROOM BOYS

The MCC party setting sail from Tilbury Docks on 15 September would compromise 17 cricketers and a manager, plus two other men with crucial roles to play if the Ashes were to be retained. They were George Duckworth, the baggage-master and scorer, and Harold Dalton, usually known by the nickname 'Woozer', the masseur. Both appointments were instigated by Hutton, though they were confirmed when his captaincy was still under threat.

Duckworth, 53, the former Lancashire wicketkeeper, had been a member of the MCC squad in Australia in 1928–29 and 1932–33, as well as managing numerous Commonwealth tours. His connections in rugby league as a journalist gave him further recognition in Australia. The role of baggage-master and scorer had been filled on MCC's tours of Australia since 1924–25 by Bill Ferguson, universally known as 'Fergie', a peripatetic Australian who undertook the same duties for other Test teams, including his home country's most recent visit to England in 1953. He was enough of a cricket celebrity to publish an autobiography, *Mr Cricket*, in 1957 and it was a further measure of Ferguson's renown that the foreword was contributed by Australian prime minister Robert Menzies.

Ferguson had submitted his application for the job in 1954–55 as early as April, but reports had reached Lord's that he had been in poor health during his most recent assignment with New Zealand in South Africa. 'He is like a prima donna who is always going to retire but finds it difficult to do so,' Aird wrote to England's 1950–51 tour captain Freddie Brown. After some intelligence gathering about the state of Ferguson's health, Aird wrote to him at the end of June. 'We have decided that the time has come when we must provide our own man from this country,' he said. 'I cannot express too strongly the thanks and gratitude of the MCC committee for all that you have done for us in the past over such a long period of years.'

At Ferguson's home in Sydney, the news did not go down well. 'Naturally I am much disappointed at the MCC committee turning me down,' he wrote. 'The papers here published that Fergie has been sacked.' He couldn't resist a barb at his successor, 'I was surprised to see Duckworth take my job, a come-down for him.' MCC sweetened the pill with a £100 donation towards a retirement gift. In any case, Hutton was keen to call on Duckworth's experience, cricket knowledge and tactical nous as much as his talent for keeping track of the score and the suitcases. 'I could always rely on George for information,' Hutton wrote. 'He knew most of the answers to my problems.' Duckworth was soon invited on to the tour selection panel, where his acumen proved crucial. 'The scorer sees more than anyone,' said Hutton,

'George was not to be confined by labels. He was guide, philosopher and friend to all who had the sense to see the worth of his experience of cricket and Australia,' wrote E.W. Swanton. Duckworth also proved a valuable bridge between players and press and, as a former Test cricketer, he commanded a respect among the players. 'He would march straight into the dressing-room at the close of play and unhesitatingly tell the team, if it were necessary, exactly what he thought of them,' said Howard.

The inclusion of Dalton was generally welcomed as a step towards a more modern approach to fitness and preparation. 'At long last, the MCC have come round to the belief that fitness for Test cricket really matters,' wrote Crawford White in the *News Chronicle*. A dapper, bespectacled figure, Dalton had been recruited on an ad hoc basis for the two Tests in Jamaica the previous winter (he was in the country as physio to the national football team) and had made unavailing efforts to get Brian Statham fit for the final match. Hutton's report to MCC requested that a masseur accompanied the team at all times on future tours, although he must have known that the post had been filled on the two previous post-war Ashes tours.

Dalton's summer job was with Essex where Bailey was a particularly enthusiastic about his work. During the next six months, Hutton would also come to value his contribution. He wrote in his retirement memoir, 'Whenever I wanted to find out something about a player's physical or mental capabilities which was not obvious on the surface I consulted Dalton. Invariably he knew better than anyone. He proved an astute psychologist and welfare officer, as well as an excellent masseur.' Others were less sure. 'He was a pseudo-medic,' Geoffrey Howard told Stephen Chalke. 'He used to walk around with a stethoscope around his neck. I don't think anyone other than Trevor took him seriously. He used to love using his hypodermic needle. I can hear Tom Graveney walking by the dressing-room door, shouting 'Give him the fucking needle, Woozer.'''

Dalton was keen to do a good job and exchanged several letters with MCC about how much equipment he would be allowed to take. Neither Duckworth nor Dalton were destined to become wealthy men as a result of their winter employment, though. Duckworth's contract was worth £300 while Dalton was paid £10 a week during the tour. While endorsing Dalton – 'a good man in a vital job' – White thought the cricketers still needed a tougher regime of physical preparation, recommending MCC call in Geoff Dyson, the chief coach of the Amateur Athletic Association: 'I know of no man better equipped to advise on methods of reaching perfect fitness and peak reaction.'

SETTING OFF

Finally, they were ready to leave. The players were instructed to be at Lord's at 6 p.m. on 14 September for a short meeting in the committee room in the pavilion before their send-off dinner in the Tavern. There they were addressed by MCC president Lord Cobham, who seemed again to demonstrate the club's obsession with avoiding more Bodyline-style controversy. 'I want you all to go out there not thinking that you are playing cricket *against* the Australians, but that you're playing *with* them,' he said. Over drinks, Gubby Allen and Harry Altham were involved in what Billy Griffith called 'heated arguments' about cricket. Len Hutton struck a bet with Allen that Vic Wilson would return home having scored more runs than Colin Cowdrey, not exactly an endorsement of the young Kent amateur's selection.

The players were about to leave their wives behind for six months, but it did not mean that spouses were able to join them. 'Although the dinner ends early it spoils the evening,' Jean Simpson, wife of Reg, told a reporter from the *Evening Standard*. A group of wives – joined by Frank Tyson's mother, Violet, visiting London for the first time – went to the cinema. 'There were too many boats and goodbyes in the film for my liking,' grumbled Edna Wardle. 'I think it is a little hard, especially as we are not allowed to accompany our husbands,' added Jean Simpson. 'This is the fourth time I have seen my husband off on one of these tours but I still do not feel any happier about it.' The couples spent the final night before departure at the Great Western Hotel at Paddington, although those who had their wives with them were sent a sharp reminder by MCC that they must ask for a split bill: the club was not prepared to fork out for bed and breakfast for the spouses.

The parting must have been particularly difficult for Keith and Joyce Andrew. They had managed to bring their wedding forward to 4 September, an event that suddenly became of interest to the national press. 'You can't go out of the house for reporters,' Joyce's mother complained on the big day. The couple had already had a taste of celebrity. Along with Tyson, they had appeared on the Sunday evening BBC show *Guess My Story*, introduced by Peter West (future long-serving anchor of the corporation's TV cricket coverage), where a panel consisting of actors Helen Cherry, Eunice Gayson, Michael Pertwee and Jack Train had to work out why the trio were newsworthy.[22] Andrew had an attack of stage fright. 'Frank and Joyce

[22]Eunice Gayson later became the first 'Bond girl', appearing in *Dr No* and *From Russia With Love*. In the former she set up one of the most famous lines in cinema history, asking Sean Connery, 'I admire your luck, Mr...?'

were as large as life, chatting away, and I was sitting on this box, of all things, and my leg was shaking. I couldn't speak,' he remembered.

The panel quickly worked out why they were there, but West thought Joyce's bright, natural manner under the studio lights meant she had the potential for a career in television. He might also have been impressed by a recent newspaper report about her second place in the All-England cookery examinations. The newlyweds cancelled their planned Cornish honeymoon and went to Eastbourne instead: four days after their return, they kissed goodbye for six months.

On the morning of the party's departure, the lobby of the Great Western Hotel was buzzing with family, well-wishers, autograph hunters and journalists. Outside, the pavements were packed with well-wishers. The previous evening – before they left for Lord's – the players had been hosted at a cocktail party by representatives of the Ronson company, each receiving a new cigarette lighter engraved with their initials. A fleet of taxis took them to St Pancras where the boat train was due to leave for Tilbury from platform 6 at 11.40 a.m.

At the station, the crowds were even bigger. Andrew and Tyson had bought a Bell & Howell 16mm cine camera, but such was the jostling that their first attempt at home movies was ruined. 'The shots of the train departure came out as though they were taken by someone suffering from an attack of beriberi,' Tyson recalled. It was at this point that most said their goodbyes. Joyce Andrew found these final moments unbearable: just before the train pulled out, she rushed away in tears. She was going back to live with her parents in Chadderton, Lancashire, and returning to her job as a proofreader with the Stationery Office.

Each couple managed these difficult moments differently: Dorothy Hutton chose not to join the throng on the platform and said goodbye to her husband in their car. Geoffrey Howard was leaving his wife, Norah, to bring up four young daughters. George Duckworth had not even told his wife, Bessie, about his MCC appointment: he left a note on the kitchen table at the 40-acre farm they ran in Warrington: 'I'm going to Australia, be back in April.'[23] Jocelyn Loader was the

[23]This is a terrific story, related in a biography of Geoffrey Howard, but the *Evening Standard* reported Bessie Duckworth as having been at St Pancras.

only one of the players' wives to travel to Tilbury, but she had travel plans of her own. The following day she was flying to Gibraltar to stay with her parents. 'Sad departures, photographers in numbers. Such excitement one finds it hard to describe,' wrote Harold Dalton in his diary.

As the train made its way into the East End and onwards through Essex, the players were reminded again of the extent of public interest and the weight of expectation. On walls and fences backing on to the track, many had painted messages or hung makeshift banners. 'Bring back the Ashes', 'Good luck Len' and 'Stick to it Boil' were just three they noted. The last would not have been seen by its intended recipient: Trevor Bailey had decided to spend the night back home in Westcliff-on-Sea and make his own way to the docks.

By the time they arrived at Tilbury, the skies had cleared and a warm sun was shining. Here was an early taste of the VIP life bestowed by selection for the tour. Duckworth dealt with all the formalities of travel, presenting the players' passports, tickets and customs documents to officials while the cricketers strolled through the mountains of luggage in the dockyard sheds, walked up the gangway of SS *Orsova*, and filed into the ship's plush restaurant for a drinks reception and five-course lunch.

For Bob Appleyard, whose previous experience at sea was as a naval petty officer sleeping 40 to a cabin, it was revelatory. 'After I married Connie in 1951, we were living on the premises of her mother's sweet and tobacco business,' he remembered. 'Now I was travelling first class on an ocean liner, dressing for dinner each night, coming into contact with people higher up the social scale.'

After lunch, it was back out on deck to pose for photographers and newsreel cameras. Hutton, his buttonhole sporting a sprig of heather tied with a ribbon in MCC colours, sent a final message to the nation. 'We know that all of you here in England will be watching our progress very carefully,' he said. 'I am very confident that this team will give an extremely good account of itself, and I hope we will retain those Ashes which we won in that very hard-fought series of 1953. This is the best team we have sent to Australia since 1932.'

Elsewhere on deck there was a reminder of that bitterly contested series in the presence of the architect of Bodyline, Douglas Jardine.

Perhaps it was just as well for their blood pressures that the Australian authorities probably didn't know that Jardine had been co-opted on to the MCC committee dealing with the planning of the tour. Cowdrey was seen in deep conversation with Jardine. He had not mellowed. 'When you get to Ceylon [Sri Lanka], Cowdrey, have a hit and get your eye in,' he told him. 'Then when you reach Australia, just remember one thing – hate the bastards.' Hutton ensured he took a break from his media duties to talk to Cowdrey's father, Ernest. 'Don't worry, I'll look after him,' he told him. The large gathering seeing the players off included officials from MCC, the counties and former players. A familiar face was the *Frankenstein* actor Boris Karloff, who kept wicket for the Hollywood Cricket Club two decades earlier, appearing twice in 1932 against a touring Australian side featuring Don Bradman.

As the 3 p.m. sailing time neared, the deck was cleared of all those who were not travelling. Among the crowds on the quayside was Denis Compton, set for several weeks of treatment on his knee before he could rejoin his teammates. 'He looked disconsolate,' Tyson thought, probably from the knowledge that he was missing out on the many pleasures of the voyage. The *Orsova*'s horn sounded a salute, the noise reaching a cacophony as other ships and tug boats joined in. And with that, she eased away from her moorings and the journey began. 'What a send-off we had – it was as if all England were present to give them good luck,' recorded Dalton.

PAPER TIGERS

Standing a little apart from the cricketers on the deck of the *Orsova* was another group of passengers whose presence was directly related to the tour. They were the journalists charged with conveying the news of the MCC's party's progress, through good days and bad, to the British public. The fact that they numbered more than 20 was an indication of the unassailable place of cricket in national life.

'It is difficult from the perspective of the early 21st century to appreciate just how powerful a grip cricket exerted on the collective sporting *mentalité* of the English in the early post-war years,' wrote the historian Peter Hennessy in his book *Having It So Good*. 'Though governed by a very small number of very narrowly recruited (in the social sense) figures around the MCC, this particular passion transcended the class divide like no other major spectator sport (except perhaps Rugby Union in South Wales).'

'Cricket was the one sport which could be followed by all classes,' wrote Charles Williams, who played for Oxford University alongside Colin Cowdrey in 1954 and became a Labour peer. 'It met the desire for something joyful and splendid. In those days, it was possible to hear a discussion of cricket in most pubs.' Post-war prime minister Clement Attlee was said to begin each working day by being briefed on the county scores.

The size of the press pack was also a sign of the primacy of newspapers as a means of bringing the latest developments – within hours of them happening – to the British public. Cricket in Australia would not be televised for another four years and, in any case, there would have been no means of swiftly transmitting that footage to the UK. There were newsreels showing a precious few minutes of a Test or tour match, but they were days out of date by the time they reached British cinema screens. There was a small amount of radio coverage, doubtless followed avidly, including 40 minutes of commentary provided by the Australian Broadcasting Commission on the Light Programme, from 7 a.m. On the Home Service there was a 15-minute summary of the day's play by E. W. Swanton and a further 10-minute analysis by Crawford White or John Arlott later in the day.

As recently as the 1928–29 Ashes tour, only two reporters, both representing news agencies, had accompanied Percy Chapman's team. Since then there had been a dramatic surge in newspaper circulations, and the familiar mastheads of the leading titles were as integral to British life as pubs and post offices. 'The reading of newspapers was a boom activity in post-war Britain,' wrote the historian David Kynaston. A country-wide readership survey carried out by the Hulton magazine group in January 1956 found that 87 per cent of Britons over the age of 16 read a morning newspaper, and that nearly 66 per cent bought one of the evening papers published in large cities and small towns alike. A remarkable 92 per cent read a Sunday newspaper.

Such a burgeoning industry had the financial wherewithal to dispatch journalists to wherever news was being made. And, as the front-page coverage of the Hutton-Sheppard captaincy saga and Fred Trueman's trials at the hands of the selection committee had demonstrated, an Ashes tour certainly fell in the category of events that demanded having a reporter on the spot, even if it was a six-month assignment involving thousands of miles of travel and sky-high expense claims.

As with the players, they were a disparate bunch. Despite their intense commercial rivalries, some were firm friends, while between others there was a mutual antipathy and suspicion. Several had played first-class cricket, others were career journalists. There were hard-nosed newsmen from the popular papers, forever in search of the next sensational story, and elegant stylists from the titles at the quality end of the market, who would not have recognised a scoop if it landed in their pre-dinner sherry.

The media contingent included two former Ashes captains: Freddie Brown, who had led the previous tour in 1950–51, a 4-1 defeat, and Arthur Gilligan, leader of a similarly unsuccessful mission in 1924–25. Brown's gung-ho optimism had made him a huge hit with the public four years earlier and his articles were to be syndicated across several Australian newspapers. It was said that the lack of national titles meant he was able to call each major stop-off point 'my favourite Australian city' without his readers seeing through the ruse. Gilligan, the former Sussex captain, was part of the Australian Broadcasting Commission's commentary team and was writing a book on the tour. Hutton maintained cordial relations with both – he had often been Brown's on-field lieutenant four years earlier – but kept a wary eye on them. At one point in the voyage he was furious to discover that one, he was too discreet to say which, had told Johnny Wardle he would struggle to spin the ball on Australian pitches.

A key figure among the writers was J.M. – Jim – Kilburn, the 45-year-old cricket correspondent of the *Yorkshire Post*. Kilburn eschewed the use of a typewriter – 'the devil's own invention' – and wrote in long-hand on press telegram forms. His match reports were elegantly composed essays; he did not comment on rumour, nor tittle-tattle, about the players: 'I am here to write about the cricket,' was his oft-quoted mantra. Kilburn had been covering his home county since 1934 and it was his second Ashes tour. On the first, eight years earlier, he had been forced to share a cabin with the *Daily Telegraph's* E.W. Swanton, two tall men shoehorned into a tiny cabin. 'We could literally not stand up in it together,' Swanton recalled.

Kilburn was close to Hutton and now assumed the unofficial role of liaison officer between the captain and the press corps. Beneath the generally friendly relations, there was an awareness of how disruptive adverse headlines could be: instructions on how to deal with reporters was high on the agenda of Hutton and Howard's first inner-circle committee meeting on board ship. Kilburn had to persuade Hutton to offer a more congenial face to the media. 'If you give them something they'll forget about what it was they wanted to ask you,' he told him. Interest in the tour in Yorkshire was at a peak: Kilburn was joined by Bill Bowes, the former Yorkshire and England seamer who had been a member of Jardine's Bodyline attack, now writing for the *Yorkshire Evening News*, and John Bapty, from the *Yorkshire Evening Post*.

The time difference between England and Australia, with play finishing around breakfast time at home, meant the evening newspapers were first to bring the action to British readers. They were eagerly seized upon by commuters, factory workers and millions who had the evening paper pushed through their letterboxes. Bowes and Bapty were not the only journalists working under deadline pressure. The *Manchester Evening News* had sent cricket correspondent John Kay, and the three London evening titles were represented by Bruce Harris (*Standard*), E.M. Wellings (*Evening News*) and Len Bailey (the *Star*). The combined average daily circulation of the trio of London papers in the second half of 1954 was 3.2 million: in 2024, the closure of the print edition of the *Standard* meant London had no evening newspaper.

The best-selling dailies in Britain were the tabloid *Daily Mirror* (average daily circulation 4,753,415) and the *Daily Express*, then still a broadsheet, (4,097,106). The *Mirror* was represented by Ross Hall, who had found plenty of news on his first tour to the West Indies the previous winter, and the *Express* by Frank Rostron. The Essex captain Doug Insole wrote that Rostron 'seldom allows himself to become too occupied by events on the field, preferring to look unashamedly about him for a "story".' The other three popular titles in a crowded marketplace were the *Daily Mail* (2,104,987), the *News*

Chronicle (1,303,786) and the *Daily Herald* (1,813,125). Their readers were well served by the trio of Alex Bannister, Crawford White and Charles Bray.

Bannister had been in the job since 1947 after wartime service which involved escaping from German capture during the Italian campaign. He had a deep distrust of the *Mail* sub-editors: 'If you gave 'em the Ten Commandments they'd cut them to four and a half.' White, described by a colleague as sporting a 'David Niven moustache', began his career in local newspapers but had been a good enough cricketer to play for Lancashire second XI. His CV included a spell as an intelligence officer in Bomber Command. Bray, who had led the way with his exclusive on the possible ousting of Hutton, had played as an amateur for Essex before the war. In the West Indies the previous winter, the locals were unimpressed with the touring journalists: in Jamaica the *Public Opinion* newspaper wrote scathingly, 'A more biased set of typewriter punchers could only be found in the offices of the late Dr Goebbels.'

Sharing with Harris the distinction of being the longest-serving member of the press contingent was the *Daily Telegraph's* E. W. Swanton. He was the senior figure of the group, in his own mind if not always in the view of his colleagues. He had reported on his first Test, for the *Standard,* in 1930 and first toured with MCC to South Africa in 1938–39. This was Swanton's third Ashes tour and his prominence and influence was already well established, not least because of his close connections with MCC. His profile owed much to the *Telegraph's* thriving circulation, which, at the end of 1954, stood at 1,048,322 a day, a substantial lead over *The Times* (220,064 in 1954) and the *Manchester Guardian* (146,048). 'The *Telegraph* was the paper of choice for the cricket-reading classes of middle England,' said Swanton's *Wisden* obituary in 2001. It was said that cricketers would ask each other 'Have you read what Swanton said today?' but his style was not to everyone's liking: 'Halfway between the 10 commandments and Enid Blyton,' thought Middlesex's J.J. Warr.

The new boy among the writers was 28-year-old John Woodcock of *The Times.* He had been on the Ashes tour four years earlier as Swanton's assistant, his trip funded by the *Telegraph's* deep pockets, a role he described as 'typist, chauffeur, chronicler, batman and butt'. He was not new to the press box, having covered the 1952 series against India as a locum for the *Guardian*, but he had been in the job at *The Times* for only a few weeks, succeeding Geoffrey Green, who had been somehow managing to combine the cricket and football portfolios.

The Times had attempted to send its cricket correspondent, Richard 'Beau'Vincent, on the previous trip to Australia, but he was afflicted by chronic homesickness before the ship had entered the Bay of Biscay and was invalided home on reaching Australia. In the next few months, Woodcock demonstrated why he would come to be regarded as one of the greatest cricket writers.

Denys Rowbotham of the *Manchester Guardian* completed the trio from the quality daily newspapers. Rowbotham was known as an assiduous watcher of the game and the first person reporters consulted in the press box when needing a reminder of an incident earlier in the day. 'He would converse, but he never took his eyes from the game and every twist and turn, technical or statistical, was entered in his notebook in his close, neat handwriting,' said a tribute from a *Guardian* colleague.

They looked enviously at their colleagues from the Sunday titles, who filed just one piece a week. Ian Peebles from *The Sunday Times* had played 13 Tests for England between 1927 and 1931, including two against Australia in 1930 in which his leg-spin earned nine wickets. 'I could not detect his googly from his leg-break,' remarked Don Bradman, who was dismissed by Peebles for 14 at Old Trafford. The Sunday job gave him time to write a number of books, including one on this tour, and he was a widely viewed as a charming, convivial companion. 'He traded in cricket stories and delicious German wine,' wrote Robin Marlar, one of his successors at the paper.

Alan Ross of the *Observer* also had a book contract and his rival authors, of which there were several on the *Orsova*, must have known that his would be the most literary offering on the shelves. 'I am as much interested in Australia as I am in cricket ... it would be a dull fellow who was not,' he wrote in his opening chapter. Ross, 32, was a poet and cut a bohemian figure, very different from his sports-writing brethren. At Oxford, where he was a contemporary of Philip Larkin and Kingsley Amis, he was a good enough cricketer to be chosen for a one-day Varsity match at Lord's in 1941, though he gave up student life to join the Royal Navy later that year.

Ross served on the Russian convoys and demonstrated extreme bravery in helping to save his ship, HMS *Onslow*, at the Battle of the Barents Sea. His first collection of poetry was published in 1947 and he joined the *Observer* as football correspondent three years later, taking over the cricket job in 1954. In the early 1960s he became a brilliant editor of the *London Magazine*, a literary publication whose prestige increased under his stewardship. Ross and Peebles were writing for a burgeoning market. Sunday newspaper readership in Britain was booming, the five most popular titles selling around 25 million copies per week. The most successful was the *News of the World*, with a weekly sale of more than eight million.

There was one notable outlier in the press pack: Margaret Hughes, due to celebrate her 35th birthday on the voyage, had been commissioned to write about the Tests by Frank Packer,[24] the combustible proprietor of Sydney's *Daily Telegraph*. Hughes was passionate and knowledgeable about cricket: she had taken a job in the advertising department of *The Star* mainly 'to see the cricket scores before the general public'. In the war she had served in the Wrens, after which she spent time in New York and then returned to work on *The Queen* magazine. She struck up a serendipitous friendship with the great *Guardian* cricket correspondent Neville Cardus and achieved her burning ambition when she earned a contract to write a cricket book.

All On a Summer's Day, with a foreword by Cardus, was published in 1953. After watching the Ashes series that summer, Hughes was desperate to see the return in Australia and wrote an enquiring letter to Consolidated Press in Sydney. Packer, in London on business, summoned her to his suite at the Savoy. He was impressed with her forthright opinions and after commissioning an article for one of his magazines, drew up a contract for her to cover the tour. Hughes had to overcome huge prejudice – 'Like a man trying to knit' was how Hutton once described women's cricket – and was roundly patronised, not least by those who mused on the extent of

---

[24]Frank Packer later expanded his media empire to include Australian television. As his successor, his youngest son Kerry signed many of the world's leading players to form a breakaway series in 1977, one of the most significant moments in cricket history.

her relationship with Cardus, then 66. 'At Lord's people have been brought round to have a look at me in the same way as they might be taken to see the Albert Memorial,' she wrote. She was nervous but reassured by small gestures such as Swanton kindly putting her heavy suitcase on the correct trolley. 'It was up to myself alone to make a success of the trip,' she wrote.

LIFE ON THE OCEAN WAVE

The SS *Orsova*, named after the Romanian port on the Danube, offered the last word in ocean-going luxury. It was impossible not to be impressed by its scale, as well as the on-board opulence. To E.W. Swanton, the size of the media contingent, the fact that England went to Australia as holders of the Ashes and the grandeur of the vessel conveyed the sense of a momentous occasion. 'It seemed that much more prestigious an expedition,' he wrote. Commissioned the previous year and owned by the Orient Line, *Orsova*'s corn-coloured hull and enormous bulk – 28,000 tons, 722 feet long, 90 feet wide and capable of a top speed of 22 knots – made it a majestic sight. The ship, which had completed its inaugural trip to Australia earlier in the year, had cost £6.5 million (more than £150 million in 2024) and had capacity for almost 1500 passengers, whose needs were attended to by a crew of more than 600. A one-way first-class ticket cost £163 (more than £3500 in 2024).

It was one of the first liners to have air conditioning, if only for first-class passengers, but the modernity jarred with some. 'She has a very new-fangled funnel and no mast – features which call forth some pungent comments from the more conservative seafarer,' wrote Ian Peebles. As the ship slipped past Eastbourne, where he had just spent his honeymoon, it was a sombre first evening for Keith Andrew. Frank Tyson felt the bonds of home loosening; that the great adventure really was happening. Six of the squad had never toured before, several had barely been out of the country. There was the potential for the whole experience to be overwhelming. 'I didn't even know half the people on the tour,' Andrew admitted.

Six players had been allocated single cabins: Hutton, Trevor Bailey (MCC acceding to his request, despite their recent disputes), Alec

Bedser and the senior amateurs Bill Edrich and Reg Simpson. Geoffrey Howard also had his own cabin. Those sharing were Peter May with Colin Cowdrey, Andrew with Tyson, Bob Appleyard with Johnny Wardle, Tom Graveney with Brian Statham, Peter Loader with Jim McConnon and George Duckworth with Harold Dalton. Godfrey Evans had been deputed to share with Compton, so presumably Vic Wilson now stood in as his roommate.

Tyson was impressed with his quarters. 'It had its own facilities, its porthole was equipped with an air scoop to maintain a constant flow of cool air into the cabin, it was well above the water line and it was only a couple of decks down from the public rooms,' he said. The writer Margaret Hughes was less taken with her accommodation. Her cabin was 'the size of a sixpence' though she was cheered to find four boxes of flowers from well-wishing friends.

There was another English cricketer aboard apart from the 17 selected by MCC. In more senses than one, he was a familiar face. Eric Bedser, the Surrey off-spinning all-rounder, was the identical twin of Alec. The pair looked so alike that even their closest county colleagues often mistook one for the other. They dressed identically and had seldom been apart – even during the chaos of the evacuation from Dunkirk in 1940 – ever since Eric arrived 10 minutes before Alec in July 1918.

Stories of their extraordinary, almost supernatural, affinity abounded: theirs was a bond that transcended normal relationships, even between identical twins. 'As long as we can remember we have never been happy apart,' Alec told their biographer, Alan Hill. That had become a problem when Alec was chosen for the first post-war Ashes tour in 1946–47: the possibility of a seven-month separation was unthinkable for both.

Fortunately, there was an 11th-hour intervention from the bookmaker and pools promoter Alfie Cope, a Surrey supporter.[25] Cope paid for Eric's passage to Australia. 'I'm going to Australia, after all – I'd almost given up hope,' Eric told the newsreel cameras. 'As you know, my brother and I have never been separated, even during our war service, and I am sure he was as delighted as I was to hear

---

[25]Cope had been responsible for introducing photo-finish technology to UK racecourses in the 1930s.

that I would be in Australia with him this winter.' When the role of baggage-master and scorer had become vacant, Eric had applied to MCC, perhaps indicating some embarrassment at being beholden to benefactors for his trip. He was employed as a net bowler and took charge of the pair's cine camera when Alec was otherwise engaged.

Gradually, a pattern to the days emerged. There was limited enthusiasm for Dalton's 7.30 a.m. PT sessions. Three players reported on the first day, only for the masseur to oversleep and be half an hour late himself. On the second day he was on time, but there were no cricketers to train. Later in the voyage the physical activity increased, though Hutton fretted about the jarring impact of hard deck timbers on fragile muscles. 'We had catching practice, played deck tennis ... it was a great way to relax,' said Tom Graveney. 'We were reasonably sensible with what we ate and drank.' Dalton made a concerted effort to underline to younger players the vital importance of fitness in the heat of Australia. He administered treatment to many of the players, but everyone wondered how long it would take him to work out that he was treating the wrong Bedser for a shoulder problem.

Hutton moved among the groups, warning the first-time tourists about the intimidating aspects of Australian crowds and the size of the Test venues. 'In particular, I tried to impress upon the fast bowlers that the ball moved little in the air, and that their main hope of early success lay in their ability to change their pace, using fielders in every conceivable way to take the wickets we wanted,' he recalled. Loader found Hutton's motivational powers rather lacking. 'He said to me "You'll have a good time on the tour and the experience will be good for you. But you won't play in a Test match." Imagine saying that to anyone?'

The team had taken a slip-catching cradle – though getting it from the luggage hold required giving the crew notice – and there were deck sports. Andrew and Graveney won the table tennis doubles and games of deck quoits proved popular. One day, the *Times* man John Woodcock got the better of Alec Bedser: 'You and your 'effin Oxford University,' muttered Bedser. The sports committee made sure that everyone was kept busy and the players mingled easily with other passengers. A lot of time was devoted to doing nothing. Relaxation was key to preparing for the demanding months ahead. 'Hutton's orders to his team were simple – take a rest from cricket,' wrote Hughes. Reg Simpson took this as an invitation to spend hours on a sun lounger. Others read or played cards and other games. The size and regularity of the meals and the quality of the food on offer astonished some players, Tyson's appetite proving particularly prodigious.

The need to rest was emphasised repeatedly. The workload of a professional cricketer in the 1950s was astonishing. They played on six days of the week throughout the summer, often travelling long distances between the conclusion of one Championship game at 6 p.m. and the beginning of the next at 11.30 a.m. the following morning. In 1954, even with injuries and constant poor weather, Alec Bedser had bowled more than 950 overs, Bailey more than 860. The batsmen expended less effort, but the fixture list was relentless: Vic Wilson had played in 35 matches, Bill Edrich 31, Bailey and Peter May 29. All of which helps to explain why, when it was possible to fly to Australia, albeit over four gruelling days, MCC still chose to send the team by boat. And there was a further reason. 'It was down to what would now be called bonding,' Woodcock explained.

The busy social side of the journey carried much of the appeal for cricketers and journalists alike. 'The genial purser on the *Orsova* found himself landed, at his table in the dining saloon, with Arthur Gilligan and his wife Penny, Ian Peebles, Alan Ross, Jim Swanton and myself. He fended us off like an old hand and seemed to enjoy it,' Woodcock recalled. The *Orsova's* captain N.A. Whinfield took his PR duties seriously, making sure he dined with as many passengers as possible during the trip. There was dancing, cabaret, film evenings, race nights and a fancy-dress party – won by Godfrey Evans as Carmen Miranda, the Brazilian-Portuguese singer known for her teetering hats made of fruit. On one evening, Hutton and Edrich – an unlikely vocal pair – performed a ribald duet for the benefit of their teammates. Edrich's party trick involved an egg, a glass of water, a tray and a broom. 'Always far more entertaining when it failed than when it succeeded,' thought Trevor Bailey.

And there were shipborne romances. A number of the passengers were young Australian women returning from a summer spent in England, some accompanied by their parents, some not. 'I have become very attached to a good-looking Sydney girl called Margaret,' Tyson wrote, instantly ignoring his mother's parting advice to be wary of 'fast' Australian girls. Other relationships were based on fertile journalistic imagination: the Bedser twins were reported to have become engaged to twin sisters from Sydney. Then someone remembered that an identical story had been published four years earlier.

Edrich's ardour was real enough. 'He was always chasing the girls,' Geoffrey Howard remembered. 'On the boat he formed quite a close attachment, and he kept in touch with her throughout the tour. I was in his cabin one day, having a few drinks and there was a photograph of his wife. And he suddenly said "I hate my wife" and threw it out of the porthole.' Bailey added, 'He was always falling in love. Bill lived in a dreamland; he never grew up.' The woman Edrich now 'hated' was Jessy, his third wife. She had loyally given evidence on his behalf during his drink-driving trial during the summer and been at St Pancras to see him off with their four-year-old son, Jasper.

The first brief stop was at Gibraltar where Jocelyn Loader was a passenger on one of the small boats that sailed out to the *Orsova*. The first chance for players to reacquaint themselves with land came on 20 September when they docked at Naples at breakfast time. Most went to visit the ruins at Pompeii – 'a city of debauchery and immorality,' Dalton noted in his diary – but a smaller party (Hutton, Edrich, Wilson, Appleyard, the Bedser twins, George Duckworth, the former Yorkshire bowler Abe Waddington, plus the journalists from the Yorkshire papers) hired taxis and travelled the 22 miles to the Caserta military cemetery.

They wandered among the Portland stone monuments, bright-white in the Italian sunshine, for some minutes before finding the gravestone they were seeking. Its inscription read 'Captain Hedley Verity. The Green Howards. 31st July 1943. Aged 38.' Verity, the great Yorkshire and England left-arm spinner of the 1930s, had died in an Italian hospital after being wounded during the battle for Sicily. In 1934, he had been chiefly responsible for England's only win over Australia at Lord's in the 20th century. Four years later, he nursed Hutton through his Test-record 364 at The Oval. 'I loved that man,' Hutton said. For Bill Bowes, the poignancy of the visit is impossible to imagine. He had been Verity's closest friend and had heard of his death while a prisoner of war in Chieti, 150 miles across Italy. A recently captured Canadian airman had conveyed the terrible news, not realising that Bowes had known Verity. A bunch of white roses, tied with Waddington's Yorkshire tie, was laid on the grave by Hutton. 'He said nothing,' recalled Kilburn. 'Nothing needed to be said.'

The *Orsova*'s next stop was Port Said, the Egyptian city at the entrance to the Suez Canal. The ship was met by a flotilla of small boats selling leather goods and other local handcrafts. If any passenger showed an interest, the item was winched up the side of the ship in a basket, with the money returning by the same method. The players stretched their legs ashore for an hour – where Bailey demonstrated haggling skills that matched the obduracy of his batting – and some recorded messages for British troops at Suez, while the press were entertained at the Union Club. The ship glided away from its moorings around midnight.

Progress had been rapid – the *Orsova* covered around 500 miles a day, which could be monitored in a daily mileage sweepstake organised by the crew – but now it slowed to a crawl as it entered the Suez Canal. The ship was greeted enthusiastically by British servicemen and their families, some of whom sailed out in small boats. Autograph sheets, packets of cigarettes and rapidly melting packs of ice cream were thrown down by the players, most reaching their intended targets.

As they left the canal there was a moment to remind the team of the portent of their mission. The pipes and drums of the 1st Battalion Scots Guards, in full dress uniform despite the intense heat, formed on a landing stage and saluted them as they passed. They played 'Will Ye No Come Back Again' and a banner was unfurled wishing the players luck. 'It was one of the most moving and blood-stirring incidents of the trip, showing that cricket is still the binder of the Empire and holds no small place in the hearts of the British people,' wrote Hughes. 'I don't know how the team standing on the bridge felt about this but I know that I had a lump in my throat.' When darkness fell, three Royal Navy destroyers flashed a good-luck message to the *Orsova*, to which Hutton responded, 'Thank you for your wishes. We will try to retain the Ashes.' For the 80,000 troops in the region, Suez was a dull but dangerous posting: during the year British soldiers had been murdered by local rebels. The announcement of a pact between Britain and Egypt in July came as a huge relief – the Scots Guards would be home for Christmas.

The ship docked at the port of Aden, a British protectorate, where Howard received a visit from Edrich. 'He has allowed things to get him down a bit,' the manager confided in a letter home. 'He is very temperamental in a way and – I think – rather homesick.' Howard admitted he was concerned he had fractured relations with Edrich by making an unguarded reference to 'police courts' in his earshot. The ship's busy social whirl was not to everyone's taste. McConnon, a quiet family man and a devout Catholic, was already showing acute signs of missing home and hearth.

The climate also presented a formidable challenge. 'We did no more than exist, stricken with the heat,' Ross wrote. 'Quoit and tennis decks were empty, the swimming pool hot, salty and stale.' Tyson postponed his daily runs round the deck. 'Even night-time did not bring relief from the blistering, following wind which blew the desert into our cabins,' he remembered. 'Below decks one could almost grasp handfuls of the torrid heat and taste the sand in it. Stepping out on to the deck was like entering an oven.'

Dalton had already been treating cases of sunburn as well as sea sickness. Now there were several cases of upset stomachs. A remarkable 14-page report entitled 'Cricket in Hot Climates', sent to Lord's before the team's departure by Dr W.J.H. (John) Butterfield of Guy's Hospital, had dealt with ailments likely to be encountered on the voyage. The document was prepared on Butterfield's own initiative as his contribution to helping the team in Australia. A triple Blue at Oxford, he was a keen cricketer and had played in the 1942 Varsity match at Lord's.[26]

His guidance on sea sickness referenced research carried out before the D-Day landings. Butterfield recommended getting tablets from the ship's doctor, drinking sugar and water, or sweet tea with no milk. 'It can strike the best of us, especially if anxious or tired, so don't feel ashamed. It doesn't kill,' he wrote. He advised limited

[26]Butterfield, later Lord Butterfield, had a long and distinguished medical career, conducting pioneering research into burns and diabetes.

exposure to the sun 'until a tan is established'. He advised that sun barrier should be used liberally and if burns did occur antihistamine cream should be applied to the sores. This had worked, he said, when he had been treating servicemen involved in Britain's nuclear bomb test programme.

To everyone's relief, the temperature cooled a little as the ship approached its scheduled stop in Ceylon (Sri Lanka) where a one-day game was to be played against an XI representing the island.[27] These whistle-stop matches had been inaugurated in 1882 and had become a regular feature of the itinerary of MCC tours of Australia since before the First World War. After two weeks at sea, they represented a good opportunity to get back into cricket gear for a none-too-serious workout. The fixture was threatened, however, by the ship's slow progress since Suez. Captain Whinfield gave orders to the engine room to increase speed and, at a rumoured cost of £1500 to the Orient Line, the *Orsova* docked at Colombo on time at 11 a.m. For the benefit of passengers disembarking to return to their jobs in the tea plantations, Hutton's squad posed for a team group on deck in their whites and blazers.

Players and press were hurried away to the Colombo Oval (now the P. Sara Oval) for a midday start. Ceylon captain, Derrick de Saram, who had scored a memorable hundred for Oxford University against the Australians in 1934, won the toss and asked MCC to bat. They quickly slumped to 59 for four, Edrich, Simpson, Graveney and stand-in captain May all falling cheaply. 'It is no easy transition from a rope ball on a gently throbbing deck to a fast turf wicket under a tropic sun,' wrote Swanton. But Cowdrey spared MCC further embarrassment with an attractive unbeaten 66, full of lovely cover drives that evoked memories of Walter Hammond, who had played on the island twice in whistle-stop matches.

May declared on 178 for eight and soon reduced Ceylon to 81 for four, but dusk fell before either team could push for a win. The ground was packed. 'All day they crowded happily around this large, green Colombo Oval, some growing out of trees, some relaxing beneath coconut palms, and they went home contented

---

[27]Ceylon was renamed Sri Lanka in 1972. It was granted Test match status in 1981.

with the driving they had seen,' reported Woodcock. Tyson, who had lost eight pounds after a stomach upset at the beginning of the week, bowled quickly – one delivery pitched, flew over wicketkeeper Keith Andrew and hit the sightscreen on the full – but to little effect. 'I am relieved the Australians did not see Tyson's ragged efforts,' wrote Frank Rostron in the *Daily Express*. Five and a half thousand miles away, Compton had a gentle workout for Cross Arrows against Barclays Bank at Lord's, scoring 20 and taking four wickets.

After post-match drinks there was an evening reception at the Great Orient Hotel. Alan Ross, who had been born in Calcutta (now Kolkata), found the island enchanting. 'Wafts of sickly scent everywhere; the jangle of music, ugly and exciting in the bazaars; men squatting in the dark, all bones, like collapsed bagpipes; the tinkle of rickshaws, the brilliant interiors of fruit shops, paw-paws glowing under bulbs, lights shining over bales of striped silk and cotton,' he wrote. 'And all the time the heat something you could put your hand through.'

Late in the evening it was time for players and press to make their way back to the harbour where they had to sidestep an encounter with a drunken Scandinavian sailor. Launches returned them to the *Orsova*. Around midnight, the great liner began to leave the lights of Colombo twinkling in the distance. Next stop, Australia.

AUSTRALIA AT LAST

There was no need for an alarm clock aboard the *Orsova* on the morning of Thursday 7 October, at least not among the cricketers. Keith Andrew and Frank Tyson scrambled out of their cabin and, at 4 a.m. under a spectacular bloodshot sky, got their first thrilling glimpse of the Australian mainland. Tug boats came out to meet them and a cloud of squawking seagulls joined the escort as land approached. Covering the last yards of its 11,000-mile, 23-day journey at a crawl, the liner docked at Fremantle's Victoria Quay at the mouth of the Swan River. Here was the gateway to Australia.

At 6 a.m., the immigration authorities conducted a medical examination so cursory that Colin Cowdrey, engrossed in a book, didn't even know he'd been through it, let alone whether he had passed or not. Margaret Hughes thought Fremantle looked like 'a Cornish coastal town', Tyson called it 'shabby'. The ship docked at 7 a.m. on what the *Evening Standard*'s Bruce Harris told readers back home in autumnal London was 'a crisp sparkling morning with a sky of unbroken blue'. A crowd of around 500 curious well-wishers and autograph hunters gathered on the quayside.

While most of the passengers disembarked, there was steady traffic up the gangway in the opposite direction. A contingent of the Australian cricket media had made the cross-country trip to attend Hutton's first press conference of the tour. His words would make the front pages of all the leading Australian newspapers the next day. The writers filed into the ship's dining-room, renewing friendships with the travelling media, and waited for the England captain to appear. There were around 50 pairs of eyes trained on him when he began to speak.

It was, all agreed, a bravura performance – witty, informative, humorous, expertly fending off awkward questions, confidently setting out his own agenda: Hutton had rarely played so many shots on an Ashes tour. 'One of Sydney's most redoubtable purveyors of cricket news and gossip was no doubt sincere when he congratulated captain and manager, Mr C.G. Howard, on the best press conference in his experience,' wrote E.W. Swanton. 'Australians this season will meet a much more matured and likeable Hutton,' said Percy Beames of *The Age*, the Melbourne morning paper. 'His interview with the press was the best and most friendly that has ever taken place with English captains.'

Hutton ranged around several topics. As the first professional captain of an England team in Australia in the modern era, he was nervous about the reception he might receive in the southern states. He repeated what he had said at Tilbury about this being the strongest MCC party since the war. He said his attack 'looks like being a little bit quick' and compared Tyson's speed to Ernie McCormick, an Australian fast bowler of the 1930s. Hutton also spoke warmly of his two young batsmen, Cowdrey and Peter May. The former, Hutton said, had the 'precious gift of seeing the ball early and is attractive in his play like Walter Hammond.' He also predicted that Australians would not have seen a bowler like Appleyard. 'I don't want to tell you too much about what he does with the ball. I don't think he'd thank me for that,' he said.

The topic of how many bouncers (usually called bumpers in Australia) should be allowed in each over was one Hutton was keen to address. He had made a pre-emptive strike before the *Orsova* reached Colombo by telling the English press contingent that he believed one short ball an over was sufficient. 'As a man who's had as many bouncers slung at him as any in the business I am strongly against a disproportionate number,' he said. 'An isolated bumper designed to take the batsman by surprise and so force him into a mistake is in my opinion a natural legitimate part of cricket. But when it reaches three, four or even five per over and one side starts retaliating it's a farce and against the spirit of cricket.'

His words had been reported extensively at home and were picked up by London-based reporters from Australian newspapers. He repeated his view now – after inquiring genially about the health of Ray Lindwall and Keith Miller – but said that umpires should be left to make their own interpretations of the law on intimidatory bowling. Nor would he strike a non-proliferation agreement with whoever was appointed Australia captain. Most thought Hutton's keenness to bring up the subject now was because he at last had retaliatory weapons at his disposal.

One small crack appeared in the PR facade. Hutton dealt tactfully with a discussion about Fred Trueman's non-selection, saying his record in the West Indies had been modest and that conditions in Australia were expected to be similar to those in the Caribbean. But George Duckworth made an unguarded remark to Alan Newman of *The West Australian*, saying Trueman's omission had come as a 'bombshell' to him. Duckworth was taken to one side by Hutton and Howard and ordered to restrict his communications with the Australian press to polite pleasantries.

Hutton's press conference has enjoyed a shelf life beyond yellowing news clippings, because of its portrayal in Cowdrey's autobiography *M.C.C.* He recalled Hutton disarming the room by downplaying England's players and prospects in broad and laconic Yorkshire tones. 'Noo, we 'aven't got mooch boolin'. Got a chap called Tyson but you won't have 'eard of him because he's 'ardly ever played ... Well we 'aven't got any batsmen really. We've got these youngsters, May and Cowdrey, but we haven't really got any batsmen ... Ah, yes, Lock and Laker. Good boolers but we've 'ad to leave 'em behind. ... What it comes to is that we're startin' out all over again. We're here to learn a lot from you.'

The passage is an entertaining read, but perusal of the following day's newspaper reports suggests it bears little resemblance to what actually happened. Hutton was upbeat about his pace attack and his young batsmen, as well as the team's chances in the Test series. And his accent? 'Hutton showed very little trace of a broad Yorkshire accent,' wrote Keith Butler of Adelaide's *Advertiser* newspaper. Newsreel footage from Tilbury confirms that, at this stage of his life, Hutton had shed his Yorkshire vowels.

On leaving the ship, the players were taken on the 20-mile journey to their hotel in Perth in a fleet of Holden saloons, the Australian-built cars that would provide much of their transport during the tour. Tyson, Appleyard, Duckworth, Tom Graveney, Brian Statham and Johnny Wardle made straight for the golf course, while others opted to look around the city. The party exuded calm, but it had been disturbed by two pieces of news, one tragic, the other destined to have implications for the rest of the tour and for the future of one of the squad's star players.

When the story of Cowdrey's innings in Colombo reached the family home in Sutton, Surrey, Ernest Cowdrey hurried upstairs to fetch a pen and paper so that he could note the scores from the next radio bulletin. His excitement at his son's progress was obvious: in the days after departure, he wrote enthusiastically to MCC to thank the club for the invitation to Tilbury. He returned to the room where he had been chatting to his brother and sat down. When his brother looked up from his newspaper a few minutes later, Ernest Cowdrey was dead. He was 52. 'He had suffered from a bad heart for some time, but his death was a great shock as well as a great loss,' Cowdrey wrote.

Cowdrey had received a telegram from a family friend on board the *Orsova*, telling him his father had been taken ill. He got a sense something more serious was wrong and had his worst suspicions confirmed by another telegram when he checked into Perth's Palace Hotel: 'My selection for Australia must have been the fulfilment of a glorious dream for him and I like to think that he was happy in the knowledge that I had started the adventure well.'

He spent the afternoon in his room, chatted to his friend May and decided there was little point in heading home. Telegrams and messages of condolence began to arrive, including one from Australian prime minister, Robert Menzies. 'You have the heartfelt sympathy of everyone in Australia,' he wrote. At dinner that night, Cowdrey's teammates came up one by one to commiserate. Hutton hung back until the players were sipping coffee after the meal. There were tears in his eyes when he laid a hand on Cowdrey's shoulder. 'I'm so sorry,' was all he said. But he did something practical, too. From that moment, he made sure that the youngest member of the party was kept constantly busy and had little time for gloomy reflection in his room. Hutton made good on the promise he had made to Ernest Cowdrey at Tilbury to 'look after' his son.

The other disturbance to the team's equilibrium was that Alec Bedser had gone down with an unpleasant attack of shingles, the sores spreading over his back. The debilitating illness was certain to put him out of the early tour matches. It transpired that it would take far longer to make a full recovery than anyone, including Bedser, envisaged. The openness in the handling of these two stories impressed the travelling journalists. 'Hutton and Howard were setting splendid examples for all future captains and managers,' wrote E.M. Wellings.

Little time was wasted in getting back into whites and two net sessions were held at the Western Australia Cricket Association ground (known as the WACA) on the day after arrival. To judge from cine footage shot on Trevor Bailey's camera, these were understandably rather gentle affairs. But Hutton was deeply appreciative that the practice pitches were excellent and mentioned it in his end-of-tour report. There was a civic reception at Perth Town Hall, followed a few nights later by a party attended by 400 people at the home of Sir Charles Gairdner, the Governor of Western Australia. Hutton continued to play a blinder in the PR game. 'Len is doing splendidly and is going to be a great success, I'm sure,' wrote Howard. 'The Aussies are all for him.' Howard was also surprised that his own duties were proving easier than he had been warned they might be back in London. 'Or else I'm only doing half the job?'

The manager was immediately confronted by a considerable logistical challenge. When he visited a local bank, he discovered that MCC had failed to wire over any funds from which to run the tour, a serious administrative blunder. Howard opened an account with the Australian and New Zealand Bank and negotiated a flexible unlimited personal overdraft of £20,000 so that he could begin to pay bills. His debts escalated alarmingly until he was able to pay in the Test-match gate receipts.

The tour matches began with a two-day warm-up against a Western Australia Country XI at Bunbury, two hours down the coast from Perth. Despite not ever looking in form, Bill Edrich scored a century and there were five wickets for Jim McConnon in a drawn game. The opening first-class fixture was against Western Australia at the WACA, beginning on 15 October. MCC had six such matches before the first Test in Brisbane and each one mattered. Naturally, the main task was to determine the 11 who would take the field at the Gabba. But to do that every player had to be given the chance to impress and, when Denis Compton arrived to swell the playing strength to 18, it would be an unusually large touring group (a point made frequently by English pressmen). There were other reasons why the games carried significance. All the states saw it as their patriotic duty to foul up the preparations of the touring team.

When the WACA became a Test venue during the Ashes series of 1970–71, it rapidly established a reputation for boasting the fastest pitch in international cricket. Sixteen years earlier, its qualities were relished by Brian Statham, who took six for 23 on the opening day, after which a century by Hutton put MCC in a commanding position. The captain later retired hurt with a thigh strain and missed his Sunday round of golf, but with Statham adding three wickets in Western Australia's second innings MCC completed a highly satisfactory seven-wicket victory on the fourth day.

Later in the week, they were back at the WACA for a match against a Western Australia Combined XI, strengthened by the inclusion of Test players from the eastern states, Neil Harvey, Graeme Hole and Test captaincy candidate, Ian Johnson. It made little difference: this time MCC won by an innings in three days. May, standing in as captain for Hutton, scored a century and there were six wickets in the match for Johnny Wardle. Hutton made careful note of the impact of Frank Tyson's pace on the WACA's rapid surface: Western Australia batsman Keith Carmody had to retire hurt after being hit on the pad by a ball from Tyson.

Leaving Perth behind, the team flew by Douglas Dakota to Adelaide. For the modern touring cricketer, air travel is a necessary and regular way of life, journeys slipping by unnoticed. But for Hutton's players flying was still a novelty. Tyson remembered 'everyone on board keeping everything crossed' but quickly realised that 'far from being exciting, flying was just plain boring'. The 1600-mile trip crossed the vast expanse of the Nullarbor Plain before they landed at Adelaide, scattering rabbits from the runway as the aircraft touched down. The flight took around six hours, but for the writers who opted to go by train the journey time was 48 hours, a trip enlivened by the occasional glimpse of exotically unfamiliar wildlife. 'Shortly after breakfast I saw an emu, looking stiff and surprised, as though caught reading someone else's letters,' wrote Alan Ross.

Notable among the welcoming party in the corrugated iron huts that served as Adelaide's airport buildings was the city's most famous resident, Sir Donald Bradman. Soon, another instantly recognisable face joined the MCC group. Two days before the start of the tour match against South Australia, Compton touched down in Adelaide, an internal flight from Sydney completing a gruelling and traumatic four-day passage from London. He had a story that emphasised the habitual chaos that surrounded his life. His car containing his kit had been stolen two days before departure and he arrived with two bulging suitcases but minus the keys to open them. When they were eventually prised open, all the cricket gear they held were a pair of dirty boots, two gloves that weren't a pair, and a bat marked 'F. Titmus'.

Other elements of his story were less amusing. As his plane approached Karachi, the second refuelling stop after Beirut, the navigator came back into the cabin and told Compton and his travelling companion, Sir William Becher, secretary of the I Zingari club, that he could not lower the front landing wheel, nor retract the rear pair. The pilot then began a series of aerial moves to try to correct the fault, a ruse that eventually succeeded in the rear wheels being raised. They could not, however, be lowered again. Using his experience in flying boats, the pilot landed the plane safely on its fuselage, eventually screeching to a halt. 'The cabin filled with sand as if we were in a storm in the desert,' Compton remembered. He also recalled the steward's voice coming over on the intercom. 'Please unfasten your seatbelts and leave the aircraft – and for Christ's sake hurry up.' No one was hurt, but the following day a jack collapsed during the repair of the undercarriage, killing one of the airport mechanics.

The journey continued via Calcutta, Singapore and Darwin. Despite having only eight hours' sleep in four days, Compton needed little persuading to play against South Australia. The decision was roundly criticised, especially by Swanton, but on the first day he hit 113 in an MCC total of 246. 'An innings which for audacity and assurance set the clock back seven years,' wrote Bruce Harris of the *Evening Standard*. No MCC XI had lost to a state side since Gubby Allen's tour in 1936–37 and Hutton's team avoided the ignominy of joining them by a mere 21 runs. Reassuringly, there were five-wicket hauls for Tyson in the first innings and Bob Appleyard in the second.

It was in Adelaide that the first serious skirmish occurred between the party and the press corps. Compton, Bill Edrich and Reg Simpson visited an ice show and afterwards had backstage photographs taken with some of the show's glamorous female dancers. The *Daily Express* cricket correspondent, Frank Rostron, was also at the show and smartly acquired the film, having a print wired back to London. The *Express* opted not to publish the picture, but it did appear in the *Star*, provoking some comment about indiscipline and behaviour on tour. Tyson wrote that Edrich received a 'please explain' letter from his wife. Howard, who was also at the show, was furious. 'A monstrous piece of mischief-making,' he wrote to Ronny Aird. At the next team meeting he warned the players about the dangers of being photographed in female company.

From Adelaide, the team journeyed to Melbourne, but two days of the game against an Australian XI at the Melbourne Cricket Ground were washed out. Howard found himself in the middle of what he called 'a storm in a tea cup' when he willingly agreed to a request to play on what should have been a rest day. The reason for the criticism, he concluded, was that the arrangement had disturbed the travel arrangements of the journalists. Swanton was a rare voice in support of the decision.

The lost time made the next fixture, against New South Wales at the Sydney Cricket Ground, even more important in terms of reaching key selection decisions before the first Test. These were the final shots of the phoney war. That being the case, eyebrows were raised when Compton, Bailey and Graveney were left out. The breakout star was Cowdrey, who made two centuries in the match. In the second innings, he opened the batting, testing Hutton's theory that his well-grooved technique was more than up to the task. In the first innings, with MCC teetering at 38 for four, master and pupil added 163. Cowdrey was particularly impressive. 'Like the careful housewife he put everything in its proper place. The full toss or long hop finished almost without exception on the boundary fence,' wrote A.G. Moyes. There were four first-innings wickets for Bedser, though it was noted how Arthur Morris treated his early overs with disdain, and four for Tyson. MCC began the last day only eight runs ahead with seven wickets in hand, the possibility of defeat looming. But Cowdrey, Hutton and Edrich batted long enough to remove the chance of a morale-sapping reverse.

The draw secured, bags were repacked and the following day the party boarded a plane for the 550-mile flight to Brisbane. They had been in Australia for six weeks: now the serious business was about to begin.

Peter May, Brian Statham, Johnny Wardle and Len Hutton read some of the good-luck messages on the boat train to Tilbury.

Crowds mass around the turnstiles at the SCG as interest in the series grows.

V

TYPHOON FRANK HITS SYDNEY

'Back there in England it's cold and wet and miserable, and the least we could have done was something to cheer them up'

A sombre Len Hutton after England's
defeat in the first Test

'If I had the chance to play the innings of my life, I would like to do it this afternoon'

Peter May to Colin Cowdrey
early in their match-changing partnership

'I'll always remember this match for the courage, sustained stamina and determination of Frank Tyson. It was one of the finest exhibitions of courageous fast bowling I have ever seen'

Australian prime minister Robert Menzies

UP COUNTRY

No one was sorry to leave Brisbane. Losing the first Test and falling behind in the series may have posed serious questions about Len Hutton's pre-tour strategy, but it put only a minor dent in morale. The captain forcibly made a point to his players: 'Now that the preliminaries are over, we are not going to lose again.' The feeling around the team was that this was not a formidable Australian side, while Hutton was confident they could not possibly drop so many catches next time. 'I simply do not believe it can happen again,' manager Geoffrey Howard wrote to MCC assistant secretary Billy Griffith in the immediate aftermath of defeat. That view was backed up by the former Australian batsman Jack Fingleton, who thought his countrymen had used up a series' worth of good fortune in one Test.

Nevertheless, the group was deflated. 'You will all be so horribly fed up and disappointed,' Howard wrote to his wife. 'I could weep for you all – all of England.' On the evening before Australia administered the last rites at the Gabba, Hutton and baggage-master George Duckworth had sought sanctuary in a river cruise. 'The Brisbane River is not attractive, but that particular evening it was heaven,' Hutton remembered. 'Duckworth and I talked about the match which was to end the following day … I was at rock bottom.' When Australia's victory was completed, his opposite number Ian Johnson tried to raise his spirits. 'You don't understand,' Hutton told him. 'Back there in England it's cold and wet and miserable, and the least we could have done was something to cheer them up.'

He was right – at home, the mood was just as gloomy. Walter Robins and Ronny Aird appeared separately on BBC television as MCC representatives to defend Hutton's gamble at the toss, but they were fighting a losing battle. Chairman of selectors Harry Altham was spotted leaving his house by a decorator working on a nearby first-floor window. 'Fleeing the country, sir?' he called out from his ladder.

The players had been hoping for a day at the Gold Coast resort of Surfers Paradise, but instead Hutton ordered them back to the Gabba for nets on the worn Test pitch. All the batsmen who had been kicking their heels had some practice and there were extended bowling spells for Bob Appleyard and Johnny Wardle. After the gamble of the spinner-less attack had imploded so spectacularly in the first Test, it was certain that one of them would be needed in the second match at Sydney in two weeks' time. There was also an intensive – and much-needed – fielding session. 'Hutton should tighten training and discipline all round,' Crawford White wrote approvingly in the *News Chronicle*. 'Too many of our men have too much time on their hands, which can be dangerous.'

The party now split into two. Those either injured or recuperating and those in need of a rest after their exertions in the Test – Denis Compton, Godfrey Evans, Trevor Bailey, Brian Statham and Frank Tyson – were allowed to go on to Sydney, while the remainder of the group boarded a flight for the 400-mile trip up the coast to the small town of Rockhampton, where they were to play a two-day game against a Queensland Country XI.

Howard put Compton in charge of the splinter group and handed over tickets for the 24-hour rail journey. 'Making Denis "Officer Commanding" is like handing over the keys of the asylum to the inmates,' said Tyson. 'With the bright lights of Sydney beckoning, there is no way Denis will tolerate such a waste of time.' No sooner had Howard disappeared in the direction of the airport, than Compton was on the phone to Col Hoy, the Queensland-based umpire who worked as a representative for Australia's domestic airline. 'Train tickets were exchanged for airline reservations and within a few hours we were on a plane heading for Sydney,' Tyson recalled. They stayed at the Rose Bay Golf Club on Sydney Harbour. Though he had to have daily treatment on his broken finger, it did not stop Compton and his teammates enjoying themselves. Tyson had a quieter time, resuming the romance with Margaret, the young woman from Sydney, that had begun on the *Orsova*.

After a bumpy flight – Hutton, Vic Wilson and Jim McConnon sought out masseur Harold Dalton for sickness tablets during a refuelling stop – the welcome in Rockhampton was characteristically warm, although the experience of Australia's rough-and-ready small country towns could be disconcerting. The *Observer*'s Alan Ross found that Rockhampton 'boasts many saloons through the swing doors of which tough men in cowboy hats push their way, as if looking for a fight, a girl, a game of dice or a rodeo.' The match was played on the Association Ground, with the pitch knitted together from clumps of turf cultivated at a nearby botanical garden. The thin outfield sat on a bed of vivid red soil – the players were not surprised to discover that this was the venue for rodeos. The heat was ferocious, but the locals cheerily packed the ground. 'One would not have been surprised if they had fired revolvers into the sky or twirled lassos,' wrote Ross.

The game was conducted amid the audible buzz of scores of transistor radios tuned to horse-racing commentaries and updates on local fishing conditions. Nothing could dent the good-humoured mood, even when, at a reception given by the mayor, Hutton stood on a chair to make a speech and said how nice it was to be in Townsville, a place 450 miles further north. The MCC batsmen galloped along at more than four an over and declared before the end of the first day. Despite the best efforts of the groundsman, the pitch had started to break up and Hutton readily agreed to waive the regulation about watering so that it could be repaired overnight.

After a Sunday off, the Queensland Country XI were bowled out for 95 and 210, though Hutton attracted criticism from the press by asking for an additional quarter of an hour so the victory could be completed. In a meaningless fixture, few could see the point. The MCC players who appeared in the match took away an unexpected souvenir: when they unpacked their bags in Melbourne their whites were stiff with a combination of dried sweat and red dust.

On the rest day, Keith Andrew, McConnon and Wardle had visited the Woorabinda reservation, a camp for Indigenous Australians 100 miles from Rockhampton. The players inaugurated a new concrete cricket pitch and a rodeo display was put on for their benefit, which included one of the camp's residents riding a bull backwards. Andrew shot some cine film of the collection of wooden huts that made up the settlement. 'This kind of camp is wholly self-supporting,' Wardle wrote in his autobiography. 'The people grow all they eat, fell their own timber, build their own houses, look after the cattle and provide their own meat. They have built their own school, their own hospital and their own gaol. A certain code of conduct is laid down by the government, and Aborigines who are judged to have lived up to it are allowed into the outside world. They are strictly forbidden to drink any form of alcohol.'

Wardle's account reveals that it was clear that the realities of life at Woorabinda were not apparent to the visitors. In 1926 the authorities in Queensland had summarily ordered hundreds of Indigenous families to move there from the town of Taroom, 120 miles away. The journey had to be made on foot. There was a further forced relocation to Woorabinda in 1942 when 254 people from Cape Bedford in north Queensland were ejected from their existing settlement when it was requisitioned by the army. They were moved by road and boat to Townsville, and then on to Woorabinda by train. They had little food and no blankets during the winter nights. Many could not adjust to the deprivations of their new settlement and died.

It is unlikely the cricketers were given a history lesson or guessed how little life had improved by the mid-1950s. The bleak Woorabinda camp was typical of how Indigenous Australians were housed in rural areas. There would have been no electricity nor running water and they had no rights – their lives were governed by administrators in an office in Brisbane. Most of the camp's inhabitants would have travelled to work as maids or stockmen on nearby farms, where they were frequently abused and exploited. Any small improvement in their conditions was still years away. In 2023, the Australian Bureau of Statistics rated the Indigenous community of Woorabinda as the most disadvantaged in Australia.

In glaring contrast, the journey from Brisbane to Sydney featured one of the highlights of the entire tour: a flight over the southern end of the Great Barrier Reef. 'No words of mine can describe it,' wrote Howard. 'One reads of coral islands and there they were below us. Tiny islands mostly but standing in the middle of a lagoon with the most lovely shades of blue one could imagine.' Alan Ross, who had embarked on a fortnight's holiday with a former wartime Navy colleague, was also awed by the experience of the reef. 'The basic feeling of unreality never leaves one,' he wrote, 'though it is submerged by the extraordinary excitement of seeing, larger and brighter even than in reproduction, the coral gardens that, throughout childhood, transfixed one in the colour plates of encyclopaedias.'

Another journalist taking time out was the *Evening Standard*'s Bruce Harris. He visited the reef in a dinghy in a group of about 40, mostly Australians, and lamented that members of his group left cigarette cartons, sweet wrappers and other waste paper floating on the surface. They also used sticks to break off pieces of coral. Ecotourism was still decades away.

In Sydney, the two sections of the MCC party were reunited for a short trip to the Australian capital, Canberra. The third flight of the day for most of the players featured some drama when, soon after take-off, Tom Graveney noticed oil spurting out of the port-side engine of the team's Dakota. When the problem was brought to the attention of the pilot, he returned to the airport. The party transferred to another plane and the journey was resumed without further mishap. 'Everyone was on tenterhooks,' recalled Dalton. In flying from Rockhampton to Brisbane, then on to Sydney, and from Sydney to Canberra, a group of novice flyers completed 1000 miles of air travel in a day.

They were heading to Canberra to fulfil a one-day charity match against a Prime Minister's XI. The fixture had been inaugurated by the cricket-mad prime minister, Robert Menzies, in 1951 with the twin aims of showing off the city and raising money for Legacy, a charity for children of Australian servicemen killed in action. It also allowed Menzies to indulge one of his favourite pursuits: spending time with cricketers.

Menzies was five years into his second period as Australia's prime minister and had won a federal election earlier in the year. He remains the longest-serving occupant of the office and was a confirmed, though not uncritical, Anglophile. Between February and April 1954, he had escorted the Queen on her triumphant royal tour of Australia. Menzies, whose office wall was adorned with a photograph of Keith Miller, was attuned to the importance of sport to the people he governed.

'Sport was fundamental to the national self-image,' wrote Gideon Haigh in *The Summer Game*. Menzies waved away objections when parliamentary proceedings were suspended so MPs could listen to the commentary of a Davis Cup tie. 'If communism was prime minister Robert Menzies' greatest public concern, cricket was seldom far from his private thoughts,' said Haigh. But he did not take it for granted that MCC would call at Canberra. The MCC archive contains personal letters requesting that the match be included in the tour programme.

Menzies assembled a strong team, including Ian Johnson, Richie Benaud, Keith Miller and Neil Harvey from the current Test team, recently retired captain Lindsay Hassett and Sam Loxton, who had played his final Test on England's previous Ashes tour. On a stormy night, there was a dinner on the eve of the game during which Hassett made a witty speech, gently goading Tyson. 'Fast – pah! I'm not scared of him and his long run,' Hassett said. 'Tomorrow, when I bat I'll hook him out of sight.' Right on cue, there was an ominous rumble of thunder and a flash of lightning that illuminated the room. 'Listen, he's just started his run-up,' said Hassett.

The match was a light-hearted affair. Fingleton umpired in a pith helmet. Play started 10 minutes late and overran when the meal breaks were inadequately policed. The whole business raised the hackles of the *Evening News*'s E.M. Wellings. 'To take a team off course for such an unprofitable event was a waste of their time and an insult to those who were attracted to watch it,' he wrote. Journalists were annoyed that no refreshment provision had been made for them. 'After the overwhelming hospitality of places like Bunbury and Rockhampton, the indifference of the capital was so exceptional,' said Harris.

It was of purely academic interest but MCC won by 31 runs in a high-scoring match which featured centuries for May and Benaud. Additional donations were made to the charity for each six and the batsmen responded to the incentive by regularly clearing the ropes. One big hit by Benaud was caught in the crowd by Field Marshal Sir William Slim, the governor-general of Australia.[28] To some observers, Hutton appeared to be still brooding over his miscalculation at Brisbane. At other times, he was more light-hearted. 'Pitches are like wives – you can never be too certain how they are going to turn out,' he remarked to Fingleton.

The captain was acutely aware that in the week since they had gone 1–0 down in the series there had been no serious work for his players. 'It seems to me that there was far too much time spent travelling and not enough in practice,' wrote Arthur Gilligan.

---

[28] Slim commanded the Fourteenth Army in Burma in the Second World War and was wounded at Gallipoli in the First World War. He was governor-general of Australia between 1953 and 1959.

Hutton must have agreed because as soon as the players arrived in Melbourne from Canberra, he organised a full and intensive net session. The following day, a four-day match against Victoria was due to start at the Melbourne Cricket Ground. It was the only first-class fixture before the second Test – some vital decisions had to be made.

HARD YARDS

Two weeks earlier, Len Hutton had kept Ian Johnson waiting while he pondered the implications of winning the toss at Brisbane. This time there was no hesitation: MCC would bat first against Victoria. Both men must have smiled at finding themselves so swiftly replicating the already infamous Gabba moment. Hutton was searching for the right combination for the second Test. He would open the batting with Trevor Bailey, while Reg Simpson dropped down the order. Tom Graveney came in for Denis Compton, Godfrey Evans returned as wicketkeeper, and Johnny Wardle and Jim McConnon seemed to be in a straight fight for the role as front-line Test spinner.

It was an important day for England to begin their reboot, but there were precious few signs of urgency. The innings crawled to 253 for eight before bad light mercifully ended the first day early. Apart from a partnership between Graveney and Colin Cowdrey, the batting was almost universally strokeless and shorn of fluency. At one point, the crowd of just under 10,000 hooted in derision at the absence of entertainment. Melbourne's capricious climate prevented more than two hours' play on the second day, but on the third, following a Sunday rest day, there was a development that was to have far-reaching consequences for the remainder of the tour – and for the destiny of the Ashes.

Just who was responsible for Frank Tyson shortening his run-up is lost in time, but several people claimed the credit. In retrospective memoirs, Compton and Bill Edrich each suggested they had played a part in the decision. Graveney thought Ray Lindwall had been involved, while Lindwall himself felt his new-ball partner Keith Miller was the instigator. 'He told him he was running too far and would be better off with a shorter run-up,' Lindwall recalled in the 1990s. 'I kind of think he shouldn't have told him.' Another theory was that Tyson had been irked when Bill Bowes wrote that his principal benefit to a bowling attack was the extended rest he gave to his partner while he took several minutes to labour through an over.

Most of the impetus, though, came from Tyson himself. Although he relied on raw pace rather than the range of skills deployed by some seam bowlers – the sledgehammer not the scalpel – he still applied intellect to his work. In the heat of Brisbane, he had found his normal run-up – around 25 yards – was sapping his stamina and reducing his effectiveness. 'I felt that if each match was going to be played under similar climatic conditions and would result in similar exhaustion then I had better adapt my technique to meet those conditions,' he said.

His run-up had been the subject of ribald comment from the Australian crowd. 'I thought he had given the game away and was going home,' remarked one wag, while another loudly assumed Tyson was seeking signs for the gents toilet. During the summer of 1954, the *News Chronicle* published a panoramic photograph across the top of its back page showing Tyson at the end of his mark (30 yards, it estimated) against Kent at Maidstone. With wicketkeeper Keith Andrew standing 20 yards back, the distance between them was more than 70 yards. Surrey batsman Micky Stewart recalled his teammate Arthur McIntyre coming out to face Tyson in a County Championship fixture: 'Arthur looked at Frank at the end of his run and Keith in the distance behind the stumps and asked, "Are you two playing in the same game?"'

Before Tyson's Test debut against Pakistan in August, Hutton had approached him in the nets. 'Don't you ever bowl off a shorter run, Frank?' he asked. In fact, he did. Tyson had operated off a more economical approach while playing in the North Staffordshire League. He was fortunate that Alf Gover, the former Surrey and England seamer, was in Australia covering the tour for the *Sunday Pictorial*. Tyson had been a regular at Gover's cricket school in Wandsworth, south-west London, and respected his coaching wisdom. In the middle of the Brisbane debacle, Gover spoke to Hutton and urged him to suggest the change to Tyson. In 2010,

Tyson told the writer Huw Turbervill in his book *The Toughest Tour* that Gover's role had become 'a bit of a myth'. 'Alf did mention to me about reverting to my shorter one, but I had been having similar thoughts.'

It had not taken Gover long to diagnose his pupil's technical ills. 'It was caused by a lack of rhythm in his run-up; in his last few strides he was straining – lengthening his strides in an effort to reach the bowling crease. This, of course, caused lack of balance and timing in his delivery and also lost him height at the moment of release,' Gover wrote in his autobiography. 'I suggested to Len that Frank made an alteration to his run-up. It was far too long and this distance was mitigated when, after the first eight paces, his feet "stuttered", the right foot dragging on the ground. I suggested that Frank cut down his run and started from the "check point" in his run-up.'

Tyson honed the modified approach in the nets and against Victoria it began to reap a handsome bounty. 'It helped me use my body weight to good advantage,' he recalled. His run-up was now 'six walking paces, 10 running strides,' according to Alex Bannister in the *Daily Mail*. In Victoria's first innings he took six for 68 and made life distinctly uncomfortable for the home batsmen. 'Extremely hostile and refreshingly accurate,' thought Denys Rowbotham in the *Manchester Guardian*. Tyson also found a fuller, more threatening length. Hutton rested him after an hour but then, keen to strike a psychological blow over Australia's best batsman, swiftly brought him back when Neil Harvey was batting. The captain was delighted to see Harvey remove his pad to restore feeling back to his throbbing leg after being hit by a ball from Tyson. Later, only Harvey's reflexes prevented him from being hit in the face by a brutish bouncer.

If his principal strike bowler's progress cheered Hutton, there was little else over which to enthuse. Neither Wardle nor McConnon impressed on their audition and MCC's fielding was again shambolic. On the huge outfield, the Victoria batsmen always knew there would be an extra run on offer while Evans waited in vain for an accurate return to reach his gloves. The final day was enlivened by a fine hundred by May, which included a fourth-wicket partnership of 120 with Cowdrey. And there was a further significant development for the second Test. Johnson pulled a thigh muscle while fielding and was rated a doubtful starter for Sydney. With Miller still not fully mobile again after a blow to the knee in Brisbane, Australia were suddenly facing an injury crisis.

RESHAPING THE TEAM

Twenty-four hours after the match against Victoria had ended in an unsatisfactory draw, the MCC players boarded an overnight train named the *Spirit of Progress* at Melbourne's Spencer Street Station and began the long haul to Sydney. At some point, the tour selection committee – Len Hutton, Geoffrey Howard, Peter May, Godfrey Evans, Bill Edrich and George Duckworth – slipped away from the inquisitive ears of teammates and pressmen, and began to discuss the make-up of the team for the second Test. Two items were at the top of the agenda: finding an opening partner for Hutton and introducing a better balance to the bowling attack.

At some point the discussion turned to whether Jim McConnon or Bob Appleyard represented the best option for the off-spinner role. Hutton expressed a preference for McConnon, but Howard and Duckworth felt strongly that in a must-win match temperament mattered as much as talent. 'Put it this way,' Howard told Hutton, 'If Jim learns he's playing, he'll pull a muscle. And if Bob learns he isn't, he'll come and cut your throat.' The task was made doubly difficult by the pallid performances of all the spinners on the tour. 'None of the slower bowlers in the touring party has so far suggested the clear conception of purpose and command of technique that would increase the team's resources to the desired extent,' wrote J.M. Kilburn in the *Yorkshire Post* after the Victoria match.

The 12 announced to the press after arrival at Sydney contained four possible changes from the team humbled at Brisbane. As expected, Evans returned for Andrew and Tom Graveney came into the middle order for the still-recuperating Denis Compton. Not for the first or last time on tour, Trevor Bailey was promoted to open the batting. 'Len seemed to think I made an ideal sacrificial lamb,' remembered Bailey. 'His theory was that, as Lindwall and

Miller were liable to remove anyone with the new ball, it might just as well be me.' Despite his flaccid performance against Victoria, Johnny Wardle was included, while Howard and Duckworth's forcible argument won the day in the debate about Appleyard or McConnon.

After his startling impact against Victoria, the inclusion of Frank Tyson was not up for debate. But it might have been. When he was selected at the MCG while Statham was rested, Tyson thought it implied that he was being prepared for a return to the ranks. In his biography of Keith Miller, *The Golden Nugget*, the Australian writer R.S. Whitington related a story that appears to have escaped the attention of other journalists on the tour. Just before the Victoria match, in the lobby of Melbourne's Windsor Hotel, Hutton fell into conversation with a group of Australian correspondents. 'You don't look happy, Len?' one of them asked. 'Would you after what happened in Brisbane?' Hutton responded. 'Who would you choose for Sydney?' he inquired. One journalist enthusiastically endorsed Tyson. In Whitington's account, Hutton initially snorted at this – 'I was hoping for a serious answer' – but was then shown a story the writer had filed to his Sydney newspaper saying that Tyson was still the bowler most feared by Australia's batsmen. Hutton went away deep in thought.

By sticking with Tyson, Hutton may also have been acting in defiance of Gubby Allen, who arrived in Sydney in time for the second Test. Allen had been a key member of the committee choosing the tour party, but had no influence over the tour selection committee. That is unlikely to have stopped him expressing an opinion that the make-up of the England attack must change after the Brisbane defeat.

Despite his lack of activity since Brisbane, Alec Bedser remained in the 12. The selection panel agreed that he was unlikely to play – the sores on his back had still not fully healed and it was now clear that recovery from shingles was a longer process than anyone had foreseen – but he stayed in the squad because of the impact his presence had on the Australians. It also left the possibility of a last-minute change of plan. 'Before the ultimate decision to omit Alec was made, I took him aside and told him he might not be included in the team for the second Test,' Hutton recalled in *Just My*

Story. 'He understood the reasons that were behind this and knew that the considerations of the committee were directed only towards winning the match.'

Australia had their own selection issues. The absence of Ian Johnson and Keith Miller was confirmed two days before the game, leading to hurried consultations between selectors Don Bradman, Jack Ryder and Dudley Seddon. There was little doubt that the captaincy would pass to opening batsman Arthur Morris, but there was an unexpected complication: he had been selected for jury service. Unsurprisingly, he was released with 'pleasure and personal good wishes' from the judge. Morris had been a regular vice-captain to Lindsay Hassett and had been promoted at short notice against West Indies three years earlier. 'If you'd like some encouragement you'll remember we lost that one,' Morris joked to English pressmen. Nevertheless, balancing the team without Johnson and Miller presented a significant problem. 'In one swoop, Australia have been crippled by the loss of their captain and best spin bowler, together with their soundest batsman, a very dangerous fast bowler and the greatest all-rounder playing cricket today,' wrote John Woodcock in *The Times*.

They called up two local players. Jim Burke, 24, would bat at No.3. He had made a hundred on debut against England at Adelaide four years earlier, but had played just two Tests since. He received the news from Miller in a phone call to the Sydney stockbroker's office where he worked, but refused to believe his New South Wales teammate was not joking. Miller felt Burke, who also offered overs of off-spin, albeit with a highly suspect action, had benefited from spending the English summer of 1954 playing for Todmorden in the Lancashire League, well away from the well-meaning advice of coaches.[29] 'He had to work things out for himself,' said Miller.

Alan Davidson, 12th man at Brisbane, came into the team, and the vice-captaincy was handed to Benaud. Another Sydney batsman,

---

[29]Burke's bowling action was described by Ian Peebles as 'like a policeman hitting a small offender with a baton.' In 1979, depressed by marital problems, impending hip surgery and a failed investment on the gold futures market, he bought a rifle and committed suicide.

Billy Watson, 23, who had scored a century for New South Wales against MCC the previous month, was named as 12th man. He was working on his father's market stall when he was told the news and immediately made his way through a throng of well-wishers for a brush-up in the nets.

For England, there had been time for hasty nets before the match began. Despite the extended discussions about the itinerary, the schedule still occasionally looked unbalanced. Hutton agonised over the composition of his XI, his chances of restful sleep not helped by the damp atmosphere that had hung over Sydney that day, creating a situation that might make it advisable for the captain winning the toss to put the opposition in. Could he take such a high-stakes gamble again? Then, on the night before the Test began, the city was drenched by a thunderstorm that rattled the windows of the team's hotel. Homes and shops were flooded and local transport was disrupted, 4.5 cm (1.5 inches) of rain falling in 12 hours. As he tried to rest, Hutton knew the pitch and the surrounding area would be covered, but that the climatic conditions would almost certainly favour the seamers.

Drizzle was still in the air after breakfast, but it had cleared by the time the players climbed into the fleet of Holden saloons that took them on the three-and-a-half mile trip from the Oceanic Hotel in the beachside suburb of Coogee to the Sydney Cricket Ground in the Paddington area of the city. Here, John Woodcock told *Times* readers, was one of 'the great cricket grounds of the world'. As John Arlott noted, the stonework of its huge pedimented scoreboard was painted light green and the Edwardian corrugated iron roofs of the vast stands, dark green. The architectural highlights of the SCG were the Members Stand, which housed the dressing-rooms, and its neighbouring Lady Members Stand, both conveying an air of elegance – the nearest Australia had to the pomp of the pavilion at Lord's. On the opposite side, rather less grand but equally important to the venue's character, was the Hill, a large expanse of grass sloping up to the scoreboard. It was here, often exposed to the pitiless sun, that the more vocal spectators sat and offered unvarnished opinions on the action.

The England players were driven through the crowds gathering outside the members' entrance and deposited behind the Members

Stand. They bustled in to change and went out to inspect the pitch. 'Juicy and good to bowl on,' was Tyson's instant verdict. Curator Bill Watt had lifted the covers at 6.30 a.m. and was relieved to find rain had not penetrated. It didn't take Bedser long to assess conditions. 'Sydney had had rain for a month and the Test wicket was protected by flat tarpaulins,' he recalled. 'The result was a piebald strip of green and brown patches and, as the groundsman had not been able to spend as much time in preparation as he would have liked, there was quite a mat of grass on the surface. It was heaven-sent for pace for when the ball hit the green patches it flew and when striking the brown it kept low. The bounce was thus inconsistent and after one quick glance I could see it was a good wicket to bowl on.'

Bedser, desperate to play, was hardly an objective observer, but he was not alone. In the *Yorkshire Evening News*, the former England seamer Bill Bowes wrote, 'If Bedser had been asked to order exactly the type of pitch and atmospherics most suited to his bowling I doubt whether he could have ordered better.' The press had picked up rumours of his possible absence. Ray Robinson of the Sydney evening newspaper *The Sun* had written the previous day, 'Some English camp followers believe there is a possibility of Test record-breaker Alec Bedser being omitted from the 12. If true this would cause one of the biggest sensations in Test history, rivalling Australia's omission of Clarrie Grimmett before the war.'

Elsewhere among the press corps there was understanding of the dilemma facing Hutton. Ian Peebles of *The Sunday Times* had a long chat with Bedser on the eve of the match. 'I said quite frankly that I would not like him to play when anything below his normal strength,' Peebles wrote. 'He had far too much to lose, as had his side, if the very real awe he had inspired in the opposition was dispelled by failure when not his real self.' Bedser could see Peebles's point, but it was clear he would still be disappointed not to be in the XI.

'Broadly, what is being decided is whether to take a chance on a recovery of form at Sydney, where he has not often had very great success, or whether to keep him in reserve this time, with an eye to launching him again at the New Year at Melbourne on the ground which has given him some of his greatest triumphs,' E.W.

Swanton wrote in his *Daily Telegraph* preview. Peebles favoured the latter option. 'My personal inclination would be to reserve him for Melbourne and let him start at full blast,' he said. Statistics certainly supported this policy. In three Tests at the SCG, Bedser had taken nine wickets at 42, while in three at the MCG the tally was a much more impressive 22 at 20.

The appearance of the pitch and the oppressive atmosphere must have made it sorely tempting to abandon the plan hatched on the train to Sydney, but Hutton stuck to his first instinct: Appleyard was in, Bedser was out. 'It seemed the wrong moment to decide that such a great bowler was past his best,' said Bowes. Woodcock agreed: 'Voices were raised in surprise and indignation. It certainly seemed a hasty decision to cast aside England's greatest potential match-winning bowler and to prefer a second spinner.' E.M. Wellings added, 'Three cheers were called for and joyously given in the Australian dressing-room.' Arlott wrote, 'Bedser, one thinks, a little wistfully, would have liked to bowl on this wicket, as grassy as any the series is likely to see.' There was a sense of witnessing a generational shift. With Miller also absent, it meant Morris, now walking out to the middle to toss with Hutton, was the only man to have appeared in every post-war Ashes Test.

As he had on his previous occasion as stand-in captain, Morris won the toss. To have the decision taken out of his hands must surely have come as a relief to the England captain – 'Hutton would not dare send Australia in again after the Brisbane lesson,' wrote Percy Beames in *The Age*. Morris put his arm cordially over Hutton's shoulder and invited England to bat first. 'After Brisbane, I doubted that any Test captain would ever again send his opponents in to bat so long as any player who had been in that match remained in Test cricket,' Arlott admitted. 'Moreover, Morris is only a deputy captain. Sydney, however, is his home ground. He is an intelligent man. He has probably added to England's invariable anxiety in facing Lindwall.' In the press box, Hassett said it was a risk he would not have dared take. Margaret Hughes saw a shaft of humour amid the tension: 'Perhaps it was because Morris was so delighted with his Christmas present of Bedser's absence that he felt he had to make a counter-present to Hutton of first use of the pitch.'

FIRST BLOOD, AUSTRALIA

A few minutes later, Arthur Morris led Australia down the pavilion steps and out towards the middle. The players trailed a few yards behind the umpires, Mel McInnes and Ron Wright. Identically clad from head to toe, the officials marched towards the pitch in military lockstep. It was still cloudy and, by Sydney standards, chilly – Morris was the only Australian not wearing a sweater. A stiff breeze blew diagonally across the ground as spectators filed through the turnstiles and sought out their favoured viewing points. While Ray Lindwall went through his usual loosening-up exercises at the Randwick End, Morris arranged a hostile field: four slips, a gully, two leg slips and a silly mid-on. Even cover hovered menacingly close. As the clock on top of the Members Stand ticked towards 11.30 a.m., Len Hutton adjusted his gaze, gave a characteristic touch of his cap, and peered beneath the peak to see Lindwall at the end of his run. 'Thus does a keeper, entering the cage, sense the tiger,' wrote Alan Ross.

There was a small release of tension when Hutton pushed Lindwall's first ball past Morris at silly mid-on and ran two. The England captain then played out six dot balls before tucking the slightly misdirected final delivery of the over off his legs for the first boundary of the match. In the absence of Keith Miller, the new ball was thrown to the bulky figure of Ron Archer at the Paddington End. At 6 foot 1 in and bowling a lively fast-medium, Archer was well placed to extract any life from the pitch. He opened with a maiden to Trevor Bailey.

For the first six overs, the players stuck to their roles like well-rehearsed actors in a play. Bailey faced only two balls from Lindwall, Hutton just three from Archer. The score had crept to 14 without loss when – whether at the instigation of captain or bowler was not clear – Lindwall switched ends. It proved a hugely significant moment. Giving Lindwall the chance to exploit the wind had made sense, but bowling into it rather than with it might assist his swing. Five balls were all that were needed to see the wisdom of the move. 'Starting well outside the off stump, the ball dipped in without warning just as Bailey pushed forward to smother the swing. His middle stump was knocked clean out of the ground,' wrote Percy Beames in *The*

Age. 'Thus Bailey's resistance had to be measured in minutes, 37, rather than runs,' said E. W. Swanton. Bailey thought it was the most distinguished duck of his career.

Peter May replaced Bailey but Hutton could take no comfort from the arrival of his deputy. May looked horribly out of touch, while Hutton was stuck on 14 for 40 minutes. May had made five off 18 balls when he turned a lifting ball from Archer to Bill Johnston at short square leg. It was grim, attritional cricket, hardly suited to the strengths of Tom Graveney, but England clung on until lunch without further setback. They had scraped together a meagre 34 in the session. The pitch, with its tufts of grass and a damp spot near a good length at the Randwick End, had been a little two-paced, but was largely blameless. The threat had come from movement in the air. It had been 'a dour struggle – as grey as the weather,' wrote Bruce Harris in the *Evening Standard.* 'Surely one of the slowest openings in all Test cricket,' thought Arlott.

There was no increase in the entertainment level after the interval. When Graveney hit Johnston through the covers, it was England's first boundary for 10 overs. Eventually, the 50 came up when Hutton pinched three off Lindwall: it had taken two hours of hard labour to reach that first staging post. But the next calamity was approaching fast. In the 29th over, bowled by the left-arm seamer Johnston, Hutton played an authentic leg glance only to see the ball's progress to the fence interrupted by a diving Alan Davidson at leg slip. Inches from the turf, he clutched the ball in his 'wrong' right hand. Hutton stood stock-still for a few seconds, unable to process what had happened. Some suspected he was waiting for the square-leg umpire to confirm the ball had carried, others that he was thunderstruck. 'There was not the remotest doubt about the legality of the catch, which was one of the greatest pieces of match-winning fielding I have ever seen,' wrote Bill O'Reilly. John Kay in the *Manchester Evening News* articulated what everyone was thinking: 'No Englishman would have made such a catch.'

Looking back at the end of his career, Davidson rated it one of the three best catches he made. When Hutton returned to the dressing-room, he slumped into his seat. 'I thought it was four runs,' he grumbled. 'You can't leg-glance nowadays without someone catching you out.' Hutton had chiselled out 30 runs off 105 balls, a minor masterpiece of defensive batting occupying two hours 12 minutes of intense concentration. But critics in the press box pointed out that, often with only two fielders in front of the bat, Hutton had never tried to wrest back the initiative from Australia.

The dismissal was the trigger for what Woodcock called 'a pathetic procession'. Next to go was Graveney, casually steering Johnston to Les Favell at third slip after labouring to 21 in 88 minutes. Swanton lamented how often Graveney seemed to get out after laying the foundations of a significant innings. Bill Edrich did not even get a spade in the ground. When Morris brought back Archer, he soon had Edrich caught by Richie Benaud at gully for 10. Edrich had been trying to get his bat out of the way of a ball that reared unexpectedly. He was the only England batsman justified in directing an accusing glare at the pitch.

The length of England's tail was demonstrated by the sight of Frank Tyson walking out at No.7. He was soon making the return journey. Morris brought back Lindwall and Tyson departed to the fourth ball of his new spell. Godfrey Evans followed swiftly, sparring at a ball from Archer and edging it to wicketkeeper Gil Langley. Evans had not scored a Test fifty since July 1952, 20 innings ago, and earned a finger-wagging from Swanton in the *Telegraph*. At tea, England had stumbled to 94 for seven, five wickets surrendered for the addition of 60 in the afternoon. 'England played like a team that was waiting for its doom,' wrote O'Reilly. 'And they got it.'

The last hope of a total that might challenge Australia lay with Cowdrey. In the second over after tea, he was dropped in the slips by Benaud off Lindwall – a rare lapse – but Cowdrey was gone in the next over anyway, edging Davidson to the wicketkeeper. One short of three figures, England were eight down and in dire trouble. With conditions still loaded so heavily in favour of the bowlers, it looked certain Australia would bat that evening, a prospect they did not relish. 'Australia were well satisfied to dismiss England at small cost in a long time: they had no particular wish to be batting,' wrote J.M. Kilburn. Several of Kilburn's colleagues felt little was to be gained by continuing the England innings. 'The England captain allowed the tailenders to potter about until the chance of saving the day had vanished,' thought Beames.

The dismissal of Bob Appleyard to a smart low catch at first slip by Graeme Hole off Davidson brought last man Brian Statham to the wicket with a message for Johnny Wardle, who had used up 41 balls in making seven. It might have been roughly interpreted as 'Get on with it, or get out.' Wardle needed no further instruction. As a left-hander, Johnston held fewer terrors for him and Wardle advanced down the pitch to hit 17 off one over (Statham scampered two off the last ball to increase the damage). Two of Wardle's swipes over the slips produced a broad grin from Johnston, in good humour after his wife had given birth earlier in the week.[30] Morris, who had wanted to take Johnston off earlier only for the bowler to talk him out of it, was less happy. As Kilburn pointed out, it did not matter that some of the runs came off the edge, the boundaries 'looked just as handsome on the scoreboard,' and, as Arlott added, 'Wardle's hearty rustic comedy relieved the grimness of the match.'

For the first time in the day, Morris moved fielders away from the bat. Benaud dropped two catches, one difficult, one more comfortable. Johnston's next over went for nine, but he had the last word, having Wardle caught by Burke at long-on. The Yorkshire spinner had made 35, England's top score, and added 43 precious runs with Statham. Nevertheless, England's paltry 154 was no-one's idea of a decent total. There was some sympathy for the challenging conditions, but little for England's faint-hearted approach. In the *Daily Express*, Sid Barnes blasted 'Timidity which would have put a dormouse to shame.'

The day had been a triumph for two of Australia's most experienced players. 'Sound, shrewd and aggressive leadership by Arthur Morris, who directed the Australian side faultlessly, made the most of the Australian bowling,' said Beames. Meanwhile, Lindwall, whose figures of 17–3–47–2 did scant justice to his contribution, had performed magnificently. 'Lindwall has not bowled better for years than he did today,' said *The Age*. The contrast with the England camp could not have been more stark. 'This was Hutton's worst moment on the tour,' said the writer Gordon Ross. The captain's mood may not have been improved by the presence at the SCG of

---

[30]Hutton presented Johnston with a five-shilling coin – a crown – as a memento of the new arrival.

MCC secretary Ronny Aird, on his way to a fact-finding mission in New Zealand, and Gubby Allen, ostensibly in Australia to seek out investment opportunities for his City stockbroking firm.

Desperate to bowl, England were now thwarted by rain that had begun falling before the end of their innings. It was still raining when the curator began his between-innings rolling of the pitch, a lack of knowledge of the regulations that prompted a sad shake of the head from Swanton. The umpires halted the rolling and asked for the pitch to be covered. Once the rain had stopped and the covers peeled away, rolling was resumed. By the time Hutton led his team out, just 17 minutes of play remained. The seam-friendly conditions merely underscored the absence of Bedser, now watching from the pavilion alongside the other missing Titan, Denis Compton.

Hutton entrusted the new ball to Statham and Bailey. O'Reilly thought the sight of Bailey marking out his run added to Bedser's humiliation. 'His omission is nothing but a ridiculous blunder for which there will be much opportunity for regret before this match ends.' Lindsay Hassett could not understand why the extra pace of Tyson had not been deployed in the murky light. England hustled through their overs and fitted in four. Morris hooked the fifth ball of the final one over square leg to the boundary, but Bailey got the next delivery to lift and it looped from Morris's glove to a relieved Hutton at leg slip. At least two writers thought the Australian captain's hand had been off the bat handle on impact. 'A piece of ill luck that may possibly have big consequences,' wrote Swanton.

Close of play: Australia 18–1 (Favell 6★), trail England by 136 runs with nine first-innings wickets in hand.

ENTER TYSON

At 23,312, the first-day attendance at the SCG had been disappointing, the dreary weather perhaps putting off uncommitted Sydneysiders. On the second day there was no such reticence. Almost double the Friday figure streamed through the turnstiles, keen to see Australia press home their hard-won dominance. One of them was David Frith,

17, later to become one of cricket's most distinguished historians and writers. Stuck in a dull job with the Commonwealth Bank, he was desperate to see as much of the Test as possible and had acquired a two-week sicknote for a minor case of pharyngitis.

Frith had been born in England, but his family moved to Sydney in 1949. He felt a strong allegiance to both countries, worshipping Ray Lindwall as much as Len Hutton. The previous morning's opening confrontation had left him conflicted: 'I suppose I wanted Len to get a few and Ray to get him out.' Sitting in his favourite vantage point in the Sheridan Stand – 'over extra cover with the pavilion to your left' – he found the suspense of the first day almost overwhelming. 'When Hutton and Bailey came out to bat I was breathing with difficulty,' he recalled. 'The tension was like nothing I'd ever experienced and if it didn't recede I feared I might not survive the day.'

Conditions seemed to be conspiring in Australia's favour. There was no hint of rain and the atmosphere was lighter and fresher. A scattering of grey clouds drifted over the ground. The pitch had 'the colour and texture of an unpolished tan shoe', according to Ian Peebles. As they made the short journey from Coogee, the England players must have been full of foreboding. They were right to be worried. Les Favell and Jim Burke instantly established a more positive tone than had been shown by the England batsmen.

Once Trevor Bailey had completed the over he had started the previous evening, Brian Statham, bowling without a fine leg or a third man, took up the attack from the Randwick End. He was uncharacteristically wayward and, after conceding 24 in three overs, swapped ends with Bailey. Hutton felt Bailey's outswing would benefit from the assistance of the cross-wind, while Statham could utilise it for his inswing. Whatever the theory, England urgently needed to reverse the momentum. After 40 minutes' play, Australia had reached 65 for one, a mere 89 behind.

Fortunately, the change of ends, allied to Bailey's formidable cricket intelligence, produced a further breakthrough. 'Bailey is a bowler who augments a not inconsiderable technique by making a very close study of his opponents' weaknesses and taking advantage of them,' wrote Peebles. Using the width of the crease to vary the angle of attack, Bailey got his reward when Favell drove carelessly at a full-length ball and was smartly caught by Tom Graveney. Denzil Batchelor said, 'Graveney holds catches at second slip as comfortably as a curate can hold a mothers' meeting.' The comparison looked less convincing when Graveney dropped a low edge from Burke off Bailey. At lunch, Australia were 88 for two and Frank Tyson had replaced Statham at the Paddington End.

In a low-scoring Test, every passage of play can be crucial, each boundary or wicket representing a potential turning point. A nip-and-tuck contest had reached another critical moment. Tyson, on whose broad shoulders rested much of England's strategy, had so far bowled 32 overs in the series for one wicket. He admitted his two overs in the morning had been 'wild and woolly'. Hutton was now relieved to hear he was feeling more self-assured. 'The approaches to the wicket were firmer and confidence was seeping back,' Tyson recalled. 'The shorter run was becoming more settled and I felt the rhythm returning, mounting to a crescendo as I crashed the ball down as fast as I could.'

But it was Bailey who made the first breach of the afternoon, having Burke caught shoulder-high by Graveney at slip for 44. Tyson struck in the next over: Neil Harvey, who had struggled to 12 off 42 balls, fending a steep lifter from the shoulder of the bat to Colin Cowdrey in the gully. Harvey's removal was more than a triumph for raw pace. 'I recalled that Keith Miller occasionally used a round-arm delivery, which moved a little off the seam,' said Tyson. He tested the idea out, dropping his arm a fraction at the point of release, and was rewarded with a prize wicket. He celebrated by beating the new batsman Richie Benaud twice for outright speed. Tyson had swiftly worked out that Graeme Hole's high backlift made him the odds-on favourite to be his next victim: theory duly became reality when Hole played an extravagant drive at a ball moving in to him and edged into his stumps.

Benaud survived but even he was not sure how. 'He was almost bowled off his body by Tyson's first violent bumper, was nearly beaten by a yorker, might conceivably have been caught by a leaping Edrich when he slashed another bumper over first slip, should have been caught by Graveney at backward short leg, and then three times failed to edge Bailey's outswing by a hairsbreadth,' wrote Denys Rowbotham. Benaud had somehow scraped together 20 when he was lbw playing back to Statham, now re-established in his customary groove after his off-colour start.

At 141 for six with tea approaching, Australia trailed by 13 with the bulk of their batting gone. Ron Archer and Alan Davidson now began to counterpunch. Shortly before Benaud's dismissal, Hutton had thrown the ball to Bob Appleyard for the first time, giving an absorbed Sydney crowd its first glimpse in the match of a wicketkeeper standing up to the stumps. Appleyard made an exemplary start, but in his fourth over Archer pulled him to the boundary and then scattered the occupants of the Hill with an on-drive for six. With that steepling blow, the sole six of the Test, Australia moved into the lead.

In three hectic balls of Statham's 15th over, Davidson square-cut for four, survived a chance to Peter May at second slip, and was bowled, hitting across a ball on leg stump. Archer and Davidson had added 52 for the seventh wicket. 'They were together only 60 minutes,' said the Australian writer A.G. Moyes, 'but it was a joyous period and a fruitful one.'

An edge for four through the unoccupied slip area by Archer took Australia past 200 and made him his team's highest scorer. 'He makes up for any lack of specialist technique by the sheer enthusiasm of his approach,' said Crawford White in the *News Chronicle*. Archer was one short of a deserved fifty when a rested Tyson returned with the new ball to end his invaluable contribution, Hutton holding a fine low catch at third slip. The impact of Tyson's pace was beginning to be felt by the Australians. 'First time I've hit the ball in the middle and been caught at slip,' Archer said when he sat down in the dressing-room. With Australia eight down and half an hour left in the day, Hutton now faced a conundrum. He wanted to keep the lead within acceptable bounds, but did not want to take the remaining wickets so quickly that he would have to begin England's second innings on what was now a gloomy late afternoon.

For the moment, he continued to push for wickets. Lindwall's belligerent 64 at Brisbane meant England believed he had lost the right to the courtesies normally extended to tailenders. He had scored 19 off 24 balls and hit two fours when Tyson bowled him an unthreatening bouncer that he edged to Godfrey Evans. The delivery was to have lasting repercussions. Hutton glanced at the pavilion clock to see 17 minutes remaining and ordered Tyson to bowl an over wide down the leg side to Bill Johnston, much to the derision of a hitherto even-handed crowd. The over took nine minutes. Once satisfied that there was no danger of England having to bat, Bailey returned to bowl Gil Langley for his fourth wicket of the innings. Australia were all out for 228, a lead of 74.

'It had been a great day for England in which encouragement surely must have outweighed disappointment,' wrote Rowbotham. 'It was a thrilling and heartening day,' said John Woodcock. John Arlott, however, warned Australia's lead might already be decisive, but conceded, 'At least Australia have been engaged in an equal challenge,' and in Sydney's *Sunday Telegraph*, the former England captain Freddie Brown added, 'In a long-range forecast, I still tip Australia to win.'

With figures of 13–2–45–4, Tyson had earned his time in the spotlight. His shorter run had 'brought a considerable increase in control with no apparent loss of pace', said Peebles. Margaret Hughes lamented that England had again dropped several catches. 'I doubt whether England will ever reign supreme until something is done about our sloppy, ragged performances in the field,' she wrote. Bailey's contribution was just as praiseworthy as Tyson's, but even he was still thinking about the absent Alec Bedser. 'It was the one Test match when the ball really swung. It was one of the very few occasions when I bowled swing rather than seam because it swung all day long,' he told BBC producer Peter Baxter for a radio documentary on the series. 'I'm quite convinced that if Alec had played in that Test match he would have played in the next one, because I picked up four wickets and I reckon Alec would have got seven.'

Bedser was not only missing the match. On the second day, he was not even at the SCG. Instead, he joined Denis Compton and Keith Miller at Randwick racecourse. Back home, in a *Daily Express* poll, 60 per cent of respondents backed the decision to leave Bedser out. But Australians remained obsessed. After the Test, a reporter asked the England captain if he missed not having Bedser in the team. 'I always miss Alec when he isn't there,' he replied. He was less diplomatic when confronted by the wife of an unnamed former Australian player at a pre-Christmas party. 'Who are the awful people who have dropped poor Alec?' she asked. 'Well, you know,' Hutton stumbled in reply, 'a good young 'un is always better than a good old 'un.'

Close of play: Australia 228 all out, lead England by 74 runs.

SYDNEY LIFE

It was during their visit for the State match against New South Wales six weeks earlier that the MCC players and the English media entourage got their first experience of Sydney. They quickly discovered it was very different from Australia's other major cities. 'Sydney had had a great influx of American servicemen during the war so it had become a much more modern sort of place,' manager Geoffrey Howard remembered. Alan Ross relished its 'bustling, noisy vulgarity'. The centrepiece was the great Harbour Bridge, opened in 1932. 'Sydney Harbour and Sydney Bridge are truly as impressive as Australians always tell the rest of the world they are,' wrote John Arlott. 'The bridge with its six traffic lanes, and four rail and tram tracks, is such that one wonders how the life of the city ever went on without it.'

With its ferries bustling in and out, and great cruise liners arriving from distant parts of the world, the Harbour was the focus of life in the city. 'It is the sea, flashing and ferrying, that holds Sydney together,' said Ross. 'Nowhere in the world do so many people live poised above the quick blues of an ocean: not in Rio de Janeiro nor in San Francisco, not in Singapore, nor in Naples.' Arlott added, 'The Harbour, many armed, varied and huge, is both beautiful and utilitarian. Home to nearly two million people, Sydney was bigger than Melbourne, a city with which it enjoyed a not-always-friendly rivalry. It also had something other Australian cities did not – a small community of recent arrivals from continental Europe.

In the mid-1950s, Robert Menzies's Liberal–Country Coalition government still enforced the 'White Australia' policy that had first become law in 1901. This was racist legislation designed to keep immigrants from the Far East out of the country. But after the Second World War there was a growing realisation that Australia had to 'populate or perish' and the rules were relaxed, though at this point only to allow the arrival of white Europeans. The influx included refugees who had been displaced in the conflict, including men and women from the Baltic states, Latvia, Estonia and Lithuania. They were met at Fremantle by Arthur Calwell, the minister for immigration, and soon dubbed 'the Beautiful Balts'. Calwell and other politicians saw the arrival of Europeans as a way of keeping the country white, while boosting its working population.

Ross's curiosity took him into a part of Sydney that instantly felt very different. 'King's Cross, the capital of New Australia, where immigrants have recreated Europe out of nostalgia. The air smells of garlic, the inhabitants dress as if in Montparnasse, the delicatessen shops and cafés stay open far into the night, and Australian is a foreign language.' While the majority of journalists were booked into city hotels, Arlott and Bill Bowes rented a flat in the district for the duration of their stay. Arlott recalled, 'It was a city where the taxi drivers knew absolutely everything and insisted on communicating it to their defenceless passengers.'

Unbeknown to them, the cricketers and journalists had first arrived in Sydney at a significant moment. On 13 November, the second day of the match against New South Wales, the state conducted a referendum on the closing hours of licensed premises and registered clubs. Voting was compulsory. Under the current law, venues serving alcohol closed at just after 6 p.m., with last orders at 5.50 p.m. This led to a phenomenon called 'the six o'clock swill' where men rushed to pubs and bars after work, and attempted to order as much beer as possible before closing time. Bodies collapsed in shop doorways after consuming several pints in a frantic 20-minute burst were a regular sight. In hotels, only residents could order a drink with a meal and then all alcohol had to be cleared from the table by 8 p.m. The vote was whether to extend opening hours till 10 p.m.

English visitors could find Australian pubs alien and intimidating. 'They are just four bare walls with no seating, modelled to take as many men as possible in a perpendicular position propping each other up,' wrote Margaret Hughes. 'Drab drink shops of the Dickens era,' thought Ross. Surprisingly perhaps, brewers opposed extending opening hours. The current system allowed them to sell huge quantities of beer with few overheads and no pressure to make their premises more welcoming. They found themselves in an unlikely alliance with the Methodist church. When the poll results were declared, there was a narrow vote in favour of extending opening time to 10 p.m., but an odd compromise was made so that bars closed from 6.30 until 7.30, thereby extending the duration of the 'six o'clock swill'.

GRADUATION DAY FOR THE OXBRIDGE BOYS

With the Test so delicately poised, relaxation was difficult. On Saturday night, Denis Compton had promised to take a group of players to a pre-Christmas barbecue at Middle Harbour, but some of the Yorkshire contingent were reluctant, 'Do we 'ave to pay?' asked one. When the cricketers arrived, they discovered that the party had been the previous night. Compton's reputation for chaos should perhaps have acted as a warning. David Frith and his brother had hot-footed it to a golf-club barbecue where, according to advertisements, some England players might be in attendance. They were not. Compton may have been responsible for that diary mix-up too.

On the rest day there was the usual dash for the golf course. Colin Cowdrey, joined by the *Daily Telegraph*'s E.W. Swanton, headed for St Alban's Church in the suburb of Epping where he read the lesson. Tyson joined Margaret on a visit to a Christmas party at the Watson's Bay naval base in the harbour. Like most Englishmen spending Christmas abroad for the first time, he found the sight of someone dressed as Father Christmas on a sweltering day incongruous. The players must have been thinking of the SCG pitch, drying out under the hot sun.

The end of Australia's first innings just before the close on Saturday meant there were no loose ends. When Len Hutton and Trevor Bailey walked to the crease on Monday morning, the objective was clearly laid out: wipe out the first-innings deficit of 74, then start to build a lead that would prove beyond Australia on a wearing pitch. It already seemed likely that turnstile operators would not be needed on the allotted sixth day. The weather was the best of the match so far, warm and sunny with less humidity, but the southerly wind was blowing straight down the ground, making it easy for a captain to decide on the deployment of his fastest bowler. The pitch, Swanton noted, 'had changed from lush green to dun'.

Ray Lindwall tried to surprise Hutton with a first-ball yorker, but the England captain was alive to the ruse. The final ball of the over sailed past gully to the fence in an unexpected act of aggression by Hutton. Oddly for a batsman predisposed to caution, Hutton had now hit boundaries in Lindwall's opening over in each of England's three innings in the series. It proved not to be a declaration of intent. When Ron Archer came on at the other end, Bailey patted back eight eminently hittable deliveries, despite there being only two fielders in front of the bat. 'An opening batsman must be able sometimes to drive the over-pitched ball,' wrote Alan Ross. He thought he detected a technical fault: 'Bailey holds his bat in such a manner as to preclude the free swing of the left elbow.'

Bailey managed one boundary, a Lindwall full toss flicked to long leg, but he had made only six in 36 minutes when he lunged forward to a ball from Archer that seamed away late and edged it to wicketkeeper Gil Langley. 'Bailey started to walk before he had completed the stroke,' said Margaret Hughes. Peter May looked more at ease, turning his first ball off his legs for three. As Lindwall reached the end of a seven-over spell before going off for boot repairs, runs began to come more easily: Hutton took nine off his final over, though not all convincingly. Alan Davidson came on for Lindwall and Bill Johnston replaced Archer – left-arm seam from both ends. 'Ten minutes before luncheon one dared to think that perhaps at last they were travelling along the road that they had found so elusive since the tour started,' wrote John Woodcock in *The Times*.

Then it all went horribly wrong. The third ball of Johnston's second over was a wide half-volley, moving away late, that Hutton flashed hard into the grateful hands of Richie Benaud in the gully. It went low and at what the *Sydney Morning Herald* called 'pistol-shot speed', but Benaud made no mistake and tossed the ball up exultantly. Lindwall thought the dismissal exposed a slight flaw in Hutton's otherwise immaculate technique. 'When he drove, his bat was a little bit away from his body,' he said. Hutton had battled to 28, but his preparatory work was in vain. In the *Daily Express*, former Australia opener Sid Barnes criticised Hutton's 'kangaroo hop' footwork. 'There is something wrong with our Len and unless it is quickly remedied England will be returning our Coronation gift of the Ashes,' he wrote. 'My own opinion is that Hutton is dislocating his fluency by striving too desperately to make a success of the captaincy – off the field.'

His replacement Tom Graveney groped for Johnston's first ball, let the second pass harmlessly by, then aimed an airy drive at the third and edged to Langley. 'He drove at it as though he were well set in a September festival at Weston-super-Mare,' said Woodcock. E.W. Swanton thought Hutton just as culpable. 'Neither of these illustrious heads was behind the line of the ball and neither stroke therefore was technically sound,' he thundered. 'I didn't see Graveney's knock – I turned my head to sneeze,' Barnes added. In the *Daily Herald*, Charles Bray wrote what many were thinking: 'Graveney's failure lends credence to the belief which is growing apace which is that he is a good county player, but not of the Test class.' Bill Bowes forecast 'a long climb back to international cricket'.

The remaining 18 balls to lunch were negotiated by May and Colin Cowdrey without further mishap, but the scoreboard did little for England's digestion – it showed them perched precariously at 58 for three, still 16 adrift. Ross enjoyed cold lobster, but the mood among the touring journalists was anything but chilled. The consensus was that two more quick wickets could see the match, and possibly the Ashes, slip from England's grasp.

The gravity of the situation was not lost on May and Cowdrey as they walked out after the interval. 'If I had the chance to play the innings of my life, I would like to do it this afternoon,' May recalled saying to his partner. 'But that was prompted by the thought that we were threatened with going two down in the series and would never be in greater need of runs.' There had been suggestions that May was failing to live up to his abundant potential and that his place might be under threat, despite his appointment as vice-captain. Cowdrey admitted, 'I was terrified, most of all perhaps, because the pitch had dried out, the atmosphere had become less heavy, the new ball had lost its shine – and technically there was no excuse for getting out. The feeling, deep down, that the game could still be won by good batting made me all the more nervous.'

What followed was one of the pivot points of the series and the first significant collaboration between two of England's greatest post-war batsmen. May – Charterhouse School, Cambridge University and Surrey – joined Cowdrey – Tonbridge, Oxford and Kent – in a fourth-wicket partnership of 116 in more than three and a quarter hours. It was not the size of the stand, though it was comfortably the biggest of the match, that impressed so much as the calm authority and impeccable judgment both brought to a situation fraught with pressure.

With Morris setting mid-on and mid-off deep, May continued to accumulate, mainly off his legs. 'Lots of May's runs come from a push shot which he deftly steers past the square-leg umpire with a casualness which belies the quality of the stroke,' wrote Barnes. 'To see May get the ball away you would think he was shelling peas.' Cowdrey was stronger on the off, producing drives that stirred memories of Walter Hammond, who had averaged 161 in five Tests at the SCG.

Despite the pitch offering them no assistance, Australia's bowling and fielding remained of the highest calibre and neither batsmen broke free. 'They batted with distinction rather than dominance, playing innumerable beautiful shots and owing little or nothing to fortune,' said J.M. Kilburn in the *Yorkshire Post*. 'There was respect in their whole attitude and they accepted without evident protest the restrictions of good length and direction.'

It was not until the 25th over, the seventh since lunch, that England finally ensured that Australia would have to bat again, but the total did not reach three figures until the 33rd, when Cowdrey drove Davidson straight down the ground, while the fifty partnership came in Davidson's next, Cowdrey this time unfurling his off drive. May reached his fifty off 129 balls when he hooked Archer to the fence, and at tea England were 129 for three, a lead of 55 with May 58 and Cowdrey 37. 'The score belies the fact that this has been a momentous session for England,' said John Arlott, 'two batsmen holding out for the whole period from a near-indefensible position.'

The afternoon had turned cooler, but, now sitting on the Hill, David Frith still got sunburnt as he watched the partnership unfold. He thought the terrace's reputation as home to cricket's most knowledgeable fans was ill-deserved. 'During the state match I overheard someone asking his mate who Peter Loader was and he replied "That's England's new leg-spinner," so I didn't think they knew everything. Nor were they as witty as legend made out.' In later decades, it became customary for photographers to linger at the close of play to capture the clearing of thousands of empty beer cans from the Hill. Such excess was not seen in the 1950s. 'It was pretty noisy, but I don't think drunkenness was a problem,' Frith recalled. 'The bar was open at the back, but if you were going to go for a drink you were going to miss the game. Everyone in the ground was a cricket fan.'

One famous cricket lover paying rapt attention to an increasingly absorbing contest was prime minister Robert Menzies, who chose to spend part of his 60th birthday at the SCG. For Kenneth McKim, a schoolteacher who had travelled more than 250 miles to get his first sight of Test cricket, the excitement was too much. At tea, he climbed the fence and walked slowly to the middle to inspect the pitch, chatting to the curator as he went about his interval chores. No one intervened and he calmly walked back to his seat. 'I just had to see the Test wicket today and I didn't care what happened to me,' he said.

May and Cowdrey had been presented with a new problem late in the afternoon session when Morris brought on Benaud. It was the start of a marathon spell of 17 overs, his longest bowl yet in a Test, interrupted only by tea. Benaud tossed his leg-breaks high into the wind, hoping to tempt the batsmen into an indiscretion, but they remained resolute, even if neither seemed entirely at ease. There was more intelligent work from Lindwall, who toiled for three hours without reward in long spells during the day. He removed his leg slip, encouraging May and Cowdrey to believe that the glance was a safe stroke, and then bowled the odd ball that dipped in late towards their pads. Before these deliveries, at a prearranged signal, Langley shifted a few yards to his left, ready to catch any shot that might be hit a shade too fine. With the pitch offering no assistance, the bowlers had to lay unorthodox snares.

In the face of these twin challenges, England's scoring rate slowed after tea, not that a fully engaged crowd seem to mind. 'It was watching batting, not the scoreboard,' wrote Denys Rowbotham. Cowdrey's richly deserved half-century arrived with a regal cover drive off Lindwall, but he had now been in for just over two and a half hours and the strain was beginning to tell. There was another landmark in Lindwall's next over when Cowdrey pushed a single to bring up the hundred partnership; it was a tribute to their vigilance that neither batsmen had once hit the ball in the air.

But Cowdrey had added only 16 in an hour and 15 minutes since tea – 'like a fluent speaker who had suddenly taken vows of silence,' thought A.G. Moyes. Now, in an effort to break the grip exerted by the bowlers, he came down the pitch to a Benaud leg-break and tried to clear Archer, positioned at a straight but deep mid-on. It was a fatal miscalculation. The ball sailed unerringly into Archer's hands. Australia had their breakthrough. Cowdrey was distraught. 'Every man jack of the 31,679 crowd rose and applauded the youngster all the way back to the pavilion,' said Charles Bray in the *Daily Herald*. 'I don't think Colin heard any of it. White of face, biting his lip and thumping his bat on the ground, he was obviously furious with himself for such an indiscretion at that particular stage of the game. He had played his part nobly. There was no need for self-condemnation.'

Back in the dressing-room, away from prying eyes, Cowdrey sat down and wept. 'I've just thrown the Test match away, Frank,' he sobbed to Tyson. 'It will be my fault.' There were sympathetic words and comfort from his teammates, though not from George Duckworth. The next time he saw Cowdrey returning from a church service, he asked, 'Been to confession, have we?' Cowdrey recalled, 'I was genuinely deceived by Richie Benaud. Perhaps tiredness had something to do with it.' He had made 54 off 182 balls and batted for 193 minutes. 'One of the most stirring battling partnerships I have seen in Test cricket,' wrote Bill O'Reilly in the *Sydney Morning Herald*. 'It is a pleasure to report that the old universities served England proudly,' said Rowbotham. Much was made of Cowdrey and May's educational backgrounds – even Barnes dubbed them 'the university boys' – but Swanton chose to salute the old professionals who had coached them at school: 'It can be said with confidence that George Geary at Charterhouse and Maurice Tate at Tonbridge would have looked on with equal pride and gratification.'

Cowdrey's greatest regret was exposing the out-of-form Bill Edrich to the potential hazards of the last six overs of the day, but he need not have worried. May remembered being reassured by Edrich's pugnacious demeanour as he walked to the middle and he made his point by quickly hitting three fours. May's scoring rate speeded up in syncopation. 'Champagne when one had prepared for indigestion tablets,' said Ross.

May ended the day two runs short of his third Test century, earning a congratulatory handshake from Lindwall as he walked off. Not the least impressive aspect of his innings was the way he refused to fret about the approaching landmark as the clock moved towards 5.30 p.m. In the *Daily Mirror*, Ross Hall called him 'a young man who today entered the portals of greatness.' O'Reilly thought he detected the secret of his formidable on-side play: 'May has a peculiar grip of the bat which has the outside edge facing straight back at the bowler as he shapes up. This is the reason why he gets the ball away on the on side of the wicket when one expects to see it go straight or towards mid-off.' Hall added, 'His was the innings of a youngster who had suddenly realised he had worn Test match short pants long enough and had decided to become a man.'

Earlier in the tour, Howard had been concerned about May's intensity off the field. 'He is, one might almost say, too keen,' he wrote to Ronny Aird, 'but that isn't really what I mean: what I mean is that he has really hardly any interests outside cricket and it is almost a pity that he hasn't because he tends to think about it too much when he is not doing particularly well.'

That night May dined with Ian Peebles at Sydney's Union Club, the *Sunday Times* man allowing him one glass of wine before sending him back to the hotel for an early night. 'This was certainly with his acquiescence, but hardly savoured of old-world hospitality,' Peebles wrote. No matter – May had work to do tomorrow.

Close of play: England 204–4 (May 98★, Edrich 16★), lead Australia by 130 runs.

'MY GOD, LINDY, YOU'VE KILLED HIM'

Who was in the box seat now? England's lead was a fragile 130 with six wickets in hand, but a tail that began at No.7. 'One would think,

England must make 100 more to give their bowlers sufficient scope to win the match,' said John Woodcock. 'It looks at the moment slightly more likely to be lost than won.' That seemed to be the consensus. 'Despite the pluck and skill of the youngsters, England have a decent old Dunkirk on their hands,' wrote Sid Barnes. 'England are still in the Test match, but only just,' said the *Daily Herald*'s Charles Bray. Barnes also had a prediction: 'It is obvious now that an extra layer of concrete will have to be affixed to a few English chins if Australia are not to win the series 5–0.'

Play began on time on the fourth morning despite heavy overnight rain, but the outfield was wet and Arthur Morris decided to delay taking the new ball. Peter May arrived early to spend a restorative half-hour in the nets and he turned the second delivery of the day from Ray Lindwall confidently past short leg for the two runs he needed to reach his hundred. Morris led the Australians' applause, joined enthusiastically by the crowd, but there was already drizzle in the air and the umpires led the players off at the end of the first over.

After a 17-minute delay, the England batsmen were insufficiently proactive in a small window before the new ball was taken, even though Bill Edrich drove Bill Johnston through the covers to bring up the fifty partnership. After eight fruitless overs, Morris could wait no longer and threw the new ball to the returning Lindwall. He needed only two deliveries to remove May with a fast, inswinging ball that hit the top of off stump – the fast bowler's holy grail. 'I was very cross with myself for getting out when we were moving towards a winning position,' May remembered. He had made 104 off 287 balls in 298 minutes.

The arrival of Frank Tyson did nothing for England's slumbering scoring rate – Edrich's aggression of the previous evening had deserted him – and the total had advanced by just 22 in 13 overs when an incident occurred that would have unforeseen consequences for the outcome of the match. Aware that Tyson had dismissed him with a bouncer in Australia's innings, Lindwall saw no breach of protocol in returning fire. But Tyson made a complete hash of dealing with the short ball. 'The height of Ray's hand seemed to suggest a different ball, but whether it was due to the overcast morning, or a badly placed sightscreen, I shall never know,' he wrote in *A Typhoon Called Tyson*. 'Sensing that it was a short ball, I tried to duck and turned my back on the bowler. Never again will I turn my back to a fast bowler.'

Tyson was struck an audible blow on the back of the skull – the ball cannoned out as far as the square-leg umpire – and collapsed in a heap. It was more than 20 years before batsmen first began to experiment with protective helmets and longer until everyone wore them. 'Felled him like a poleaxed ox,' wrote Denzil Batchelor. Tyson temporarily lost consciousness with, as Ian Peebles noted, 'His arms flinging outwards in the relaxed fashion that means complete oblivion.' Lindwall rushed up the pitch in some distress and the Australians gathered around the prostrate figure. Edrich arrived from the non-striker's end: 'My God, Lindy, you've killed him.'

There was similar concern in the England dressing-room. 'We were all worried to death,' said Tom Graveney. 'It was a terrible blow.' Lindwall was admonished in print by Bill O'Reilly: 'Fast bowlers everywhere should be encouraged to keep that bouncer for the recognised batsmen who are quicker on their feet than most bowlers.' But the Australians believed it was far from Lindwall's fastest ball and the fault lay with Tyson's befuddled response. 'It was the slowest bouncer you've ever seen,' said Morris. 'He played about three shots before it hit him.' In the press box, Peebles and Woodcock agreed there was little prospect of Tyson playing any further part in the match.

He got to his feet groggily and was led off, still clutching his head, by two ambulancemen. He instantly had a blinding headache. Manager Geoffrey Howard accompanied him to a hospital two miles away in Macquarie Street, furiously shooing away press photographers as Tyson was escorted into the building. The incident underlined to Howard his responsibility for the welfare of the players. He was already fretting that Reg Simpson, in bed with a temperature of 104°, might have polio. There was no need to worry about Tyson. He had a sizeable lump on his head, but was cleared to return to the ground. At his own expense, Tyson joked, 'The thickness of the Tyson skull was proved beyond doubt.'

Back at the SCG, England's prospects looked no brighter. Having scored just 16 in the session, Edrich became overly obsessed with surviving until lunch. The consequences were predictable. In trying to withdraw his bat from a harmless delivery from Ron Archer wide of off stump, he deflected it on to his stumps. Another setback came in the second over of the afternoon when Godfrey Evans, dropped off the first ball he faced, edged Lindwall to Archer at slip.

There was astonishment in some quarters at the sight of Tyson now walking out to resume his innings. Lindwall put a comradely arm round his shoulder and there was warm appreciation from the crowd. When he drove Archer straight to the boundary, the stroke was greeted by prolonged cheers. 'We greatly underestimated this very tough young man's stamina and courage,' wrote Peebles. Tyson soon lost Johnny Wardle, lbw to Lindwall's off-cutter, and two overs later was himself outfoxed by Lindwall's slower ball. Since the start of the day, England had lost five wickets for the addition of only 46. They led by just 176. It had been a shocking collapse, undoing much of May and Cowdrey's diligent reconstruction work.

The first innings had underscored the value of tailend application. Bob Appleyard, still to get off the mark when Tyson was out, greeted last man Brian Statham with the words, 'We'll get this up to 300, Brian.' Joined in a cross-Pennine alliance, they made a contrasting pair. 'Appleyard played straight down the line, while Statham threw his bat at the ball, making some curious strokes and some splendid ones,' wrote A.G. Moyes. Peebles, who sometimes dusted off his leg-spin to bowl in the nets, added, 'Appleyard has always practised his batting with commendable earnestness and now reaped the fruits of his application. He batted with an orthodox solidity that would have gained the approval of Wilfred Rhodes himself, while Statham gave evidence of enterprise and eye rather than accepted practice.' With minimum footwork, Statham hit straight drives for four off Lindwall and Archer, while Appleyard square-cut Alan Davidson to the fence.

As so often the case with unexpectedly prolific last-wicket stands, Australia quickly lost their collective sense of humour. Moyes thought Morris had erred tactically in persisting with his seamers. Eventually, Johnston switched to spin and Richie Benaud was also introduced. 'No doubt the batsmen passed a vote of thanks to Morris for keeping his straight bowlers in action for so long when the slow man was so clearly desirable,' said Moyes. Appleyard and Statham had added 46 and batted for nearly an hour when Statham was caught behind by Gil Langley off Johnston.

England were all out for 296. To win the match and take an almost certainly unassailable 2–0 lead in the series, Australia had to score 223. There were still two and a half days left; time did not enter into the calculation. Also on Australia's side was the placid nature of the pitch. 'The wicket is easy,' said Arlott. 'All the life in the pitch at Sydney inherits from the water used in the preparation. That gives, especially to this amount of grass, a green quality which may last the first two days, but, after that, and with Sunday intervening, it dries out and the wicket becomes easier with time, slow and bland, defying lift.'

At 3.20 p.m., Morris and Favell set out on their mission. They walked into a firestorm. Neither Tyson nor Statham fitted the stereotype of the perpetually angry snarling fast bowler, a role honed to perfection by Fred Trueman, but both Hutton's new-ball spearheads were clearly fired up. 'I was in an ugly mood,' said Tyson, still nursing a headache. 'Statham oozed aggression,' wrote Arthur Gilligan. Hutton thought he detected a changed mood in Tyson. 'When he came out of his concussed state I swear there was a new light in his eyes as if a spark had been kindled deep down inside him,' he recalled. 'The blow seemed to trigger off something, perhaps a new willpower, a fresh determination, perhaps even a desire to get his own back.'

Statham began into the breeze from the Paddington End. Favell nearly played on to his first ball, survived a loud appeal for leg-before off the second and cut the fourth through Bill Edrich's hands at first slip. 'A chance a Test match player should have taken,' thought Moyes. Tyson opened at the Randwick End with the wind at his back. Morris, a veteran of 40 Tests, looked discombobulated at being assailed by high pace from both ends. 'Morris carved and slashed as though trying to quell a bush fire,' said Peebles. 'It seemed as though he must have a pressing appointment for tea,' added Swanton.

In the frenetic atmosphere, runs came quickly – 27 in 25 minutes before the interval. Morris deflected a Tyson full toss for a four to long leg where a black cocker spaniel collected the ball before May could retrieve it. A boy managed to persuade the dog to drop it at Wardle's feet. In the last over before tea, Morris tried to hook a ball from Statham that kept fractionally low and was lbw for 10.

Tyson struck again in the first over after the break, Edrich this time holding on to a stinging slip catch above his head to remove Favell for 16. Australia were 34 for two and Hutton sensed an opening. But in what Peebles called a 'snakes and ladders' Test match, Australia now fought back. Neil Harvey was beaten by his first two balls from Tyson and Jim Burke took several blows on the body, but they remained resolute. The scoring rate slowed to a crawl. Despite the perilous nature of the contest, both batsmen were jeered by the crowd. 'Hey Burkey, you're so like a statue I wish I was a pigeon,' came the cry from the Hill, an old joke dusted off and repurposed.

Bailey and Appleyard gave Statham and Tyson a breather and, in the final session of the fourth day, Wardle was finally given a bowl. In the last over, Harvey took advantage. 'Harvey hit him like thunder through extra cover and then flicked a strong four down to long leg,' reported Arlott. In the final 80 minutes, Australia had managed just 38 runs. Swanton predicted, 'If that is to be their pace tomorrow, the end, whatever it is, will be a long time coming.'

There were two visitors to the England dressing-room at the close. Lindwall and Morris were both keen to check on Tyson's health, but he assured them getting hit was 'purely accidental'. He may have still been dizzy when he opened the attack, but R. S. Whitington thought he had 'bowled faster than any modern bowler can bowl'. Lindwall and Morris must have been dismayed when a further examination cleared Tyson to bowl the next day.[31]

Close of play: Australia 72–2 (Burke 13*, Harvey 26*), need another 151 runs to beat England.

TYPHOON BLOWS IN

Most pundits were keeping their options open, but not Tom Goodman of the *Sydney Morning Herald*. 'Australia should win the

---

[31]Strict concussion protocols now operate in Test cricket. At Lord's during the 2019 Ashes series, Australia's Marnus Labuschagne replaced Steve Smith as a full substitute after he had been hit on the head by a ball from Jofra Archer.

second Test at the Sydney Cricket Ground today,' he assured his readers. 'It does look as if the team has the batting strength with Lindwall as No.9 and Langley as No.10 to see this match through.' He was not alone. The now somnolent SCG pitch, yellowing in colour like an old newspaper, was reckoned to provide the best reason for Australian optimism and English gloom. The two captains from the previous Ashes series in Australia were in agreement. 'It is not possible to imagine the pace bowlers who comprise England's spearhead causing a rout on this dead-slow wicket,' wrote Lindsay Hassett. Freddie Brown agreed, 'The pitch at the Sydney Cricket Ground has ceased to help pace bowlers.'

But when Len Hutton assessed conditions on arrival at the SCG he found two factors in his team's favour. First, it was a cool day with little prospect of stamina-sapping heat. Second, the wind was blowing straight down the pitch, offering valuable assistance to his fast bowlers. Hutton pondered how best to use the conditions to England's advantage. One way was to deploy his heavy artillery, Frank Tyson and Brian Statham, in short bursts from the Randwick End with the wind at their backs, while instructing Trevor Bailey, Bob Appleyard and the hitherto underemployed Johnny Wardle to apply a tourniquet to the run-rate at the Paddington End. The other was to assail the Australian batsmen with pace from both ends. He chose the latter course. 'Attack with both barrels,' as E. W. Swanton called it.

Tyson was given the wind, Statham asked to operate into it. Godfrey Evans geed up his teammates. 'We shall be there at the finish,' he called out as they walked to the middle. The crowd was sparse, building to just over 14,000, and the Hill around a third full, plenty of room for sunbathers to stretch out either side of the scoreboard. Prime minister Robert Menzies watched from the pavilion, content that matters of state could wait until the end of this enthralling contest. Jim Burke and Neil Harvey middled the first exploratory balls of the morning with an ease that spread reassurance around the home dressing-room. Alan Ross predicted that by tea-time Australia would be 2–0 up. Then Tyson shifted the game – and the destiny of the Ashes – on its axis.

Hutton had seen the portents. 'After one ball Evans and the slips exchanged significant glances and moved back several paces,' he recalled. 'I never saw Evans so far back.' The third ball of Tyson's second over was a yorker of blistering pace that crashed into the base of Burke's off stump. New batsman Graeme Hole lasted four balls before he was victim to the same devastatingly simple ploy. 'Hole was still at the top of his backswing when Frank hit his wickets,' remembered Bob Appleyard. It didn't matter how slow the pitch was – by bowling yorkers, Tyson was taking the surface out of the game. Suddenly, Australia were 77 for four, still 146 short of the finish line.

Hutton still had to conserve the resources of his potential match-winners. Trevor Bailey came on for Statham and, after three more overs, Tyson was replaced by Statham. Soon after Australia had brought the hundred up, Appleyard was given his first opportunity of the day in place of Bailey. He almost bowled Richie Benaud with his first delivery. Harvey and Benaud were both straining against their natural instincts, but Benaud also knew that his best chance of scoring was against the slower bowlers. He tried to sweep the first ball of Appleyard's second over, but succeeded only in top-edging it high into the air, towards Tyson, waiting, Swanton reported, 'In a sort of no-man's land behind the square-leg umpire.'

Possibly Benaud had not seen enough of Appleyard to appreciate his subtleties. 'He varies his pace and makes the ball hold up at the last second before dipping in to the batsman,' said Alan Ross. The ball flew so high that Arthur Gilligan reckoned Tyson would have had time to take his sweater off and still complete the catch. The wind had been a blessing to Tyson when he was bowling, but now, as the ball swirled towards him, it became a hazard. 'There was a heart-stopping moment when I realised I had gauged it wrongly,' he recalled. Sinking to one knee, and with his hands away from his body in defiance of the coaching manual, he clutched the ball. 'At the last moment he lunged forward on bended knee, extending his hands as if for the sacrament. The ball found them miraculously,' wrote Ross. Amid the growing tension, Harvey completed an outstanding fifty off 115 balls. At lunch, Australia were 118 for five, having scored 46 in a morning session of sustained suspense that might have been directed by Alfred Hitchcock.

The interval gave Tyson and Statham a chance to recharge, and Hutton immediately had them back in tandem. It took only until the third over of the new session to reap the benefits. Ron Archer had joined Harvey after Benaud's dismissal, but he had made just six when he shaped to cut a Tyson delivery that jagged back viciously off the seam and plucked out his middle stump. 'All the cricketers in England who had been the victim of Lindwall at his fastest were revenged in that fleeting second,' wrote Margaret Hughes. Archer glared in turn at the pitch and his shattered stumps before departing.

Quickly, things got better still for England. Alan Davidson looked determined to get the scoreboard moving, but the second ball of Statham's next over was a sharp lifter that flew from the edge in the direction of the gap between first and second slip. The need for Bill Edrich or Tom Graveney to go for it was removed when the diving figure of Evans flew across – 'like a bird veering in flight,' thought Tyson from third man – in front of both to clutch the ball in his gloves. For half a second it looked as if it might pop out as he landed heavily on the turf, but he deftly transferred the ball from his left to right hand and clung on, holding it triumphantly aloft as he rolled gymnast-like on the ground. 'The sort of near-impossible wicketkeeping catch which can, and often does, win matches,' wrote Bruce Harris. Ross added, 'Davidson himself might have caught such a catch; if not conceivably anyone else. The ball flew from the bat-maker's name as if it had come in contact with a spring.'

The crowd had been hushed – John Arlott even detected the sound of a crying baby – but there was a buzz of expectation as Ray Lindwall strode out. The renewal of hostilities with Tyson after the previous day's flashpoint was a subject of feverish expectation. Lindwall had made so many critical interventions with the bat on his country's behalf that, at 127 for seven, his partnership with Harvey seemed key to Australia's fading hopes. He quickly collected eight runs off Statham, but then Harvey took a single off the second ball of the next over to bring him into direct opposition with Tyson. The Hill urged Tyson to unleash a retaliatory bouncer. He was more canny than that. The first ball came back sharply off the seam and Lindwall just kept it out. As Tyson walked back to his mark, A.G. Moyes was on the microphone in the Australian Broadcasting Commission commentary box:

There is quite a murmur going around the crowd now as they are probably remembering that yesterday Tyson was unfortunate to get in the way of one from Lindwall. He turned his back completely on a ball that got up and of course we all know that he was knocked out and had to be assisted from the field. Tyson to Lindwall, outside the off stump, AND HE'S BOWLED HIM! It came back on him and knocked his off stump right out of the ground. Lindwall is out, bowled Tyson for eight. Harvey is 55, 10 sundries, and Australia eight for 136. Well that's the fourth time this morning that Tyson has hit the stumps. His figures now five for 54.

But Harvey was still there, now with 55 off 137 balls and producing what many thought was the innings of his life. 'All the time he was playing it in the middle of the bat,' remembered Colin Cowdrey. 'It was one of the greatest innings I have ever seen.' Harvey relished the battle. 'The havoc Tyson was playing with batsmen at the other end seemed to bring out the best in me,' he wrote in his autobiography. The rush of wickets since lunch had brought the visitors to life. 'Every time a wicket fell, we rushed around the dressing-room hugging each other and making the most awful din,' said Geoffrey Howard. It was all too much for Jim McConnon, who shut himself in the toilets until the match was over. The frenetic atmosphere also got to the scoreboard operators. At one point the name of Dr F. Rosati appeared in the slot reserved for Australia's next batsman. Dr Rosati was merely being asked to report to the main gate.

Harvey had given a masterclass in keeping the strike and shielding his partners, but with eight men out and Australia still 87 short of their target, the time now came to attack. Some felt Harvey could have taken the initiative earlier, others that Benaud, Archer, Davidson and Lindwall should have been instructed to occupy the sheet-anchor role while Harvey went on the offensive. Now he began to turn down singles and find the boundary more frequently. 'The more desperate the situation became for Australia, the more devastating was Harvey,' Hutton recalled. Gil Langley did not offer much support. The eighth ball he faced was a devastating inswinger from Statham that snapped the base of the off stump.

Best Match Figures by an England Bowler at the Sydney Cricket Ground

Wickets	Bowler	Overs	Balls per over	Runs	Series
11	M.W.Tate	89	8	228	1924–25
10	G.A. Lohmann	67.1	4	87	1886–87
10	H. Larwood	49	6	124	1932–33
10	**F.H. Tyson**	**31.4**	**8**	**130**	**1954–55**
10	G.A. Lohmann	94.2	6	142	1891–92
10	T. Richardson	57.5	6	204	1897–98
10	A.R. Caddick	45	6	215	2002–03
9	G.A. Lohmann	51	4	52	1887–88
9	R. Peel	51.3	4	58	1887–88
9	J.T. Hearne	58.1	6	141	1897–98
9	A. Fielder	57.5	6	170	1907–08
9	D.V.P. Wright	51	8	198	1946–47
9	M.W.Tate	79	8	207	1924–25

Last man Bill Johnston walked to the crease – 'all arms and legs in comic discordance,' wrote Woodcock – alongside an umpire carrying a replacement stump. 'An embarrassing accompaniment,' said Ross. Johnston's bat, bound together with tape, looked like a museum exhibit, but he proudly boasted that it was the one he had used while topping the averages on the 1953 Ashes tour. In 17 innings, Johnston had hit 102 runs and been dismissed only once. Three years earlier, at Melbourne, he had put on 38 for the last wicket with Doug Ring to steer Australia to a one-wicket win over West Indies. 'Nor is Johnston nearly such a duffer with the bat as his general deportment and expressions of comic bewilderment convey,' said Swanton. England were not home yet.

Ramping up the tension further, there was a delay while drinks were taken. Harold Dalton, the MCC masseur, had been extolling the virtues of the sherry-and-eggs concoction he had been mixing up for Tyson and Statham. Vic Wilson brought out swiftly prepared tumblers of the sticky mixture for Hutton's strike bowlers. An invigorated Statham came close to dismissing Johnston with the first three balls he faced. Off the final delivery of the over, the No.11 wanted a single, but Harvey loudly turned him down. Australia needed 78. For context, the highest 10th-wicket partnership to win a Test match at this point was 48 by South Africa's Dave Nourse and Percy Sherwell against England at the Old Wanderers in Johannesburg in January 1906.[32]

Harvey chose this moment to launch a thrilling assault on Tyson, taking 11 off the next over, including a hooked four that bounced clear of Trevor Bailey's grasp at long leg. Harvey made no contact with the final ball of the over, but, by pre-arrangement with Johnston, ran anyway and scampered home. Under pressure, England's fielding was creaking again. 'There were not many agile athletes among us,' admitted May. Statham bowled an exemplary over that cost just two and, before the final ball, Evans came up to the stumps to prevent another scrambled single. Not that Johnston seemed to mind facing Tyson. He flicked the first ball one-handed off his hip for four with what Swanton called 'a gesture of superb disdain', then stole a single off the second.

No quantity of sherry and eggs could disguise the fact that Tyson and Statham were labouring. 'I'll try to hang around, at least for your hundred, because I think Frank's had it,' Johnston remembered saying to Harvey. Hutton had key decisions to make. Statham was now running in from the Paddington End like a commuter forlornly chasing a bus accelerating away into the distance. After a spell of 6–1–17–2, he was rested, but when he was replaced by Bailey, Harvey's eyes lit up. The second ball was driven back over Bailey's head for four. A pull-drive off the seventh penetrated a one-saving field and also found the boundary. 'Another quarter of an hour of Harvey in this form would have meant acute crisis, if not actual defeat,' thought Ian Peebles.

Harvey could not conjure a single off the last ball, however, giving Tyson another crack at Johnston. The last pair had put on 35 in almost 40 minutes. Near exhaustion meant it would have to be his last, but Hutton persuaded Tyson to have one more over. Statham approached his partner: 'Try one a little closer to his body and a little shorter, Frank.' Moyes was back behind the ABC microphone:

---

[32]The record is now 78 by Sri Lanka against South Africa at Durban in 2019. During the Ashes series later that year, Ben Stokes and Jack Leach scored 76 for the last wicket to take England to a thrilling victory.

Here's Tyson to Johnston – Johnston plays a one-handed shot, it's a tennis shot that goes straight through to the fence for four. Crashing against the boundary, right in front of the main pavilion stand. Now Johnston is 11, Harvey is 92, 10 sundries, nine wickets down for 184. Somebody please pass a nerve tonic. [laughter in the commentary box.] Here's Tyson to Johnston, Johnston tried to play the same type of shot and he's touched it and he's caught by Evans, and the match is all over. There's an appeal and Johnston is out caught Evans, bowled Tyson for 11, England wins, Australia dismissed for 184. Congratulations England, England levelling now the Test series.

England had won by 38 runs. Tyson and Statham walked off side by side, captured in one of cricket's most famous photographs. At the pavilion gate, Statham stood back to let his partner walk in first, while Tyson insisted they should exit together. After a little pantomime dance, Tyson led the way. More than one visiting journalist remarked that while the game may not look all that close on the scorecard, that was not how it had felt in the last gripping hours of a classic Test match. Menzies was the first visitor to the jubilant England dressing-room. 'England deserved to win,' he said. 'But I'll always remember this match for the courage, sustained stamina and determination of Frank Tyson. It was one of the finest exhibitions of courageous fast bowling I have ever seen and I am glad it had a just reward.'

The captains were equally effusive. 'It was a great exhibition of fast bowling by Tyson and Statham. They are young men of character, you know, as well as of bowling ability,' said Hutton. 'A fine show of fast bowling by Tyson and Statham,' said Arthur Morris. 'Tyson has a lot of guts. He was always a menace to the batsmen.' Australia's captain also paid glowing tribute to Harvey's defiance. 'Harvey was one of the heroes of an epic,' wrote Hutton later. But Harvey was more rueful: 'We should have got them and got them easily.'

Once the clamour had subsided and the only sound around the SCG was the hammering of typewriters in the press box and the incessant hum of nearby telegraph machines, many reflected that England's stirring win was not merely founded on the bowling of Tyson and Statham. In the first innings Wardle and Statham had added 43 for the last wicket; in the second Appleyard and Statham made 46. Those partnerships had laid the foundations of victory.

For the Australian writer R.S. Whitington: 'This was a day to remember, like the days at Edgbaston and Old Trafford must have been in 1902,' he wrote, 'the kind of day that lifts cricket, Mount Everest-like, above most other games men play.'

Peter May and Colin Cowdrey leave the field during the partnership that turned the match in England's favour.

Frank Tyson goes down in a heap after being hit on the head by a bouncer from Ray Lindwall.

SECOND TEST

Sydney Cricket Ground   17, 18, 20, 21, 22 December, 1954

ENGLAND FIRST INNINGS

			Balls	Mins	4s	6s	Out at
*L. Hutton	c Davidson b Johnston	30	105	132	3	—	3/58
T.E. Bailey	b Lindwall	0	28	37	—	—	1/14
P.B.H. May	c Johnston b Archer	5	18	12	—	—	2/19
T.W. Graveney	c Favell b Johnston	21	74	88	1	—	4/63
M.C. Cowdrey	c Langley b Davidson	23	71	76	1	—	8/99
W.J. Edrich	c Benaud b Archer	10	23	21	1	—	5/84
F.H. Tyson	b Lindwall	0	13	14	—	—	6/85
†T.G. Evans	c Langley b Archer	3	3	3	—	—	7/88
J.H. Wardle	c Burke b Johnston	35	62	70	5	—	
R. Appleyard	c Hole b Davidson	8	17	20	—	—	9/111
J.B. Statham	not out	14	18	23	—	—	10/154
Extras	5 lb	5					
All out (54.3 overs, 257 mins)		**154**					

ENGLAND SECOND INNINGS

			Balls	Mins	4s	6s	Out at
*L. Hutton	c Benaud b Johnston	28	54	77	4	–	2/55
T.E. Bailey	c Langley b Archer	6	33	36	–	–	1/18
P.B.H. May	b Lindwall	104	287	298	10	–	5/222
T.W. Graveney	c Langley b Johnston	0	3	2	–	–	3/55
M.C. Cowdrey	c Archer b Benaud	54	182	193	6	–	4/171
W.J. Edrich	b Archer	29	109	96	4	–	6/232
F.H. Tyson	b Lindwall	9	37	43	1	–	7/239
†T.G. Evans	c Lindwall b Archer	4	10	23	–	–	8/249
J.H. Wardle	lbw b Lindwall	8	19	25	–	–	9/250
R. Appleyard	not out	19	64	63	1	–	
J.B. Statham	c Langley b Johnston	25	39	53	5	–	10/296
Extras	6 lb, 4 nb	10					
All out (104.3 overs, 463 mins)		**296**					

AUSTRALIA BOWLING

Lindwall	17	3	47	2	31	10	69	3
Archer	12	7	12	3	22	9	53	3
Davidson	12	3	34	2	13	2	52	0
Johnston	13.3	1	56	3	19.3	2	70	3
Benaud					19	3	42	1

Australia won the toss and decided to field   Hours of play: 11.30 a.m.–5.30 p.m.
Umpires: R.J.J.Wright (Victoria), M.J. McInnes (South Australia)

AUSTRALIA FIRST INNINGS

			Balls	Minutes	Fours	Sixes	Out at
L.E. Favell	c Graveney b Bailey	26	45	58	2	–	2/65
*A.R. Morris	c Hutton b Bailey	12	15	18	2	–	1/18
J.W. Burke	c Graveney b Bailey	44	87	105	1	–	3/100
R.N. Harvey	c Cowdrey b Tyson	12	43	72	–	–	4/104
G.B. Hole	b Tyson	12	23	31	1	–	5/122
R. Benaud	lbw b Statham	20	51	64	2	–	6/141
R.G. Archer	c Hutton b Tyson	49	89	128	6	1	8/213
A.K. Davidson	b Statham	20	56	60	2	–	7/193
R.R. Lindwall	c Evans b Tyson	19	23	37	2	–	9/224
†G.R.A. Langley	b Bailey	5	12	21	1	–	10/228
W.A. Johnston	not out	0	6	8	–	–	
Extras	5 b, 2 lb, 2 nb	9					
All out (55.4 overs, 310 mins)		**228**					

AUSTRALIA SECOND INNINGS

			Balls	Minutes	Fours	Sixes	Out at
L.E. Favell	c Edrich b Tyson	16	27	32	2	–	2/34
*A.R. Morris	lbw b Statham	10	16	25	1	–	1/27
J.W. Burke	b Tyson	14	88	102	1	–	3/77
R.N. Harvey	not out	92	190	251	9	–	
G.B. Hole	b Tyson	0	4	4	–	–	4/77
R. Benaud	c Tyson b Appleyard	12	47	51	–	–	5/102
R.G. Archer	b Tyson	6	19	27	–	–	6/122
R.K. Davidson	c Evans b Statham	5	6	5	–	–	7/127
R.R. Lindwall	b Tyson	8	8	9	1	–	8/136
†G.R.A. Langley	b Statham	0	8	13	–	–	9/145
W.A. Johnston	c Evans b Statham	11	17	40	2	–	10/184
Extras	7 lb, 3 nb	10					
All out (53.4 overs, 293 mins)		**184**					

ENGLAND BOWLING

Statham	18	1	83	2	19	6	45	3
Bailey	17.4	3	59	4	6	0	21	0
Tyson	13	2	45	4	18.4	1	85	6
Appleyard	7	1	32	0	6	1	12	1
Wardle					4	2	11	0

ENGLAND WON BY 38 RUNS

The match was scheduled for six days but completed in five

Attendances: First day: 23,312. Second day: 44,879. Third day: 31,679. Fourth day: 20,909. Fifth day: 14,575.

Total: 135,354

Twelfth men: W.J. Watson (Australia), J.V. Wilson (England).

Sources: Barry Valentine, Charles Davis (sportsstats.com.au), cricketarchive.com, Richard Cashman

They have been thousands of miles from home, but the England players enjoyed a riotous Christmas lunch at the Oceanic Hotel in Coogee.

VI

CRACKS APPEAR IN MELBOURNE

'I don't think I can play today, I'm not feeling too well'
        Len Hutton on the opening morning of the third Test

'At times he looked like Hutton and at others like Hammond'
                        John Arlott salutes England's
                young century-maker, Colin Cowdrey

'One of the greatest Test bowling performances of all time'
        Bill O'Reilly on Frank Tyson's match-winning spell

CHRISTMAS DOWN UNDER

Geoffrey Howard was not looking forward to Christmas. The MCC manager wrote home on 24 December – a day of oppressive heat and humidity in Sydney – making the observation that Australians' main contribution to the festive season appeared to be 'a very considerable over-consumption of beer'. Frank Tyson had fitted in some shopping with his girlfriend from the *Orsova*, Margaret. 'Every shop in every street seems to have a loudspeaker, each providing a different contribution to the conflicting cacophony of carols,' he recalled in his tour memoir. Christmas Eve was Colin Cowdrey's 22nd birthday, a poignant moment given the death of his father three months earlier. As if he did not already have enough to do, Howard carried in his briefcase a list of people to whom he was expected to send official Christmas cards from the team. They included the Earl of Rosebery and Viscount Cobham, incumbent and future presidents of MCC, the former England captain Douglas Jardine, and senior figures at the Orient Line and the British Overseas Airways Corporation.

Christmas Eve provided the highlight of the holiday for Tyson. Along with baggage-master George Duckworth he boarded a bone-shaking tram to the Sydney suburb of Kensington to visit the neat bungalow that was the home of Harold Larwood and his family. Larwood, who had just turned 50, had been the spearhead of England's pace attack in the Bodyline series 22 years earlier. Though a demonised figure in Australia at the time, he had emigrated in 1950, finding a warm welcome and making a contented new life. Duckworth, a teammate on that tempestuous tour, stopped off en route to pick up bottles of beer. The *Manchester Evening News* had already dubbed Tyson 'the Larwood of 1954', and they toasted his success at the SCG. 'Harold said he admired me – but I admired him more,' Tyson wrote. As they left, Larwood told him, 'When you hear 50,000 Aussies shouting at you, you know you've got 'em worried.'

The team spent Christmas Day at the Oceanic Hotel in Coogee, their base since arriving in Sydney. Cowdrey was up early to attend a service at a local church. When they had stayed at the Oceanic the previous month during the State match against New South Wales, Howard had complained about the slow service. So it proved again: by the time the Christmas lunch was ready, the waiters had gone home. The players, many already well refreshed, didn't mind at all. 'A hilarious party. Best to draw a curtain over it. Just say it was hilarious,' Howard remembered. These high-spirited occasions were not to the liking of Len Hutton, though he probably recognised the benefits to morale. More than one player remembered him enduring rather than enjoying the horseplay.

After lunch, some of the team made their way to the beach. Duckworth was recognised by the lifeguards, all fellow rugby league enthusiasts, and they conspired to play a prank on Norman Preston, the editor of *Wisden*, who was happily enjoying a swim. 'Let's have an incident,' Duckworth said to his friends. 'Go and pick up Norman as though he were in trouble.' Preston was dragged from the water, loudly protesting that he was perfectly all right.

It was not all fun and games. 'For the individual, Christmas can be hard to manage on tour,' wrote John Woodcock of *The Times*. The MCC party had been away from their families for more than three months, with another three remaining. Wives and children had recorded messages for the players. Brian Statham discovered that his baby son, Terence, had cut his first tooth. 'I was thrilled beyond measure to hear the voices of my wife and two sons sending me Christmas greetings,' Johnny Wardle remembered. 'It made me feel, without a shadow of a doubt, that the right place for a husband and father at Christmas time is at home with his family.'

Bob Appleyard had made a recording which was transferred to a 78 r.p.m. vinyl disc and delivered to his wife and daughters in Bradford in time for the holiday; it remained a treasured family keepsake. 'Hallo, Connie. Hallo, Rosemarie and Elizabeth. What a thrill this gives me,' Appleyard said. 'Thinking of you and the children in our own home gives me the nearest image of the festive season. I feel so happy that my voice is amongst you now. It's a very full life we lead here, but it could not quite make up for moments such as these.' Hutton was not the only one who found the drunken jollity and the late-arriving turkey a trial. 'It was the worst Christmas Day I have ever had,' Appleyard told his biographer, Stephen Chalke.

The *People* Sunday newspaper arranged for Tyson to speak to his mother Violet at home in Middleton via radio-telephone. At a distance of 10,000 miles, and with journalists hovering in the background at both ends of the line, it was a stilted six-minute exchange, but one that nevertheless cheered them both up. 'Congratulations, love, we're all very proud of you in Middleton and everywhere else,' said Violet. When the call ended, she wiped tears from her eyes.

In 33 years as a cricket correspondent, Woodcock would become familiar with spending the festive season in a hot climate. 'Partly because it is the height of summer, Christmas in Sydney or Melbourne or Johannesburg or Adelaide has an unreality that carols piped into the hotel lift and cardboard reindeer suspended from the ceiling are unable to dispel,' he wrote in 1981. Woodcock's friend Alan Ross spent Christmas Day with friends at Palm Beach and noted how the spread of suburban bungalows was beginning to rob the area of much of its natural beauty. 'Their houses are whimsical, their shopping centres heavy with the stench of petrol and exhausts,' he wrote.

On Boxing Day morning hangovers were being nursed. Dr John Butterfield's 'Cricket in Hot Climates' report, prepared for the benefit of the players, dealt with the subject of recovery from alcoholic excess. He had several tips, including delaying the first cigarette of the day when hungover. 'After liberal hospitality, try to prevent hangover by drinking more than 1 pint of fruit juice, or more than 1 pint of water + 1 salt tablet,' Butterfield wrote. 'This must be done before going to bed, after the party. Empty your bladder before going to bed.' There followed his bullet-point advice: 'If you have a hangover in the morning – 1. Take two Alka Seltzers in water or crush two aspirins in water + salt tablet; 2. Drink a lot of water; 3. Try to take some breakfast; 4. Lie down for half-hour after breakfast; 5. Don't smoke yet.' He added, 'Remember, a hangover means that the body needs: 1. Water, lots; 2. Salt; 3. Something to soothe the stomach, head; 4. Probably more rest.'

Butterfield's report had been mailed to Howard from Lord's and arrived during the Brisbane Test. 'I very much enjoyed reading the pamphlet on cricket in hot climates and will take the first opportunity that arises to let the boys have the benefit of it,' he wrote to MCC assistant secretary Billy Griffith. 'I shall obviously have to spend a little time abbreviating it or I shall get howled down!'

It may have been the second hangover of the week for some. On the evening after their series-equalling victory in the second Test, the whole squad had been treated to dinner at Prince's in Martin Place, one of Sydney's swankiest restaurants, by Henry Sayen, a millionaire American businessman who had become an unofficial mascot to the team. Sayen, born in Pennsylvania and resident in New Jersey, had made seven first-class appearances, including one for the Gentlemen of England, in the English summer of 1908. In 1953 he had attracted considerable publicity after attending the drawn Lord's Test against Australia. 'Somehow the newspaper boys had got on to my "Gentlemen of England" record and the idea of a Yankee coming to London just to watch a single game of cricket tickled their fancies no end,' Sayen recalled.

MCC had rolled out the red carpet, offering not only a five-day pass to the pavilion, but opportunities to wine and dine with many of the great and good of the game. Sayen became fast friends with secretary Ronny Aird. On the final morning of the match – his passage home on the *Queen Mary* was booked for the following day – with England facing defeat, he asked if he could address the team in the dressing-room. 'I apologised for offering an unknown Yank's opinions upon them and then I explained my little scheme for easing up the tension of such a grim situation.'

Sayen offered a range of financial incentives, including £5 for any player making a fifty and a $500 bonus if the team turned the situation around and won the match. They did not quite manage that, but a heroic rearguard action ensured England escaped with a draw and Trevor Bailey and Willie Watson collected their fivers. Sayen – 'an evangelist aflame with the thrill of his cause,' said Alec Bedser – was thrilled. 'Like going to the races and trying to lose,' he said. His talismanic qualities had also been on display before the final must-win Test in Jamaica in the 1953–54 series. Once more, he set out a range of cash bonuses for stand-out performances, doubling the sums on the last day, and was happy to pay out when Hutton's epic double-century set up England's victory. He even had to dash back to the hotel when his wad of dollar bills threatened to run out.

With his deep pockets and status as a lucky charm, it is not surprising that everyone was delighted to see Sayen arrive in Sydney. He had been in touch with Hutton before the opening Test. 'I believe that Len has heard from Henry Sayen offering $20 to the chap who tries hardest in the Test match,' Howard wrote to Aird. 'If he had sent it to the person who is most trying it could have been awarded forthwith!'

Sayen was travelling against medical advice after recently undergoing major surgery and had to abandon plans to watch the third Test. Normal protocols about outsiders in the dressing-room were abandoned for Sayen and the Australian press proved as curious about his cricket obsession as their Fleet Street counterparts had been in 1953. His dining companions included prime minister Robert Menzies and Sir Donald Bradman. Sayen sent a wreath to the grave of Victor Trumper and was caricatured by Arthur Mailey, the former Test leg-spinner who was a talented cartoonist. As Australian wickets fell on the final day, Sayen danced delighted jigs with Aird. But no amount of pleading could persuade him to extend his stay. 'I was feeling pretty unwell and I felt that if it meant I had to die, I had better be at home for it,' he said.

HOW DO YOU SOLVE A PROBLEM LIKE ALEC?

Hangovers or not, most of the team had to be up on Boxing Day morning for the trip to the coal-mining town of Newcastle. The three-day match against Northern New South Wales had been shorn of first-class status, but was a fixture of significance for two of the biggest names in the MCC squad. Neither Alec Bedser, now recovered from shingles, nor Denis Compton, whose broken finger had healed, had played since the first Test a month earlier. Both needed to prove their readiness for the third, beginning at Melbourne on New Year's Eve.

Not all the players travelled – Len Hutton handed captaincy duties to Peter May – and on 27 December, while the opening overs were being bowled 100 miles away in Newcastle, Hutton accompanied Frank Tyson, Brian Statham, Trevor Bailey, Keith Andrew and Geoffrey Howard to the White City Stadium in Sydney's Rushcutters Bay, where Australia's tennis players were taking on the United States in the final of the Davis Cup. It was one of Howard's great talents as a manager, deeply appreciated by the players, that he was able to arrange treats on this scale. 'To get tickets for even one day is like winning the lottery,' Tyson said.

Fuelled by the emergence of brilliant young players Ken Rosewall and Lew Hoad, both members of the Davis Cup team, interest in tennis in Australia was at an all-time high – inducing anxiety in cricket administrators – and the match attracted a daily attendance of 25,578, then a record for the competition. Once again demonstrating his deft touch when it came to sport, prime minister Robert Menzies had made the draw for the singles on court on Christmas Day. Australia had won the tournament for the previous three years, but they were about to surrender their crown to the Americans. 'The loss of the Davis Cup was a much bigger blow than the defeat of their cricketers at The Oval in Coronation year, because really they are a nation of tennis players,' wrote Margaret Hughes. It put pressure on Australia's cricketers to restore national prestige.

Several English journalists did not make the trip to Newcastle – the *Times* sports desk sent Woodcock to cover the Davis Cup – but the agency dispatches conveyed good news about Compton, who made a fluent 60 before being stumped. The news on Bedser was initially less reassuring. When May won the toss and put Northern New South Wales in, Bedser was given the new ball but had to labour into a wind that was stiff enough to blow the bails off three times. He was given just 10 overs and took a solitary wicket.

In MCC's response to Northern NSW's 211, May scored a brilliant hundred, his fifth of the tour and his fourth in successive matches, and there were encouraging signs of progress in Bedser's rehabilitation in the second innings. He took three for 18 in a devastating spell. Writing in the *Newcastle Sun*, the distinguished Australian writer Ray Robinson said, 'The ball which bowled Roger Wotton was a leg-cutter which pitched on the middle and leg stumps and hit the top of off stump – a Bedser special which has dismissed many famous batsmen, including Sir Don Bradman and Lindsay Hassett.'[33] It was reported that May then took Bedser off so that he did not finish the match off too quickly and deprive the locals of entertainment. His replacement, Johnny Wardle, came in for heavy punishment.

On the third day, MCC completed a nine-wicket win and then travelled back to Sydney to rejoin their teammates. That night, the squad boarded an overnight train to Melbourne, arriving just as

---

[33]Bedser had bowled Bradman for a duck at Adelaide in the 1946–47 series with a ball which the Australian reckoned was the best to take his wicket in his career.

the city streets were coming to life. They checked in to the elegant surroundings of the Windsor Hotel and, following a rest and lunch, the players strolled over to the Melbourne Cricket Ground for afternoon nets. This crowded programme was hardly the ideal preparation for a critical Test match starting the next day, a point made forcibly by Howard in his end-of-tour report to MCC. Their earlier visit for the state game against Victoria had prepared them for the scale of the venue, but it still inspired awe. 'After the building congestion which surrounds most of England's major cricket grounds, the vastness of Australian sporting venues is an eye-opener,' wrote Tyson. 'Not only are the playing areas larger, but the parking areas for cars are far more extensive. Everything is on a bigger scale.'

Hutton was visibly distracted, lost in thoughts on selection and strategy. The fibrositis which had plagued him during the English summer had returned to add to his woes. He had also developed a heavy cold. The sense of expectation around the remaining Tests had been cranked up since England's win in Sydney. At 1-1 with three to play, a contest for the ages was developing, but that only increased the pressure on the principal performers.

Both teams named 12 players. Australia had made three changes. Ian Johnson returned to the captaincy while Keith Miller took over the all-rounder's slot from Alan Davidson. Miller, out of action since the first Test, was still suffering with a knee injury and harboured grave doubts about his ability to bowl more than a few overs, but his talismanic properties were such that the selectors were prepared to take the gamble. There was also a new wicketkeeper. Gil Langley, whose clean glovework had earned plaudits at Sydney, suffered an eye injury from a flying bail during Queensland's match against South Australia over Christmas and was ruled out. Len Maddocks of Victoria was called up as a replacement. The slightly built Maddocks, 28, did not have Langley's wicketkeeping polish, but would bolster the batting.

For England, Compton replaced Tom Graveney, while Bill Edrich, despite being wretchedly out of form, was chosen to open the innings with Hutton after the failure of the experiment with Trevor Bailey. The news of Edrich's promotion provoked a furious reaction from the overlooked Reg Simpson. Bedser remained in the squad, his return on his favourite ground, probably in place of Johnny

Wardle, widely taken as read. 'I do not think that any sensations need be expected this time regarding England's most famous bowler,' wrote Swanton. 'To leave Bedser out at Sydney was one thing and sufficiently grave at that; to dispense with his services on this ground is another matter.' Bill O'Reilly agreed: 'I take it for granted that Bedser will play tomorrow for the one overpowering reason that the England selectors could not be half so foolish again as they were in Sydney.'

But Bedser was not sure he enjoyed his captain's full confidence. On the third morning at Newcastle, he had fallen into conversation with E.M. Wellings of the *Evening News*. 'He was a worried and depressed man,' wrote Wellings. 'Not enough people had expressed faith in him, though I was able to tell him that there were still quite a lot of us who regarded him as the world's number one bowler. And despite the success of Tyson and Statham in Sydney, that was indeed my view of his prowess.'

In a tight-knit squad of players, Bedser must have been sensing the mood. Publicly, Hutton remained supportive, privately, he was having his doubts. 'The thought that Alec might not be up to his best owing to his illness, and past his peak owing to length of service, was unpalatable and hard to face,' wrote *The Sunday Times* correspondent Ian Peebles. 'Yet everyone was uncomfortably aware that the moment must come when that life and fire which comes from youthful elasticity diminishes, and the bowler of pace knows that nothing can replace it.' Those words encapsulated Hutton's deepening concerns. In his final autobiography, *Fifty Years in Cricket*, published in 1984, Hutton claimed he first began to suspect that Bedser's powers were waning while on the voyage to Australia.

Hutton set great store by the cricketing wisdom of baggage-master and scorer George Duckworth. 'George drew my attention to the number of no-balls Alec bowled, which suggested he was untypically straining to get to the wicket. Also, although he was still a fine catcher in the gully positions, he was rather slow in the field.' Duckworth was convinced there was a historical precedent for Bedser's decline. On the Bodyline tour 22 years earlier, Maurice Tate of Sussex, a medium-pace bowler of the same type as Bedser, had been selected alongside the pace quartet of Harold Larwood, Bill Voce, Bill Bowes and Gubby Allen. Tate had taken 55 Test wickets in Australia and inspired similar levels of respect as Bedser. Under Douglas Jardine, like Hutton convinced that outright pace was the best means of victory in Australia, Tate was not selected throughout the series. On the follow-up tour of New Zealand, a selector told him he was 'getting too old'. Duckworth could not help but divine a link between Tate and Bedser. As Hutton sank deeper into contemplation, the fate of one of England's greatest servants remained uppermost in his conflicted thoughts.

A MORNING OF DRAMA – AND REGRETS

Within a few short hours on the morning of New Year's Eve 1954, a series of events occurred at the Windsor Hotel and at the Melbourne Cricket Ground that remain some of the most extensively chronicled and pored over in the history of Ashes cricket. Yet there remain grey areas, elements not wholly understood, and confusion among some of those who were closest to an unfolding but largely unseen drama. In many subsequent accounts, failing memories, self-serving half-truths and sloppy ghostwriting have led to the historical record being seriously flawed.

The most consistently reliable version came from MCC tour manager Geoffrey Howard in his 2001 memoir *At the Heart of English Cricket*, written by Stephen Chalke. Howard, then 90 but with a pin-sharp memory, recalled an early-morning visit to Len Hutton's room. The England captain, wearing a woollen vest, was sitting upright in bed, staring blankly at the wall. 'I don't think I can play today, I'm not feeling too well,' he said. A doctor was called, but he could find nothing to prevent Hutton playing in the Test match. By this time a small gathering had formed around the bed – baggage-master George Duckworth and the senior players Denis Compton, Bill Edrich and Godfrey Evans. Masseur Harold Dalton also made an appearance – 'LH very queer,' he noted in his diary.

'He seemed to be on the verge of cracking up. It was difficult to know what was in his mind, but he told us he didn't feel very well, thought he had a temperature – it might be better if he didn't play,' Evans recalled. 'We told him he must play,' Compton added. 'He seemed to be in a very disturbed state indeed as if suddenly things had got too much for him and he couldn't or wouldn't go on. Bill Edrich, Godfrey Evans and myself stood and sat around his bed in some bewilderment and dismay.' Edrich persuaded Hutton to order room-service breakfast and eventually, without yet committing to playing, he was coaxed into a car bound for the MCG.

There was irony in the identity of the teammates now imploring Hutton to play. The previous evening, the captain had been sipping coffee in the hotel foyer with fellow Yorkshireman Bob Appleyard. 'Denis Compton, Godfrey Evans and Bill Edrich came down the steps all dressed up,' Appleyard remembered. 'This was the night before the Test match. Len said, "Look at those three, they're going out and the excuse will be that they've got to relax before a match." Then he said, "This is the time to be thinking about the match." And he was.'

It was not unusual for Hutton to be overwrought on the eve of a Test. 'Hutton was the greatest worrier I ever met,' wrote Jim Laker. 'Just before the start of a Test match he used to live on his nerves in a way which was alarming to watch. It wouldn't surprise me to learn that he was up half the night before a Test because he could often have a sharply nervous edge on the first morning.' There is no question, Hutton was feeling the strain. 'Mine is not always a very pleasant job,' he had told reporters in Sydney. The endless round of social events, speeches, press conferences, concern about the team, not to mention his lack of runs, was exacting a heavy toll. And, at the halfway point in the tour, he was feeling as acutely homesick as any of the players under his command. 'He relied a great deal on Dorothy and, by Melbourne, he was missing her terribly,' said Howard. 'There were times on the tour when I had to pack his bags for him because he wasn't ready.'

Whatever these multiple issues, Howard was convinced one problem was at the heart of the captain's personal trauma – how to tell Alec Bedser he was not playing in the third Test. When the players had left the bedroom, Howard said quietly, 'If you like, I will tell Alec.' But Hutton insisted, 'No, it's my job.' Time was running short. Fortunately, the Melbourne Test started at midday, with the naming of teams half an hour earlier. That 30-minute window was a boon to the panicked England management and senior players. Hutton had still not said he would play. 'We don't care a bugger what you do Leonard, but you must go out on to that field,' Evans told him bluntly. Several accounts give the unsung Duckworth the most credit for cajoling Hutton out of his room.

On arrival at the ground, Edrich and Evans took Hutton out to look at the pitch – 'a brown strip of plastered marl and soil on which the battle would soon be joined,' John Kay told *Manchester Evening News* readers. Hutton returned looking 'rather doleful', added Kay. Back in the dressing-room, Hutton asked Bedser, Compton and Trevor Bailey to conduct their own inspection. 'I assumed wrongly that the attack had been restructured for me to play,' Bedser recalled in 1986. Compton remembered Bedser pressing his thumb into the pitch and saying, 'Yes, I reckon I can bowl well on that. I'd like to play.' He then made an un-Bedser-like additional comment, 'If I do, I'll be trying.' Compton added, 'It was always a certainty that Alec would be trying.'

It must have been when Hutton got back to the dressing-room that he relented. 'All right, I'll play,' he told Edrich and Evans. By the time Bedser, Compton and Bailey returned from the middle, the England team had been pinned up on the back of the door. 'It's a vivid picture in my mind,' Howard said. 'I'd been delayed at the hotel and I'd only just arrived. Alec was standing in front of the door on one side, Johnny Wardle on the other. They were both changed and ready, both with their blazers on, looking at the list to see who was playing.' Wardle was in, Bedser was out.

Alec Bedser lived to be 91 – 'It is as if an old and mighty oak tree has fallen at last,' Christopher Martin-Jenkins wrote in *The Times* on his death in 2010 – his place in cricket history, and more especially in Ashes lore, unchallenged. But he never forgot that moment in the visitors' dressing-room at Melbourne, nor did he forgive Hutton for failing to complete the apparently simple task of telling him in advance. 'I don't mind being left out, but I want to be told,' Bedser told Hutton's biographer, Donald Trelford. 'He didn't like to tell you. That's what it amounted to really.' Howard agreed: 'Len knew he was going to hurt Alec and Len didn't like hurting people.' Howard believed he should have insisted on being the one to break the news.

The incident reheated the debate about the inherent differences between amateur and professional captains. That may explain why Edrich, the amateur captain of Middlesex, also offered to break the news to Bedser. In Australia four years earlier, MCC had been led by the amateur, Freddie Brown. Howard added, 'If Freddie had been captain he'd have taken Alec to one side on the eve of the match. "I'm afraid I'm going to have to leave you out", he'd have said, and Alec would have accepted it ... Alec was used to the master-servant relationship. It was much harder to take from Len.'

The tour selection committee had initially been enthusiastic about recalling Bedser, but quickly saw that finding a place in the team for him was an intractable problem. Wardle may have been underused in the second Test, but on a Melbourne pitch expected to break up on the last two days his wrist-spin had match-winning potential. After Brisbane, no one was keen to deploy four seamers again and it was unthinkable to jettison Tyson, Statham or Bailey.

All the senior players thought Bedser should be left out. The final decision, however, remained with Hutton. He had confided in his close friend, J.M. Kilburn of the *Yorkshire Post*. 'I knew he was being dropped before Bedser did,' Kilburn wrote. 'Len wasn't always as tactful as he might have been because he was shy of doing what he had to do. Leonard couldn't bring himself to do it.'

Hutton later wrote that he detected a lack of confidence in Bedser that morning, but he also accepted that the issue could have been better handled. 'Alec Bedser emerged from the inevitable discussions surrounding his omission with much sympathy,' he said. 'For his sake I was glad he did not reach the stage where he came in for criticism, because of any deterioration in his own splendid record of bowling performances.' In his book *Twin Ambitions*, Bedser wrote, 'Len had said nothing to me about his intentions. I wished he had. He has since told me and has written in his book that he agonised over the decision and if he could have the chance of a "replay" he would act differently and at least put me in the picture. I honour Len for being so frank.'

When the England team news was conveyed to the press box, Hutton was sharply criticised. 'He [Bedser] had been too great a cricketer to be treated in this way,' wrote John Arlott. The Australian A.G. Moyes added, 'A man who has done as much for England as Bedser deserved something better than to be thrown aside like an old cricket boot.' In *The Times*, John Woodcock said, 'England entered the match without Bedser, whose dismissal for an unsuccessful spinner seems precipitate and hard to reconcile.'

Others were more reluctant to condemn. Former England captain Arthur Gilligan wrote, 'Trying to put myself in Len Hutton's position, I realised the skipper's anxiety to have a balanced attack. Tragic it was to see Big Alec as a spectator. I feel that in view of the success of Tyson and Statham at Sydney, there was no room for him in the team.' Peebles did not think Bedser had been dealt with unfairly. 'It had to be remembered that until the last moment it was an evenly balanced question as to whether or not he would play,' he said. 'It is difficult to see why his inclusion in the 12 should have been an indignity.'

The story had one unexpected postscript. In a number of books published subsequent to the tour, the story of Bedser's dramatic axing and its clumsy handling has been relocated to Sydney. It is true that he was in the 12 for the second Test, and also that he conducted an inspection of the pitch before the toss, but he had been forewarned by Hutton that he would not play and accepted that his recovery from shingles was not sufficiently advanced. It was at Melbourne that time was effectively called on the career of one of England's greatest cricketers.

A STAR IS BORN

John Woodcock told *Times* readers he thought he detected the ghost of a smile on Len Hutton's face when he won the toss and informed Ian Johnson that England would bat first. The captains had been greeted by warm applause from all round a rapidly filling Melbourne Cricket Ground when they walked to the middle at 11.30 a.m. Hutton made a gesture to the stands intended to convey that England were batting. But if he was feeling happier, the rest of his team were not. 'As Australia took the field, you couldn't help feeling a kind of gloom about things, with Len apparently exhausted and without all his usual nerve, and Alec so tactlessly, even woundingly, omitted from the side,' Denis Compton remembered.

The mood might have been lightened if they had been privy to a breakfast conversation between Keith Miller and Sir Donald Bradman. Miller warned the chairman of selectors his still-painful knee might prevent him from bowling at all. 'Give it a go, Keith, and if you feel any reaction, stop bowling,' Bradman advised. At the MCG, Miller bumped into prime minister Robert Menzies in a corridor under the members' stand. 'Why don't you try a couple of overs?' Menzies asked. 'It's vital we get a good start.' In the dressing-room, Miller had his knee bandaged, jogged through his action and announced he was ready to at least have a trial over.

Johnson was relieved. The previous night he had given an off-the-record briefing to the journalist R.S. Whitington that Miller's knee would allow him to bowl only in an emergency. Before he left Sydney, his doctor told him he should attempt no more than short spells. Ray Lindwall's fitness problems went unpublicised. Still debilitated from the hepatitis that had laid him low before the first Test, he was now nursing a strained leg muscle.

Nevertheless, under sparkling blue skies and a hot sun, Lindwall opened the bowling from the Pavilion End. The gates of the MCG had been open since 9 a.m. and the crowd was building towards its 65,000 limit. At a cost of £A600,000 (around £7 million in UK currency today), the largest cricket ground in the world was being redeveloped as the main stadium for the 1956 Olympic Games. The old Public Stand had been demolished, leaving a gaping hole on one side and cutting the capacity by 20,000. It meant there were no reserved seats and that the area available to members was reduced by a third. Australian spectators generally had a relaxed approach to being in place for the opening ball, but the pressure of space may have led to prompter arrivals.

It was just as well they were in their seats. The start was sensational. Lindwall's first ball was a poorly directed inswinger, but as it flashed past his pads, Hutton overbalanced and came perilously close to falling on his stumps. Len Maddocks was a fraction late with his dive and the ball scuttled down to the boundary for four byes: no Test wicketkeeper could have had a more ignominious start to his career. It was the opening salvo in a thrill ride of a morning. By the end of the over, England were 11 without loss after a cover-driven three by Hutton and a leg glance to the boundary by Bill Edrich.

There were cheers when the ball was thrown to Miller at the start of the second over. It was just like old times. Lindwall and Miller v Hutton and Edrich: a four-way confrontation that could have taken place in any Ashes Test since the Second World War. Miller posted three men close on the leg side and opened with a fiery maiden, striking Edrich a painful blow above the elbow. At the end of the over Miller assured Johnson his knee felt fine and he could continue to operate at full pace. The battle was on.

With the third ball of his second over, Miller struck. Heedless of the waiting trap, Edrich turned the ball off his legs to where Lindwall took a smart low catch, tumbling to the ground as he clung on. In prime form and on his 25th birthday, Peter May should have been bursting with confidence, but instead looked uncomfortable and was almost bowled by Miller off the fifth ball he faced. It was a temporary reprieve. 'Lindwall always seems to have a special ball up his sleeve with which to greet May,' noted Ian Peebles. This one was no exception, rising sharply from a good length and moving away a fraction, it hit May on the glove and lobbed to Richie Benaud in the gully. May had failed to score – his third dismissal of the series without reaching double figures – and, head down, missed the pavilion gate by 10 yards as he trudged off.

It had become customary for Colin Cowdrey to arrive with England facing ruin. He got off the mark with an edge past third slip for four and followed that with a leg-glance to the boundary, but before the recovery mission could be properly launched Hutton had joined the procession. The England captain was lured into following a perfectly directed away-swinger from Miller and edged low to Graeme Hole at first slip. His scores so far in the series were 4, 13, 30, 28 and now 12. Diagnosing a technical fault, Alan Ross wrote, 'Hutton now affects to play on the off past point, rather than mid-off, which widens the margin for error when the left foot is not across and the ball is still new.'

In the *Daily Express*, Sid Barnes condemned England's top order as 'weak-kneed'. He wrote, 'There is no excuse for batsmen who attempt glances and cuts in the opening overs of a Test before they can possibly be in command of the situation.' John Arlott moved from the press box to the MCG's trustees' room, where a large pair of Japanese-manufactured binoculars had been mounted on a stand. 'The strength of the glasses is such that the eye can detect a fly on the batsman's cap, the grain and trademark of his bat.'

He saw an expression of grim defiance from new batsman Compton as he faced his great friend, Miller. Compton drove him past extra cover for three – the first runs Miller had conceded – but Miller's high action was extracting lift from the firm pitch and the fifth ball of his fifth over rapped Compton on the glove and flew to

Neil Harvey in the gully. 'Through the binoculars, it was possible to see Compton's face screw up as he threw off his glove,' said Arlott. In some pain, Compton was sent to hospital for an x-ray, a worrying reminder of the first morning at Brisbane. 'Internally and externally, he must be one of the world's most photographed men,' observed Peebles. This time there were no broken bones, but at 41 for four, England were suffering their own fractures.

Trevor Bailey was like a minister in a wartime cabinet, forever dealing with a crisis. Typically, he got his head down, although the scoring did not so much slow as come to a juddering halt. Miller and Ron Archer, who had replaced Lindwall at the Pavilion End, bowled five successive maidens. In a desperate bid to ease the pressure, Bailey pushed Archer towards mid-off and set off for a single. Archer swooped on the ball, swizzled in one thrilling movement, but directed his throw wide of the stumps with Bailey yards short of safety. Had he hit, half the England team would have been out before the scoreboard had registered 50. As it was, they reached lunch without further mishap, though still teetering at 59 for four.

It had been Miller's morning, a fact generously acknowledged by the crowd as the Australians left the field. He had defied a gloomy medical prognosis to bowl unchanged for figures of 9–8–5–3. There had been just two scoring strokes off his bowling, both in his fourth over, which included the dismissal of Hutton. 'These Australian fast bowlers seem to possess rare and almost magic powers of making a straightforward wicket seem a terror,' wrote Arlott. 'Today it was Miller who did so by bowling of such swing, movement off the pitch, lift, change of pace and accuracy that the England batting was held in chains for the entire hour and a half to lunch.'

Melbourne veterans recalled a similarly singular performance by England's Sydney Barnes in the New Year Test of 1911–12 when he bowled throughout the morning for figures of four for three. But those had been six-ball overs, and Barnes's approach and action involved much less physical strain. As always with Miller, it was the manner of his performance as much as the cold statistics that left a lasting impression. More than one journalist noted that he did not even seem to know where his mark was, he merely turned at an approximate point and ran in again. 'Vitality poured from him like the sunshine from the sky,' wrote J.M. Kilburn in the *Yorkshire Post*.

Typically, Miller shrugged off the plaudits: 'I've bowled just as well at Manly Oval and been hit all over the place.'

Miller radiated charisma. The back page of *The Age*, Melbourne's morning newspaper, that reported his first-day heroics also carried a large advertisement for the men's haircare product Brylcreem, featuring Miller swinging a bat next to his immaculately coiffured head. In reality, his slicked-back hair, unfashionably long for the time, seldom stayed in place for long on the field. The gesture with which he swept it from his eyes became one of his trademarks. Miller had been a wartime pilot in the Royal Australian Air Force, flying bombing raids over Germany (Edrich, one of his wickets that morning, had been decorated for bravery as a wartime pilot). When asked in the 1980s about the stresses of playing in the Australian Test team he memorably answered, 'I'll tell you what pressure is. Pressure is having a Messerschmitt up your arse. Playing cricket is not.' As Benaud wrote in a tribute after Miller's death in 2004, 'He made the game come alive simply by being on the field.'[34]

But he could not continue his marathon spell into the afternoon and, from the first deliveries after the resumption, it was clear that the pitch had lost its early firmness. There was now little encouragement for the seamers. 'The afternoon was completely different cricket,' Cowdrey remembered. He confirmed this with a flurry of fine strokes and reached his second fifty of the series with a single off Benaud. Rock-like in defence without missing an opportunity to attack, he had given a lesson to England's vastly more experienced top-order batsmen. 'Cowdrey might have come down from another planet when he started to bat, so superior did he look to those who had gone before,' wrote Margaret Hughes. 'He stood guard over the deceptively swinging ball like a broody hen over its chicks,' said R.S. Whitington.

Cowdrey became bogged down after reaching his fifty, just as he had at Sydney. The dead-slow off-spin of Johnson and Bill Johnston's left-arm medium-pace seemed to contain hazards that Miller, Lindwall and Archer had not. At 115 he lost Bailey, who swept hard at an invitingly short ball from Johnston: the leg-side close fielders

[34]For his book on the Victory Tests, a series played in England in 1945, the author Mark Rowe conducted research which showed Miller flew less than eight combat hours on two missions.

took evasive action, but Bailey merely mistimed the ball into his pads from where it looped in the air. Maddocks, who had not flinched, sprawled in the dust to take a notable first Test catch.

For 40 minutes, Cowdrey was stuck on 56, as if the metallic number alongside his name on the scoreboard needed a spot of oil. Failing to heed the lessons of Sydney, where an impetuous shot had led to those dressing-room tears, he attempted to loft Johnson over Archer at mid-on. Arlott watched in horror as the fielder's 'immense leap' reached the ball, but could only tip it, goalkeeper-style, over his head from where it trundled to the fence.

Having broken the spell, Cowdrey collected two more fours before tea and by the interval had moved to 68. But at 130 for five England were still in trouble and frittering away the advantage of winning the toss. Miller had not bowled at all in the afternoon, but in response to the urgings of the crowd Johnson brought him back early in the final session. Stiff and with a sore knee, he could not rekindle the magic. When Godfrey Evans hit him over mid-on for four, Miller walked down the pitch and shook the batsman's hand. After two unthreatening overs, he was withdrawn.

It was a symbol of Cowdrey's authority that he was not flustered when a short ball from Lindwall hit him over the heart (at 14 stone he was well padded against such incidents). He merely leaned forward to the next delivery and drove it majestically through the covers for four; eye, feet and bat working together in symphonic harmony. 'At times he looked like Hutton and at others like Hammond,' thought Arlott. 'One could see him cheerfully passing the time of day with his opponents,' noted Swanton. 'He seems to have the art of playing hard without looking grim and unhappy about it all.'

The innings had a further benefit: it lifted the mood of the captain. After his dismissal, Hutton had sat in the corner of the dressing-room, pads still buckled, lost in gloomy recrimination. As Cowdrey took command, Hutton joined the players in their viewing area. 'I sat next to Len for long periods and he kept repeating, "What a beautiful shot,"' Geoffrey Howard wrote. Cowdrey was a confirmed Hutton disciple. 'One of the most encouraging things of all about him is his ability to study the skipper's technique,' Howard had earlier noted.

After the departure of Evans for 20 and Johnny Wardle without scoring, Cowdrey had Frank Tyson for company as he entered the

'90s. 'He moved towards his century as though unaware of the scoreboard's existence,' wrote Neville Cardus. Cowdrey eased to the milestone with a late cut for three off Johnson, a straight drive for four off Archer and, next ball, a scampered three wide of mid-on. 'To my dying day I shall remember the on-drive off Ron Archer which gave me three runs and took me to the coveted three figures, my first in a Test match,' Cowdrey wrote in *Time for Reflection*. 'As I ran the first, the noise was deafening. As they sized up whether the two runs could be made into three, so it died to a complete hush and as we ran for the third all hell seemed to break loose, except it was far from hell! It was my happiest moment and the kindness of the reception had to be heard to be believed.'

Les Favell, fielding on the boundary, remembered the ovation as spine-tingling. Crawford White of the *News Chronicle* called it, 'One of the most touching expressions I have seen. It had a warmth and feeling about it that I always imagined an Australian crowd might reserve for the greatest performances of a Bradman.' Cowdrey was the youngest England batsman to score a Test century in Australia since J.W. Hearne, aged 20, in 1911. There was a congratulatory handshake from Johnson.

Hutton called the innings 'astonishingly mature' and Tyson 'icily superb'. Howard added, 'It really was an innings of great concentration, superb defensive technique and magnificent strokemaking and what a charming boy he is. It has not in any way affected him and he remains the completely unspoilt young cricketer.' A pithy telegram arrived from Sir Pelham Warner, 'Cowdrey, Melbourne, Magnificent, Warner.'

In 2016, in an interview with the former England captain Mike Atherton, one of his successors as cricket correspondent of *The Times*, and to mark his 90th birthday, Woodcock chose Cowdrey's maiden Test century as the one innings he would like to see again. 'It was the most marvellous innings. I don't think he ever played better than that again,' Woodcock said, 'but there's no footage of it and I can't remember it as well as I would like to. But I remember how I felt watching it at the time.'

The warmth of the reaction from the Melbourne crowd may have had something to do with the human story behind the performance. Cowdrey had arrived in Australia in October to be greeted by the news of the death of his father. He had shown remarkable fortitude and resolve to become one of the successes of the tour. In the MCC archive there is a letter from Cowdrey's mother Molly asking the club to convey a message to her son. 'He must not worry – there is nothing to worry about – nor must he be sad, for he must carry on and "play the game" with even more determination than ever now, as his father would have wished him so to do.'

But he could not remain unbeaten to the close. With just over half an hour left, Cowdrey shouldered arms to a wide ball from Johnson that hit a crack in the pitch and turned viciously back behind his legs to bowl him. It was the third time in the series he had been out without playing a stroke. There was no flourish from the tail this time: Statham and Tyson went quickly, and five minutes before the 6 p.m. close England were all out for a deflating 191. There was no time for the Australian reply to begin.

Close of play: England 191 all out.

PITCH BATTLE AT THE MCG

To non-cricket lovers the sport's enduring obsession with pitches is baffling: nothing remotely similar exists in any other sport. In the build-up to and during a Test, the properties of the 22 yards of turf that form the match's battlefield are picked over with the sort of rigour normally found only in forensic pathology or major fraud investigations. But this is not a ruse to baffle the uninitiated – the qualities of the surface have a material influence on the progress of a cricket match.

A pitch can be hard and true, assisting pace bowlers; damp and tinged with green, helping the seamers; or dry and dusty, to the benefit of spin bowlers. If a surface lacks any of those characteristics, batsmen may prosper, especially if the bounce is consistent and the ball reaches them at a predictable height. And the surface must not deteriorate so quickly that the contest is over too soon. This matters for financial as well as for sporting reasons.

By 1954–55, the authorities at the Melbourne Cricket Ground had become concerned about the condition of its pitches. Two weeks before the start of the Test, they sidelined curator Bill Vanthoff and called in Jack House from Melbourne's Albert Ground to prepare the pitch. This was motivated in part by the way the wicket had behaved during MCC's match against Victoria earlier in December. Officials were worried about the damage that could be wrought by Frank Tyson on a surface that began to break up too quickly. It was not until 2009 that the England fast bowler Steve Harmison coined the term 'chief executive's wicket' to describe a pitch prepared to last as long as possible to maximise revenue. But even in a less commercial age, the men running the MCG had one eye on their profit margins.

Tyson and Brian Statham had given the surface a close examination after their net session on the eve of the Test. Tyson recalled that in an attempt to quicken up the Test pitch the curator had not followed his usual practice of planting couch grass in the square, but he noted, 'This policy had certainly removed the cushioning effect of the coarse grass and its root system, but in doing so it had also robbed the wicket of its main binding agent.'

The Victoria-New South Wales Sheffield Shield match over Christmas had lasted a full four days, but the pitch had to be repaired during the game. There were already cracks in the surface. In his preview for the *Daily Express*, former Australia batsman Sid Barnes wrote, 'It is a pretty safe bet that the Test pitch will start to go apart at the seams after the first three or four days. Time without number the first team to bat on the Melbourne Cricket Ground has won.' In the *Manchester Guardian*, Denys Rowbotham went into great detail, highlighting that 'Since England's last tour of Australia the Melbourne wicket had changed slightly in character. The chief visible difference has been a disarming widening of the cracks, of which most Australian wickets are full, and which normally affect their playing behaviour unbelievably little,' he explained. 'However, the edges of the cracks in the Melbourne wicket recently have tended to crumble and the wicket as a whole to break up badly after the fourth day.'

In *The Age*, cricket correspondent Percy Beames also pointed out that, even at the start of matches, cracks were typically a feature of Melbourne pitches. 'Those cracks have been proof of a solid foundation and a guarantee of the lasting qualities of the pitch,' he explained. 'Only a few cracks have opened up on the pitch that will be used today. This suggests that once the upper crust begins to wear, the under-surface may begin to work through for the pitch to break up. Spin bowling could become a force late in the game.'

When Australia began their attempt to overturn England's undernourished 191 on New Year's Day, the behaviour of the pitch was uppermost in the minds of the players. Tyson began from the Pavilion End, Statham from the Southern Stand End. There was incident from the get-go. Tyson had an appeal for lbw against Les Favell turned down by umpire Mel McInnes off the fourth ball, the same batsman then top-edged Statham's first delivery wide of second slip – shutting the stable door, Len Hutton immediately deployed a third – and was hit a blow on the hand by Statham's next ball. Then Tyson got something better than a near miss, trapping Arthur Morris lbw for three with one that kept almost unplayably low.

Keith Miller emerged to what Arthur Gilligan called 'a tornado of cheering', but Favell hogged the strike, consigning the leading man to the supporting cast. Favell played some good shots and some streaky ones, while never suggesting he might be in for the long haul. When Trevor Bailey replaced Statham, Miller – who had seemed preoccupied by flies buzzing around his head – square-cut him gloriously for four. Statham, however, was merely having a breather before switching to the Pavilion End. The first ball of his new spell moved away from Miller, found the edge, and Godfrey Evans held a superb low catch in front of first slip.

'The indications were that the wicket had not relapsed into the docility that local cricketers had expected,' wrote E. W. Swanton in the *Daily Telegraph*. 'The odd ball from the fast bowlers was taken by Evans head high: and what made batting difficult was that quite a few kept low.' The point was emphasised in Statham's next over when Favell was lbw to a delivery that grubbed along at ankle height after pitching. Australia were 43 for three and in serious trouble. 'The pitch has two paces,' Alan Ross noted, while Ian Peebles, with the authority of a former Test cricketer, explained, 'It was firm and fast but, whether as a result of the method of preparation or the regulation covering them, the ball came from it at differing heights. This is the most disconcerting feature a batsman can find in any pitch, however agreeable it may be in other respects.'

Neil Harvey and Graeme Hole attempted to rebuild, identifying the lunch interval as their first objective. They did not make it. Hole's selection ahead of Jim Burke had been the subject of some criticism from Australian journalists, who felt the team lacked batsmen with sufficient defensive resilience. The strength of the argument was underlined when Hole played over a Tyson full toss and was bowled, a victim again of his high backlift. Australia were 65 for four at the interval, six runs better off than England had been at lunch on the first day, also for the loss of four wickets.

Tyson and Statham were reunited after lunch, but could not make further incisions. It was a day of formidable heat. 'Imagine a tempest raging inside one of the tropical greenhouses at Kew Gardens and you have a feel of Melbourne Cricket Ground when Australia batted,' wrote Bruce Harris. 'Usually a breeze brings relief from the heat; this one added to everyone's discomfort when the hot wind puffed into our faces.' In the afternoon, the skies turned grey and the sun disappeared, but that brought no relief. Accurate bowling and unpredictable bounce ensured run-scoring was desperately difficult. Richie Benaud was jeered by a crowd who failed to appreciate the twin challenges.

Eight overs into the afternoon session and after a drinks break, Hutton introduced Bob Appleyard. His third ball had the doubly rewarding effect of beating Harvey in the air with mesmerising flight and off the wicket with sharp spin: it pitched on leg stump and cannoned into off. Appleyard, his selection once again the subject of press criticism, had removed Australia's best batsman. Of more long-term significance, he had confirmed that he was ready to play a key role in the series. 'I had a setback at the start with the rib injury, but by Melbourne I was starting to sort out how to bowl in those conditions,' he recalled.

Clearly struggling against Appleyard, new batsman Ron Archer edged the first ball he faced between wicketkeeper and slip for four. He was no more at ease in Appleyard's next over, but Benaud was the spinner's second victim, caught at backward short leg by Vic Wilson, fielding for Denis Compton. Local boy Len Maddocks came to the wicket to enthusiastic applause, but was utterly bamboozled by Appleyard's first ball. He survived, just.

A stethoscope would have been needed to detect the run-rate, but Archer and Maddocks survived until tea with Australia 132 for six. Appleyard had taken two for 17 in six overs, but, bafflingly, Hutton replaced him with Johnny Wardle. The decision was given some credibility, however, when Wardle switched to round the wicket in his second over and bowled Archer with a faster ball that barely left the ground after pitching. Smarter fielding might have removed Ray Lindwall before he had scored, but he was yorked by Statham before the miss could prove too costly.

There were 64 minutes left in the day when Ian Johnson joined Archer: Australia were eight down for 151, still trailing by 40. Yet Hutton seemed paralysed by concerns about having to negotiate an awkward evening spell against Lindwall and Miller. His own stuttering form may have been a factor. England began to take their time and appeared to give up on the idea of taking wickets. 'They had Australia right on the floor then unhappily let them get up again,' wrote Alf Gover in the *Sunday Pictorial*. 'I felt that Australia's later batsmen should have been shot out long before close of play.' Australia ended the day only three runs behind. To make matters worse, England's fielding had become shambolic.

'No catches went to hand that were not taken, but almost the whole side were terribly slow over the ground,' wrote Swanton. 'Both at cutting off and chasing the hit there was an amount of fumbling that no school coach would have allowed to pass unreprimanded, while the throwing was as haphazard as ever.' Ross bemoaned England's 'matronly slowness', calculating that more than 20 runs came from strokes that should not have yielded even singles. 'Evans was made to jump all over the place for ragged returns,' added Harris.

Once again, the discussion returned to the pitch. Before the start of the second day Hutton had said to Vanthoff, 'This wicket won't last another three days. It is so dry.' Statham remembered, 'By Saturday evening the pitch had gone from light brown to dark grey in colour and wide cracks were running all over it. If ever a wicket was drying away to nothing, it was this one.' Tyson said the approaches to the pitch were so hard that spikes or studs could not penetrate. 'Several times Brian Statham had skated and fallen along his run-up, only saved from injury by his suppleness and litheness.' Statham had a gash in his leg after one tumble. Another slip ended with him performing a cartwheel.

Bill O'Reilly wrote, 'Melbourne's pitch deserved no bouquets and will get none. During their partnership, Harvey had gestured to the pitch and said to Benaud, 'I don't think we'll be able to play on this on Monday.' Interviewed by Gideon Haigh for his book *The Summer Game*, Johnson recalled, 'We went in on Saturday and the wicket was doing all sorts of things. When I was in with Len [Maddocks] towards the end of the day, you could see the ball starting to fly off the cracks.'

Close of play: Australia 188–8 (Maddocks 36*, Johnson 12*), trail England by three runs.

HUTTON'S GO-SLOW

Late on Saturday afternoon, the patience of the Melbourne crowd snapped. Hoots of derision were heard around the MCG. Angry spectators began to jeer and boo the England players. If Len Hutton was bothered, it did not show. Nor did it deflect him from his course. It was not just the fear of a tricky half-hour of batting or inept fielding that allowed Australia off the hook in the closing stages; reducing the game to the pace of a funeral procession was all part of Hutton's master plan for retaining the Ashes.

The figures did not lie. On the opening day, Australia had bowled 67.6 eight-ball overs. On the second, England laboured through 54. 'One very important item restricted the swing and rhythm of the cricket – the inordinate time that England took to bowl an over,' wrote E. W. Swanton. 'The crowd showed their resentment at the interminable conferences and slow crossings-over and they had one's sympathy.' In *The Times*, John Woodcock criticised 'A good deal of dawdling between overs, to the open disapproval of another great concourse'. He also thought the tactic backfired. 'In the end, instead of a useful little lead, England were only just ahead.'

There were mitigating factors, the steadily soaring temperature being one. Hutton also claimed the incessant hubbub from the stands meant he could only communicate with his bowlers at close quarters. But he would sometimes leave his position in the slips and walk to Frank Tyson, Brian Statham or Trevor Bailey as they paused at the end of their run-up. They might discuss field placings, but equally they might chat about nothing at all. 'Are you all right?' was the captain's most frequent question.

In his book *Fifty Years in Cricket*, published in 1984, at a time when Clive Lloyd's West Indies were under fire for their over-rate, Hutton mounted a sterling defence. 'I strongly refute any suggestion that with cold-blooded deliberation I put a restraint on the over-rate as a tactical policy,' he wrote. But that's not how the Australian broadcaster Alan McGilvray remembered it. He recalled Hutton becoming 'moderately inflamed' early in the tour when he suggested Australia were favourites. '"No way! We will win," he came back. I asked how he could be so sure. "Because we'll give them less balls to hit than they give us," he replied.'

That version accords with the memories of the men under Hutton's command. 'He deliberately slowed the over-rate down, but at the end of the day we generally got them out,' said Tyson. 'He'd walk from slip to the end of a bowler's run and say, "How are you, Frank?" And then walk back again, which would enable you to have a breather.' Statham recalled, 'One of his pet theories was to make the opposition wonder where they were going to get the next run and generally to slow the game down and make them think about it. It wasn't unknown for him to slow the game down in other ways and, to be honest, I didn't feel one way or the other about it.'

Some journalists were slow to understand what was happening. At Sydney, Margaret Hughes had written, 'There was a great deal of consultation with bowlers and different field placing and it seemed a pity that Hutton had not got his field set at this stage of the tour.' In the *Daily Herald*, Charles Bray agreed, 'The field should be worked out for each bowler before the match begins. Long conferences between the captain and bowler create a feeling of uncertainty and sloppiness which affects the team as a whole.' But it was not carelessness or a lack of planning – quite the opposite.

Alec Bedser remembered, 'In 1954 my brother Eric was broadcasting and it took 14 minutes once for Tyson and Statham to bowl two overs. Eric timed it because he used to have to sit and try to fill in. Len came to me once when we were playing New South Wales and said, "You bowl your overs too quickly." I knew what he meant of course, but I claimed innocence and said, "Why? What do you mean?" He said, "The less balls you bowl, the less runs they're going to get." So I said, "Have you ever thought that the more balls I bowl the more wickets I'm going to get?"' Bedser's Surrey teammate Peter Loader was more blunt. 'It was dreadful the way he slowed down the over-rate. I'd been brought up at Surrey under Stuart Surridge, where the idea was to get on with it, because the more balls you bowled the more people you got out. His cutting down the overs was a bloody disgrace. I was embarrassed. I'd think to myself, "Here is one of the great cricketers of the world, and he's got it wrong."'

Australian criticism was almost universal. At Brisbane, the recently retired captain Lindsay Hassett had complained to Geoffrey Howard: 'This isn't the clean potato.' The manager knew what was going on. 'Len was pretty adept at keeping the overs down,' Howard said. 'He spent a lot of time placing the field.' Speaking in the early 1990s, Ian Johnson added, 'This is the greatest problem in cricket today and I'm afraid Len started it. Len slowed it down to 90 balls an hour against our 112; that was absurdly slow. I think it was to break the concentration of the batsmen. We used to reckon that 60 runs an hour was even time, so that if there were 120 deliveries an hour that meant a run every two balls. But if the rate is slowed to 90, it's quite obvious that if you score at the same rate you're only going to make about 40.'

Nor did it go down well in some quarters at home. The issue came up at a meeting of MCC's cricket sub-committee in March, by which time Hutton's team were in New Zealand. Clearly, Gubby Allen had been irritated by the tactic during his recent trip to Australia. His research revealed that the MCC teams of 1932–33 and 1936–37 (the latter under his captaincy) had bowled around 10 overs per day more than the current bowling attack. The minutes noted, 'It was agreed that such a slowing-down of the tempo not only deprived spectators of an hour's cricket, but might well do grave harm to the game.'

Hutton insisted he was merely borrowing from Australia's playbook. 'Now and again I had a chat with one of them, a ploy I copied from the master tactician himself, Bradman,' he said. 'Tyson and Statham deserved all the help I could give them in field placings.' And support came from an unlikely quarter. In the Melbourne *Age*'s front-page 'Collins Street Calling' column, John Hetherington wrote, 'One radio commentator's persistent sniping at Len Hutton for delaying Test play on Saturday by conferring with his bowlers and resettling his field made little sense. True, only 54 overs were bowled against 67.6 by Australia in England's innings on Friday. What of it? Australia can learn nothing from England about using every trick within the rules to win the Tests. Hutton's idea was to get our side out as cheaply as possible. It seemed to work.'

WATER TORTURE

On the second evening, the teams attended an Australian Board of Control dinner, with prime minister Robert Menzies the star guest. Afterwards, several players moved on to a barbecue. Harold Dalton, the MCC masseur, had been asked by Len Hutton to monitor the social lives of Frank Tyson and Brian Statham, and prevent his prize assets accepting too much Australian hospitality. Dalton noted disapprovingly in his diary that Tyson was 'semi-inebriated' when got back to the Windsor Hotel at 2.30 a.m.

The rest day turned out to be anything but. Those who had managed any sleep awoke to ferocious temperatures. By 9 a.m. in Melbourne it was already 29.5°C (85°F). At midday it had reached 36 (98). By 2 p.m., the thermometer peaked at 40 (105.1). Blistering northerly winds, measured at 50 m.p.h., ramped up the levels of discomfort. In the city's suburbs, the wind tore down trees and fences, and brought power cuts. Further afield, the situation was more serious. Grass, scrub and forest caught fire and around 20,000 men were thought to be involved in an effort to control the blazes. Livestock was lost, towns evacuated. Around 30,000 acres of land were thought to have been affected. 'It started off as just a fire, but now it is a catastrophe,' said first constable H.W. Harley from Tarrayoukyan, 220 miles from Melbourne.

Some of the cricketers went ahead with their plans. A contact of Trevor Bailey's – 'he has more connections than a switchboard,' said Tyson – arranged for the England players to go surfing off Point Leo. They enjoyed the water, but it soon became too hot for swimming. 'Even bathing could not bring physical comfort,' Tyson recalled. 'The north wind whipped up the sand which stung the legs like wasps.' The following day, Geoffrey Howard wrote home, 'Yesterday was an absolute stinker – one of the hottest days I have ever known.'

The weather provided a reminder of the potentially devastating power of the Australian climate. 'Sunday was one of those days we never know in England,' said Statham. When the players drove back into Melbourne from the beach, they found scores of overheated cars steaming by the roadside. Nevertheless, the coast provided a refuge for many Melburnians: thousands spent the night on the beaches as a way of escaping the stifling city. Victoria was not the only state hit by the scorching temperatures. In the hills outside Adelaide, the governor of South Australia Sir Robert George narrowly escaped death when the family's summer home was destroyed in the worst bush fire the state had known.

'It was as if the steam in a laundry had been turned on the city and left on all day,' wrote Margaret Hughes. John Arlott thought it 'as hot as the draught from an oven'. Similar to Hughes, he found the only coping strategy was to shut all windows and doors, pull down the blinds and stay indoors. Later, Hughes ventured out. 'At five o'clock I went to a tea party; we sat in the garden until midnight and it was as warm at that time as it had been all day.' She voiced what many must have been thinking. 'I don't think it would have been possible to play cricket under these conditions, so it was just as well that the furnace blast happened on the Sabbath.'

Undeterred, Keith Miller and Ray Lindwall played golf with Ossie Pickworth, a leading professional who had recently won his fourth Australian Open title. 'During the round we both told Ossie that the wind would take out any moisture that remained in the pitch and make the cracks even wider,' Miller remembered. 'We expected the game to be over by Monday night, we told him.' At home in the Melbourne suburb of Middle Park, Ian Johnson also fretted: 'I was thinking "God, what's the wicket going to look like on Monday?"'

At the MCG, Jack House, the curator drafted in by the ground authorities, and Bill Vanthoff, the man he had usurped, shared the concerns of the Australian captain. World cricket was governed by rules and regulations set out by MCC in London and there was no ambiguity or wriggle room in the wording of law 10. 'Under no circumstances shall the pitch be watered during a match,' it read. House surveyed the strip he had prepared as it baked in the heat. 'Someone's going to be killed on this wicket,' he told Vanthoff. 'We can't leave it like this. I'm going to give it a bit of a fizz.' He unspooled the curator's hosepipe, turned on the tap and began to douse the Test pitch.

Vanthoff wanted none of it. He rushed away to telephone Percy Beames, cricket correspondent of *The Age,* an old Australian Rules football teammate. 'Percy, something terrible's happened,' Vanthoff said. 'Jack House has flooded the square. He's put too much water on.' The story – retold by Gideon Haigh in *The Summer Game* – took another twist when Beames relayed the information to the paper's editor, Harold Austin. He wanted to know if he thought it was an attempt to influence the outcome of the match in Australia's favour. Beames didn't think so, whereupon Austin, keen to preserve cricket's reputation, said they would not publish the story. Instead, the back page carried a short piece outlining the expected condition of the pitch after Saturday's play. For those in the know – and the fact that rebuilding work meant the passing public could look into the MCG and see the watering meant that many *did* know – there was a pointed sign-off paragraph. 'After the Test match begins the pitch cannot be watered,' it read. 'Rolling can only take place before the start of play each day, or between innings.'

Johnson was an early Monday-morning arrival at the MCG. He ran his spikes along the clearly damp surface of the pitch, then summoned Arthur Morris. 'This has been watered,' he told his deputy. When the England players turned up, Tyson went up to the radio commentary position in the Members' Stand and instantly noted something was amiss. 'I saw that the colour of the Merri Creek soil on the square was not the dried, baked grey I had expected – but black, as though it were damp,' he wrote. Hutton remembered, 'There was enough moisture in parts to rise above the welts of their shoes.' Brian Statham added, 'Our spikes sank into the soft turf and with the slightest pressure you could draw a line with the welt of your boot.' When Johnson shared his suspicions with umpires Mel McInnes and Colin Hoy, McInnes's response was, 'Say nothing to anybody.'

Play began in a surreal atmosphere: nobody was quite sure how the pitch would behave. The players had taken it in turns to study it minutely, like art dealers examining an old master they suspect is a fake. Hutton was keen that none of his players were looking for excuses. 'Let's win the game first and complain if we have to afterwards,' he told them. By the end of Tyson's opening over, Len Maddocks and Johnson had eased Australia into a three-run lead. Mercifully, the heat had subsided: it was considerably cooler than Sunday's peak.

It was also clear that the demons in the surface had been tamed, at least for now. The ball bounced at a predictable height, there were no shooters, nor steep lift for Tyson and Statham. That the wicket area was now damp was shown when Statham borrowed a pen-knife from McInnes to scrape the accumulated detritus from his spikes. The change in underfoot conditions made it hard for him to keep his feet. He tumbled three times in his opening spell and was only saved from injury by his suppleness.

Singles were taken that could have been prevented with more athletic fielding, but England succeeded in removing Maddocks in the sixth over when he tickled a ball from Statham to Godfrey Evans. The debutant had made 47 and it was clear that, for all his wicketkeeping excellence, Gil Langley might struggle to reclaim his place. Maddocks was the first Victorian to keep wicket against England in Australia since Jack Blackham in the 1890s. On the rest day, a local woman had presented him with a notable good-luck charm: a silk spotted handkerchief dated 27/5/88 that had been given to her as a child by Blackham.

The arrival of last man Bill Johnston to the usual broad grins all round meant the only sensible course of action was to attack. Johnston raced to double figures, inspiring his captain to hit Trevor Bailey for three fours in an over. Australia's lead crept up, but eventually Johnston aimed an over-optimistic blow at Statham and was bowled for 11. Statham finished with five for 60, his best Test figures to date. Johnson was unbeaten on 33 and Australia had made 231, a lead of 40. Their last two wickets had added 80. 'A score usually worth the first three English batsmen,' said Alan Ross.

Hutton and Bill Edrich had five overs from Ray Lindwall and Keith Miller to negotiate before lunch. Miller beat Edrich three times with balls that lifted and shaped away outside off stump in a probing opening over, but the pair survived. After the break, Lindwall and Miller were soon replaced by Ron Archer and Johnston, bowling his left-arm spin. At 21, Archer was comfortably the youngest member of Australia's seam attack, and his strength and youthful vigour made him look more likely to break through than the greybeards who had taken the new ball. Instead it was Johnston who beat Edrich with a sharply spinning delivery just as England cleared the first-innings arrears. It was cold comfort, but 40 represented England's best opening partnership of the series so far.

Peter May had been making a habit of following a poor first-innings score with a significant contribution in the second. He was cautious at first but two beautiful straight drives – the second applauded by the bowler Miller – showed he was finding his range. Hutton's painful progress at the other end was attracting the derision of the MCG crowd. 'Hutton has batted since Brisbane rather as one who, long word-perfect in several languages, now seems increasingly to hanker for the dictionary,' wrote Ross. When Hutton took a single off Miller in the penultimate over before tea, he doffed his cap and offered his bat to the stands as an invitation to anyone who could do better.

Any hope that this signalled the end of Hutton's poor run was ended in the third over after tea when he was lbw to a ball from Archer that darted back in to his pads. England's lead was a precarious 56. Colin Cowdrey survived a shout for lbw in the same over and in the next was warned by Lindwall for backing up too soon. 'This he did in the most courteous way, holding the ball as his arm came over to deliver and merely showing it to Cowdrey, who was some three yards down the wicket,' E.W. Swanton reported. He reminded *Daily Telegraph* readers that at Sydney in 1947 the Indian bowler Vinoo Mankad had taken the bails off to dismiss Bill Brown in a similar incident.[35] 'Lindwall would have been quite justified in running out Cowdrey,' Swanton added. 'The incident illustrated something one is always looking for nowadays and not infrequently noticing: that whatever strange stuff we may hear and read about modern toughness in sport, there is room yet for chivalry and the unwritten law.'

What little aggression England showed came from May – Cowdrey was content to let his partner take the lead – and the vice-captain reached his half-century by hitting Benaud through mid-on in the 43rd over. Gradually, May blossomed. In his Sydney hundred, most of his runs had come from shots square of the wicket. Now it was his driving – off, on and sometimes gloriously straight – that attracted rave reviews. 'One classic boundary hit back past bowler Miller flashed through the field leaving the two men close to the bowler gaping open-mouthed,' wrote Bill O'Reilly. 'And the fact that the impact of bat and ball was almost noiseless was proof enough that the stroke had been timed to perfection.' He would have had more runs but for the continued excellence of Australia's fielding. Denzil

---

[35] When a bowler runs out a batsman who is backing up too far, it is still known as a 'Mankad'.

Batchelor compared May's footwork with that of the great American heavyweight, Joe Louis. O'Reilly thought batting of this quality stripped away partisanship. 'Class performers of his high standing have no nationality while they entertain so liberally.'

May lost Cowdrey on 128 when the hero of the first innings dozily watched a harmless ball from Benaud spin back on to his stumps and dislodge a bail. Sensing an opening, Johnson summoned Lindwall for another burst before the close. Denis Compton had a bandaged thumb, a left hand that was not properly healed and no serious match-practice for six weeks. Lindwall's assault included a particularly brutish bouncer, but Compton withstood the test. In fact, he might have collected more than 10. In the *Daily Herald*, Charles Bray chastised him for 'clock-watching rather than picking up some easy runs late in the day.' But the day belonged to May, who earned a glowing testimonial from Swanton. 'There was a confidence and maturity about his batting today that I had not seen in the play of any young English batsman on a comparable occasion since the war.'

Close of play: England 159–3 (May 83*, Compton 10*), lead Australia by 119 runs.

BLAME GAME

Harold Austin had shown unusual restraint for a newspaperman in opting not to publish Percy Beames's exclusive about the pitch watering, but all through the day on Monday the MCG press box throbbed with feverish speculation. 'Pressmen could be seen rushing here and there, chatting together in groups, snatching phones,' wrote Margaret Hughes. When a Sydney evening paper ran with the story about the laws being transgressed, Austin saw no further reason to keep it out of *The Age*.

The right-hand side of Tuesday morning's front page – next to more serious news about Sunday's bush fires – carried a story by Beames under the headline 'Test pitch watered during game.' There were no back-covering phrases such as 'it is alleged,' nor cautious deployment of the word 'reportedly'. Beames stated as fact that the Melbourne pitch had been watered on Sunday in a clear contravention of regulations.

Beames had asked Keith Miller for an off-the-record briefing at Monday's lunch interval. At the same time, two Australian players went to see Jack Ledward, secretary of Australia's Board of Control, to point out that it was obvious that the strip had been watered. 'When the Australia and English players took the field yesterday they were amazed to find that Saturday's cracks in the wicket had closed up,' Beames wrote. He said the cricketers had been swapping jokes about the ground's 'local shower'.[36]

Curators Jack House and Bill Vanthoff denied any knowledge, House speculating that the pitch had sweated under the covers on Sunday evening. Melbourne Cricket Club secretary Vernon Ransford, a veteran of 20 pre-First World War Tests, said he was 'upset and disturbed' that such a report had appeared. House's denials had to be weighed against the pre-match assessment of the pitch he had given to R.S. Whitington. 'If conditions are cool over the weekend it may last until Monday,' he predicted. 'But if they are hot it will crack badly by Monday.' Whitington added, 'Players from both teams noticed that the surface of the pitch on the Monday morning was quite soft. They also said that grass cuttings, which had obviously got there from spraying, were lying in the footholds made by the bowlers. Players also said that the cracks which were almost half an inch wide on the Saturday had been closed and that young green grass was growing between them.' It was unarguable that for most of the third day the pitch had played blamelessly and that the first signs of uneven bounce did not occur until the final session.

English officials kept their counsel. 'We have not taken any action,' was all manager Geoffrey Howard would say. Although it was not reported, a meeting did take place between Howard, Hutton and the ground authorities. They got nowhere: Hutton's end-of-tour report to Lord's said 'little satisfaction' was gained at the meeting. Meanwhile, MCC secretary Ronny Aird and Gubby Allen, still on their goodwill visits, politely refused invitations to comment. 'They realised that the watering, if it helped one side more than the other, could only help England,' wrote Whitington.

---

[36]The watering controversy became enough of a *cause célèbre* to warrant a mention in Harold Pinter's 1957 play *The Birthday Party*.

Diplomatic silence did not stop Aird and Allen visiting the press box during the day in search of more details. A joint inquiry was launched by the Melbourne Cricket Club and the Victoria Cricket Association. Vanthoff, House and the ground's nightwatchman were interviewed, but, oddly, no players. The club's assistant secretary, A.B. Cuttriss, was sent to the press box to deliver the inquiry's verdict. 'Statutory declarations have been made by the two curators and by the watchman employed to guard the pitch at night that neither the pitch nor any portion of the ground has been watered since the commencement of the match,' said the official statement. Beames stood by his story and protected his source.

There were potentially serious implications for the series. If it was proved that the pitch had been watered, the match could be declared void. That possibility was raised by Swanton on the front of the *Daily Telegraph*. Neville Cardus thought it was the only option if the story was proved. In an effort to disprove the watering story, Melbourne Cricket Club called in two civil engineers from Melbourne University, one a specialist in soils. They wrote a long and detailed explanation of how a combination of climatic circumstances over the weekend and the tarpaulins covering the wicket had drawn moisture to the surface and closed the cracks. Despite the undoubted knowledge of the experts, the cricket fraternity remained sceptical. By that time, however, public interest had moved on – and the Test had been thrillingly decided.

ANYBODY'S MATCH

As a former England captain, Arthur Gilligan recognised a pivotal moment when he saw one. 'The result of this match depended almost entirely on this partnership,' he wrote, referring to the unbroken fourth-wicket alliance between Peter May and Denis Compton. The pair had added 31 risk-averse runs on Monday evening, but with a lead of just 119, England needed them to hang around. Neither did. Runs came at a trickle, just 14 in the first eight overs of the day, with Bill Johnston, bowling with a gentle mesmerising left-arm loop from the Pavilion End, proving particularly hard to get away. May's fluency deserted him completely. He was nearly stumped off the first ball of Johnston's fifth over and dismissed by the next one, a well-spun ball that flicked his pad en route to off stump.

Compton soon followed. His hand injuries had restricted his strokeplay – 'like Samson shorn of his hair,' thought Alan Ross – and on 23 he leg-glanced Ron Archer and was caught behind by Len Maddocks. It had become a wearingly familiar method of dismissal for Compton: he did not even bother to check if the catch had been completed. Ian Peebles, a Middlesex teammate before the war, thought Compton was planting his left foot too far inside the line of the ball when playing the shot.

Godfrey Evans, dropped second ball by Ray Lindwall at short leg, tried to wrest back the initiative and when he hit Johnston for two fours in an over, Ian Johnson changed tack. Lindwall and Keith Miller returned and the new ball was taken. It was a mistake. 'Nowadays captains of all cricket teams around the world take the spinner off directly somebody starts to hit him – and Johnson is no exception,' wrote Margaret Hughes. 'Surely this is how the great spinners took their wickets?' There was nothing in the pitch for the seamers, and Evans and Trevor Bailey survived comfortably until lunch.

Soon after the resumption, Evans touched a Lindwall outswinger to Maddocks, leaving England 211 for six, a lead of 171. But if Australia thought that put them back on top they had reckoned without Johnny Wardle. He did not look happy against pace, but when Johnston returned Wardle saw it as an invitation to chance his arm. Johnston had been impressively parsimonious in the morning, but now Wardle hit him to the boundary four times in an over.

'It was Wardle who thrust the pressure on bowlers instead of allowing them to bowl to any length they thought most profitable on a slower, easier and less reliable pitch,' wrote R.S. Whitington. As John Arlott pointed out, these were not slogs: only one shot was airborne. 'He directed the ball with much skill through the few gaps in the outfield.' Similar treatment was meted out to Johnson, a late cut and two sweeps bringing three more fours. Wardle was bowled aiming to sweep Johnson again, but his 38 off 45 balls changed the tone of the day.

This might have been the moment for Bailey, on 14 off 93 balls, to take on the role of aggressor. His inactivity was already provoking boos from the crowd – not that he seemed in the least perturbed. 'Unfortunately for England's needs, this has the effect of driving him even further into his shell,' wrote E.W. Swanton. 'Bailey would not budge either his feet or his bat,' said Hughes. 'We want this ground for the Olympic Games, you know,' shouted one spectator. 'Bailey's innings was described as unintelligent,' wrote A.G. Moyes. 'Well, if Bailey is against you, most disparaging names seem to fit him, for no one in the game today can be so annoying and aggravating. But not unintelligent. That's not Bailey.' Breaking out of a defensive mindset could be harder than it appeared. 'Bailey embraced his responsibility with monastic devotion,' said Arlott, 'revelling in sackcloth and ashes.'

Nevertheless, England's last three wickets mustered just 22, the sole highlight being Neil Harvey's sensational catch to remove Frank Tyson. His lofted cover-drive off Johnston looked worthy of four runs, but Harvey jumped to palm the ball into the air then swivelled round to take the catch with his back to the pitch. At just before 4 p.m. England were all out for 279. Australia needed 240 to retake the series lead. 'The watering of the pitch definitely helped England's batsmen in the second innings,' said Whitington. And the benign behaviour of the surface after the weekend had given the match a split personality. 'It made a mockery of the game's conduct, conflict and struggles on Friday and Saturday,' said Denys Rowbotham in the *Manchester Guardian*. Ian Johnson agreed: 'It was like losing the toss twice.'

There was another big crowd – more than 57,000 – and while they had been even-handed in applauding Wardle's innings there was no doubt where their allegiances lay. When Les Favell and Arthur Morris walked out to begin Australia's second innings, they were greeted by a burst of loud, encouraging cheers. 'In the Bradman era this total would have been laughed at by the Australians; today it will be blood, sweat and tears,' said Hughes.

Tyson began from the Pavilion End, but bowled too short and the pitch, though drying on a sunny afternoon, was still docile. It took a change to bring the first chance, Bailey failing to cling on to a caught-and-bowled opportunity from Morris. But Australia's vice-captain was gone in the next over. He drove uppishly at Tyson and Cowdrey, positioned at silly mid-on for just such an eventuality, tumbled athletically to hold the ball inches from the ground.

A murmur of surprise greeted Richie Benaud's appearance at No. 3, prompting speculation about the reasoning behind the change in the order. Some suspected Miller was still feeling listless (Moyes reminded his readers of the foolishness of playing golf in Sunday's heat), others that Benaud grew agitated while waiting to bat at six. A third possibility was that Johnson wanted two aggressive young batsmen to make substantial inroads into the target that evening.

That theory was given credence by the approach of Favell and Benaud. Runs came more quickly, both men found the boundary – Benaud lifting Bob Appleyard for a one-bounce four – and ran swiftly between the wickets. Len Hutton ordered his bowlers to slow the tempo, a tactic that paid off in frustrating the hyperactive Favell. When Appleyard offered a temptingly flighted off-break, Favell lifted his head, played over the ball and was bowled. 'The ball was a beauty and one to nibble wormholes through any incoming batsman's confidence,' wrote Lindsay Browne in the *Sydney Morning Herald*. Harvey couldn't have been concerned, because he collected six runs from his first two balls from Appleyard.

Nor was Benaud prepared to play for the close. In Appleyard's next over he smashed him high and straight. Umpire McInnes at first signalled a six, but there was doubt about whether the ball had bounced inside the fence. The matter was referred to a policeman on duty by the sightscreen, who ruled that the ball had definitely bounced. 'For this splendid constabulary impartiality he was roundly but good-naturedly booed,' wrote Peebles.

The only remaining incident was the appearance of a well-refreshed spectator zig-zagging around the outfield, holding up play for five minutes. Benaud and Harvey remained unfazed. Hutton gave Wardle a consolation over. He found no help from the pitch, but it was clear that the surface was drying out. How it might behave tomorrow was a matter of fierce conjecture.

Close of play: Australia 75–2 (Benaud 19*, Harvey 9*), need 165 runs to win.

RETURN OF THE TYPHOON

'Tyson bowled like a clot.' Harold Dalton, the MCC masseur, did not mince his words in his diary entry for Monday 3 January, although the verdict seemed harsh, given that he had only delivered four overs.

Dalton blamed Tyson's inertia on his late return from Saturday night's barbecue. The following evening, Dalton was outraged again. 'Tyson up drinking beer with a woman in the bedroom,' he scribbled. Tyson's room-mate Keith Andrew telephoned Len Hutton and the captain came to investigate. Tyson remembered it rather differently, recalling the incident as a demonstration of Hutton's man-management skills. 'Len was a great psychologist. It wasn't what he said, but what he didn't say,' he wrote. 'I remember at the Windsor in Melbourne, four of us and some girls, at 10 o'clock one night. Len poked his head in, "Are you all right?" he said. It was what he didn't say that counted. "I'll see you in the morning." Within an hour we were all tucked up in bed, fast asleep.'

Perhaps Tyson didn't think he would be needed on the fifth day at the MCG. England's chances of snatching a win seemed to rest with Bob Appleyard and Johnny Wardle. 'The wicket, hurt maybe by imputations as to its character, seems to have withdrawn all favours from the fast bowlers,' said E. W. Swanton. He couldn't resist adding that the best England bowler for such a surface was Alec Bedser. Denys Rowbotham added, 'England's only chance of victory tomorrow, indeed, seems to depend on whether Appleyard can spin the ball still more on this mysteriously unpredictable wicket.'

There was no consensus, but most observers plumped for a home win. 'Australia are on the way to victory, unless the wicket deteriorates,' said John Arlott. E.M. Wellings disagreed. He told *Evening News* readers, 'England appear to have the better chance, and I fancy they will win provided this peculiar self-irrigating pitch does not unearth another mysterious and secret reservoir.' The symmetry with the second Test at Sydney was remarkable. Then, Australia had been 72 for two at the start of the fifth day, needing another 151. Now, they were 75 for two, 165 away from victory. 'Advantage had been first with one side and then the other during the first three days of this thrilling match,' said Arthur Gilligan. 'It could never be described as a classic match apart from a few purple patches, but for fluctuating fortune, thrills and tough fighting, few surpassed it.'

To the dismay of the MCG's caterers, it was clear there would be no need for the sixth day. Once again Melburnians turned up in vast numbers: more than 50,000 were in attendance, taking the match aggregate past 300,000. Some opted to miss the morning and come along later for the potential excitement of the denouement.

Even with the bulldozers in attendance, the MCG was the most imposing cricket ground in the world. But size wasn't everything. Many players did not relish the Melbourne Test.

'To walk into the harsh Melbourne sunlight from the shadowy dark of the dressing-room and find yourself facing the largest crowd you have seen at a cricket match is like entering a gladiatorial ring, and loud though the applause for you may be, you cannot escape the conviction that secretly all the thumbs are pointing downwards,' wrote Hutton. Keith Miller was Melbourne born and had played for Victoria before relocating to Sydney in 1947, but he was not a fan of the MCG either. 'It is certainly imposing with its huge stands, but it is too much of an amphitheatre,' he said. 'When playing there I always feel like an early Christian thrown to the lions.'

That was always assuming you could get past the gatemen. During the match against an Australian XI in November, Denis Compton had been refused entry on the first morning. It was too much to expect the heroically disorganised Compton to remember his pass, but after an argument lasting a few minutes he simply vaulted over the turnstile. Colin Cowdrey was also detained after leaving the ground to play squash. When MCC returned to play Victoria in December, there was a similar incident when Appleyard, Vic Wilson, Bill Edrich and Brian Statham were denied entry on their return from a net at Melbourne Grammar School.

If there were any such incidents on the fourth morning of the Test they went unreported: England had a full complement of players when Hutton led them out. All eyes were on Appleyard, but Hutton did not so much as glance in his direction. Instead, he threw the ball to Tyson. Hutton had a hunch that his quickest bowler might now be more effective from the Southern Stand End, from which Keith Miller had caused such havoc on the first morning. It meant Tyson was running up a slight slope, with a gentle wind blowing into his face, but neither troubled him. By four minutes past 12, he had made the initial incision.

Neil Harvey set the scoreboard moving by collecting two for a leg-side nudge off the first ball of the morning. Off the seventh, he played a leg glance which seemed destined for the boundary before Godfrey Evans dived across – 'like a flying trapezist,' wrote John Woodcock – and held an astonishing catch, just above the ground and inches from Colin Cowdrey's bootlaces at leg slip. 'He gathered in the most extraordinary wicketkeeper's catch I have ever seen,' remembered Tyson. Cowdrey leapt into the air. 'I don't know what I'm doing up here – do you think I should have gone for it?' he asked the prostrate wicketkeeper. 'It didn't matter who had gone for it as long as someone had,' Evans wrote. 'If ever there was a turning point, that was it,' said Tyson.

Evans's acrobatics had a double benefit. They lifted England's fielding out of the geriatric trough it had occupied since the first morning at Brisbane, while simultaneously instilling a sense of fatalism in the Australian dressing-room. 'Tyson's first over was like the very sounding of Australia's doom,' said Denys Rowbotham. Just as vital in adding to Australia's foreboding was the next over from Statham, in which three balls in succession bounced barely above ankle height. Miller survived, but Statham's following over was even more hazardous and a boundary off the inside edge did little for the batsman's security of tenure.

Fast bowlers form predatory partnerships. One may harvest the wickets while the other performs the groundwork. Tyson now capitalised on the unsettling effects of Statham's relentless, probing accuracy. The first ball of Tyson's third over of the day was short and wide of off stump – 'the first bad ball I had sent down all morning,' he reflected – but Richie Benaud, in attempting to hook, sent it cannoning into his stumps via a bottom edge. 'This was an irrational stroke for the hour and the pitch,' wrote Woodcock. Benaud found a bail lodged in his pads as he walked off and threw it angrily aside as he passed the England slips.

New batsman Graeme Hole took a single off his third ball, bringing Miller down to face Tyson. If Tyson felt the delivery that removed Benaud was his worst, the fifth one of the same over was his quickest. From Miller's flailing edge it flew like a tracer bullet high to Hutton at second slip. The England captain palmed it into the air and Bill Edrich, several feet deeper at first slip, reacted instantly to grab the ball inches from the ground. Nothing could have demonstrated the transformation in England's fielding more than this combination between two 38-year-olds.

Australia were reeling at 87 for five. In 28 minutes' play, they had lost three wickets for the addition of 12 runs. Hole and new batsman Ron Archer did not so much steady the ship as bail out a few puddles of water. The score had advanced by 10 when Hole, having jabbed down on three successive Statham yorkers, was offered the chance to drive by the same bowler and edged to Evans. The carnage continued in Tyson's next over: first Len Maddocks was yorked for a first-ball duck, then, two balls later, Ray Lindwall was leg-before to one that kept low, also without scoring. Tyson now had six wickets. 'Batsmen came and went so fast that it seemed at times that only a movie camera with some 24 exposures a second could be sure at keeping up with the details,' wrote Lindsey Browne in the *Sydney Morning Herald*.

Match-winning spells such as this often gather a momentum of their own. 'At times like this, sportsmen seem to operate on instinct,' recalled Tyson. 'I felt like a jockey riding a runaway Derby winner,' Hutton remembered. But the captain now had to make a decision. Tyson and Statham had each bowled five overs. England were two wickets from victory, Australia's target still a distant 142 runs away. Should he give them a rest? Hutton had a chat to his vice-captain Peter May and decided to keep them going for a while longer. Bill O'Reilly thought Tyson could go on all morning. 'Tyson's great assets in the mechanics of bowling are supplemented by an outstanding bowler's temperament which urges him on long after one expects a bowler of his pace to be looking for a rest.'

Ron Archer and Ian Johnson collected 10 off the next two overs, but they were merely postponing the inevitable. Archer was yorked by one from Statham that deflected from his pads and when Johnson ran a single off the second ball of Tyson's next over it brought Bill Johnston to the striker's end. Michael Charlton[37] was at the microphone for the Australian Broadcasting Commission:

Johnson four, Johnston yet to score, just gives Bill Johnston the strike. Australia nine for 111. And Tyson bowls to Bill Johnston now and beats him just outside the off stump, there's an appeal for a catch, and he's gone! A great catch by Evans, diving across, Evans rolling around on the ground, Bill Johnston out caught Evans bowled Tyson for no score and Australia all out for 111.

---

[37]Charlton later moved to the UK and became one of the best-known faces on BBC News, reporting on the assassination of President Kennedy and the first moon landing. He presented *Panorama* for several years.

England had completed an astonishing victory by 128 runs: Tyson's final figures were seven for 27. In a session lasting 79 minutes, eight Australian wickets had fallen for 36. 'Nothing more dramatic has happened in modern Test cricket,' wrote Lindsay Hassett. A stunned Johnson shook Tyson's hand before walking off. His team's limitations against extreme pace had been ruthlessly exposed. Tyson's figures were the best by an England fast bowler in an Ashes Test since Tom Richardson took eight for 94 at Sydney in 1897–98. His fifth-morning spell was 6.3–0–16–6. 'One of the finest exhibitions of fast bowling I have ever witnessed,' said Neil Harvey. 'One of the greatest Test bowling performances of all time,' thought O'Reilly. Appleyard, billed as the potential match-winner, had not even touched the ball in the field.

Best Figures by an England Bowler in Australia

	Overs	Maidens	Runs	Wickets	Ground	Series
G.A. Lohmann	27.1	12	35	8	Sydney	1886–87
G.A. Lohmann	43.2	18	58	8	Sydney	1891–92
W. Rhodes	15	0	68	8	Melbourne	1903–04
L.C. Braund	29.1	6	81	8	Melbourne	1903–04
T. Richardson	36.1	7	94	8	Sydney	1897–98
J.C. White	64.5	21	126	8	Adelaide	1928–29
F.H. Tyson	**12.3**	**1**	**27**	**7**	**Melbourne**	**1954–55**
W. Bates	26.2	14	28	7	Melbourne	1882–83
R.G. Barlow	34.2	20	40	7	Sydney	1882–83
J.A. Snow	17.5	5	40	7	Sydney	1970–71

Tyson modestly refused invitations to lead the team off. Instead, he waited for Statham and they linked arms before leaving the scene of their triumph. 'Brian Statham bowled better than I did. I just had the luck to get the figures,' Tyson said. Johnson agreed: 'Both Tyson and Statham bowled extremely well,' he said. 'I emphasise them both because although Tyson got the figures, Statham, in my opinion, bowled just as well. We can have no excuses.' Evans, too, deserved his share of the plaudits. 'Evans collected every catch within his range,' wrote J.M. Kilburn in the *Yorkshire Post,* 'and one or two that would have been out of it by normal standards.'

A section of the crowd came across the playing area to look at the much-discussed pitch. There was loud laughter when one of the groundstaff began to douse it with a hose. Other spectators gathered in front of the dressing-room area, and called for Hutton and Tyson to appear. Thousands more remained in their seats, numbed by what they had witnessed. 'They were stunned into silence, the whole thing was over so quickly,' remembered Geoffrey Howard. 'They just sat there in their seats, eating their lunch and drinking their beer while we celebrated in the dressing-room. It was the most magic day of my life.' The usually resourceful MCC manager had been unable to find anywhere to buy champagne. Keith Tolhurst, a former Victoria player, came to the rescue and the toasts were not only frequent but also free.

An hour after the conclusion, Bruce Harris of the *Evening Standard* found Hutton in the players' lunch room, finishing a meal with Miller, Lindwall and Johnston. Hutton paid tribute to Tyson. 'It was a lovely bit of bowling, wasn't it? I want to congratulate the Australian crowd. They behaved wonderfully in defeat. No, I'm not making predictions even now about the destiny of those Ashes – there is a lot of cricket to be played yet.'

Back home in England, the victory was front-page news and a timely boost for a country recovering from a weekend of snow and freezing temperatures while contemplating the threat of a national rail strike. In Middleton, Violet Tyson again had a house full of visitors. Learning a lesson from Sydney, she remembered to get up and have an early breakfast. She sent her son a telegram. 'Well bowled, Frank, keep it up.' Across the Pennines in Pudsey, Dorothy Hutton said she had no plans to cable Melbourne. 'I've been too busy,' she told reporters. 'In any case I shall be writing later today.'

Tyson experienced a sense of anticlimax once the champagne had run out. With Keith Andrew, he went to the cinema in the afternoon, only remembering halfway through the film that he had forgotten an interview request from Australian commentator Alan McGilvray. When he got back to the Windsor Hotel, he made a note in his diary: 'Perhaps the luckiest and certainly the happiest day of my life.'

THIRD TEST

Melbourne Cricket Ground   31 December, 1954 and 1, 3, 4, 5 January, 1955

ENGLAND FIRST INNINGS

		Balls	Minutes	Fours	Sixes	Out at
*L. Hutton	c Hole b Miller	12	32	37	1	—	3/29
W.J. Edrich	c Lindwall b Miller	4	11	17	1	—	1/14
P.B.H. May	c Benaud b Lindwall	0	6	7	—	—	2/21
M.C. Cowdrey	b Johnson	102	247	239	15	—	8/181
D.C.S. Compton	c Harvey b Miller	4	9	11	—	—	4/41
T.E. Bailey	c Maddocks b Johnston	30	118	118	3	—	5/115
†T.G. Evans	lbw b Archer	20	63	72	2	—	6/169
J.H. Wardle	b Archer	0	9	15	—	—	7/181
F.H. Tyson	b Archer	6	28	32	—	—	10/191
J.B. Statham	b Archer	3	17	23	—	—	9/190
R. Appleyard	not out	1	2	2	—	—	
Extras	9 b	9				
All out (67.6 overs, 295 mins)		191				

ENGLAND SECOND INNINGS

		Balls	Minutes	Fours	Sixes	Out at
*L. Hutton	lbw b Archer	42	141	146	3	—	2/96
W.J. Edrich	b Johnston	13	52	65	1	—	1/40
P.B.H. May	b Johnston	91	183	199	8	—	4/173
M.C. Cowdrey	b Benaud	7	55	51	—	—	3/128
D.C.S. Compton	c Maddocks b Archer	23	101	89	2	—	5/185
T.E. Bailey	not out	24	144	163	2	—	
†T.G. Evans	c Maddocks b Miller	22	41	41	2	—	6/211
J.H. Wardle	b Johnson	38	45	41	7	—	7/257
F.H. Tyson	c Harvey b Johnston	6	27	33	1	—	8/273
J.B. Statham	c Favell b Johnston	0	6	8	—	—	9/273
R. Appleyard	b Johnston	6	10	8	1	—	10/279
Extras	2 b, 4 lb, 1 w	7				
All out (100.5 overs, 431 mins)		279				

AUSTRALIA BOWLING

Lindwall	13	0	59	1	18	3	52	0
Miller	11	8	14	3	18	6	35	1
Archer	13.6	4	33	4	24	7	50	2
Benaud	7	0	30	0	8	2	25	1
Johnston	12	6	26	1	24.5	2	85	5
Johnson	11	3	20	1	8	2	25	1

England won the toss and decided to bat   Hours of play: 12 p.m.–6 p.m.
Umpires: C. Hoy (Queensland), M.J. McInnes (South Australia)

AUSTRALIA FIRST INNINGS

		Balls	Minutes	Fours	Sixes	Out at
L.E. Favell	lbw b Statham	25	35	53	4	–	3/43
A.R. Morris	lbw b Tyson	3	9	17	–	–	1/15
K.R. Miller	c Evans b Statham	7	8	21	1	–	2/38
R.N. Harvey	b Appleyard	31	71	100	4	–	5/92
G.B. Hole	b Tyson	11	24	32	1	–	4/65
R. Benaud	c sub b Appleyard	15	54	78	–	–	6/115
R.G. Archer	b Wardle	23	53	70	2	–	7/134
†L.V. Maddocks	c Evans b Statham	47	140	162	2	–	9/205
R.R. Lindwall	b Statham	13	15	20	1	–	8/151
*I.W. Johnson	not out	33	85	117	3	–	
W.A. Johnston	b Statham	11	15	22	1	–	10/231
Extras	*7 b, 3 lb, 2 nb*	12					
All out (*63.3 overs, 355 mins*)		**231**					

AUSTRALIA SECOND INNINGS

		Balls	Minutes	Fours	Sixes	Out at
L.E. Favell	b Appleyard	30	61	76	2	–	2/57
A.R. Morris	c Cowdrey b Tyson	4	14	36	–	–	1/23
R. Benaud	b Tyson	22	63	91	3	–	4/86
R.N. Harvey	c Evans b Tyson	11	31	32	1	–	3/77
K.R. Miller	c Edrich b Tyson	6	17	22	1	–	5/87
G.B. Hole	c Evans b Statham	5	24	17	–	–	6/97
R.G. Archer	b Statham	15	22	43	1	–	9/110
†L.V. Maddocks	b Tyson	0	1	4	–	–	7/98
R.R. Lindwall	lbw b Tyson	0	2	1	–	–	8/98
*I.W. Johnson	not out	4	13	21	–	–	
W.A. Johnston	c Evans b Tyson	0	3	4	–	–	10/111
Extras	*b 1, lb 13*	14					
All out (*31.3 overs, 185 mins*)		**111**					

ENGLAND BOWLING

Tyson	21	2	68	2	12.3	1	27	7
Statham	16.3	0	60	5	11	1	38	2
Bailey	9	1	33	0	3	0	14	0
Appleyard	11	3	38	2	4	1	17	1
Wardle	6	0	20	1	1	0	1	0

ENGLAND WON BY 128 RUNS

The match was scheduled for six days but completed in five.

Attendances: First day: 63,814. Second day: 65,515. Third day: 63,040. Fourth day: 57,418. Fifth day: 50,483.

Total: 300,270

Debut: L.V. Maddocks (Australia).

Twelfth men: J.W. Burke (Australia), J.V. Wilson (England).

Sources: Barry Valentine, Charles Davis (sportsstats.com.au), cricketarchive.com, Richard Cashman

Australian players raise a glass to toast the arrival of 1955: Left to right: Ian Johnson, Ron Archer, Jim Burke, Arthur James (masseur), Bill Johnston, Les Favell, Graeme Hole.

Colin Cowdrey hooks Ron Archer to the boundary during his brilliant first-innings hundred.

Godfrey Evans sprawls to take the catch and Brian Statham has removed Keith Miller in Australia's first innings at Melbourne.

All alone and still unknown, Frank Tyson prepares to leave Northampton at the start of the tour.

VII

ADELAIDE AND THE ASHES

'I think he was the fastest bowler I ever faced — he was probably the fastest bowler I saw in my career'
Ray Lindwall on Frank Tyson

'I've got a feeling someone is in for a nasty half-hour'
Keith Miller to his teammates before the
start of England's run-chase

'The buggers have done us again'
Len Hutton as England collapse in pursuit of victory

IDEAS ABOVE HIS STATION

Low key might be the kindest way to describe Frank Tyson's departure from Northampton. On 14 September, 1954, the day before MCC set sail for Australia, he stood on the London-bound platform of the railway station in his adopted home town and waited to begin the first part of his journey towards a new life. It would be seven months and more than 35,000 miles before he saw Northampton again.

Tyson wears a smart suit and a natty trilby: an overcoat is slung over his arm. Just to the left, and slightly behind him, a railway porter sits on a mail-bag trolley, puffing on his pipe. Otherwise the platform is practically empty. Nobody has come to see Tyson off – 'they stayed away in their droves,' he later wrote – apart from the representatives of the *Northampton Chronicle & Echo*. 'He could be a young soldier in mufti. He could be a film noir gumshoe,' said Gideon Haigh in a speech to launch Tyson's tour memoir in 2005. 'But he's a young cricketer waiting for his train to London, without agent, ghostwriter, life coach or spiritual guru in sight.'

Although the photograph is clearly staged, there is nothing fake about the indifference of the Northampton public. Selection for an MCC tour undoubtedly conferred a level of celebrity, but for now Tyson was still a relatively anonymous figure. By the time the England team left Melbourne after his second successive match-winning performance, all that had changed. Taking 19 wickets in two Tests at a pace that had shocked and intimidated Australia's leading batsmen catapulted Tyson to sporting stardom. At home he was front-page news, leaving journalists suddenly scrambling for biographical background. The *Empire News* and *Manchester Evening News* signed him up for columns at £10 a time. In Sydney, a sports equipment manufacturer announced the launch of a new ball, 'The Typhoon', in his honour. Tyson was thrilled: 'I shall take some home and try flogging them around the clubs.'

His widowed mother, Violet, welcomed the newsreel cameras. 'It's been all very exciting,' she said. 'As a mother I'm very proud and I'm sure all England is.' She showed a Pathé News reporter the Indian clubs her son swung each evening to strengthen his arm muscles. Tyson died in 2015, aged 85, but the aura that became attached to his name in these few weeks endured. 'His place in the pantheon was never disputed,' said his *Wisden* obituary.

Tyson was not a fast bowler for the purists, like Fred Trueman, Dennis Lillee or Michael Holding. His short, energetic run-up, requiring huge physical effort, might be compared among modern-day pacemen to the Indian, Jasprit Bumrah. 'He is a tremendous force of human nature,' said Neville Cardus. 'In technique I did not think he was the equal of Larwood, Lindwall and Miller,' wrote the former Australian batsman Jack Fingleton, dismissed three times by Larwood in the Bodyline series. In a review of the 1954–55 series in *The Cricketer*, Fingleton returned to his theme: 'Tyson has not the variations that Larwood possessed. He has no control of the bumper and he does not move the ball as Larwood did, but in sheer pace, tenacity and stamina I thought I could well have been watching Larwood again.'

In his tour book, John Arlott provided a graphic description of Tyson at work during the devastating fifth-morning spell at Melbourne:

He turned, leant forward, as if peering at the batsman and, after three stammers of the feet, launched himself up a stretch-striding and accelerating run of 18 long paces. His body, thrown forward until the last few yards, heaved back and then, again, forward with the delivery, his hand following behind the released ball as if with an extra valedictory impulsion and his body hurled three or four leaping yards down the pitch after it.

The *Sydney Morning Herald*'s Lindsey Browne also mentioned that long follow-through and Tyson's 'comic-strip bully's attitude' as he looked at the batsman. Despite his physical presence, he did not cut a menacing figure. 'Without a cricket ball in his hand he wouldn't cause a ripple in a bird bath,' wrote Ross Hall in the *Daily Mirror*. Joyce Andrew, wife of Tyson's roommate Keith, recalled his habitual clumsiness. 'If he came to the house, you had to watch out,' she remembered. 'He'd break anything he sat on. I used to have a special chair for him.' The press made much of his English literature studies at Durham University and Tyson's ambition to be a schoolteacher at the end of his cricket career. He struck up a friendship with Arlott based on their mutual love of mooching around Australia's second-hand bookshops.

His elevation to superstardom had been as rapid as the deliveries that propelled England towards their two great victories. The previous winter had found him a long way from the packed Test grounds and broiling temperatures of Australia. Weekends included net sessions at the indoor cricket school run by the former Surrey and England seamer Alf Gover in south-west London, imbibing precious wisdom on fast bowling. During the week he worked on a willow plantation in Leicestershire owned by the bat-making family of Surrey captain Stuart Surridge.

Freddie Brown, the Northamptonshire captain, had thought Tyson's pace fell away during the course of a day and recommended a winter of stamina-building hard labour. Felling willow trees certainly provided that, as Peter Loader, an MCC teammate in Australia, had discovered. 'After the first three days you'll want to run away and die,' Loader warned Somerset's Ken Biddulph. 'Your hands will be sore and bleeding and your back will ache more than you can imagine. But it does get better.' As well as the manual work there was steak every night and plates piled high with bacon and eggs at breakfast. For Tyson, the benefits soon became obvious.

As he reached peak performance in Australia, teammates as well as opponents began to regard him with something close to awe. 'He was too fast for them,' said Peter May, recalling the Melbourne Test. 'I fielded in the slips in that match and Frank's pace was such that I would not have backed myself to hang on to anything snicked at me.' Tom Graveney recalled the devastating spell at Sydney. 'I was at slip and I was 50 yards back. I was nearer the gate to go off the ground than I was to the batsman.'

The Australians agreed. Although Brian Statham regularly achieved high speeds during the series, Arthur Morris, who had to face-down Tyson's withering new-ball assaults, reckoned that facing Statham after an over from Tyson was like tackling the medium-fast Trevor Bailey after Statham. 'I think he was the fastest bowler I ever faced – he was probably the fastest bowler I saw in my career,' said Ray Lindwall. Morris, added, 'All fast bowlers are fast enough, but Tyson has that extra yard and you've hardly time to pick your bat up.'

Plenty of informed judges endorsed that view. The author David Frith, who wrote a history of fast bowling, thought that in the 1954–55 series Tyson 'surely bowled as fast as any man in history'. During England's Ashes tour 20 years later, when Dennis Lillee and Jeff Thomson were inflicting heavy defeats and broken bones on a traumatised England batting line-up, John Woodcock of *The Times* accepted a lift back to his hotel during the Adelaide Test from Sir Donald Bradman. "'And who is the fastest you've seen?" I asked the Don, thinking he would probably say Harold Larwood for the havoc he had caused on the Bodyline tour,' Woodcock remembered. 'Instead, without a second thought, he replied: "Oh, Frank Tyson."'

Perhaps Tyson's secret was that he loved his work. 'To bowl quick is to revel in the glad animal action; to thrill in a physical prowess and to enjoy a certain sneaking feeling of superiority over the other mortals who play the game,' he wrote in *A Typhoon Called Tyson*. 'Oh yes, there have been better fast bowlers but I doubt whether there has been one who derived more pleasure from bowling fast.'

UNLUCKY JIM

Thanks to the joint efforts of Geoffrey Howard and Len Hutton, relations between the MCC party and the travelling press corps remained largely cordial. It helped that England were winning. 'It is so much pleasanter for a correspondent overseas to follow a winning than a losing side,' said Bruce Harris of the *Evening Standard*. 'Besides "the office" likes it that way.' Howard's work was praised in a letter to assistant secretary Billy Griffith from Crawford White of the *News Chronicle*, sent in the early weeks of the tour. 'He seems to have the knack of letting everybody know exactly what is happening and is not afraid to give frank background material to help things along. Len, too, is doing a fine job and is a different man to the one who toured last winter.'

Soon after the third Test, however, there was a full-blown and, at times, ugly row between MCC and one of Britain's best-selling newspapers. The problem emanated not from Australia, but less than four miles from the Grace Gates, in Fleet Street. It began on 11 January, the final day of MCC's drawn game against a Tasmania Combined XI at Hobart. In attempting to stop a stinging drive from Neil Harvey, Jim McConnon, the Glamorgan off-spinner, fractured the little finger of his right hand. The Australian journalist Ray Robinson was smart enough to remember it had been from a shot by Harvey's brother Clarence, in the match against Queensland in November, that McConnon had suffered the blow to the groin which had ruled him out for several weeks. Misfortune, as well as the Harveys, seemed to be following him around.

Hutton thought the blame lay partly with the cheap ball being used in the match, a concern MCC had raised with the Australian Cricket Board. There were three types of ball on the tour: the best quality for the Tests, a less expensive one for the state matches and a low-grade variety for the country games. 'Cheap balls are hard compared to the best hand-stitched ones, the risk of injury being much greater using the former,' Hutton wrote in his end-of-tour report. It was a cheap ball that had injured McConnon in Tasmania, although Hutton estimated such cheeseparing had saved the Australian authorities a mere £50.

McConnon was examined by John Colquhoun, a Melbourne surgeon, who wrote to Howard confirming everyone's worst fears: 'I agree with you that he has been damned unlucky ever since his arrival in Australia and I am of the opinion that he will not be of any further use to the MCC for the remainder of the tour.' McConnon would be in plaster for six weeks.

Howard consulted the timetables and found the P&O liner *Strathmore* was sailing from Fremantle on 23 January. He decided to send McConnon home. Given the player's incapacity, it did not seem a particularly controversial move. As Howard reported to Lord's, McConnon would like to have stayed long enough to watch the fourth Test at Adelaide, but that could not be fitted around the departure dates of the liners. A fractured finger was not the only consideration.

'The poor chap has had a rotten tour. There is no doubt about that, although he is not, I am bound to say, a terribly good tourist,' Howard wrote to Billy Griffith. 'He finds it awfully hard to "muck in" with the blokes and tends rather to make heavy weather of minor injuries. His general attitude towards life is that of a person who thoroughly enjoys a little ill health.' Howard admitted his remarks might appear harsh, though, adding, 'I like him very much as a chap. He is quiet, modest, almost too modest and unassuming, but he is not really very well equipped physically and mentally for a tour like this. He just is not tough enough.'

The matter may have ended there had it not been for a back-page column by Desmond Hackett, one of the best-known sportswriters in the country, in the *Daily Express* on 27 January, the eve of the fourth Test. Hackett wrote, 'Let us hope too that England play with a bigger heart than the MCC officials have shown in handling the unhappy case of Jim McConnon, who has been ordered home for the sad and single reason that he broke the little finger of his bowling hand.' According to Hackett, McConnon had asked to be allowed to stay until after the fourth Test, to see what he felt would be a famous England victory, and was willing to pay the difference between the cost of the sea passage and the air fare. 'Bluntly, it is not cricket,' was his verdict on MCC's penny-pinching attitude.

At Lord's, the article sparked fury. Questions were asked about Hackett's source. It was thought McConnon might have been collared by a freelance in Perth before boarding ship. By 3.30 p.m. that day MCC had issued a statement denying most of the story: McConnon had not been forced to leave the tour, had not asked to stay on until the end of the Australian leg and had certainly not offered to pay the difference for his travel (one of Howard's letters noted that McConnon was particularly careful with money).

In a letter to Howard, Griffith described the report as 'one of the wickedest pieces of journalism it has been my misfortune to read.' The outrage did not stop Hackett wading back into the story on 2 February, citing the volume of correspondence – a pile of letters 'cricket-stump high' he claimed – the *Express* had received on the subject. 'Cricket lovers from all over Britain have risen to demand the full story of Jim McConnon,' he wrote. 'They write with the venom of a Frank Tyson special.'

This prompted another rebuttal from MCC and a phone call to the club's lawyers to discuss the possibility of taking legal action against the newspaper. After studying the advice, MCC president Viscount Cobham wrote to Griffith, 'Dearly as I would love to go for this vile publication I have a feeling that we would lose more than we would gain.' Later, he described the *Express* as 'nothing short of the scum of the earth'. In Australia, Howard agreed: 'How I hate newspapers of the *Express* type.'

Sensing a chance to have a dig at their rivals, the *Daily Mail* contacted MCC to ask if Roy McKelvie, one of the paper's leading writers, could be granted an exclusive interview with McConnon when the *Strathmore* docked at Tilbury, and the BBC asked him to appear on the *Sportsview* programme.

When the ship arrived on 20 February, Griffith travelled to Tilbury to form an official welcoming party. He was at McConnon's side when he gave a press conference, followed by a newsreel interview, denying stories that he had been forced home. 'The specialist who had examined my broken finger out there said it was better for me to come home and the matter was agreed with the tour manager, Mr Howard,' he said. Hackett was also at Tilbury and claimed to have landed an exclusive interview with the returning bowler before Griffith could get to him. Griffith told Howard the piece was a complete fabrication. 'The thing is too utterly fantastic and diabolical to bother you with any more,' he wrote. And with that the story blew over.

McConnon returned to Wales, where he had an injury-hit summer for Glamorgan, taking just 48 wickets. He returned to his best in subsequent seasons, but never again earned international recognition. The man who had been chosen ahead of Jim Laker, one of England's greatest bowlers, returned to relative obscurity. As the author David Woodhouse said, 'Jim McConnon is now remembered, when he is remembered at all, for not being Jim Laker.'

JOHNSON UNDER PRESSURE

In Tasmania, they were delighted to welcome Len Hutton. In the summer of 1954, Bill Jeanes, secretary of the Australian Board of Control, had written to Lord's conveying the earnest hope of Tasmanian cricket officials that the MCC captain would visit the island. Neither of his immediate predecessors, Walter Hammond and Freddie Brown, had bothered to do so. Hutton responded promptly: 'It is my intention to play or be present at all the country matches.' It demonstrated that despite the cut-throat intensity he brought to retaining the Ashes, Hutton appreciated the role of an MCC tour as a flag-waving exercise.

The two matches were laid-back affairs – Tasmania's elevation to the Sheffield Shield was more than 20 years away – and the Combined XI were bolstered by the inclusion of Test players from the mainland, Neil Harvey, Richie Benaud, Alan Davidson and Les Favell. The match was drawn, but drew an attendance of more than

20,000, the biggest crowd for a first-class game in Tasmania. In the second match, MCC beat Tasmania by 243 runs, but Hutton managed the clock so efficiently that the game did not finish until 15 minutes from the end of the last session, maximising the entertainment.

There were two more matches – against a South Australian Country XI at Mount Gambier, a coastal town near the border with Victoria, and the return state fixture against South Australia at Adelaide Oval – before the fourth Test began on 28 January. But the England captain now retired to the Pier Hotel in the seaside suburb of Glenelg, seven miles from Adelaide, to husband his resources and plan his strategy. 'A retreat such as this ensured that he could, without giving offence, avoid meeting well-meaning people, who would want to talk cricket,' wrote Hutton's biographer Gerald Howat.

The tour selection committee's main topic for discussion was the underperforming batting. Bill Edrich had not made a significant contribution since Brisbane, whereas Tom Graveney had scored a century against Tasmania. 'I was in great nick, the ball kept whistling off the middle of the bat which was very nice,' Graveney recalled. 'I felt I had just about done enough to get back in the side. For the first time in my cricketing career I'd gone out and trained, worked hard to get fit, run up and down the sands at Adelaide, and I wasn't picked. I was livid.' England named an unchanged team.

That relative serenity was not replicated in the Australian camp. Once again, the wisdom of promoting Ian Johnson to the captaincy ahead of Keith Miller was called into question. After the third day of the Melbourne Test, when Johnson hit an unbeaten 33 batting at No. 10, Bill O'Reilly had written, 'Johnson needs to make some well-defined contributions like this to make his place in the team certain. In placing himself No. 10 on the batting list, hiding himself at mid-on in the field and using himself generally as second-change spin bowler, he had not, until yesterday, done much to clinch his position.' Miller, meanwhile, had made a scene-stealing performance with the new ball on the opening morning.

Johnson did not have many fans in the England dressing-room either. 'Off the field "Johnno" was charming and likeable,' wrote Edrich. 'On it he was a greenhorn with only moderate cricketing ability – a combination guaranteed to tear the inside out of any international team.' Nor was there much respect for his slow, floaty off-spin, delivered with a suspiciously bent elbow. 'All we players contend that Ian throws, although no Australian would agree,' said Godfrey Evans. 'As he passes muster with the umpires, perhaps it is a matter of opinion.'

When Johnson was appointed just before the first Test at Brisbane it seemed a triumph for expediency. The captaincy was decided on a vote by the individual state cricket boards. Their preferences were not made public, but R.S. Whitington believed that the six Victorian and South Australian delegates voted for Johnson, the three from New South Wales for Miller, while Queensland's two votes went to Arthur Morris. Johnson then required just one vote from Western Australia or Tasmania to carry the day. Sydney's *Daily Telegraph* was sharply critical of the process: 'There is a strong feeling among cricket enthusiasts that horse trading on a state basis rather than objective valuation of cricket skills have dominated selectors' discussions.'

Some sympathy was due to Johnson. 'He was unlucky to come to the captaincy at a time when the great team of a few years earlier was in decline,' wrote Gerry Cotter in his book *The Ashes Captains*. 'Yet his leadership was not the inspirational sort that will lift a team when times are rough; he was solid and dependable but unoriginal, rarely one for taking a gamble.' In contrast, John Arlott felt Miller's leadership had 'a touch of genius'. Miller was in the process of leading New South Wales to a hat-trick of Sheffield Shield titles. The commentator Alan McGilvray believed only Don Bradman rivalled Miller in his ability to watch a few minutes of cricket and come up with a piercing appraisal of the strengths and weaknesses of the players involved.

But Miller lacked Johnson's establishment credentials. Johnson's father Bill was a Melbourne wine and spirit merchant, and had been a Test selector: his father-in-law Dr Roy Park[38] played one Test for Australia in the 1920–21 Ashes whitewash and had been a schoolmate of prime minister Robert Menzies at Wesley College, the prestigious Melbourne school also attended by Johnson. There was no doubt

[38]Park made a first-ball duck in his only innings and bowled one wicketless over. It was said that his wife dropped her knitting as he prepared to face his first ball, bent down to pick it up and missed most of his Test career.

that Johnson was well equipped to handle the various social and diplomatic demands of being a tour captain, which might help to explain his appointment before the 1954–55 Ashes series.

Soon after Len Hutton's team had headed off to New Zealand, Australia were due to make their first tour of the West Indies. The trip had been arranged at the instigation of Sir Hugh Foot, governor of Jamaica, and endorsed by Menzies. The prime minister saw it as a chance to enhance Australian prestige overseas, while in the Caribbean there was a desire for a more chivalrous contest after the rancour of MCC's 1953–54 visit under Hutton. Whitington, Miller's biographer, believed this in part explained the preference for Johnson. Whitington wrote, 'My belief is that Bradman was genuinely convinced that Miller was not the man the board should appoint to lead Australia on an overseas tour and that, if he were appointed to lead her now at home, this would be the inevitable and unavoidable consequence.'

Whitington felt the administrators made a key miscalculation. As in England, there were concerns about the game's falling popularity. Few cricketers could match the youthful charisma of the tennis stars Lew Hoad and Ken Rosewall. A Test team led by a figure with the zest and *joie de vivre* of Miller might have been exactly what Australian cricket needed. However, the board members were mostly conservative, cautious and unimaginative characters, and, Whitington said, 'They would be unlikely to appreciate (as indeed Bradman appears not to have done) that the very qualities of Keith's which won the admiration of overseas people (from Royalty to ragamuffins) and would help Australia now, were the ones being advanced against him – his fearlessness, positiveness, independence of thought and action, and his frankness.'

A CAUTIOUS START

Ten days before the start of the fourth Test, the Australian selectors announced their team for what had become a must-win match. The headline was that vice-captain Arthur Morris had been discarded – to howls of outrage – along with Graeme Hole. Morris's replacement at the top of the order was Colin McDonald, 26, of Victoria. It would be his seventh Test, but his first against England. He was at the cinema with Len Maddocks when Victoria teammate John Power came rushing down the aisle with the good news. Two years earlier, McDonald had scored a century against South Africa at Adelaide. 'I am glad it is being played there,' McDonald said. 'It has pleasant memories for me.' Hole was replaced by Jim Burke. In Adelaide, there was dismay that local hero Gil Langley had not been reinstated as wicketkeeper: instead, Maddocks kept his place to add ballast to the batting. Alan Davidson was the 12th man.

Australian writers and pundits were in agreement that home batsmen needed to show greater resolve against Frank Tyson and Brian Statham. They noted how many had been dismissed playing cuts, hooks and glances: few seemed to want to get into line. An English journalist thought he had diagnosed the problem. 'They are strokemakers,' wrote the *News Chronicle*'s Crawford White. 'Their training has not built the discipline the circumstances demanded.' One distinguished former Australian Test player turned journalist disagreed. Arthur Mailey, the great leg-spinner of the 1920s, felt recalling a mainly defensive batsman such as McDonald when the match needed to be won was faint-hearted. 'What Messrs Tyson and Statham really need is a sound thrashing,' Mailey said.

In contrast to their bickering opponents, England's build-up was serene. It seemed indicative of the crisis engulfing Australian cricket that MCC strolled to an innings victory over South Australia. There were seven wickets for Peter Loader, bowling impressively even if his Test chances were limited, and centuries for Denis Compton and Peter May. Les Favell's place in the Australian XI was suddenly in doubt after he was dismissed twice for low scores by Alec Bedser.

Adelaide was in the midst of a heatwave, making the Pier Hotel, with its cooling breeze blowing off St Vincent Gulf, an inspired choice for the MCC party. After the win over South Australia, Hutton sensibly throttled back on preparations and gave his men some extra time off. That still left two days in the nets to tune up for the Test, though there was some surprise when Bedser was seen bowling at the Australians.

Arthur Lance, the Adelaide Oval curator, was preparing his first Test pitch and he predicted it would hold few terrors for batsmen. Lance told journalists that he thought the team winning the toss would win the match. In contrast to the thrillers at Sydney and Melbourne, a high-scoring contest was expected – the short square boundaries increasing that likelihood – bringing the possibility of a draw into the calculations of both captains. That would be good enough for England to retain the Ashes.

The sweeping vista of the ground was highly impressive. 'Not a discordant note anywhere,' had been the verdict of the great England opener Jack Hobbs. 'The Adelaide Oval is the best and finest, the most beautiful cricket ground I have ever seen,' manager Geoffrey Howard had written in a letter home in October. Arthur Gilligan thought only Newlands in Cape Town stood comparison. The view over to St Peter's Cathedral was magnificent. The giant scoreboard, first used in 1911, was one of the most impressive structures on any cricket ground.[39] A line of Moreton Bay fig trees, originally planted to stop people getting a free view of the action, added a softer touch to the panorama. The Adelaide Hills shimmered in the distance. The players appreciated the superb practice facilities and nets, and were also well looked after by the dressing-room caterer, Johnny Leith. 'It was a pleasure to play cricket in such surroundings,' said Tyson.

As at Melbourne, play did not start until midday. At the toss, Johnson, using an 1891 penny featuring the formidable countenance of Queen Victoria – a memento of his Second World War service in the Pacific – opted to bat first after Hutton lost the toss. The England captain made a whirling motion above his head to indicate to the dressing-room that they would be bowling. Then a second toss was made, purely for the benefit of a photographer who had fluffed his shot first time around. Geeks were delighted to point out that Australia had now won 84 tosses to England's 83. The England players were unsure of the make-up of the Australian XI and were not enlightened until Hutton returned from the middle, clutching the team sheet.

The withdrawal of Lindwall, who had suffered a leg injury during Queensland's Sheffield Shield match against Victoria, meant the promotion of Davidson and a late recall for the discarded Morris. He would open the innings with McDonald. Favell, originally named

---

[39]The scoreboard is still hand-operated and is a heritage-listed building.

in the team, had arrived at the ground to be greeted by chairman of selectors Sir Donald Bradman: 'Les, you're 12th today. I think you'll agree your form has not been good just lately.' With Langley also missing, there were no South Australia players in the side, news greeted by much local anger. 'When the announcement was made over the public address system that I was 12th man there were loud murmurs of disappointment around the ground,' Favell recalled.

It had been clear to Hutton when he conducted his first inspection of the pitch an hour earlier that the heat would play a major role in his strategy. The temperature was nudging 31°C (90°F) when he led his team from the pavilion – side-on to the pitch at this ground. 'Many spectators wore panama hats and carried parasols as protection against the temperatures,' wrote Bernard Whimpress and Nigel Hart in their centenary history of Adelaide Oval. 'The men were in shirtsleeves and one reporter noticed the Bishop of Adelaide, the Right Rev. B.P. Robin, clad in white jacket, shorts and long socks.' Bruce Harris noted, 'The women wore dresses as light and airy as convention allowed.' Ian Peebles was concerned the match might become an endurance contest unless there was a break in the weather. Sid Barnes called the ground 'a cauldron of heat'. There had been no rain in Adelaide for more than three weeks. Back in England there was snow, fog and floods as millions switched on their radios to hear the BBC's early-morning update.

Tyson opened the bowling from the Cathedral End with three slips, a gully, two leg slips, cover, mid-on and a deep square leg. McDonald and Morris, untroubled, collected four runs off the over. One leg-side catcher was taken out for Statham and four runs were added to the total, but there was real aggression from McDonald in Tyson's second over when he crashed one boundary past gully and another through the covers.

A hot wind added to the discomfort for the players, as it had at Melbourne. In 1877, James Southerton, a member of the England team in the inaugural Test match, described the Adelaide wind as 'almost hot enough to set your clothes on fire'. Hutton had little option but to shuffle his bowlers frequently to conserve their physical resources. Tyson bowled three overs and Statham just two before they were succeeded by Bob Appleyard and Trevor Bailey, but they were soon back. A pattern of frequent bowling changes emerged.

R.S. Whitington sensed the England captain's agitation: 'Hutton, in the covers and at mid-on, was giving those outward manifestations of inward unsettlement that the observant have come to recognise – touching his cap, staring at the ground, starting forward to begin the issue of an order, then mentally cancelling it, making mental surveys and appreciations of his field settings.'

Hutton had contributed to his team's struggles by dropping Morris at leg slip in the first over of Statham's second spell. The Australian vice-captain mistimed an attempted pull, but the ball arrived more slowly than Hutton anticipated and the chance was spurned. Fifty came up in the last over of a taut but undistinguished morning. As Hutton had predicted, there was too much at stake for either side to cast aside caution. 'I expect it to be as tense a struggle as an English Cup final at Wembley which, because of the gravity of the occasion, never produces the best football,' he said in his pre-match press conference.

There was a little more action to engage the crowd in the afternoon. In the first over McDonald drove Statham through the covers for a boundary that took the score to 55: the highest opening partnership of the series by either team. In Statham's next over Morris made a hash of an attempted hook and had to swat the ball away as it threatened to drop on to his stumps. The reprieve was temporary. Facing Tyson in the next over, Morris went back to a ball that lifted and it brushed his glove on the way through to Godfrey Evans. Morris had made 25, but his successor, Burke, was rendered almost completely strokeless.

McDonald, meanwhile, was justifying his recall. Adelaide's lower bounce and absence of swing suited his game. McDonald saw the introduction of Johnny Wardle as a signal to attack: if Hutton fretted about deploying spin he might end up overworking his seamers. The logic may have been sound, but the execution was faulty: McDonald pulled against the spin and sent the ball looping towards Denis Compton at wide mid-on. He took a couple of steps backwards, but was off balance when the ball arrived and he dropped the catch. Len Bailey of London's *Star* blamed female spectators screaming in the members' area for putting Compton off as he shaped under the ball.

The veterans Hutton and Compton had both now spurned eminently catchable opportunities. They were seen to exchange sheepish glances. E.M. Wellings of the *Evening News* had no sympathy: 'Men who could find so much time for golf while their fielding remained weak cannot complain if I question their cricket judgment,' he grumbled. 'They were sent out to represent England at cricket, and golf, race meetings and other diversions should not have been allowed to distract them.'

Like Morris, McDonald could not capitalise on his let-off. In the next over he tried to turn an Appleyard off-break off his legs, but could only push it into the grateful hands of Peter May at forward short leg. McDonald had hit 48 on his return and forced a re-evaluation of criticism of the selectors. In the last over before tea, England claimed their third wicket of the session when Burke, who had crawled to 18 off 74 balls, was taken smartly by May at short leg off Tyson. On an unhelpful pitch and in stifling conditions it had been a notable effort by England. 'Hutton had directed operations with craft and wisdom,' wrote Peebles.

There was more of the same after tea. Bailey, who had not bowled since before lunch, returned to tempt Neil Harvey with a ball of drivable length which he edged to Edrich at first slip. At 129 for four with 75 minutes left for play, and Keith Miller and Richie Benaud together, it felt like the moment for Australia to take on England's toiling bowlers. But both were hamstrung by the gravity of the situation. Miller was clearly hampered by a blister on the first finger of his right hand: several times he grimaced as he jerked his hand off the bat handle. Two runs came from the first four overs of the partnership. 'Benaud and Miller were like a couple of old hens scratching around,' said Gilligan. 'I cannot remember when Australian batsmen were so negative.'

Among the Australian writers, A. G. Moyes saw it as a missed chance to seize control of the game. Just 42 runs came in the 100-minute final session. During the day, England's five bowlers had been rotated in 20 different spells. Barnes thought Hutton had managed them 'with the meticulous care of an art dealer handling delicate Dresden china'. There are many aspects of 1950s Test cricket which would be unrecognisable to modern audiences, but perhaps none so immediately obvious as scoring rates. Australia's puny first-day total was of an order sometimes reached in slightly more than a session in the 21st century. At Edgbaston in 2005 England hit 407 runs on the opening day; at Brisbane in 2006–07 Australia launched the series by scoring 346, losing only three wickets in the process. The attacking approach reached its apogee in the 2023 series in England where the home team rattled along at 4.74 runs per over. On this day in 1955 at Adelaide Australia slumbered at 2.77 off 58 eight-ball overs.

Close of play: Australia 161–4 (Miller 26*, Benaud 12*)

ONE EYE ON THE DRAW

To relief all round, Saturday was cooler. Coping with extreme heat is an issue for every England team touring Australia, and days such as the opener at Adelaide took a considerable toll on their physical resources. Dr John Butterfield's medical advisory report for the MCC party dealt extensively with the demands of extreme temperatures and recommended several courses of actions, especially for bowlers.

He was a strong advocate of the use of salt tablets, especially at the end of a day in the field. Butterfield cited the recent example of the British runner Jim Peters at the Commonwealth Games in Vancouver, who had collapsed with severe dehydration at the end of the marathon. To bowlers and wicketkeepers, he suggested immersing hands in cool (not iced) water at the lunch and tea intervals. 'Leave wrists wet if possible,' he wrote. He recommended applying camphor ice, eau de cologne or after-shave lotion to the backs of hands. For fast bowlers he advised 'foot draining', which meant lying back for at least a minute with their bare feet raised above their heads, resting on a wall. Butterfield supplied a helpful diagram. This technique, he said, had been used by the Desert Rats fighting in north Africa during the war.

Although the temperature was less of an issue, Len Hutton stuck to his policy of deploying his bowlers in short bursts. Brian Statham and Frank Tyson resumed the England attack, but, by the fifth over, the ball was with Johnny Wardle and Bob Appleyard bowled the sixth. To add to his mastery of flight, Appleyard now had a stiff breeze at his back. The combination proved too much for Richie Benaud, who gave May his third short-leg catch of the innings off the seventh ball of Appleyard's opening over. New batsman Len Maddocks arrived at the middle to loud cheering. A local newspaper had appealed to spectators to forget their disappointment at his inclusion ahead of

Gil Langley and offer their full backing to Maddocks. He joined Keith Miller, but they were not together for long: Miller had made 44 when he misjudged a ball from Appleyard and offered Trevor Bailey a comfortable catch at midwicket.

Despite the warmth of his welcome, Maddocks looked woefully out of touch – 'The edges of his bat saw more service than the middle,' wrote the *Daily Telegraph*'s E.W. Swanton. Before he had got off the mark, Maddocks almost gifted Appleyard another wicket, but May, at short leg, was guilty of a rare fielding lapse and dropped the chance. He made amends after Hutton gave the new ball to Tyson during the last over before lunch, holding a smart catch at third slip to remove Ron Archer. England were relieved to see the back of Archer, who had hit the first six of the match into the members at square leg. At the interval, Australia had reached 221 for seven. 'Below standard for this pitch,' thought John Arlott.

When Alan Davidson edged Trevor Bailey to Godfrey Evans soon after lunch, Australia were in danger of posting a seriously undernourished total. But Ian Johnson's pre-match quotes had been bullish, promising that Australia would head to the final Test in Sydney with the series level. He must also have been heartily fed up of the flak aimed in his direction since the defeat at Melbourne. With Maddocks a willing accomplice, the captain led a counter-attack, in particular targeting Wardle, who bowled three overs for 23 in mid-afternoon. They had added 49 for the ninth wicket when Maddocks pushed Statham to Appleyard at midwicket and set off for a quick single. Johnson sent him back, but he was still yards short when Appleyard picked the ball up, took a moment to compose himself and lobbed a throw high over Evans's head. Amid stiff competition, it was one of England's worst fielding moments in the series.

Roared on by a fully engaged crowd of just under 44,000 (the largest at the ground since the explosive third Test during the Bodyline series), Maddocks and Johnson steadily increased Australia's total. Maddocks brought his 50 up off Tyson – 'to an ovation that must have echoed far across the city,' said Swanton – then hooked the same bowler for four and drove Statham imperiously through the covers. The 300, a distant milestone when Davidson was out, came up in the 95th over. 'Maddocks's innings,' wrote Bill O'Reilly, 'could be held up as a shining example of intelligent application of fundamental batting principles.' The sluggish pitch had so neutered the threat of Tyson that Johnson goaded the England bowler to attempt more bouncers.

The partnership had reached 92 before, in the last over before tea, Johnson lofted Bailey to Statham at mid-off. He had made 41 with five fours and gone some way to resuscitating his reputation. Immediately after the break, Maddocks was run out by a fine throw by Wardle from long leg. His 69, easily the top score of the innings, earned him a standing ovation: Australia were all out for 323 at 4.21 p.m.

The wickets were shared between Tyson, Bailey and Appleyard. The wicketless Statham had been struggling with a problem that might, if unremedied, have had serious implications. After months of running in to bowl on Australia's rock-hard grounds, the toenail was shearing off the big toe of his left foot. 'I dealt with this injury in my own skilled manner,' Statham recalled, 'first of all cushioning it with a wad of cotton wool and Vaseline.' The home-made cure had sufficed in the West Indies during the previous winter, but not now: Statham bowled in great pain during the first day. Gubby Allen suggested a solution he had used himself on two Ashes tours: cutting a hole in the leather toecap of the boot. It proved a perfect solution, though Statham wondered if the sight of the end of his sock protruding through the boot proved off-putting to the Australian batsmen.

England had just short of an hour and a half to negotiate when Hutton and Bill Edrich walked out to face Miller and – in Ray Lindwall's absence – Ron Archer. Hutton took seven from Miller's opening over and 16 came off the first two, but thereafter the rate slowed closer to England's customary level of progress. Johnson brought himself on from the Cathedral End after two overs from Archer and immediately settled into a rhythm. He stayed on to the close, conceding just three runs off nine overs of gently probing, generously flighted off-breaks. 'Hutton and Edrich thrust forward at him with limp bats, intent only on survival,' wrote Swanton.

When Hutton was on 20 he survived a confident shout for a catch behind off Davidson: the sound the Australians heard was the England captain's bat hitting the ground, not the ball brushing its edge. Percy Beames of *The Age* felt England already had an eye on the draw. They made it to the close without losing a wicket, though in the final over Edrich almost gave a slip catch off a sharply spun ball from Benaud.

Close of play: England 57–0 (Hutton 34*, Edrich 21*) trail Australia by 266 runs with all first-innings wickets in hand

MORE PITCH BATTLES

After the imbroglio over the pitch at Melbourne, it was hoped the fourth Test could pass without a row about the wicket. Unfortunately, that proved impossible. Curator Arthur Lance had been battling with the lack of growth of couch grass, which was needed to bind pitches together, and in its absence winter rye grass had continued to sprout. Lance's solution was to 'plug' it by dropping blocks of turf from elsewhere on the ground into the barren spots, but, 'By the end of play on Saturday the pitch was showing signs of unevenness,' said Percy Beames in *The Age*. 'In many places slight depressions could be seen.'

Early in England's first innings, Len Hutton began to fuss about the pitch. He was worried that left-armer Alan Davidson was creating rough outside the off stump which would make life awkward for England's right-handed batsmen when facing Ian Johnson's off-spin. He spoke to Johnson and to umpire Ron Wright. Johnson was in no mood to back down. If any bowler was damaging the pitch it was the heavy-footed Frank Tyson, he retorted. Hutton said that was irrelevant, but Johnson pointed out that Bob Appleyard could exploit Tyson's rough when bowling to the left-handed Neil Harvey. Voices were raised. Wright examined the mark made by Davidson's studs and ruled it was not dangerous.

Davidson began to veer away from the danger area soon after releasing the ball, which might have been taken as a victory for Hutton. The England openers neurotically patted down the pitch after each delivery. Irritated fielders told them to get on with the game. In Australia's first innings, Hutton had again slowed down the over-rate: excessive prodding of the wicket seemed to be just another time-wasting tactic to the Australians. 'It is feared that the unevenness of the wicket surface will become much more pronounced within the next two days,' said Beames. The anticipation of Monday morning's resumption was made all the keener.

Most of the England players spent the rest day in the Barossa Valley, the wine-growing region to the north-east of Adelaide. They visited the Hill-Smith vineyard and later the Lindsay Park horse stud. Tyson accepted an invitation from John Arlott to dine at an elegant house in the hills overlooking the city. 'It proved to be a lively dinner party with stimulating intelligent conversation,' he wrote. It was hard to stop thinking about cricket, however. England could be either poised to clinch the Ashes or face the unnerving possibility of heading back to Sydney with the series squared and the outcome still in the balance.

Before the cricket could begin on Monday morning, there were ceremonials. To mark Australia Day, Johnson raised the national flag, while the teams stood in line and the crowd sang *Advance Australia Fair*.[40] 'I regret to say none of us was able to join in because we hadn't a clue about the words,' wrote Margaret Hughes. The holiday meant there was another big crowd – a little under 40,000 – and the partisan atmosphere was boosted by two significant moments in the opening overs. Johnson began from the Cathedral End and struck with his seventh ball, turning an off-break through the gap between Edrich's bat and pad as he stretched unconvincingly forward. It was not much consolation that 60 was England's best start of the series. In the fourth over of the morning, Richie Benaud made a further incision when Peter May failed to deal with a top-spinner that reared up from the pitch like a snake shooting from a charmer's basket. He could only fend it in the direction of slip where Ron Archer took an outstanding diving catch.

At 63 for two only 45 minutes into the day, England were on the cusp of a crisis. Fortunately, Colin Cowdrey's short Test career had already encompassed plenty such moments. He looked calm and unflustered from the start. 'Cowdrey's mature mastery still astonishes one,' wrote Denys Rowbotham in the *Manchester Guardian*. The pitch remained occasionally treacherous, but perhaps not as much as its appearance suggested: it reminded Hughes of 'the sawdust-covered floor of the old barnstorm theatre'. Johnson kept himself and

---

[40]It permanently replaced *God Save the Queen* as the Australian national anthem in 1984.

Benaud going, but turned to Bill Johnston, bowling spin, and Alan Davidson – who delivered the only over of seam in the morning – as lunch approached. There was even an exploratory over of Jim Burke's occasional off-spin.

During the interval, Johnny Wardle and Tom Graveney left the ground to sneak a look at the Australian Tennis Championships taking place at nearby Memorial Drive: Ken Rosewall was meeting Lew Hoad in the men's singles final. This seemed an absurd piece of scheduling and attendance at the tennis duly suffered. The stewards on the gate would not let the cricketers in and – though they were wearing their MCC blazers and whites – the gateman at the Adelaide Oval refused them re-entry as well. As had happened at Melbourne, Geoffrey Howard was summoned to vouch for them.

In the morning, England had scored only 54 off 25 overs, hitting a paltry four boundaries. There was no change in the pattern in the afternoon: the first 12 overs of the session brought just 16 runs. 'It must have seemed tedious to most of the crowd,' Rowbotham conceded. But to those with an appreciation of the finer points of defensive batting, this was a gourmet banquet. Since Cowdrey's emergence as a Test player of immense potential, it had often been noted how much his textbook technique resembled that of Hutton. Now it was possible to simultaneously study teacher and star pupil. They showed acute judgment in what to leave alone – the balls that spun the most viciously were often harmlessly wide of off stump – what to kill stone dead with bat angled towards the ground and what could safely be played with their pads. Occasionally the ring of close fielders was kept interested, but Hutton and Cowdrey mostly steered clear of alarms.

Cowdrey had often pretended to be Hutton when playing cricket with his father as a boy – now he was 22 yards away from his hero in a match that could decide the destiny of the Ashes. Throughout the tour, Cowdrey had benefited from Hutton's advice in the nets and when they had batted together. It was a debt he never forgot. 'He was a terrific technician,' Cowdrey recalled. 'His secret was to think early and go late. That would be the thing I learnt from him, get your antennae out. We didn't talk much when we were batting together. We'd meet in mid-wicket and he'd say, "Well done, well done."'

Hutton's footwork that day was a PhD submission in its own right. R.S. Whitington likened him to the American middleweight,

Sugar Ray Robinson. 'To those who have batted under such circumstances against persistently penetrative and exceedingly accurate bowling, Hutton's masterly demonstration was as much a delight as an education,' Whitlington wrote. His opponents may have been critical of aspects of his captaincy, but they were united in admiration of his batsmanship. 'His technique was the finest I've ever had the opportunity to bowl to,' said Davidson. 'The way he went on to the back foot first, shifting his weight, and then was still able to go forward. His technique should have been recorded on film as one of the finest there has ever been. I never saw him hurry; great players never hurry.'

Hutton had brought up his fifty with an all-run four to fine leg in the morning and seemed, as the afternoon wore on and he allowed himself odd moments of aggression, to be moving inexorably towards his first century of the series. But on 80 Johnston dragged down a long hop that demanded to be hammered to the boundary. Hutton was through the stroke slightly too soon, but it was still hit with considerable force. To general disbelief, Davidson at short leg somehow clung on to an astonishing catch. 'The ball was simply a blur,' Davidson remembered, 'but I instinctively anticipated its path. Afterwards I was told it would have cut me in half had my hands not been there.' Peebles lamented, 'Once again superlative fielding had cut Hutton off when fully set.' Hutton had batted for four and a half hours, faced 294 balls and had put on 99 with Cowdrey. But England still trailed by 161: more hard graft was required.

Fortunately, Compton proved up to the task. Before and after tea he hunkered down with the well-set Cowdrey in a show of determination entirely at odds with his cavalier reputation. England's slow climb towards parity was aided by unimaginative captaincy from Johnson, who kept his spinners on too long and failed to vary his lines of attack. The run-rate slowed to a crawl, however, as both batsmen struggled to time the ball on a pitch of uneven pace.

'Only if a batsman was absolutely over a half-volley was it ever safe for him to drive,' said Rowbotham. As the crowd began to jeer, Cowdrey grew agitated and attempted a few rash shots. 'It is hard to visualise the strain that this sort of occasion makes on a young man just 22,' empathised Swanton. Soon, 12th man Vic Wilson was trotting out to the middle with a replacement bat and two bananas.

'Skipper thought you might be hungry?' Wilson said. Cowdrey did not need a new bat nor a banana – this was Hutton's way of telling him to block out the crowd noise and redouble his efforts. He got the message. Cowdrey and Compton saw England through to the close without further alarms. 'Short of unexpected disaster tomorrow, England should be safe from defeat in this match,' wrote Rowbotham.

Close of play: England 230–3 (Cowdrey 77*, Compton 44*), trail Australia by 93 with seven first-innings wickets in hand

A FEW BOB'S WORTH

The Adelaide Oval press box thrummed with its usual level of agitated activity: the hammering of typewriter keys, the shouts of 'copy' to summon the boys responsible for transmitting words to newspaper offices, the telephone conversations with nit-picking sub-editors, the noise of the nearby telegraph machines transporting pictures and words around Australia and across the globe to England.

Yet not everything was quite as normal. Two regulars were missing from the contingent of English journalists, while there was one new face – and a famous one at that. With England in the ascendancy and interest soaring at home, the *Daily Mirror* had despatched Peter Wilson, reputed to be the highest-paid sportswriter in Fleet Street, to Adelaide. Wilson arrived in time to cover the state match against South Australia and take in some of the Australian Tennis Championships: tennis vied with boxing as his favourite sport.

Wilson, who wrote under the banner 'The Man They Can't Gag', was the son of F.B. 'Freddie' Wilson, a stalwart of the *Times* sports desk and a former cricket captain of Harrow School and Cambridge University. Peter was also educated at Harrow and had a florid turn of phrase – his colleague, Norman Giller, wrote that he could sink a bottle of whisky without spilling a syllable – and a grand manner that made him an unlikely character to be one of the faces of Britain's biggest-selling left-wing daily.

There was space in the press box because of the unexpected absence of two of the tour's most acute observers, John Woodcock of *The Times* and Alan Ross of the *Observer*. Woodcock had been taken ill at a barbecue in Tasmania and was immediately rushed to hospital in Hobart, where he was found to have a duodenal ulcer. *The Times* had to summon Stewart Harris, who had recently rejoined the paper as assistant to Australia correspondent Roy Curthoys in the Melbourne bureau. Although Woodcock was sufficiently recovered to be at the ground by the time the Test began, he was not rushed back to work.

Ross, meanwhile, was a patient in Adelaide's Calvary Hospital after an operation for appendicitis. He was laid up for a fortnight, wrestling with the heat, but cheered by visits from friends, fellow journalists, and also Geoffrey Howard and Colin Cowdrey from the MCC party. 'If one has to be ill anywhere I can, from all points of view, thoroughly recommend Adelaide,' he wrote. Ross followed the Tests on a bedside radio and, like Woodcock, was able to make it to the ground for the final day.

When they emerged a few minutes before midday, the players were greeted by an outfield filled with seagulls. A small boy's effort to disperse the birds proved wholly inadequate. The early fourth-day exchanges were a mirror of events 24 hours earlier. England, desperately keen not to lose an early wicket, contrived to lose two. Compton and Cowdrey had emphasised their determination to push on with their fourth-wicket alliance by tuning up in the nets. They might have been better making do with a cup of tea in the dressing-room. Ian Johnson had delayed taking the new ball the previous evening in the hope that overnight covering might draw some moisture to the surface of the pitch. He made the switch after three deliveries of the second over, giving Keith Miller the chance to exploit the extra shine and bounce. He needed one ball. Compton went back to a delivery that ducked back in late and was lbw for 44. Cowdrey at least managed to add two to his overnight score before he edged Alan Davidson to Len Maddocks. England were 91 behind with just Trevor Bailey left of the front-line batsmen.

With Bailey at the crease, it might have been the signal for a period of dogged retrenchment. Instead, Godfrey Evans, the other new arrival, came out bristling with intent. He raced into double figures and shrugged off being dropped at slip by Jim Burke. When he lofted Davidson into the unattended deep, the England batsmen ran five and were weighing up a sixth when Arthur Morris finally retrieved the ball like an ageing Labrador. 'His innings was more than a cheerful wallop,' wrote Woodcock's locum Harris. 'There was skill and decision in everything he did, not least his running.' The 50 partnership came up one ball after the drinks interval and, although Evans was out later in the over for 37, made in better than even time, England were now appreciably closer to Australia's total.

Johnny Wardle played himself in for three balls from Richie Benaud then smashed the fourth over long-on for an enormous six which scattered spectators on the Hill in front of the scoreboard. 'From hit to pitch that clout could not have been less than a hundred yards,' said E.M. Wellings. The Adelaide Oval may have had short square boundaries, but its straight ones were longer than average: Arthur Gilligan reckoned Wardle's blow was one of the longest hits in world cricket. But rather than continue Evans's display of initiative, the seventh-wicket pair retreated. The scoreboard operators might have been in danger of nodding off. In the penultimate over before lunch, Bailey collected two off the struggling Ron Archer and England passed 300 for the first time in the series.

The afternoon session was even more soporific. Nine runs came in the first seven overs. Wardle broke the monotony with successive fours off Johnson, but was caught and bowled when trying for a third. As journalists noted, Bailey was often at his best with a proactive batsman at the other end. With the arrival of a struggling Tyson, Bailey lapsed into an apparent slumber. This was a repeat of his Melbourne innings, when he seemed unable to switch to the role of senior partner with the advent of the tail. Davidson bowled five successive maidens. 'The 25 minutes in which Bailey and Tyson scored one run apiece touched the depths of sporting entertainment,' wrote E.W. Swanton. A single off Benaud's 34th over brought the scores level, but another 26 balls passed before England moved into the lead.

By that time Tyson had gone, soon to be followed by Bailey. Brian Statham then provided Benaud with his fourth wicket and England were all out for 341, a neither-here-nor-there lead of 18. Australia had a tricky 40 minutes to negotiate before tea, but Morris and Colin McDonald did not look daunted. Runs came at a steady clip.

The pitch offered Tyson and Statham no encouragement. After five overs, Hutton turned to Appleyard from the Cathedral End.

Appleyard's use of flight and faster pace through the air presented a different challenge to Johnson's slow off-spin and Benaud's leg-breaks. 'He is not a spinner in the proper sense: rather he runs the ball off the first and middle fingers,' explained Swanton. 'While that is generally enough to give a little turn he has always that manipulation of the action which gives birth to flight.' Members of the press pack from southern newspapers had been slow to appreciate Appleyard's attributes: he felt they were still obsessed with the non-selection of the Surrey pair Jim Laker and Tony Lock. Now, he was about to present an unanswerable case.

The fifth delivery of his opening over was short and wide outside off stump. Morris rocked back and cut it hard into the ground from where the ball reared up and smashed into the face of Cowdrey, close in at gully. He collapsed as if picked off by a sniper. Cowdrey was the day's second victim of the Adelaide Oval's scarred and pockmarked square. 'The state of the infield made accurate and quick ground fielding extremely difficult, and it concealed dangers for fielders in the close positions,' said Wellings. He thought the ground 'unfit for a match of such importance'. Earlier, Johnson had slipped and fallen on his elbow, keeping him out of Australia's attack for most of the day. As Cowdrey lay flat out, play was held up for five minutes. Masseur Harold Dalton came out and eventually Cowdrey was led off clutching his bloodied face. The image was the main picture on the front page of the following morning's *Daily Telegraph*, despite attempts by an angry Appleyard to shoo photographers away. An x-ray later revealed a broken nose.

Morris was clearly distressed and the delay disturbed his concentration. Appleyard gave his next ball a little more air and the batsman, playing a fraction too soon, lobbed back a return catch. 'The Yorkshireman's spin and accuracy opened a mental chasm in Morris's mind as deep as a Himalayan gorge,' wrote Sid Barnes in the *Daily Express*. Australia were 24 for one at tea.

Hutton kept Appleyard going and rotated his seamers from the River End. There was no sign of Wardle until Hutton chose to prey on frayed nerves near the close. Appleyard did not concede a run until the final ball of his third over. He struck again with the first of his fourth.

This time Appleyard defeated Burke's forward push with an off-break that slipped between bat and pad, cannoning into the leg stump: 'a beauty,' wrote Bill O'Reilly. 'Hutton, that shrewd campaigner, knew that Johnson was too slow to take full advantage of the pitch, whereas Appleyard, who pushed the ball through much faster, would succeed,' wrote A.G. Moyes. His relentless accuracy also offered no respite, frustrating batsmen such as Neil Harvey, keen as always to keep the score moving. Harvey had made only seven when he aimed an ugly against-the-spin heave at a short ball and was bowled.

In any circumstances it was a poor shot, but in the current state of the game it was criminally reckless. Head bowed, Harvey trudged back to the pavilion. Appleyard had lopped off the head of the Australian batting with clinical efficiency: in effect they were 36 for three. Miller arrived to join McDonald, who had been observing events at the other end with mounting alarm. Knowing that Miller's finger was now painfully infected, Hutton brought back Tyson: 'A scene of superb struggle,' wrote Harris. Miller seemed unsure whether he preferred the physical pain of facing Tyson or the mental challenge presented by Appleyard. Tyson pressed down hard on the accelerator – Moyes thought he was bowling 'faster than any man since Larwood'.

But McDonald and Miller could not be shifted, and there were no more breakthroughs for England. Appleyard's figures were 10–5–13–3. How the game stood at the close was hard to call – but writers from English newspapers remained wary of Australia's ability to climb off the canvas. 'Four times today did the gods of cricket shift their favours and tonight they left us guessing still which side they will select to win,' said Harris. 'Although England's position is the stronger, there are several possibilities yet as to the outcome,' thought Swanton. 'Another day of strange and varied fortune left both teams warm in hope and slightly clammy in anxiety,' wrote the *Yorkshire Post*'s J.M. Kilburn. In the *Daily Herald*, Charles Bray added, 'Australia are not in a hopeless position but they are in a dangerous one.' Hutton could not resist returning to Saturday's row over the bowlers' rough: 'Appleyard might yet win the match on the pitch made by Alan Davidson.'

Close of play: Australia 69–3 (McDonald 29*, Miller 12*), lead England by 51 runs with seven second-innings wickets in hand

A DIFFERENT KIND OF HERO

Early in the tour, Bob Appleyard was the subject of a few lines in one of manager Geoffrey Howard's frequent letters to Ronny Aird at Lord's. 'He seems a little bit worried and nervous about his health, and that, of course, is easily enough understood in view of his medical history,' Howard wrote. 'I do not think he is going to be very easy, and is, in fact, the only member of the party who has not thoroughly settled down.' It was true that the rib injury suffered during the stop-over in Ceylon had delayed his adjustment to Australian conditions, but the independently minded Appleyard was not struggling with other aspects of touring life: he was merely different.

Appleyard's emergence from a two-year struggle to recover from tuberculosis naturally gave him a different perspective to some of his teammates. The hectic social life enjoyed by Denis Compton, Bill Edrich, Godfrey Evans and others held no appeal. He shared a room with the quiet farmer Vic Wilson. 'I would say that Bob was quite a lonely individual on tour,' Trevor Bailey told Appleyard's biographer, Stephen Chalke. Appleyard did not agree with that assessment: he was just happily self-contained and dedicated to his cricket. He did, though, earn an unexpected nickname. 'Whenever I met anyone who offered to show me around their company, I would go along and take anyone who was interested with me,' he said. 'So they started calling me "the factory inspector".' In Adelaide, there had been a more glamorous outing when he and Colin Cowdrey dined at the home of Sir Donald Bradman, who had asked to meet them. 'It was such an honour to be invited,' Appleyard recalled. 'We just listened in awe, like a pair of apprentices with their master.'

After hours of diligent work in the nets, by the fourth Test he felt he had reached a level of consistent performance not previously attained in his career. 'Everything had come together,' he said. 'I'd got used to eight-ball overs and, because it was so warm all the time, I could bowl short spells and I didn't stiffen up so much afterwards. I had to work hard to perfect my control of flight, my changes of pace and direction, and by Adelaide I really felt in control.'

His teammates were deeply appreciative of what his unusual bowling style offered the team. 'The warm climate suited him and he admitted that he had not felt so well for years, and for that reason he seemed to let himself go,' said Godfrey Evans. 'Dip – that was what was most remarkable about Bob's bowling,' added Bailey. 'I'd never come across a bowler of his pace with dip before, and I've never seen it since.'

Appleyard's inspirational story gained great public interest. He became a champion for TB sufferers across Australia. 'I'd visited a couple of sanatoria for tubercular patients,' he remembered. 'Some of the lads were getting ready for coming out and they'd got tickets for the Test. They were all sitting at a certain place on the ground. And when I was fielding down there they all cheered, "Come on Lofty."'

What was not commonly known was that Appleyard's life had contained challenges beyond even his astonishing recovery from TB. His mother had left the family's Bradford home when he was seven and his sister died when he was in his early teens. His father, a traumatised First World War veteran, remarried and had two daughters, but when war was declared in 1939 he could not face a repeat of the conflict. After sending Bob, then 15, to visit his grandmother, he gassed the entire family. On his return home, it was Bob who discovered the bodies. Later in life, Appleyard had to endure the death of a son and grandson from leukaemia. Chalke's award-winning biography was called *No Coward Soul*, part of the title of the final poem written by Emily Brontë before her death from tuberculosis, aged 30, in 1848.

Appleyard's success late on the previous day meant there was a general expectation that he would be at the forefront of England's renewed efforts on the fifth morning. 'England thus still has a slender chance of victory,' wrote the *Manchester Guardian*'s Denys Rowbotham, 'and more than a slender chance if Appleyard can dislodge Miller and McDonald early tomorrow morning.' But, just as he had at Melbourne, Len Hutton put his faith in pace.

His intuition was instantly rewarded. Colin McDonald, so admirable in defence the previous day, played across Statham's third delivery, a full toss, and was bowled. In Statham's next over, Keith Miller played forward to a ball that kept low and was also bowled. Then Tyson, back off his long run, trapped Richie Benaud with a half-volley to which, head in the air, he offered a shot whose exact intention was hard to define. In 21 minutes, Australia had lost three wickets for the addition of seven runs.

It got worse. Len Maddocks was lbw to Statham in his next over and Tyson then had the limping Ron Archer caught behind. Batsmen had been shuttling in and out of the Australian dressing-room with alarming regularity, but finally there was respite and a five-over spell in which no further wickets fell. Alan Davidson demonstrated to his colleagues what might be achieved with a mixture of calmness and resolve. Bill Johnston, promoted above his injured captain, made the most of being dropped by Evans off Statham. The hundred came up in the 37th over, but eight wickets had been lost in getting there. Johnston immediately aimed a cross-batted shot at Tyson and skyed a catch to Appleyard at mid-off.

Ian Johnson had needed an injection in his injured elbow to allow him to bat – still, the general was more up for the battle than some of his troops. He must have known the situation was hopeless, but Australian cricket teams are hard-wired to fight until the corpse stops twitching. Davidson and Johnson negotiated the two remaining overs before lunch and the first four after the break. When Davidson edged Tyson to the boundary it was the first four of the day. The temperature hovered around 32°c (90°F), but Hutton drove his strike bowlers on until lunch. Appleyard was finally given the ball after the interval, but it was his Yorkshire teammate Johnny Wardle who delivered the final blow when Davidson failed to make contact with a tempting long hop and was lbw.

Australia were all out for 111, the same miserably apologetic total they had made in the second innings at Melbourne. Seven wickets had fallen for 42 between the midday start and 2.30 p.m, a performance of shocking ineptitude. 'The Australian batsmen completely lacked the guts to fight their way out of trouble,' said Arthur Gilligan. Bill O'Reilly admitted his notebook had barely been able to keep up with the procession in the morning. 'It was much more difficult, however, to try to account for the extraordinary attitude our batsmen developed towards the tense situation,' he wrote. John Arlott called them, 'A rabble in retreat.' England needed a routine 94 to win, secure a 3–1 lead, clinch the series and retain the Ashes. Hutton's long-cherished dream was within touching distance.

'THE BUGGERS HAVE DONE US AGAIN'

Injured or not, Ian Johnson led Australia out. Ron Archer, struggling with a leg muscle strain, was also in the group. Johnson could not bowl, nor throw. His lack of mobility would be a hindrance in the field, but this was a public show of defiance. The Australians were fired up by a pugnacious pep talk from Keith Miller. 'I've got a feeling someone is in for a nasty half-hour,' he said. He never made a better prediction.

The clock was approaching 2.40 p.m., but time was the last thing on Len Hutton's mind. He would have been quite happy to come back tomorrow if that's what it took to get the job done. At least he was out in the middle, now waiting to take the first ball from Miller from the River End. As the England team left the field at the end of Australia's second innings, Hutton had moved alongside Denis Compton. '"Denis, I don't feel like going in again ... would you mind going in first?"' Compton recognised the haunted look Hutton had worn in his hotel room on the first morning at Melbourne. 'It looked to me as if Len had almost had enough, as if the mental strain of the whole thing was becoming almost unbearable.'

Compton said that of course he would open the batting, at the same time pointing out his lack of experience in the role. When the players got back to the dressing-room he began to pad up, but, glancing over, saw that Hutton was doing the same. 'I went across to him and asked him if he still wanted me to go in first. "Oh, no, no ... I'll be going in first." In a moment of irritation I felt he might have communicated his change of mind to me, but Len seemed so exhausted and under so much pressure that it was understandable he should overlook things.' Compton thought this incident was a graphic demonstration of the stress of elite sport: 'I can always remember his look of anguish as I sat there, padded up and ready to go in.'

The England captain's steel had not entirely deserted him. Peter May asked who would go in at No.4 given Colin Cowdrey's broken nose and blackened eyes. Hutton replied coldly that there would be no change in the batting order. Hutton reduced the target by three when he pushed Miller's fourth ball past Johnson at mid-off. That brought Bill Edrich up to face Miller. In the

Australian Broadcasting Commission box, Charles Fortune was at the microphone:

'So Hutton's away with three runs, England nought for three, needing 94 runs to win the Test match and the rubber. Miller turns, comes back, bowls, and Edrich is out, bowled. [loud crowd noise] Edrich bowled. Played right over the top of one pitched well up to him. Had his middle peg knocked back. England one for three, Edrich bowled Miller no score.'

With Archer not fully fit, Alan Davidson took the new ball from the Cathedral End. May, the new batsman, collected three runs before the focus turned back to the magnetic figure of Miller at the end of his mark. The second ball of the over was a delicious outswinger that Hutton edged low to second slip where Davidson dived to catch the ball almost off Archer's bootlaces. With both openers gone, England were 10 for two. Lindsay Hassett sympathised with Hutton. 'Three times in the last three Tests,' he wrote, 'Davidson has caught Hutton and on each occasion the catches were of such an outstanding nature that Hutton might honestly consider himself cheated by fate.'

One came off the over and four from Davidson's second. Cowdrey then square-cut Miller to the fence, but was rapped a painful blow on the thigh by the next ball. The follow-up was devastating. Cowdrey played at another late-shaping outswinger and Archer at first slip made the catch look easier than it was. Now it was 18 for three: suddenly the fate of the Ashes was back in the balance.

Disbelief mingled with despair in the dressing-room. The recuperating Woodcock had been invited to share the triumph, but now he was witness to moments of sporting drama denied to his press-box colleagues. 'Len was sitting in the dressing-room,' Woodcock recalled. 'He had taken his shirt off, and had a towel round him. He still had his pads on.' Godfrey Evans remembered the taut atmosphere: 'Nobody spoke, although facial expressions told their own story.' Appleyard joined Hutton away from the viewing area – 'We got to the stage where we couldn't watch' – and, over and over, Hutton kept repeating the same words. 'The buggers have done us again,' he said. He was becoming convinced Miller, his old nemesis, was about to spirit away the prize he had worked so long to achieve. The normally phlegmatic Compton was furious. 'I'll show you who's done who,' he said, snatching his bat and walking out to the middle. England still needed 76.

Arthur Gilligan articulated what many were thinking: 'It was a good job for England that Ray Lindwall was not at the other end.' The tension got to even the most experienced observers. 'I have seen every [Ashes] Test in Australia since 1932 and never have I known such excitement as today's,' wrote the *Evening Standard*'s Bruce Harris. 'How many heart stoppages there were, I cannot estimate. My own came to a halt repeatedly.'

An extra touch of theatricality was added by four Royal Australian Air Force Gloster Meteor jets roaring over the ground. Locals interpreted this as a sign of encouragement to the former Second World War pilot, Miller. His concentration disturbed, May spooned an attempted drive off Miller towards mid-off. The bowler pivoted and sprinted after the ball, but it dropped out of his reach. Some things proved beyond even his superhuman powers.

Gradually, England drew the fire from Australia's furious onslaught. With figures of 7–1–20–3, Miller had to take a breather. Archer, gamely but ineffectively, bowled from one end, while Richie Benaud and Bill Johnston were also introduced into the attack. Benaud thought he had May leg-before, but his appeal was turned down by umpire Ron Wright. Miller wasn't quite finished. May drove Johnston's penultimate ball before tea hard and low through extra cover where Miller, sprawling inches from the turf, held an astonishing catch in his left hand. He rolled over and over as the Adelaide crowd celebrated this unexpected revival of hope.

From the vantage point of the dressing-room, however, it was clear that the ball had slipped from Miller's grasp as he completed his gymnastic tumbling. Compton thought so, too, and urged May to stand his ground. But communication was difficult above the tumult. 'We could see that the ball bounced out of Miller's hands and hit the ground,' said Frank Tyson. May looked to Miller for confirmation that he had completed the catch and when the fielder nodded he walked off. Miller later said he was certain he had control of the ball for long enough. None of the England players agreed. Hutton wanted Geoffrey Howard to lodge an official protest. 'It was the most unworthy thing that I ever saw Keith do on a cricket field,' said

Tyson. Tom Graveney recalled the incident more than 50 years later: 'Keith may have put it down, but I'm sure he wouldn't have cheated.'

Nevertheless, England were 49 for four at tea, still a tantalising 45 from victory. The Compton-May partnership had sapped Australia's belief. 'May and Compton got right down to the job,' wrote Gilligan, 'head down, bat straight and steady, playing every ball on its merits.' Compton could only admire his great friend's heroic bowling performance. 'It was a typical piece of Miller's inspired aggression,' he said. 'He was hostile, very quick, accurate. Off a docile and placid wicket he was moving the ball both ways.'

Trevor Bailey's pin-sharp cricket brain saw that this was not a moment to get bogged down, even if all-out attack would be reckless. Instead, he and Compton plotted a middle course, collecting runs sensibly whenever opportunities presented themselves. Eventually, Johnson was left with no option except to bring back Miller. Bailey was crowded by five close fielders, but no one in world cricket was less likely to get flustered. After his three overs had cost 14, Miller was withdrawn. England now needed just 11.

Finally, Hutton allowed himself a smile. 'I wish that bugger Hawke were here to see this,' he said to no one in particular, a reference to that famous Lord Hawke speech – 'Pray God no professional shall ever captain England' – given almost exactly 30 years earlier. Hutton made his way down to the radio commentary position where Alan McGilvray was at the microphone, broadcasting to England as well as Australia.

England were four runs from victory when Bailey was anticlimactically lbw to an invitingly floated slower ball from Johnston. Evans had been trying to focus on reading a book to shut out the feverish anxiety of the dressing-room. Now he was needed in the middle. 'My only thought was to finish it off as quickly as possible,' he remembered. He wondered why Compton seemed strangely reluctant to run between the wickets, later discovering that he had been offered £5 to hit the winning run. Miller summoned up the energy to test Evans with a sizzling bouncer, but as McGilvray described, there were no more causes for alarm:

Now the scores are level, five for 93, Compton 34, Evans two. Scores level. It's a tie as it stands with five wickets in hand. Miller to Evans, it's hit high and hit for four. It's gone away to the boundary for four. Five wickets for 97 and England have won this match by five wickets. A good shot by Evans brought four. The crowd swarming all over the ground now, around the players, around Compton, they are running all over the ground to add their congratulations. England won the fourth Test and the Ashes.

McGilvray then introduced Hutton, congratulating him on winning the Ashes, his captaincy and the job he had done. 'Thank you very much indeed, Alan,' replied Hutton. 'At this moment of course we are feeling pretty tired and I really don't know what to say except that all the team are very happy indeed at the result, as I know you all will be at home. Thank you very much.''

Four years earlier at Melbourne, Compton had been at the crease when England defeated Australia for the first time since the Second World War. At The Oval in 1953 he had hit the runs that won back the Ashes in Coronation year. Now, he had completed a notable hat-trick. 'The most satisfying 34 runs I ever made,' he said.

At 5.20 p.m. on a sunlit Adelaide afternoon, England had retained the Ashes. It had been an epic day of Test cricket – compared by John Arlott to 'the plot of a novel'. After the catastrophic defeat in Brisbane, Hutton's men had clinched three successive victories in matches of nerve-shredding tension that had tested to the limit their mental strength as much as their cricketing talent. For Hutton, the first professional in the role, it was a momentous, era-defining achievement. He became the fifth England captain to win a series in Australia in the 20th century. In the next 70 years, only four men would match that feat. It is one of the most exclusive roll calls in sport.

Two further facts burnish Hutton's CV. Of England captains to win in Australia, only Johnny Douglas in 1911–12 did so after losing the first Test. And Hutton didn't just win an away series – he had already wrested back the Ashes at home in 1953. Under Hutton, John Arlott wrote, 'England lost their inferiority complex bred by Australia's immense post-war power.' However, since 1955, winning successive home-and-away series against Australia has proved beyond all but Mike Brearley and Andrew Strauss.

Hutton conducted a 40-minute press conference and posed for photographs that would appear in many of the following morning's

English papers. There was no ticker-tape presentation, no trophy, no replica of the Ashes urn to flourish triumphantly, no supporters to salute, no round of TV interviews, no lap of honour. At the end the crowd had gathered sportingly in front of the pavilion, but it soon dispersed. Within half an hour the Adelaide Oval was empty, seagulls picking through the detritus of picnic lunches and discarded newspapers that blew across the ground. The England players packed up their kit and climbed into the waiting Holden saloons for the journey back to the hotel: it was time for the celebrations to begin.

'A NEW ERA IN ENGLISH CRICKET'

No one knew how Bill Edrich had got up there and no one was quite sure how he was going to get down. Sitting on top of a 20-foot-high marble pillar in the lobby of the Pier Hotel, Edrich, glass of champagne in hand, serenaded the cheering crowd below. He had made his hazardous ascent for a bet – £100 he claimed – but after shinning down he agreed to a further double-or-quits punt on the toss of a coin. This time he lost.

Edrich was not blessed with a great singing voice, but that did not stop him deploying it. 'Bill loved parties and he brought to them the same zest and enthusiasm which epitomised his cricket,' Trevor Bailey recalled. 'He considered that a good one should never end before dawn and he was always prepared to provide a cabaret act to delay the break-up.'

As England's victory party got into full swing, Edrich belted out a few popular songs. Hutton joined him and the pair reprised a somewhat bawdy duet first heard aboard the *Orsova*. The players dedicated a lusty version of 'For He's a Jolly Good Fellow' to Hutton. The captain responded with 'On Ilkley Moor Baht 'At'. Within hours, Edrich went missing for 48 hours with an old RAF colleague. He returned only just before the team were due to leave for Sydney, and had to be dressed and shepherded to the coach by Denis Compton.

Everyone agreed it was a good party. 'I had to sign for 100 bottles of champagne at about a guinea each,' manager Geoffrey Howard recalled. 'And I was so busy that I never even had one glass myself.'

Bruce Harris of the *Evening Standard*, who claimed to be the only man present who had also attended the celebrations to mark the triumph under Douglas Jardine 22 years earlier, a notable double, thought it 'good humoured' and noted that none of the hotel guests were offended. From the hotel most of the team went to another party at the home of a family who had entertained them during their stay in Adelaide. There was some concern that Frank Tyson had joined Edrich on the missing list, but a search found him fast asleep under a grand piano. That merciless morning spell had taken its toll.

At the press conference earlier, Hutton had acknowledged that the rapid conclusion of the Test had come as a surprise. 'It was entirely unexpected,' he said, 'which is why cricket is so fascinating a game. I expected we should have to make 160 to 170 runs to win and I must say, funny though it sounds, it would have been easier to do that than make 90-odd.'

Talking to the assembled press he had been thoughtful and generous, particularly when discussing the heroic efforts of Miller. 'I think he is the finest new-ball bowler in the world,' he said. 'He has troubled me a lot – and I wish he would concentrate on his batting.' While on the subject of the veterans, he praised Compton's coolness in a crisis and saluted the prehensile work of Davidson, describing him as the best close-to-the-wicket fielder playing today.

His main theme, though, was youth and the shining performances of England's new stars. 'Test cricket is a young man's game,' he said. 'Credit must go to Tyson, Statham, May and Cowdrey. And, of course, Evans has again kept wicket magnificently. England has an extremely good attack in prospect with Tyson, Statham and Trueman, and spinners of the class of Lock, Wardle, Appleyard and Laker.' Hutton believed that May and Cowdrey were the best two young batsmen in the world and he paid particular tribute to Cowdrey: 'He has the best temperament I have seen in any young cricketer for a long time,' he said.

At home in Yorkshire, it was a day to remember. John Boyd-Carpenter, the Harrogate-born minister of transport, had announced the building of Britain's first motorway to link St Albans and Sheffield, a 150-mile stretch of road that was expected to cost £200 million, but next to the lead story in the *Yorkshire Post* was a picture of Hutton, bat over his left shoulder and making a V sign with his right hand. At the bottom of the page was a heart-warming story about Hutton's sons, Richard,[41] 12, and John, 8, both pupils at Wood Hall, a prep school near Wetherby in West Yorkshire. They had raided their pocket money to send a telegram to their father: 'Hooray! Love, Richard and John.' Richard asked headmaster J.W. Catlow if the school could have an afternoon off in recognition of England's triumph. 'It is not every school which has Len Hutton's two sons, and so, of course, I had to grant their wish,' Catlow said. The *Post*'s leader column joined in: 'We are especially proud of Hutton, who has bypassed the wealth of criticism which followed him to Australia, shaken off the dust of cricket pedants and statisticians, and shown himself to be incomparably England's captain.'

Sir Pelham Warner, who had captained the MCC teams in Australia in 1903–04 and 1911–12 (though on the latter tour he was ill and missed the entire Test series), said, 'I think we are seeing the beginning of a great era in English cricket.' Robert Menzies, who had watched so much of the series and dined with Hutton and Johnson after the third Test, was in London for the Commonwealth Prime Ministers' Conference. 'He suffers the natural disappointment of Australians but he is a cricketer and loves cricket so the winning and losing is nothing. It is the game,' said Menzies' spokesman. 'He is most impressed by the bowling performance of Tyson and Statham and regards them as the best fast-bowling pair since Jack Gregory and Ted McDonald in the twenties.'

At Lord's, MCC flags were raised over the pavilion within minutes of victory being confirmed on the early-morning BBC broadcast. 'Well done. Magnificent performance,' read the club's telegram to the team. Assistant secretary Billy Griffith was in good humour as he fielded calls from press and public. It was just as well the club had upgraded plans finally to make Hutton a member of MCC. No one wanted to mention that, if some senior figures at the club had had their way, Hutton would have been removed from the captaincy before the team even set sail. The plot was now a footnote in history.

[41]Richard Hutton followed his father in playing for Yorkshire and England. He made five Test appearances in 1971.

FOURTH TEST
Adelaide Oval   28, 29, 31 January, 1, 2 February, 1955

AUSTRALIA FIRST INNINGS

			Balls	Minutes	Fours	Sixes	Out at
C.C. McDonald	c May b Appleyard	48	117	160	5	—	2/86
A.R. Morris	c Evans b Tyson	25	90	110	1	—	1/59
J.W. Burke	c May b Tyson	18	74	81	1	—	3/115
R.N. Harvey	c Edrich b Bailey	25	42	64	3	—	4/129
K.R. Miller	c Bailey b Appleyard	44	142	151	4	—	6/182
R. Benaud	c May b Appleyard	15	66	104	2	—	5/175
†L.V. Maddocks	run out	69	165	169	7	—	10/323
R.G. Archer	c May b Tyson	21	27	37	2	1	7/212
A.K. Davidson	c Evans b Bailey	5	11	17	—	—	8/229
*I.W. Johnson	c Statham b Bailey	41	62	94	5	—	9/321
W.A. Johnston	not out	0	0	1	—	—	
Extras	b 3, lb 7, nb 2	12					
All out (99.1 overs, 501 mins)		**323**					

AUSTRALIA SECOND INNINGS

			Balls	Minutes	Fours	Sixes	Out at
C.C. McDonald	b Statham	29	95	126	1	—	4/69
A.R. Morris	c & b Appleyard	16	27	39	1	—	1/24
J.W. Burke	b Appleyard	5	19	27	1	—	2/40
R.N. Harvey	b Appleyard	7	21	21		—	3/54
K.R. Miller	b Statham	14	50	47	1	—	5/76
†L.V. Maddocks	lbw b Statham	2	20	28	—	—	7/79
R. Benaud	lbw b Tyson	1	4	5	—	—	6/77
R.G. Archer	c Evans b Tyson	3	7	17	—	—	8/83
A.K. Davidson	lbw b Wardle	23	56	76	4	—	10/111
W.A. Johnston	c Appleyard b Tyson	3	19	35	—	—	9/101
*I.W. Johnson	not out	3	30	31	—	—	
Extras	b 4, lb 1	5					
All out (43.2 overs, 234 mins)		**111**					

ENGLAND BOWLING

Tyson	26.1	4	85	3	15	2	47	3	
Statham	19	4	70	0	12	1	38	3	
Appleyard	23	7	58	3	12	7	13	3	
Bailey	12	3	39	3					
Wardle	19	5	59	0	4.2	1	8	1	

Australia won the toss and decided to bat   Hours of play: 12 p.m.–6 p.m.
Umpires: R.J.J.Wright (Victoria), M.J. McInnes (South Australia)

ENGLAND FIRST INNINGS

			Balls	Minutes	Fours	Sixes	Out at
*L. Hutton	c Davidson b Johnston	80	294	270	5	–	3/162
W.J. Edrich	b Johnson	21	88	92	2	–	1/60
P.B.H. May	c Archer b Benaud	1	10	9	–	–	2/63
M.C. Cowdrey	c Maddocks b Davidson	79	315	296	9	–	5/232
D.C.S. Compton	lbw Miller	44	140	124	5	–	4/232
T.E. Bailey	c Davidson b Johnston	38	136	145	2	–	9/341
†T.G. Evans	c Maddocks b Benaud	37	28	36	5	–	6/283
J.H.Wardle	c & b Johnson	23	68	67	2	1	7/321
F.H.Tyson	c Burke b Benaud	1	29	22	–	–	8/323
R. Appleyard	not out	10	12	18	2	–	
J.B. Statham	c Maddocks b Benaud	0	8	7	–	–	10/341
Extras	b 1, lb 2, nb 4	7					
All out (140.6 overs, 552 mins)		341					

ENGLAND SECOND INNINGS

			Balls	Minutes	Fours	Sixes	Out at
*L. Hutton	c Davidson b Miller	5	6	11	–	–	2/10
W.J. Edrich	b Miller	0	2	2	–	–	1/3
P.B.H. May	c Miller b Johnston	26	75	71	1	–	4/49
M.C. Cowdrey	c Archer b Miller	4	10	9	1	–	3/18
D.C.S. Compton	not out	34	97	115	1	–	
T.E. Bailey	lbw b Johnston	15	49	57	2	–	5/90
†T.G. Evans	not out	6	5	3	1	–	
Extras	*b 3, lb 4*	7					
5 wickets (30.4 overs, 139 mins)		97					

Did not bat: J.H.Wardle, F.H.Tyson, R. Appleyard, J.B. Statham

AUSTRALIA BOWLING

Miller	11	4	34	1	10.4	2	40	3
Archer	3	0	12	0	4	0	13	0
Johnson	36	17	46	2				
Davidson	25	8	55	1	2	0	7	0
Johnston	27	11	60	2	8	2	20	2
Benaud	36.6	6	120	4	6	2	10	0
Burke	2	0	7	0				

ENGLAND WON BY FIVE WICKETS

The match was scheduled for six days but completed in five.

Attendances

First day: 29,136. Second day: 43,983. Third day: 39,876. Fourth day: 26,298. Fifth day: 23,206. **Total:** 162,499.

Twelfth men: L.E. Favell (Australia), J.V.Wilson (England).

Sources: Barry Valentine, Charles Davis (sportsstats.com.au), cricketarchive.com, Richard Cashman

Delight in the England dressing-room after Godfrey Evans hit the runs that meant the Ashes were safe. Left to right, Trevor Bailey, Keith Andrew, Bob Appleyard, Johnny Wardle, Bill Edrich, Tom Graveney, John Woodcock (*The Times*) and Colin Cowdrey.

Len Hutton offers a Churchillian gesture – and gives one of the bats he endorsed a little product placement – after England's victory in Adelaide.

Tyson goes through his paces in Auckland for the benefit of scientists trying to measure how fast he bowled.

VIII
RETURN TO SYDNEY

'When I'm asked who was the best, and greatest, captain I played under, I'd say Len Hutton'

England wicketkeeper Godfrey Evans
on Hutton's captaincy

'He was an excellent manager. He looked after a very happy team and he did an awful lot to make it a happy team'

Trevor Bailey pays tribute to manager Geoffrey Howard

'"Pad up, Tom. You'd better come in with me." That was how I became an England opening batsman'

Tom Graveney on his sudden promotion in the fifth Test

CAPTAIN LEN

What were the qualities that Len Hutton brought to captaincy? What attributes did he have that enabled him to get the better of Lindsay Hassett, by the barest of margins, in 1953 and Ian Johnson, emphatically, in 1954–55? Perhaps Hutton's greatest virtue as a captain was his razor-sharp tactical acuity. 'There were certain things he understood about the game, simply by talking to him about technique and about various players, and about the bowling he had at his command,' said R.E.S. Wyatt, the former England captain who was a member of the selection panel that appointed Hutton in 1952. 'You knew he wasn't going to let you down. From a tactical point of view, and for appreciating the weakness of the opposition, he was very good.' Bob Appleyard, a key bowler in the 1954–55 triumph, added, 'He had a marvellous aptitude for seeing and reading the game, the batsman's faults and weaknesses. He had an insight into the game better than anyone I've ever played with.'

That cricket wisdom had been imbibed from his earliest days as a professional in the Yorkshire dressing-room of the 1930s. When Hutton made his County Championship debut, a few weeks before his 18th birthday at Edgbaston in May 1934, his teammates included Herbert Sutcliffe, Arthur Mitchell, Maurice Leyland and Hedley Verity, all players with an innate understanding of cricket's nuances and complexities. The tyro made 50 (and took three wickets), but was perplexed by Warwickshire's lanky slow left-armer George Paine. 'Maurice came down the pitch between overs and gave me a valuable hint or two,' Hutton remembered.

Witnesses to Hutton's formative years recalled how he would observe the strict hierarchical etiquette of the time, rarely speaking, but listening closely and squirrelling away knowledge for future use. He later understood that the absence of the captain – changing elsewhere in the amateurs' dressing-room – was a blessing. The seasoned professionals were free to formulate their own tactical plans. 'Almost all my boyhood was spent with older men,' he told Donald Trelford, the editor of the *Observer* who produced a biographical tribute to Hutton after his death. Trelford asked how he had spent his coming-of-age birthday in June 1937? 'In an opening partnership of 315 with Herbert Sutcliffe,' Hutton answered instantly. 'And Herbert was furious when I got out.'

It was this unforgiving approach that he brought to the England captaincy and especially to achieving the summit of his ambitions in 1954–55. 'It was as if his whole Test career had been dominated by a need to beat the Australians at their own game on their own turf and lay the ghost of Bodyline bowling forever,' Trelford wrote. 'He embodied and recreated the spirit of pre-war Yorkshire cricket in order to achieve it.'

This method earned the respect, if only qualified admiration, of his rivals. 'We won the first Test so easily and England fought back,' said Neil Harvey. 'That takes a bit of good leadership. You've got to have fellows who want to play for you. If they're not going to play for you, you're not going to be a good captain. Len had them wanting to play for him. And he led from the front.'

'He was a good, solid captain. He didn't make any tactical mistakes that I can recall,' Hassett remembered. 'Len was unimaginative as a captain, but very sound: he rarely took an initiative and he rarely made a mistake,' Johnson added. 'He wasn't so much a slow thinker as a cautious thinker. Before he tried anything he wanted to make sure that he'd really thought about it. He made very, very few mistakes.'

Cautious, pragmatic, wary of risk-taking: these are recurring observations on Hutton's captaincy: 'He only gambled on certainties,' said Trevor Bailey, his vice-captain on the 1953–54 tour of the West Indies. 'He was a bit on the cautious side,' admitted Wyatt. 'His attitude was not to give anything away, not to take any risks.' Nevertheless, England's success justified Hutton's approach. 'When I'm asked who was the best, and greatest, captain I played under, I'd say Len Hutton because he was so good,' said Godfrey Evans. 'He wasn't always popular with everybody, but he had a method of getting the best out of people, which is where I think he had it over most.'

England's Ashes Wins after Falling Behind

Series	Host	1st Test	2nd Test	3rd Test	4th Test	5th Test	6th Test	Result
1888	England	A	E	E	–	–	–	2–1
1911–12	Australia	A	E	E	E	E	–	4–1
1954–55	**Australia**	**A**	**E**	**E**	**E**	**D**	**–**	**3–1**
1981	England	A	D	E	E	E	D	3–1
2005	England	A	E	D	E	D	–	2–1

However, there was no consensus about his captaincy. Bill Edrich claimed that, under pressure, Hutton's decision-making was flawed. Jim Laker agreed. 'He sometimes flapped on the field,' Laker wrote. 'He made wrong decisions under pressure and sometimes he failed to do what had to be done.' Both cited the final afternoon of the fourth Test against Australia at Headingley in 1953 when, they claimed, Hutton had to be roused from a trance-like state and ordered to make the bowling changes that would halt Australia's comfortable progress towards victory. Defeat that day would have meant the Ashes were lost. Edrich also thought Hutton was poor at delegation, even after he had offered, during the voyage to Australia, to take on some of the duties and share the burden. 'Len's idea of skippering was to take all the responsibilities on his own shoulders and in the end the weight of them ruined him as a cricketer,' said Edrich. 'His nervous health was stretched to breaking point.'

Hutton found the demands of motivation and man-management a constant challenge, though Brian Statham felt he was successful in establishing *esprit de corps*. 'The atmosphere on that tour was very good and the atmosphere in the dressing-room was tremendous,' he said. 'It came from the manner in which the tour had progressed and the way we'd tackled the Test matches, and got stuck in and had a real go.'

Peter Loader, who took regular wickets in the state matches without coming near to a Test call-up, disagreed. 'After we had won the Ashes at Adelaide we were all invited to different parties to celebrate and I went to the toilet and Len was next to me. "Hello lad," he said, "Did you have a good tour?" It was almost the only time he spoke to me off the field for the whole tour,' Loader recalled.

And it was not just the fringe players who could feel ignored. Alec Bedser was laid low by illness when the team arrived in Australia: 'I had these shingles and I lay in bed in Perth for 10 days and he never came to see how I was all the time I was lying there.'

In contrast to these assessments, John Arlott felt Hutton did nurture the men under his command. 'He was unobtrusive in his captaincy, although he had all the subtleties, a deep knowledge of the game, an instinctive, if slightly avuncular, affection for his players, and an immense willingness to understand their problems and help to solve them,' Arlott wrote. 'Thus, his handling and guidance of Frank Tyson in Australia in 1954–55 was an essential part of that player's, and the team's, success.'

Peter May, Hutton's deputy in Australia, saw how much the leadership drained Hutton's resources. 'He was a very shy person and suddenly to be the first professional captain of England was a hell of a job for him, being the person he was,' he said. 'Colin Cowdrey agreed: 'The man-management was very hard for him. He had a great intuition as to whether someone liked him or not, and if they didn't he was liable to go back into his shell and be quite evasive. He wasn't too keen on the good-time lads and he could cold-shoulder them a bit.' Yet that comment also offers a clue to Hutton's success. He thoroughly disapproved of the hectic social lives of Edrich, Evans and Denis Compton, but recognised that all three were key players and, reluctantly, tolerated their choices.

All the players – and manager Geoffrey Howard – noted how Hutton would appear to drift off in the middle of talking to them, as if losing his thread. If he ended a sentence with 'You know what I mean?' they rarely did. Often Howard would find him in his room, with the radio on, staring at the wall. 'None of us knows him and none of us ever can do,' Howard wrote.

Results did little to mollify Hutton's sternest critic in the media. 'The pleasure of both the West Indies and Australia tours has been greatly marred for me by the feeling of hostility and distrust which has surrounded both parties under Hutton's command,' E.W. Swanton of the *Daily Telegraph* wrote in a letter to MCC secretary Ronny Aird. Neville Cardus was also frequently critical of Hutton's hard-nosed pursuit of success, but was forced to admire the way he masterminded England's comeback in Australia. 'I doubt if Hutton has so far received all the praise due to him for the way he declined to be shaken by his blunder at Brisbane,' wrote Cardus, 'a blunder "after the event" for there was reason when he won the toss for the bold action he risked in asking Australia to bat first.'

At the end of the series, before some members of the team left for home and the squad was reduced in size, the players presented their captain with a clock inscribed with the words they had most often heard him say in Australia. It read simply: 'Are you all right?'

THE VOICE OF CRICKET

In millions of English households it became an early-morning ritual. As the first kettle of the day whistled on the hob, radios were tuned to the Light Programme, where Test match commentaries were – in a bewildering feat of technology – broadcast 10,000 miles across the globe, live from Australia. Through the whine and the crackle, on a cold English winter's morning, it was possible to get a thrilling sense of the blinding sunshine, the shimmering heat and the great sporting drama as Len Hutton fended off Ray Lindwall and Keith Miller or Frank Tyson and Brian Statham laid waste to the Australian batting.

The voices of the Australian Broadcasting Commission team were, naturally, mainly home-grown, notably A.G. Moyes and Alan McGilvray, but Michael Charlton sounded English and Charles Fortune was born in England, even if he was now based in South Africa. Then there were the summarisers, Vic Richardson and Arthur Gilligan, Ashes adversaries in the 1924–25 series. McGilvray recalled their chemistry: '"What do you think, Arthur?" was the lead-in to a never-ending torrent of arguments and discussions that seemingly knew no bounds. They captured a nation and held it spellbound through the glorious days of Bradman and Hammond, Brown and Bedser, Miller and Lindwall, and a small army of the game's champions.' John Woodcock remembered it slightly differently: 'It was said that the two of them seldom allowed an over to pass without at least one "I quite agree, Arthur" and "Absolutely, Vic."'

Later in the morning, the BBC broadcast a summary of the day's play, and this time the voice was instantly familiar to English listeners: John Arlott. Since his first radio cricket commentary on the 1946

Test matches against India, Arlott had become synonymous with the game. He came from a highly unusual background, having made the improbable career transition from policeman on the beat in Southampton to BBC radio poetry producer. The Welsh poet Dylan Thomas was a friend and a fan. 'My dear John,' he wrote from a villa in the Apennine mountains in 1947. 'It was very good to hear from you. Though I hear your voice every day from Trent Bridge at the moment. You are not only the best cricket commentator – far and away that; but the best sports commentator I have heard ever: exact, enthusiastic, prejudiced, amazingly visual, authoritative and friendly.'

Arlott had never been to Australia, but he accepted an offer to write colour pieces for the *Evening News* in London (though he and the paper's cricket correspondent E.M. Wellings were far from friends), write a tour book, and broadcast for the BBC. It was a lucrative assignment, but as a freelance he could not afford the luxury of spending time aboard the *Orsova*. Instead, he flew out just before the first Test in Brisbane. On the way, there were stops in Karachi, Delhi, Calcutta, Hong Kong and Japan. He gathered material for travel articles and gave a series of lectures – in Tokyo he introduced students to his literary hero, Thomas Hardy.

As these assignments demonstrate, Arlott was far from a conventional cricket journalist. Before his departure, he had conducted a tour of English cheese regions. This led to a book, *English Cheeses of the South and West*. He was a knowledgeable and enthusiastic wine drinker (he later became wine correspondent of the *Guardian*) and used some of his downtime on the tour to visit Australian wineries. By the mid–1950s, Arlott was already a well-known public figure. In 1953, he had been part of the BBC radio team covering the Coronation and he was also one of the faces used to advertise Brylcreem hair-care products. The fact that the other personalities from cricket the company hired were Denis Compton, Keith Miller and Godfrey Evans says a lot about Arlott's level of celebrity.

Arlott also regularly appeared on the BBC radio programme *Any Questions?*, in 1953 speaking with measured humanity on the subject of homosexuality, then still illegal in Britain and recently the subject of a virulent campaign by the police, right-wing press and Tory home secretary Sir David Maxwell Fyfe. During the tour, he also appeared on the Australian version of the programme – often alongside leg-spinner-turned-journalist Bill O'Reilly. 'I talk about sex: it seems to work,' he wrote to his secretary Valerie France.[42] 'They have asked me to be on the programme every week until I leave.'

Other aspects of the trip were not so convivial. 'My father did not like Australia,' his son, Timothy, said. That view is supported by some of Arlott's letters home. To BBC cricket correspondent Rex Alston he wrote, 'The cricket is interesting throughout Australia, but otherwise it is a dull country: the people much of a hearty sameness and none of the things that interest me available in more than driblets – virtually no second-hand bookshops, bare bones of worthwhile architecture, no pottery, no glass, no pictures.' Similar thoughts were conveyed to Valerie. 'Australia is bright, brash, noisy but the country is all the same,' he said. 'They are nice people but there is no variety. I have a fancy to write a book about Australia. The Australians would hate it, but I would be out of the country by then.'

The broadcasts were well received and demonstrated Arlott's skill and flexibility, reining in his lyrical instincts to provide short, sharp bulletins of each day. 'Quite admirable' was Alston's verdict. 'In the words of Kenneth Adam (at an OB party last night) "John has disciplined himself extremely well in the cause"! I think you are quite right to take us through the day's play without too much statistical detail, and then to finish as you did with an assessment of the position and maybe a prophecy.'

As with many of the players, Arlott suffered badly from homesickness. A Christmas phone call home to his wife and children in north London ended in tears at both ends of the line. There were compensations in wine, even if his passion was the subject of press-box teasing by O'Reilly and Jack Fingleton. After the Adelaide Test he visited practically every vineyard in South Australia with Bill Bowes of the *Yorkshire Evening News*. 'Australian wine-making had far to go in those days – many of their products were sugary imitations of the French or of sherry and, as such, were all but undrinkable,' Arlott recalled in his autobiography. 'But there was good stuff to be found and it was duly discovered, enjoyed and remembered.'

---

[42]Valerie France became Arlott's second wife in 1960.

Arlott flew home via Fiji, Hawaii, San Francisco, Chicago and New York, and almost immediately found himself fighting the parliamentary constituency of Epping for the Liberal Party: he did not win and was free to carry on his never-less-than hectic freelance career. He did not tour Australia – nor anywhere else – again, though he did make a brief reappearance to commentate on the Centenary Test at Melbourne in March 1977.

LOSING FOCUS

In his press conference after victory in Adelaide, Len Hutton underlined his desire to ram home his team's advantage and complete a 4–1 victory in the fifth Test in Sydney. Hutton knew his history. Douglas Jardine, his regular reference point, had won the Bodyline series by a thumping 4–1 margin, as had Percy Chapman in 1928–29 and Johnny Douglas in 1911–12. Hutton found the idea of emulating them hugely seductive, but he was exhausted, physically and mentally worn out by the demands of a tour that had been in progress for nearly five months. And there was another factor inhibiting his ambitions.

Eight days after the end of fourth Test – during MCC's second state match against Victoria at Melbourne – Dorothy Hutton arrived to join her husband for the remainder of the tour. 'It is NOT a good idea to have wives [on tour],' manager Geoffrey Howard wrote to his own spouse, Nora. 'From the moment they arrived, the husbands have virtually left the party and I strongly disapprove! It is not right in principle and I shall say so.' Dorothy Hutton had been joined on her journey by Jean Evans, wife of wicketkeeper Godfrey. On the other hand, Howard's antipathy to the arrival of wives did not extend to Trevor Bailey's partner, Greta. 'Trevor's wife arrived on Friday and has produced a most marked difference in the young man,' he said in a letter to Lord's. 'His appearance is altogether cleaner and smarter, and it is possible to get into his room without kicking things to either side. His baggage is still tied up with string and he is not altogether in control, but he is a good deal nearer so.'

MCC tolerated the idea of players being joined by their partners on tour, but without much enthusiasm. A minute of the selection sub-committee on 3 May, 1954 recorded, 'That under no circumstances should the suggestion be entertained concerning financial aid to players for wives to visit Australia during the tour. Any applications for wives to join the team for a limited period should, however, receive the consideration of the MCC Committee.'

The topic was sensitive. One month into the tour, the *Daily Herald* ran a story on the subject with quotes from Jackie Graveney, wife of Tom. After it was published, she wrote anxiously to Billy Griffith at Lord's claiming she had been misquoted. Griffith offered a sympathetic response, 'Please do not worry about it and rest assured that we here at Lord's pay very little attention to the cricket news in papers like the *Daily Herald*.'

There were a number of reasons for Howard's annoyance at Hutton's sudden distance from the main business of the trip: for one, it added to his already formidable workload and that of baggage-master George Duckworth. Some of the players noticed a difference, too. Bill Edrich thought it was poor reward for the support he had given the captain during the past few months. 'It was noticeable that when the Ashes had been retained after the fourth Test, Len, free of his anxieties, had little time for the colleagues who had tried to help him in his lone battle,' Edrich said. 'He had an unhappy knack of dropping people.'

Retaining the Ashes merely added to the volume of correspondence. Howard said, 'I remember asking him at one point if he'd had any letters of congratulation. "I've been unindated," he said. He wasn't a great user of words. "Unindated." And he opened up his case and there were hundreds of them.' Howard drew up a standard letter of thanks that Hutton could quickly top, tail and sign.

Many years and tours passed before there was a softening in official attitudes to wives – and, later still, children – on tour (although, with the advent of air travel, the duration of the trips became shorter). On the 1962–63 Ashes tour, England captain Ted Dexter attracted heavy criticism when his wife, Susan, a well-known fashion model, accompanied him to Australia. 'As wife of the MCC captain Mrs Dexter modelled, wrote and televised so profitably that the weekly earnings were said to be £100,' wrote E.M. Wellings. 'Dexter, and hence the team also, earned adverse publicity when, on arrival in Sydney by air with his wife in the party, he asked the television unit for payment for an interview.' When the players' families arrived in Australia during the 1974–75 Ashes tour, John Woodcock wrote in *The Times*, 'It is no more a place for them than a trench on the Somme.'

In the 21st century, it would be unthinkable for wives and children not to be around for substantial parts of an Australian tour and, likewise, when Australia visit England. For Hutton, Evans and Bailey paying for their partners to travel to Australia was a considerable expense, out of the reach of most players, and the captain was certainly all too aware of the cost. 'Len's main interest was in securing Dorothy satisfactory accommodation,' Howard remembered. '"Best possible terms" he was after.'

Hutton was always conscious of money and believed that rewards for professional cricketers were too low, given the high profile of the sport. During the Melbourne Test, he used his speech at an official dinner given by the Australian Board to complain about the difference between the profits of the board and remuneration of the performers who the public paid to see. The Australian all-rounder Keith Miller was an admiring member of the audience. He recalled, 'Len was in cracking form. "You rich men get all the money – why don't the players get more? Miller and Lindwall have done so much for Australian cricket – what are you going to do for them?"'

In retirement, Hutton combined a successful career in business and the media. 'Len brought to the problem of acquiring money all the thought, tenacity and concentration which epitomised his batting, and it was hardly surprising that he should be a success in the commercial world,' wrote Bailey. 'He was certainly the only cricketer I knew who read the stocks and shares before the sports page.'

THE MANAGEMENT

When Geoffrey Howard collected MCC's share of the gate money for the third Test at Melbourne, he could afford to relax a little. The match drew a five-day attendance of 300,270, paying receipts of £A47,933 (worth £38,346 in UK currency), a record for a match in Australia despite the MCG's reduced capacity and the loss of the sixth day. And with that the tour manager could pay off the overdraft he had arranged with the Perth branch of the Australia and New Zealand Bank after the team's arrival in October. From here on the tour was in profit.

Managing the finances of the 1954–55 tour was not the least of Howard's achievements, and just one more aspect of the brief he handled with the skill of an administrator who combined talent, charm, diplomacy and popularity in equal measure. 'I have had a certain number of letters from other sources in Australia and I am sure you would be delighted to hear the nice things that are said on all sides about the team and its manager,' MCC assistant secretary Billy Griffith wrote to Howard, soon after the victory in Melbourne. 'Everybody is delighted with the splendid job you are doing personally and we all here send our congratulations.'

The view was fully endorsed by the players. 'Geoffrey was a brilliant manager,' said Tom Graveney. 'He was the best manager of all – he did it all himself.' Trevor Bailey agreed: 'He looked after a very happy team and he did an awful lot to make it a happy team.' Bob Appleyard added, 'He had a great relationship with Len Hutton and I think he took a lot of the weight from Len's shoulders.' When Hutton became a slightly detached figure after the arrival of his wife, Howard found himself working more closely with vice-captain Peter May. 'Helpful and unruffled, he made the whole thing work,' May later wrote. 'He had no assistant manager, no accountant.'

Howard went out of his way to help journalists. When the team left Perth for Adelaide early in the tour, a local pressman wrote, 'Adelaide will like manager Mr Geoffrey Howard. In Perth he has been voted by officials as the best-looking MCC manager to tour Australia and the most co-operative by English and Australian cricket writers accompanying the team. Mr Howard looks more like an English film star than a cricket manager.' Howard cut out the article and sent it to his father in England. 'This chap knows his stuff,' he wrote.

Apart from his administrative talents, he was able to maintain friendly relations with the players while commanding their respect and being able to mete out discipline when appropriate. The meetings of the Saturday Night Club, at which attendance was compulsory, had become essential to maintain morale. 'We used it to let off a bit of steam,' Howard remembered. 'One time in Australia Bill Edrich and Godfrey Evans arrived late. They'd been to the races and they were full of grog. We were in the middle of the fines. Bill got up to speak and words wouldn't come out. He was smiling away and young Colin Cowdrey was sitting there looking at him thinking "What's wrong with him. This isn't the man I know."'

Although the players had to attend many stuffy official functions, Howard was adept at arranging treats, including trips to the races and tennis tournaments. Four years earlier, the MCC management had decided that Sydney's famous oysters were too expensive for the tour budget. Howard thought differently and ruled oysters could go on the bill. Brian Statham in particular took full advantage of the munificence. In a detailed end-of-tour report for MCC, Howard listed the problems found in many Australian hotels. When service was slow and value poor, he allowed players the freedom to visit local restaurants.

Still, his workload was staggering. 'At every stop there was baggage to be unloaded and reloaded, hotel bills to be settled, local dignitaries to be greeted,' wrote Howard's biographer Stephen Chalke. During his wartime service in the RAF, Howard had been in command of more than a thousand men in the Egyptian port of Alexandria. He drew on those experiences. 'A six-month cricket tour has so many likenesses with six months of soldiering,' he told Chalke. 'For one thing, you have these short periods of action and, just like in war, people have to deal with all the time in between. Some go and have a few beers, others fall to philosophising.'

He could not please everybody, though. In the *Daily Telegraph*'s smartly published post-tour collection of E.W. Swanton's reports, criticism of Howard made at the time of the selection of the tour party was re-published, without amendment. It prompted an angry note from MCC secretary Ronny Aird to Swanton. 'The last sentence is unworthy of a journalist whose writing is respected as much as yours is,' Aird wrote.

In fact, Swanton had no personal criticism of Howard – he had loaned him his secretary, Margaret Harper, to help deal with the increased volume of correspondence after the series had been won – but he did believe that a different style of manager was needed: 'In all the seven MCC tours that I have been on, the manager has been really little more than a secretary subsidiary to the captain. As you know, I think there is an urgent need for a different approach to the whole problem and it is made no less immediate by the fact that we have just won the rubber.'

However, there was no criticism of Howard at Lord's, especially when – after all the wrangling with the Australian cricket authorities about low entrance fees and percentages of receipts – the manager returned with a surplus of around £9500 (more than £200,000 now). 'It has been a fascinating experience,' Howard wrote to Billy Griffith late in the tour. 'It has taught me a great deal and kept me occupied in mind and body.'

No less than the players, he had to deal with the strains of a long separation from his family. As well as regular letters to his wife, Nora, Howard found time to keep in touch with his four daughters at home in Cheshire. The day after victory in Adelaide, he wrote, 'It is quite a long time since I wrote to you, because I have been very busy helping Len Hutton to win the "Ashes". It sounds as though your daddy is a dustman! It is lovely to think that we are getting near the end of our time in Australia. I am *so* tired of standing upside down.'

In 2001, when Chalke was working with Howard on his book, they drove down to Hampshire for a reunion with John Woodcock of *The Times*. 'I've spent 17 Christmases in Australia, Geoffrey. I've been out there with every England side in the last 50 years and your tour was the happiest of them all,' Woodcock said. 'It was so well managed, you were so level-headed and you only had George Duckworth to help you.'

GRIM DAYS IN SYDNEY

'With the series decided, all the pizzazz seems to have gone out of this tour,' complained Frank Tyson when the MCC party arrived in Sydney to prepare for the second state match against New South Wales, closely followed by the fifth Test. A feeling of anticlimax was understandable – the team were victims of their own ruthless efficiency in killing off the series with a match in hand. The end of February was approaching: although the players would not begin to arrive back in England until early April, thoughts were inevitably turning to home.

Hangovers had just about cleared up after the victory at Adelaide when MCC played a two-day, non-first-class match against a Victoria Country XI at Yallourn, 90 miles from Melbourne. The town had been built to house power-station workers and there was also an opencast brown coal mine less than a mile from the Yallourn Oval where the match was played. 'The pitch for the game was quite good, but the general match facilities were absolutely dreadful,' Tyson wrote. 'The air was thick with dust and everything we touched seemed filthy.' Flies were numerous and huge: Peter Loader swallowed one while running in to bowl. Choking, he was forced to leave the field.

As on previous up-country excursions, the cricketers and the travelling press entourage were received with generous hospitality. On the rest day there was a party out in the bush. 'Barbecues are a favourite means of jollification among Australians, presumably because meat is so plentiful,' wrote Bruce Harris of the *Evening Standard*. There were steaks and chops of a size not seen in the average butcher's shop window in an English high street. Loader insisted there was even more meat on the fly he had swallowed.

But there was an unfamiliar face in the MCC line-up: with several players nursing injuries, manager Geoffrey Howard was pressed into service, 25 years after his three-game career with Middlesex. 'I had an awful match,' he confessed in a letter home. 'My knee came up like a balloon on Saturday and today I pulled a thigh muscle in my left leg.' He might have been better touring the streets of Yallourn: the planned town was laid out in the manner of the English garden cities designed by his grandfather, Ebenezer.

They left the flies and the coal dust behind to return to Melbourne and the second state match against Victoria. Rain made play possible on only the middle of the three days, making a draw inevitable. In their post-tour reports for MCC, Howard and Len Hutton were insistent that Australian tours were a month too long and that the second fixtures against the states should be culled. With just 13,000 people inside the vast stadium to watch the sole day's play, they may have had a point, but the attendances for the first Victoria match had peaked at only 18,000. More successful with Melburnians had been MCC's match against an Australian XI in November, which had a second-day attendance of 36,380.

Back in Sydney, the aggregate turn-out for the pre-Test New South Wales match was down by 25,000 on the first meeting in November, reinforcing the views of the manager and captain. It was a pity, because the locals missed a superb game, featuring the bright, attacking cricket which had been notably absent from the no-quarter attrition of the Tests. Brilliantly led by Keith Miller, making his point forcibly to the Test selectors, NSW won by 45 runs with an hour to spare. 'Miller's captaincy in this match was the best exhibition of thoughtful manoeuvring I have seen this season,' wrote Bill O'Reilly. 'I think that Len is slightly in awe of him,' Tyson admitted.

This was MCC's first defeat by a state since 1936–37 and Margaret Hughes took the opportunity to criticise Hutton. 'The match proved that there is still one captain left who plays cricket in the true spirit,' she wrote. 'Miller realises more than anyone that cricket should be regarded as a game and that it is more important for the spectators to be satisfied than the match shall not be lost.' There was a row after Hutton led his team off when, with NSW's 19-year-old batsman Bobby Simpson on 98 not out, spots of rain began to fall. Hutton said he had the agreement of the umpires, but the officials offered a different version of events. When play resumed, Simpson took an ugly swipe at a ball from Johnny Wardle and was stumped without adding to his score.

On Wednesday 23 February, two days out from the start of the Test, the weather forecast on the front page of the *Sydney Morning Herald* was warm and humid, with rain predicted in the northern border districts and showers on the northern coast. There seemed no cause for concern, but the tone changed a little 24 hours later, when punters were praised for their pluck in attending the races at Canterbury in a non-stop downpour. Another day on and it was clear that New South Wales was being engulfed in a natural disaster described by state premier Joe Cahill as 'near catastrophic'.

The Hunter Valley took the full force of the torrential rain that fell for hours without a break. The town of Singleton, 130 miles from Sydney, was evacuated and thousands of people were moved from their homes in Maitland in anticipation of the Hunter River bursting its banks. A shortage of food and blankets was reported in the towns of Trangie and Warren, but floodwater had closed airfields across the state, hampering aid efforts. The planes that could take off were deployed to spot people on rooftops. A family of three died when their truck was swept away by a torrent of water. More heavy rain was the alarming forecast in the following morning's paper.

By Saturday, the death toll was reported to have risen to 16, with the cost of damage estimated at around £A1 million. The *Morning Herald* and its sister Sunday paper, the *Sun-Herald*, launched an appeal to help the stricken areas. Howard organised a collection among the MCC players that raised £A50 and a donation of £250 was wired from Lord's. The Queen sent a message of sympathy to the people of New South Wales.

The stories were grim. At Maitland, two men drowned when they fell from a rope ladder lowered by a helicopter trying to rescue them from the top of a railway signal box. In the town of Dubbo, more than 300 people were unaccounted for and 11,000 residents were expected to be without food by the evening. In overcrowded centres used for housing the homeless, there were outbreaks of gastritis. Maitland asked for supplies of typhoid vaccine to be despatched urgently.

Amid these appalling headlines, the fate of a cricket match became inconsequential, but there was no question of the fifth Test being called off. The rain had been less severe in Sydney, but it was still heavy and constant. 'Even in the worst days of our last English summer there had not been a comparable period of sustained gloom,' said Ian Peebles. 'At the moment it looks like being a Test match on water skis,' wrote Alan Ross. Typically, Ross considered the wider picture, noting that only days previously the flooded areas had been concerned about bush fires after a prolonged drought. He recalled a comment made by his room-maid: 'The world will end not with an atom bomb, but with a flood.'

The authorities at the Sydney Cricket Ground were confident that the match could begin within hours of the rain stopping. 'The drying rate of the SCG has improved tremendously since rubble drains were put down across the field some years ago,' said Alan Barnes, secretary of the NSW Cricket Association. But it did not stop. On what should have been the first day, the players dutifully reported to the ground. The first thing the England players noticed on entering the SCG was that the adjacent No. 2 ground was under water. 'When we reached our dressing-room we discovered that the

333

main oval was in a similar condition,' wrote Tyson. 'It was a vast lake with an island of tarpaulins in the centre.'

With no toss possible, the captains did not have to name their teams. That suited England, who had Colin Cowdrey recovering from flu – he had been sent away to recover in a nursing home to avoid spreading the bug around the team – Trevor Bailey with a broken finger suffered against Victoria and Tyson under treatment for a sore knee. Australia had called up Billy Watson, who had been in the XII for the second Test, and the Queenslander Peter Burge in another effort to shore up their fragile batting. Lindwall was back, but Bill Johnston had been axed. There was doubt about wicketkeeper Len Maddocks, who was suffering the after-effects of inoculations for the forthcoming West Indies tour, which meant Gil Langley had to fly in as cover. When Maddocks was declared fit, there was a debate about how much of his £A80 match fee Langley was due. He got £A20.

It was similarly bleak on the second day. Although Hutton and Ian Johnson turned up to inspect the playing area, there was no chance of the match beginning. The loss of the receipts from what was always the best-attended day of the match caused Howard to downgrade his estimates of the overall tour profit. On Sunday, the rest day, the sun came out to mock the cricketers and would-be spectators, but by Monday morning it was raining hard again. No Test in Australia had seen the first three days abandoned, but it quickly became clear that an unwanted record was about to be established. The England players did not leave their hotel.

Tuesday was dryer. When Hutton and Johnson walked to the middle at 11.30 a.m., Peebles noted, 'The pitch was a dry white in the midst of a very green field, with ominous muddy patches where the water lay close to the surface. The roller circling the outfield left large brown skid marks.' Provided there was no further rain, it was announced that play would start after lunch. In modern-day Test cricket every effort is made to make up for time lost to bad weather with extended playing time and the use of floodlights, but no such devices existed in the 1950s. There were just 13 playing hours left when the captains walked out to toss: a draw – and the end of Hutton's ambitions to sail home with a 4–1 victory – seemed certain.

GRAVENEY COMES GOOD

For the third time in the series, the captain winning the toss – this time Ian Johnson – invited the opposition to bat first. This caused less of a stir than Hutton's grave miscalculation at Brisbane or in the previous SCG Test when stand-in Arthur Morris had rolled the dice. Johnson rightly calculated that his only chance of victory was to bowl England out cheaply in the still-damp atmosphere. After recently being confirmed as the man to lead Australia in the Caribbean, Johnson needed to make a bold statement. A 3–2 Ashes defeat would look a lot better on his CV than 3–1.

With fewer than 7500 people in the ground, the tension that had been a feature of the series had drained away, though Ray Lindwall v Len Hutton could never be a mundane contest. Once again, their opening exchanges were explosive. Lindwall's field was so attacking that Hutton might have been able to shake hands with the entire Australian team before facing the first ball. Added to the usual umbrella of wicketkeeper, slips and the leg trap, there was a silly mid-off and a forward short leg. Hutton gracefully glanced Lindwall's second ball to the untenanted boundary at fine leg (continuing his series habit of first-over fours), then hit the next square off his legs for two more. The fourth delivery dipped in late towards Hutton's pads and this time his clip travelled knee-high to the debutant Peter Burge at leg slip. The new boy's first touch of the ball as a Test player was to catch the England captain, albeit after a nervous juggle.

As the Australians took the field, Lindwall had outlined his plan to lay a snare for Hutton with an inswinger. 'As he's got older, he's inclined to fall across to the off side when playing to leg,' Lindwall told Burge. 'Sure enough, Hutton hit Ray's fourth ball to me,' Burge recalled. 'The ball rolled around in my arms and I grabbed it to my chest. I didn't stop shaking for an hour after taking that catch. I used to sell programmes at the Gabba and watched Hutton as a boy, and now I'd caught him in a Test match. I couldn't believe it.'

Watching phlegmatically from the non-striker's end was Tom Graveney, in exile since his failure in the second Test, but now tasked with solving England's chronic need to find a dependable opening pairing. In a newspaper article during the 1953 Ashes, Sir Donald Bradman had expressed the view that Graveney possessed the technical attributes to open the batting. Now that theory was about to be put to the test. While it was acknowledged that Bill Edrich had been fortunate to retain the role during the series – 'He was finished. Exhausted. Shot his bolt,' said Graveney – it might have been expected that the specialist opener Reg Simpson would be given a further opportunity. However, it was not only Simpson's love of sunbathing that made Hutton unwilling to restore him to the team. 'Reg was a back-foot player,' explained Trevor Bailey. 'Len was always worried about the ball that was going to nip back. That's why he was always on the front foot. Simpson was a marvellous player of fast bowling, because he was a good back-foot player.'

In Graveney's frequent retelling of that morning's events, he was unsure if he was even in the XI when Hutton returned to the dressing-room after losing the toss. 'Then Hutton came across and said, "Pad up, Tom. You'd better come in with me." That was how I became an England opening batsman. I had played in the spot a few times before, but without really fancying the job.' If he was fazed, he did not show it. Nor was he troubled by Hutton's early departure. In alliance with Peter May, Graveney began to build one of the most crowd-pleasing partnerships of the tour. In Miller's opening over, Graveney drove him straight to the sightscreen with an imperious flourish. 'It was in the nature of a trailer, which, for once in a way, was truly indicative of the picture to come,' wrote Ian Peebles. He collected nine from Miller's next over, providing a booster-shot of confidence. After the game against NSW, Hutton had expressed regret that Graveney had not been given opportunities to open earlier in the tour: faith in Edrich's relish for battle had far outweighed his paltry contributions with the bat.

But Graveney knew there was more to it than that. He was aware that his captain did not fully trust him, did not think he took the game seriously, nor made the most of his abundant talent. It was said that Hutton was wary of Graveney's ruddy complexion, not because it implied – as with Simpson – a fondness for sunbathing, but an enjoyment of a bucolic lifestyle in rural Gloucestershire. That suspicion spread to the press box. Alan Ross thought the fourth-day start meant this was, 'Not a Test match, except statistically. That probably accounts for Graveney's lovely batting.' E.M.Wellings added, 'With nothing at stake and no particular stress and strain on the players, the circumstances exactly suited Tom Graveney.' A suspicion that a stylist somehow cared less about the game than individuals with fewer natural gifts would later unfairly dog the England career of David Gower.

Yet no one disputed the beauty of Graveney in full spate. Neville Cardus wrote that if cricket were destroyed and only Graveney survived, it could be recreated 'from his way of batting, from the man himself'. He reached his fifty off 76 balls with six fours and at tea England were well set at 95 for one. The only alarm had come when May lofted Ian Johnson uncomfortably close to Les Favell at deep mid-off. 'England disported themselves in the manner of conquerors,' wrote Ross. After tea, May completed his fifty off 121 balls, the first time he had reached double figures in a first innings in the series – a lopsided statistic for England's most prolific batsman.

Throughout, it was the quality of Graveney's driving – off, on and straight – that enchanted the crowd as well as some of his critics in the media. 'On so slow a pitch, Graveney could employ his high Edwardian backlift and still play the faster bowlers with an almost negligent ease,' said John Arlott. 'Full of style and confidence, he stood at the non-striker's end, tall, legs crossed, leaning serenely on his bat.' Ross, as usual, looked for technical reasons and decided Graveney was now getting his head over the ball in synchronised alignment with his feet.

The player himself had no fancy theories. 'It was one of those days when everything went right,' Graveney wrote in *Cricket Through the Covers*. 'Each time I stretched my left foot down that easy paced strip, the ball seemed to be there to drive.' The Australian R.S.Whitington evoked Jack Hobbs and Victor Trumper, the most rarefied company, in describing the innings. May was playing scarcely less fluently: in one Davidson over he stroked him through the covers twice. With all the elegance of their strokeplay it was easy to overlook the power regularly on display. On a still-sodden outfield, the ball had to be hit hard to reach the boundary.

Graveney progressed to his century – 'like a king to his coronation,' said Whitington – and got there with a thrilling flourish. He was on 85 when he faced the 38th over of the day, Miller's 10th. The second ball was driven for four, the fourth was sent racing through the covers, the sixth hit straight back past the bowler. Graveney, Miller and Lindwall had been regular golf partners in the past few months – they had played 18 holes the previous day – and this was the sort of batting of which Miller thoroughly approved, even if it was at the expense of his figures. With Graveney three short of his hundred, Miller bowled him a leg-stump long hop: the batsman was so surprised he failed to accept the gift. The act of generosity was repeated next ball and this time Graveney pulled the ball to the unguarded fine-leg boundary for his second Test hundred, his first against Australia.

It looked as if he might go on, but, with the close of play looming, he drove hard back to Johnson and the Australian captain clung on to the catch. 'Johnson would have suffered grievous injury if he had not caught it,' said A.G. Moyes. The fielders lined up to offer congratulations. 'It was not merely that he made a hundred, but that he made it in a manner to warm the heart of any cricketer,' wrote Arlott. 'His 111 was as exquisitely fashioned as an object by Fabergé,' said Ross. A pale-looking Colin Cowdrey edged his first ball from Johnson to Len Maddocks, and, when Richie Benaud returned to bowl the final over in murky light, Peter May was caught by Davidson at slip. Three wickets had fallen for eight runs in the last 25 minutes, removing a layer of gloss from England's day.

Close of play: England 196–4 (Compton 0*)

'GEORGE' BEST

Amid the hubbub of England's Adelaide victory party, Sir Donald Bradman scanned the room and, breaking off his conversation with Len Hutton, he found the cricketer he was looking for, quietly nursing a drink in the corner: 'I hope that man gets the credit he deserves,' he said. He was looking at Brian Statham.

Amid the small forest of newsprint generated by the exploits of Frank Tyson, it was easy to overlook the sterling contributions of his new-ball partner. Statham, 24, had no headline-grabbing nickname that could compete with 'Typhoon' – he was known as 'George', the 'Whippet' or the 'Greyhound'– but with 18 wickets at an average of 27.72, most taken from the less advantageous end, he was an essential component of England's success.

This was recognised by those in the know. 'Statham got more out of the pitch in the way of lift and life than did any other bowler in the match,' wrote Bill O'Reilly after the second day's play of the fifth Test. 'Statham has bowled wonderfully well on this tour. If a vote were taken among the Australian batsmen I feel certain that he is the one who would be voted the most dangerous of the English attack.' Nor did he go unappreciated by Hutton. 'No captain could wish for a better man in his team,' he said. 'He bowled with the stamina of a lion.'

Statham was 6 foot tall, but otherwise not the strapping fast bowler of popular legend. He did not boast Tyson's light-heavyweight's shoulders or the coalface slab of Fred Trueman's muscular back. But he was exceptionally supple and light on his feet – hence the Whippet and Greyhound nicknames – qualities that served him well when he struggled to keep his feet on the treacherous run-ups in the third Test at Melbourne. He was also double-jointed: when taking off his sweater, he could coil his right arm over his right shoulder and reach down to the base of his back.

Physically, he had much in common with 21st century-titan James Anderson, England's record wicket-taker, with whom he now shares the name of the ends at Old Trafford. Statham's athleticism also meant he was an excellent fielder – John Woodcock thought him the best fast-bowling fielder he ever saw – and a more capable batsman than his figures suggest.

In his long career – he made two further Ashes tours and played his final Test in 1965 – Statham became a byword for precision. 'He was so accurate that on soft turf the marks where he pitched were usually grouped like rifle shots around a bullseye,' wrote John Arlott. In the tour match against a South Australian Country XI at Mount Gambier, he bowled six batsmen without conceding a run. 'If they miss, I hit,' he once said – and he became forever linked to that quote. 'He rarely pitched short, preferring to concentrate on line and length, gaining movement off the wicket to make the batsman play at every delivery,' said Denis Compton. 'You ignored a ball from Brian at your peril. Only occasionally would he slip in a bouncer, disguising it so cleverly that it brought him many wickets.' In the 1954–55 series, Statham was also genuinely fast. 'His speed in that Australian summer was not far short of Tyson's,' said Arlott.

His popularity was sealed by his habitual affability off the field. Trevor Bailey admired his ability to rustle up pancakes in a hotel kitchen and toss them without dropping them. 'No one could wish to travel with a better tourist and companion,' said Alec Bedser. And he was also greatly appreciated by Tyson: 'In Brian Statham I had a partner whose effort and support were unstinted, whose work was beyond praise and who, on many occasions, was the less fortunate, but far better half of the Tyson–Statham combination.'

LINDWALL REACHES HIS CENTURY

The new regulation on pitch-covering, used for the first time in this series, had kept the state treasurers happy and helped to maximise revenue. But it had robbed the game of one of its most intriguing aspects. As John Woodcock pointed out, in previous series a match starting on the fourth day after prolonged rain would have taken place on a very different surface. 'Many were saying how much more excitement would be in store had the pitch been left at the mercy of the weather,' wrote Woodcock. 'It certainly seemed unfair that bowlers unsure of their grip should be faced by batsmen playing on a pitch zealously guarded from the rain.' The era of the 'sticky' wicket was disappearing into history.

There was a further benefit to England from the exhilarating partnership between Graveney and May: it insured them against the possibility of defeat. When Trevor Bailey joined Denis Compton, still to get off the mark, to face the last seven balls of Richie Benaud's uncompleted over from the previous evening, the platform had been erected for an acceleration of the scoring rate to offer the opportunity of an afternoon declaration. But Hutton hadn't got the memo. When Bailey and Compton began sluggishly there was an assumption that they were just taking stock of the pitch and the bowling, but they seemed stuck in first gear, Compton in particular looking out of touch in what seemed certain to be (and was) his final Test innings in Australia.

In the *Daily Telegraph*, E. W. Swanton thought the morning session 'could best be described as boring'. Ray Lindwall and Keith Miller took the new ball in the third over, but offered little threat. It was the left-armer Alan Davidson, shaping to move the ball away but then dipping it back into the right-hander, who provided the greatest threat. After one over in which Compton looked baffled, the batsman went into deep conversation with Miller, as if seeking a lesson on dealing with swing bowling. In the 90 minutes of the morning session, England added only 51. A crowd that was building to almost double that of the first day began to grow restive. 'All indications from the Hill that increased activity would be welcome were resolutely ignored,' wrote J.M. Kilburn in the *Yorkshire Post*.

Although he was not out in the middle, Hutton still copped the blame for England's torpor. Some writers claimed to have spotted Compton looking to the players' viewing area for permission to increase the scoring rate but being told to carry on in the same vein. An annoyed Swanton sent a question to the dressing-room demanding to know whether the batsmen were operating under orders. Word came back that they were not, and that Hutton was 'not dissatisfied' with the approach. Then Compton was dropped at mid-on by Johnson off Lindwall and, in the next over, at slip off Benaud. Something snapped. Compton took his cap off and handed it to one of the umpires. 'Suddenly he was recognisable in appearance and style,' wrote Woodcock.

Shedding the cap seemed to lift a burden from Compton. 'For 40 minutes of a blue and beautiful afternoon he showed Sydneysiders a last broad glimpse of his genius,' added Woodcock. From 26 off 122 balls, he flicked a switch and added 58 off the next 78. Benaud, unfortunate not to dismiss Compton earlier, now felt the full force of his transformation. One over was hit for four fours – a cut, a drive and a brace of sweeps – but a drinks break interrupted his momentum and soon the entertainment with Johnson holding on to a sharp return catch off possibly the hardest hit of the innings.

The fifth wicket had added 134, but had only briefly offered anything worth remembering. With tea approaching and a declaration widely expected, the focus shifted from the England batsmen to an Australian bowler. After dismissing Hutton the previous afternoon, Ray Lindwall moved to 98 wickets against England. No Australian fast bowler had claimed 100 victims in Ashes contests and, at 33, this seemed likely to be his last opportunity. He was helped by England's sudden conversion to the benefits of throwing the bat. Godfrey Evans became Lindwall's 99th England victim, but he was still one short of the landmark when the last over before tea began.

Johnny Wardle smashed the second ball high in the direction of Davidson at long-off and the player recently described as the best fielder in the world by Hutton positioned himself underneath the ball – and dropped it. Fortunately for Lindwall, Bailey remained in a generous mood. When the bowler ran in to bowl his sixth ball, the England batsman stepped aside and offered him a clear sight of all three stumps. Even with that open invitation, the ball seemed to be heading down the leg side until it glanced off Bailey's gloves and on to the stumps. Lindwall had his 100th Ashes wicket, but only after a moment of unexpected chivalry from Bailey, who was the first to shake his hand. 'Bailey made himself many friends, who will be slow to forget the gesture,' wrote Bill O'Reilly in the *Sydney Morning Herald*. 'There was a school which deplored the suggestion of collusion,' said Swanton. 'Personally, I welcomed it.' Not everyone agreed. 'His record is now just a paper record,' fumed Len Bailey in the London evening paper, the *Star*.

For others, the late burst of action did not excuse the tenor of the play earlier in the day. 'Compton, Bailey kill the Test' was the headline in the *Daily Express*. 'What a grand opportunity Hutton thus lost to leave Australia with the plaudits of an appreciative Sydney crowd instead of raucous heckling,' wrote Sid Barnes. 'It is a pity this match ever started. In my book Tests are Tests and should never be allowed to plumb the depths of shabbiness reached today.'

There was an unexpected postscript. It turned out that Lindwall was not finished at all. He toured England for a third time in 1956 and was still in action when MCC returned to Australia in 1958–59. In the final match of that series at Melbourne, he dismissed Bailey twice for a duck in what turned out to be the final Test of the England all-rounder's career. Lindwall retired with 114 Ashes wickets.

WARDLE SENDS AUSTRALIA SPINNING

It was an easy-to-miss statistic, but England's 371 for seven declared was their highest total of the series. Australia were left with an hour and 40 minutes to bat on a bright, sunny penultimate afternoon: no one foresaw any problems. Here was 'a game doomed to inconclusiveness before it was able to begin,' according to Denys Rowbotham in the *Manchester Guardian*. When Colin McDonald hit Frank Tyson's fourth ball for six, it confirmed there was no assistance in the pitch for England's seamers. Statham still used his four overs well. One ball to the debutant Billy Watson came back so sharply that it shaved the leg stump, evaded Godfrey Evans and went for four byes. A similar delivery struck Watson a painful blow in the groin. After four overs, Bob Appleyard replaced Tyson, though he quickly gave way to Johnny Wardle.

The fifty came up in the 12th over, but Watson's first Test innings ended two runs later, when he was deceived by Wardle's off-break and bowled. The Yorkshire spinner had been restricted to deploying his orthodox slow left-arm so far in the series, but now he had Hutton's blessing to wheel out his wrist-spinning variations. It was soon obvious that the Australians had little idea how to combat this unexpected new threat. 'Watson was the only one to be bowled, but not the only one to be beaten,' wrote J.M. Kilburn. 'Wardle, mainly unchallenged, bowled some admirable overs of mixed spin and flight.' But the only further wicket before the close fell to Tyson when Les Favell was beaten by a yorker.

Close of play: Australia 82–2 (McDonald 45*, Harvey 12*), trail England by 289 runs with eight first-innings wickets in hand

On the final day of the series, there was a reminder of the relative unimportance of sport. The estimated cost of the damage caused by the New South Wales flood had risen to £A15 million. Homes in the worst-affected towns and farms had been buried under putrid brown slime and sand. As the clean-up operation continued, the appeal fund stood at £A400,000 with £312,000 promised from the British government.

With their bags packed for a midnight flight to New Zealand, the England players made a final journey to the SCG. The idea of forcing a victory seemed fanciful, but Tyson struck in the opening over when Neil Harvey was through his shot too soon and the bowler grabbed the return catch. It was Tyson's 28th and final wicket of the series. Wardle opened from the other end, but when his fourth over of the day went for 13, Hutton switched him around. Colin McDonald and Keith Miller had added 44 for the fourth wicket and seemed to be leading Australia clear of potential embarrassment when McDonald called Miller for an ill-judged single. 'Some thought it a bad call, others that Miller began too slowly,' said A.G. Moyes. Godfrey Evans still had time to collect Colin Cowdrey's poorly aimed throw and run Miller out.

McDonald had looked easily the most composed of Australia's frontline batsmen and, on 72, may have begun to entertain thoughts of a century. It might explain why he failed to notice that Hutton had moved Peter May deeper at square leg to intercept his favourite sweep shot. McDonald obligingly hit Appleyard straight into May's hands. That was 138 for five and the moment for Wardle to take command. He bowled with a teasing flight and a length that offered batsmen the possibility of the drive if they were brave enough. None were. 'Our players groped and floundered against the cheerful sandy-haired Wardle,' wrote Tom Goodman in the *Sydney Morning Herald.* 'Some of them made crude strokes and some fell into obvious traps.' Richie Benaud stretched forward and was bowled through a huge gap between bat and pad. Peter Burge pulled a short ball straight to Appleyard at midwicket and the same combination saw off Len Maddocks. Alan Davidson was caught behind, though plainly did not think he had hit the ball. Wardle had his first Test five-for.

Five runs were needed to avoid the follow-on when Ray Lindwall came out to join Ian Johnson. They approached the task sensibly, inching the total forward in singles, until – on 221 for nine – the Australian captain apparently believed that a deficit of 150 was sufficient. As Lindwall hit the ball to Compton at cover, Johnson set off for a single, but was sent back: he turned, but could not beat Compton's throw to the bowler's end. On the way off, Hutton told him that Australia would be batting again: they were one run short of safety. Johnson now faced not just the embarrassment of miscalculating the follow-on score, but the possible ignominy of losing by an innings after winning the toss. The moment had historical resonance for Hutton: Australia had not been asked to follow on since the Oval Test of 1938 when he had made his world-record score of 364. 'There was some excuse for failing to get within distance of *that* tally, but none at all for scoring only 221 on a good pitch at Sydney,' wrote Moyes.

England had five minutes short of two hours to heap more humiliation on their hosts. They made a good fist of it. There was no grumbling about a sluggish over-rate now: Tyson bowled off three paces and still knocked the bat out of Watson's hands. Watson was given an uncomfortable examination of his Test credentials by Statham, and eventually edged him to slip where Tom Graveney took a superb catch. Another Graveney slip catch, this time off Wardle, removed the wretchedly out-of-form Favell. Then Harvey was caught and bowled by Wardle to leave Australia 29 for three.

McDonald and Miller used up enough time to quell thoughts that England might stage a fantastical heist, and Hutton seemed reluctantly to agree that the draw was now inevitable when he asked Graveney to bowl his very occasional leg-breaks. McDonald duly presented him with his first Test wicket by edging to Evans. Miller and Benaud, convinced that Australia were safe, made some bold attacking shots, but Miller missed one huge attempt to hit Wardle out of the ground and presented him with his seventh wicket of the day.

The clock on the SCG pavilion showed two minutes to six when Hutton collected Burge's boundary hit from the fence and carried the ball back to the middle. It took a moment for the crowd to realise what was happening: the England captain intended to bowl the last over of the series. Hutton had been a promising leg-spinner at the start of his career, but now his bowling was rarely seen and his only Test wicket had come before the war. Benaud and Burge collected risk-free singles before the sixth ball was too short to ignore and Benaud aimed a huge and ugly slog: he missed it and was bowled. Alan Ross wrote, 'England's captain, stoically denying himself the luxury of a smile, took his cap and walked from the field with the air of one who could have taken wickets as easily as that at any time he chose.'

FIFTH TEST

Sydney Cricket Ground   25, 26, 28 February and 1, 2, 3 March, 1955
No play on the first three days

ENGLAND FIRST INNINGS

			Balls	Minutes	4s	6s	Out at
*L. Hutton	c Burge b Lindwall	6	4	3	1	–	1/6
T.W. Graveney	c & b Johnson	111	158	166	14	–	2/188
P.B.H. May	c Davidson b Benaud	79	188	184	8	–	4/196
M.C. Cowdrey	c Maddocks b Johnson	0	1	1	–	–	3/188
D.C.S. Compton	c & b Johnson	84	204	188	8	–	5/330
T.E. Bailey	b Lindwall	72	183	198	4	–	7/371
†T.G. Evans	c McDonald b Lindwall	10	13	16	–	–	6/359
J.H. Wardle	not out	5	8	8	–	–	
Extras	*1 b, 3 lb*	4					
7 wkts dec (*94.6 overs, 387 min*)		**371**					

Did not bat: F.H. Tyson, R. Appleyard, J.B. Statham

AUSTRALIA BOWLING

Lindwall	20.6	5	77	3
Miller	15	1	71	0
Davidson	19	3	72	0
Johnson	20	5	68	3
Benaud	20	4	79	1

Australia won the toss and decided to field   Hours of play: 11.30 a.m.–5.30 p.m.
Umpires: R.J.J. Wright (Victoria), M.J. McInnes (South Australia)

AUSTRALIA FIRST INNINGS

			Balls	Minutes	4s	6s	Out at
W.J. Watson	b Wardle	18	56	62	1	–	1/52
C.C. McDonald	c May b Appleyard	72	156	170	5	1	5/138
L.E. Favell	b Tyson	1	3	2	–	–	2/53
R.N. Harvey	c & b Tyson	13	32	37	1	–	3/85
K.R. Miller	run out	19	36	54	2	–	4/129
P.J.P. Burge	c Appleyard b Wardle	17	34	32	2	–	7/157
R. Benaud	b Wardle	7	9	5	1	–	6/147
†L.V. Maddocks	c Appleyard b Wardle	32	62	64	4	–	8/202
A.K. Davidson	c Evans b Wardle	18	68	70	2	–	9/217
*I.W. Johnson	run out	11	22	32	1	–	10/221
R.R. Lindwall	not out	2	7	10	–	–	
Extras	10 b, 1 lb	10					
All out (*60.4 overs, 277 mins*)		**221**					

AUSTRALIA SECOND INNINGS (following on)

			Balls	Minutes	4s	6s	Out at
W.J. Watson	c Graveney b Statham	3	20	27	–	–	1/14
C.C. McDonald	c Evans b Graveney	37	70	81	3	–	4/67
L.E. Favell	c Graveney b Wardle	9	15	11	2	–	2/27
R.N. Harvey	c & b Wardle	1	9	7	–	–	3/29
K.R. Miller	b Wardle	28	44	42	4	–	5/87
P.J.P. Burge	not out	18	37	31	2	–	
R. Benaud	b Hutton	22	35	22	4	–	6/118
Extras		–					
6 wkts (*28.6 overs, 116 mins*)		**118**					

Did not bat: †L.V. Maddocks, A.K. Davidson, *I.W. Johnson, R.R. Lindwall

ENGLAND BOWLING

Tyson	11	1	46	2	5	2	20	0
Statham	9	1	31	0	5	0	11	1
Appleyard	16	2	54	1				
Wardle	24.5	6	79	5	12	1	51	3
Graveney					6	0	34	1
Hutton					0.6	0	2	1

MATCH DRAWN

Debuts: W.J. Watson, P.J.P. Burge (Australia)

Attendances

First day: –. Second day: –. Third day: –. Fourth day: 7,402. Fifth day: 13,537. Sixth day: 8,905.
Total: 29,844

Twelfth men: R.G. Archer (Australia), J.V. Wilson (England).

Sources: Charles Davis (sportsstats.com.au), cricketarchive.com, Richard Cashman

BEDSER'S SAD FAREWELL

And that, more or less, was that. In the pavilion, the NSW Cricket Association gave each MCC player a silver cigarette box. Vice-captain Peter May made presentations on behalf of the players: an inscribed clock for Len Hutton; a silver salver, signed by all the players, for manager Geoffrey Howard; a cigarette case for masseur Harold Dalton; and a travelling clock for baggage-master and scorer George Duckworth, perhaps as a reminder of his all-too-familiar cry, 'Bags outside your rooms by 7 a.m.' Hutton and Howard gave each of the players an inscribed pewter tankard.

Among Howard's duties in the previous weeks had been to make travel arrangements for the members of the team not going on the two-Test trip to New Zealand. Two of the squad's biggest names were heading for home. Denis Compton was flying to South Africa, where he would be reunited with his wife before he returned to London, and Alec Bedser and twin brother Eric were booked to sail home on the *Orsova*.

The man who had begun the series as the most respected bowler in the world could not wait to leave Australia. The two months since his exile from the Test team was confirmed, before the third Test in Melbourne, had been among the most miserable of his career. 'For Alec Bedser at the moment I have nothing but the greatest sympathy,' manager Geoffrey Howard wrote to MCC assistant secretary Billy Griffith on 1 January. 'It has been for him a wretched tour in every way so far, beginning with his illness and resting, at the moment, on his exclusion from the last two Test matches. That he has taken it well goes without saying: that he feels it strongly equally goes without saying and I am very, very sorry for him.'

With the series won and Frank Tyson nursing an injury, there had been speculation that Bedser might be summoned to give a farewell performance in the fifth Test at Sydney. 'We had thought that Bedser might be played, not only because he bowled well against New South Wales, but also as a delayed tribute to his greatness, which has meant so much to English cricket in post-war years,' wrote A.G. Moyes. But Hutton was not given to shows of sentiment and when Tyson was declared fit there was no question of him not being in the XI.

Bedser retained several staunch allies among the English press contingent. E.M. Wellings of the *Evening News* saw his exclusion as some sort of conspiracy. 'The most disappointing feature of the sorry business was that Len Hutton should have so readily heeded the campaign being waged against Alec Bedser,' he wrote after the up-country game at Newcastle between the second and third Tests. 'I have long been a great supporter of Hutton, but in this case I consider he was badly at fault and showed surprising weakness. The idea had obviously become implanted before the tour started.'

That was a reference to Bedser's absence from the tour selection committee, a puzzling omission in view of Bill Edrich's inclusion. Another issue was that on the outward voyage Bedser had refused the role of senior professional when offered it by Hutton. It was an ill-defined job, up to the holder to make of it what he would, but it involved monitoring younger players and acting as a buffer between the squad and the captain. The reason for his refusal, Bedser claimed, was that the duties associated with the job should be carried out by the captain, especially now the job was held by a professional.

When Bedser took five wickets against South Australia immediately before the fourth Test, Wellings returned to his argument. 'After taking the first two wickets and having a third intended victim badly missed, he languished in the field while nearly 100 runs were scored,' he wrote. 'In the second innings he was never brought back after a shattering early spell, which appeared to prove that he could still make better use of a new ball than any other bowler in the world.'

It seemed certain there would be no comeback. 'It could well, I suppose, be the end of a great cricketer's Test-match career,' Howard had written. 'The whole business was hateful and in a way one almost yearns to be proved wrong; but I do not see how we could have done better at Sydney [in the second Test] with him because to have used him effectively must have meant that Tyson and Statham were off for longer periods than they should have been and the Australian batsmen's discomfort against them is all too manifest.'

When the fifth Test ended with Hutton's comedic dismissal of Benaud, there were the usual end-of-match rituals and goodbyes. Like many of his media colleagues, former Australia batsman Jack Fingleton was still at work. 'When the last flag on the grandstand had long been furled, I looked up from my press work and saw the saddest sight of all,' he wrote. 'In the gloaming I saw a man in civilian clothes treading the pitch as if he were a pilgrim in Mecca. He walked, at last, towards the pavilion and then turned and "took one long and lingering look, and took a last farewell" before he, too, went into the pavilion for the last time. It was Alec Bedser.'

TAKE THE LONG WAY HOME

'Oh, it doesn't matter about New Zealand,' an official of the New South Wales Cricket Association told Geoffrey Howard as the fifth Test approached its conclusion. An idea had been mooted to add an extra day to the match, partially to make up for the three days lost to rain. 'I'm sorry. We can't. We're due to play at Christchurch,' the MCC manager had said. The response told much about the condescending view of New Zealand cricket in Australia. Many Australians seemed not to like the idea of visitors heading across the Tasman Sea. 'On more than one occasion I was left with the unpleasant impression that by visiting New Zealand we were in some way flouting or slighting Australia,' wrote Douglas Jardine in 1932–33.

After first visiting for what expanded into a four-Test series in 1929–30, England made nine more trips tacked on to the end of Ashes series.[43] It was not until the mid–1970s that England toured New Zealand without first having been to Australia, and although the difficulties of travel partly explained this, it was also a reflection of the weakness of New Zealand cricket.

---

[43] The inaugural series was treated so casually by MCC that another England team was contesting a Test series in the West Indies at the same time – only the second instance of a country playing two series simultaneously.

That did not mean they were not enjoyable visits. After months of high-stakes intensity in Australia, the calmer life – on and off the field – proved highly appealing. 'It is good to say that life in New Zealand is *great*,' Howard wrote home. 'They are very friendly and very hospitable, but they do *not* press everything on you. So far not one person has said "How do you like New Zealand?" or "How do you like our beer?" And all the better for that.'

This final section of the MCC's winter assignment was an exercise in flag-waving and sporting diplomacy as much as it was about cricket. Secretary Ronny Aird had made an extended fact-finding visit in advance of the team, and the detailed report he presented once back at Lord's conveys a genuine desire for the advancement and improvement of cricket in the country. 'They're desperately keen to have you,' Aird told Howard. 'You must give them a good time. And make sure they see Tyson.'

The squad's arrival at Christchurch was delayed three hours by poor weather conditions, but they soon settled in. 'It is wonderful to be here in New Zealand after the rack of Australia,' Howard reflected. 'It is so quiet and climatically so much more invigorating. Our last day or two in Sydney were difficult for the manual workers [fast bowlers], because of very high humidity and a good deal of heat.' Tyson was more succinct: 'This is a beautiful country,' he said after the drive into Christchurch from the airport. They were quickly back in action in a three-day game against Canterbury at Lancaster Park, a seven-wicket win featuring another Tom Graveney century.

The first Test was at Dunedin, on the south-east tip of New Zealand's South Island. 'The only major outpost of civilisation between us and the South Pole is the city of Invercargill,' wrote an awed Tyson. It was the inaugural Test match at the Carisbrook ground. The facilities were basic and the pitch looked slow. Len Hutton knew that the inexperienced New Zealand batsmen had spent the past few weeks apprehensively reading headlines about Tyson and Brian Statham. He won the toss and asked them to bat. It was a day of pitifully slow scoring. In eight minutes short of five hours, New Zealand were bowled out for 125. Only Bert Sutcliffe – 'clearly a class above the other batsmen,' thought Tyson – looked as if he belonged in the international game, hitting 74.

England were scarcely more fluent on the second day. They established a lead of 84 for the loss of eight wickets, but Hutton's plans were disrupted when the next two days were wiped out by rain. When the final morning dawned sunny, he declared and handed responsibility for securing victory back to his bowlers. They responded by bowling New Zealand out for 132, Tyson taking four for seven in eight overs. It left England needing a routine 49 to win.

The second Test was at Auckland's Eden Park on the north island. En route, there was a tour match against Wellington, won easily with another Graveney century. Tyson and Statham both missed the game, but received a visit from scientists at the Royal Aeronautical College of New Zealand, who were conducting an experiment on measuring bowling speeds. They asked each of them to bowl a ball with a metal coating, which registered as it passed through a sonic beam. As it did so, the ball gave off a high-pitched whistle, the duration of which could be measured and translated into miles per hour. Tyson was measured at 89 m.p.h., Statham at 87. However, both wore two sweaters on a chilly day and bowled without a proper run-up because of the sodden outfield. Neither thought the result remotely accurate. It would be decades before reliable speed guns could be deployed to give accurate measurements of bowling speeds.

From unspectacular beginnings, the second Test turned out to be one of the most remarkable in history, though not for any reason that is fondly remembered in New Zealand. In another stodgy, low-scoring contest, England struggled in response to New Zealand's 200 all out. Hutton, recovering from a virus, dropped down the order to No.5, and England were still 36 in arrears when he was joined by Tyson, batting at No.9. 'Stick around for a while, Frank, we may not have to bat again,' Hutton told him when he arrived in the middle. Tyson dismissed the remark as another example of his captain's hard-to-read sense of humour. Later, he would reconsider: 'I can only presume that having already batted for two hours or more, Len was more awake to the problems of the pitch and conditions than his dopey teammates.'

Hutton's 53 and Tyson's unbeaten 27 steered England towards a
lead of 46. And the captain was right: they did not have to bat again.
New Zealand's second innings began on the stroke of 3 p.m: by 5.04
p.m., when Statham sent Johnny Hayes's middle stump flying out of
the ground, it was all over. New Zealand had been bowled out for
26. It was – and remains – the lowest score in Test history, four runs
fewer than South Africa made against England at Port Elizabeth in
1895–96 and at Edgbaston in 1924. There was an appealing neatness
to the conclusion of New Zealand's shambolic second innings: they
were 22 for eight with Johnny Wardle and Bob Appleyard, who had
taken four wickets and narrowly missed taking a hat-trick, in harness,
but Hutton brought Tyson and Statham back, recognising that the
partnership which had achieved so much together during the tour
should be symbolically reunited at its end.

This was a deep and lasting embarrassment for New Zealand, as
Sutcliffe reflected later. 'I still cannot fully explain it,' he said. 'Bad
batting, of course. Good bowling, undoubtedly. Lack of resolution,
almost certainly. And perhaps the intensity of the struggle earlier
had taken something out of our rather inexperienced and diffident
batsmen. It really was an extraordinary affair.'

In England, the news passed many by. Britain's national newspapers
had been forced off the streets by a strike of maintenance workers
seeking a £2-a-week pay rise. The dispute lasted for nearly a month.
In any case, most of the press pack covering the tour were on their
way home in what turned out to be a far-sighted decision by their
sports editors. The New Zealand leg of the tour added more than
three weeks to MCC's already gruelling schedule, but it was a success
in PR and financial terms. An estimated £16,000 was raised for
cricket in the country.

Now thoughts could properly turn to home. The squad had
already splintered with the departure of Alec Bedser and Denis
Compton from Sydney. There were more offshoots. Hutton and
Godfrey Evans had opted for a leisurely sea cruise home with their
wives, and returned to Fremantle to travel aboard the SS *Oronsay*.
As had been planned for months, the bulk of the team were flying
home via the United States. On the day of departure, news was
cabled to New Zealand that Statham's mother Florence had died

at home in Manchester, aged 65. There was a tragic symmetry with the death of Colin Cowdrey's father, news of which had been cabled to the player on the day of the team's arrival in October. Alarmingly, Cowdrey had heard that his mother Molly was unwell at home in Surrey, so he opted to take an earlier flight home with Graveney, though fortunately there turned out to be no cause for concern.

For the remaining players there were stopovers in Fiji, Hawaii and San Francisco before they were met off the plane in New York by Henry Sayen, the team's unfailingly generous American benefactor. Tyson and Trevor Bailey were invited to Sayen's home in Princeton, 50 miles from New York, while the rest of the team flew out and landed at London airport on 5 April. The newspaper strike meant their arrival had not been publicised and there was a smaller crowd than might have otherwise been expected. Cowdrey and Graveney joined the jostling crowds of autograph hunters. The homecoming would anyway have been overshadowed by a bombshell piece of national news: prime minister Sir Winston Churchill announced he was to step down and hand over to foreign secretary Sir Anthony Eden.

'We were a team all the time,' Peter May told reporters. 'Everyone did his bit and I am only disappointed that Len Hutton is not here today to share in this great moment.' Hutton had cabled through a long message from the high seas. 'I am very sorry not to be here with the team and so complete what has been a wonderful tour in every way,' he wrote, before returning to his now familiar theme of the emergence of a new group of young players in May, Cowdrey, Tyson and Statham. Nor did he forget the contribution of his shipmate Evans. Tyson and Statham arrived three days later, and Bedser two days after that.

A month later Hutton walked down the gangway at Tilbury. Coincidentally, Compton flew in from South Africa on the same day, swiftly denying reports that he was about to retire. Before the England captain left the *Oronsay*, he was greeted by Aird bearing a red and yellow tie, and a pass that confirmed Hutton had become the first professional to become a member of MCC while still playing. It was a long overdue honour and the delay hardly reflected well on the club. At official functions in Australia, Hutton had quietly asked Howard not to wear his members' tie, feeling the embarrassment of not having his own. It wasn't even a new tie – unable to locate one before leaving London, Aird presented Hutton with his own.

At Leeds City Station that evening, Hutton was reunited with his sons, Richard and John, after eight months apart. The homecoming was quiet and informal. Only half an hour earlier, Eden, who had called a general election after taking over from Churchill, had launched the Conservative party's campaign at Leeds Town Hall, but there were no crowds for the returning Ashes hero. The family were driven home to Pudsey by Hutton's brother, Edmund, while a borrowed van dealt with a large pile of luggage. Hutton told a *Yorkshire Post* reporter that he had a television appearance the following day, but hoped to be back in the nets at Headingley before the end of the week.

Life moves swiftly and inevitably on to the next challenge in professional sport, and that was true even in an era when fixture lists were not influenced by the need to fill TV schedules. The South Africans, England's Test opponents in the summer of 1955, had already arrived and launched their tour uncertainly with a defeat against Worcestershire. By the time Hutton returned to England, the men who had served under him in Australia had already embarked on a new campaign.

In the opening game of the season, Cambridge University v Surrey at Fenner's, beginning on 30 April, May had scored 72 and the still-smarting Tony Lock had taken 10 victims in Surrey's easy win. Johnny Wardle, the left-arm spinner chosen ahead of Lock for Australia, also collected 10 wickets in Yorkshire's victory over MCC at Lord's. Frank Tyson's first action of the summer was against Yorkshire at Bradford, bringing him into direct opposition with Fred Trueman. Both were overshadowed by the spinners, Bob Appleyard and George Tribe. Colin Cowdrey began with successive hundreds for MCC against Oxford University and for Kent against a Northamptonshire attack led by Tyson. In the West Indies, meanwhile, Ian Johnson's Australians were 2–0 ahead in their series in the Caribbean.

There was a scramble to publish the first of an astonishing 12 books covering the tour. Arthur Gilligan's *The Urn Returns* won by a short head, and it was reviewed alongside John Arlott's *Australian Test Journal* and *Ashes Triumphant* by Bruce Harris in the May issue of *The Cricketer*. More titles would keep the magazine's reviewers busy in the coming months.

Rather more quirky was a record released by the Trinidadian calypso artist Lord Kitchener, titled 'Lord Kitchener on the Ashes'. Lord Kitchener, real name Aldwyn Roberts, had come to England on the *Empire Windrush* in 1948. He was already a successful performer in his homeland and soon became well known in the UK. In 1950, he was involved in the composition of the famous calypso 'Victory Test Match' (better known as 'Cricket, Lovely Cricket'), although the song was released by his fellow Trinidadian Lord Beginner (Egbert Moore) to mark West Indies' sensational first victory over England at Lord's. Roberts' song about the 1954–55 series was a paean to the Ashes triumph with the chorus, 'Good captaincy from Len Hutton but the honours must go to Typhoon Tyson.' He referred to England as 'we', even while writing calypsos about the racism and discrimination experienced by the first wave of the Caribbean diaspora.

Lord Kitchener's single and the pile of tour books were an indicator of the impact and importance of England's victory, as well as cricket's place in the national culture. Some Test series – even those for the Ashes – do not live long in the memory, but the contests in the Australian summer of 1954–55 earned a lasting place in the crowded history of the sport. They belong with those other immortal series of 1894–95, 1902, 1932–33, 1974–75, 1981, 2005 and 2023. With three epic victories following a crushing defeat in the opening match, England under Hutton achieved something extraordinarily rare: a come-from-behind win on Australian soil. For Hutton, the triumph proved a lasting memorial that stands as tall and proudly today as it did more than 70 years ago.

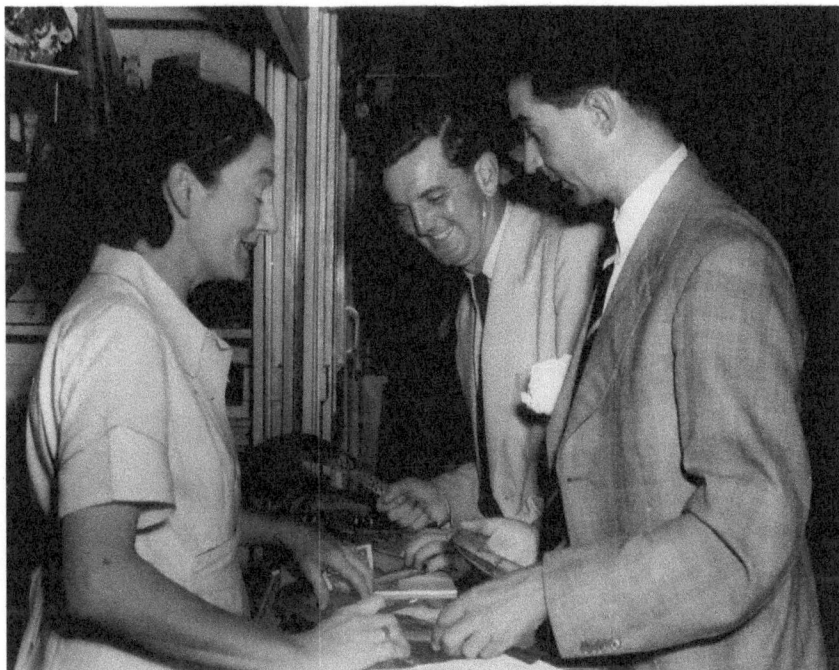

Some last-minute souvenir shopping for Reg Simpson and Tom
Graveney at the airport before they leave for New Zealand.

Photo by Alec Iverson/Fairfax Media via Getty Images

Home at last: Godfrey and Jean Evans and Dorothy and Len Hutton arrive at Tilbury aboard the Oronsay, a month after the rest of the team.

POSTSCRIPT

On 7 June, 1955 – two days before the first Test of the summer against South Africa at Trent Bridge – there was a significant demonstration of the status now enjoyed by Len Hutton after England's victory in Australia. At 10.15 p.m. on the BBC Home Service, John Arlott introduced a half-hour programme called *Captain of England: Len Hutton*. The national broadcaster – every bit as much part of the establishment as MCC – was paying due tribute to the professional leader who had pulled off a great sporting triumph.

Arlott had assembled an impressive cast: Hutton's former Yorkshire and England colleagues Bill Bowes, Maurice Leyland and Norman Yardley, Reg Perks of Worcestershire, who had bowled at Hutton when he made his first century in 1934, the former England wicketkeeper Les Ames, the noted coach Alf Gover, plus Denis Compton and Colin Cowdrey, England teammates from the recent tour. E. W. Swanton offered a measured view from the press box and a dash of showbiz glamour was added by Wilfred Pickles, the radio presenter and comic. 'Now I'm not a sports expert, but I'm a Yorkshireman and I love cricket, and I do reckon I know something about people,' said Pickles. 'To me Len Hutton is not just the captain of England or a record-breaker – he's a real person and a pal of mine. And as a person and as a pal, he'll do for me.'

The voice of the ordinary cricket lover was provided by Walter Flesher, a gamekeeper on the Yorkshire Moors. He gave short shrift to Hutton's critics. 'Only a little while ago there was some fella writing in a paper about Hutton's field placings in Australia and all the mistakes this chap thought he'd made,' he said. 'If ever a man might have been shaken and had his confidence upset it must have been Len 'utton after that Brisbane match, and yet he went on and stuck to his own plans and eventually succeeded. Military generals are judged on their ability to force ultimate victory and I suggest cricket captains should be similarly judged.'

The night before Arlott's programme was aired, MCC held a dinner to celebrate the winter's success at the Dorchester Hotel in Park Lane. Not all the players could make it. A national rail strike was wreaking havoc with the travel plans of cricketers. Frank Tyson and Keith Andrew were stuck in Coventry, where Northamptonshire were playing Warwickshire. Tyson sent a telegram of apology: 'Regret that foot platers not sympathetic to dinner platers.' The strike also left Tom Graveney marooned in Portsmouth. In his speech, MCC president Lord Cobham revived memories of the Ashes series for those who had not been in Australia. 'Those cold frosty mornings in the winter,' he said, 'when we crept from our beds, risking frostbite, turned on our radios, then woke the baby.' Each of the players was given an inscribed cigarette case, but the gifts may not have been met with much enthusiasm – several months later MCC wrote to Graveney reminding him that his was still awaiting collection at Lord's.

Swanton's contribution to the radio programme revisited familiar themes. 'I'm sure many people find it difficult to assess his performance as England's captain because so much of the comment on the matter has not been objective,' he said. 'People's thinking on this has been coloured by his being a professional. What the era of Hutton's captaincy has done is to emphasise that the man who ought to be captain at any given time is the one with the best qualifications.'

Cowdrey was looking to the future not the past. 'I'd like to wish him not only good fortune this year in the Tests against the South Africans, but that he may be free from his back trouble,' he said. 'I wish him that good health so that any young player who is fortunate enough to play under him will have the chance to benefit from his long experience in the way I did in Australia.'

By the time the programme was broadcast that already sounded like wishful thinking: Hutton had been ruled out of the first Test with arthritis in his lower back, Peter May stepping up to take his place as captain. Bulletins on Hutton's bad back had featured regularly on the sports pages in the five weeks since the season began. He was chosen to lead MCC against the South Africans at Lord's in May – after his rushed elevation to the membership, he was now qualified for that honour – and was warmly applauded when he walked out to open the batting with Graveney towards the end of a bitterly cold first day.

The atmosphere soon turned sour, however. With MCC three without loss and the clock at the Nursery End showing 6.28 p.m., the touring team hurried to their fielding positions to fit in another over before the close. Hutton turned on his heel and headed for the pavilion, followed at a distance by a bemused Graveney. South African captain Jack Cheetham remonstrated with umpires Frank Chester and Frank Lee. Contacted by Frank Rostron of the *Daily Express* the next day, Hutton denied any sharp practice. He explained that the Lord's clocks were showing different times and that he had merely been using a clock elsewhere on the ground as his guide.

It proved to be a passing storm. By Tuesday morning the headlines had switched to Hutton's confirmation as England captain for all five Tests against South Africa – the first time the selectors had felt emboldened to appoint a leader for an entire home series since C.B. Fry before the Triangular tournament against Australia and South Africa in 1912. 'We decided to honour Hutton because no man likes to feel that he is on approval from match to match, and Hutton has well earned the job on his successes,' said Gubby Allen, who had taken over from Harry Altham as chairman of selectors.

But Hutton spent the day on the masseur's table and did not resume his abruptly interrupted innings, nor bat again in the match. He was back in action a week later for the Whitsun weekend Roses match at Old Trafford, making two low scores, and his last opportunity to prove his fitness for the first Test match came against Surrey, the all-powerful county champions, at The Oval. It proved a miserable experience – Peter Loader, bristling after being overlooked in Australia, dismissed Hutton for a duck and one. Before the match ended, his withdrawal from the first Test, and May's promotion, had been confirmed.

Hutton was back in action by the following weekend, and there seemed genuine reason for optimism that he would be fit for the second Test when he hit 85 against Kent at Hull. It proved ill-founded. Although Hutton was included in the Yorkshire team for the return match against Surrey at Headingley, an announcement came from Lord's on Sunday 19 June that he would take no part in the remainder of the series.

It was front-page news and the lead story in *The Yorkshire Post*. Hutton was disappointed, but explained, 'The trouble is rheumatism. I was free from it in Australia, but it started again when I began playing this season. Test cricket demands a high level of physical fitness and in addition to my back trouble I have been having trouble with my arm. Coming back to this climate has not helped my back trouble either.' He was immediately co-opted on to the selection committee and made a return rail trip to London with May to help select the England team. To complete his misery, the following day he was dismissed twice by Alec Bedser, another disgruntled member of his winter tour party. Hutton's plight elicited a flood of more than 500 letters to his Pudsey home, many suggesting remedies for back conditions. 'A popular cure was to place a nutmeg in my pocket,' he recalled. 'I was sent enough nutmegs to start a business.'

Later that week, as May led England into the second Test at Lord's, Hutton celebrated – if that was the right word – his 39th birthday. His persistent health problems had naturally prompted speculation about his future. 'Has record score-maker played last innings for England?' was the strapline above the main headline on *The Yorkshire Post*. 'I shall be surprised if he plays for England again,' wrote Eric Stanger, the paper's second-string cricket writer. 'In fact, I think, he would be wise to call it a day even if, as we all hope, his health is fully restored.'

'If my back does not improve this will be my last season in cricket,' Hutton admitted. Nevertheless, he believed his best cure was to carry on playing for Yorkshire, which meant he spent his birthday in Northampton. It seemed like a sensible course of action when he made 194 against Nottinghamshire at Trent Bridge the following week. 'Attacking the bowling with fluent grace and power, he took 14 in one over from Smales, including a six, and scored his last 94 in 65 minutes,' reported the *Daily Telegraph*. But when the Yorkshire team moved on to Bournemouth, Hutton was laid low again. 'I was virtually a prisoner in my own bed,' he said. A local osteopath was needed to ensure he could make the journey from the team hotel to the ground. After being dismissed for a duck in the first innings, he made only two in the second.

It turned out to be his last appearance for Yorkshire, his farewell to the County Championship, and his last top-level cricket match (he played in three more first-class games, one in 1957 and two in 1960). 'In the almost rural setting of Dean Park, Bournemouth, before the chestnuts, the conifers and the retired colonels, a great England player passed unobtrusively from the scene,' wrote his biographer Gerald Howat. For Hutton the melancholy journey home recalled the one he had made from Hove in 1939 when Britain was on the brink of war. 'Long before I left Bournemouth I had come to terms with the fact that I could not carry on,' he said. In his final autobiography, *Fifty Years in Cricket*, Hutton revealed that he had been taking up to 16 painkilling tablets a day just to get on the field. At the end of the season he visited a Leeds hospital where his back was encased in plaster from neck to waist. Within days, the pain eased and he was able to stop taking the pills.

Although Hutton later wrote that he knew his career was over during those excruciating days in Bournemouth, the formal announcement of his retirement did not come for more than six months. It followed an appointment with the orthopaedic surgeon Reginald Broomhead at a hospital in Leeds. Broomhead told him his back problems could recur at any time. Hutton ascribed the issue to years of leaning over a bat. There was also no doubt he was exhausted from the physical and mental strain of successive winter tours, which had made huge demands on his constitution. 'Len Hutton has been through the cricket mill,' Arlott said at the end of his radio tribute. 'Notice the broken nose, the beaten-in knuckles, the tired, drawn face after a tense day in a tightly fought Test match, the concentration of captaincy.'

But opinions differed as to whether he had intended to carry on. There was a school of thought that, with his ambition of winning in Australia achieved, he could afford to relax a little and give fuller rein to his strokeplay. 'I do look forward to the future, and playing bright cricket, and hitting the ball and really enjoying it, perhaps when I haven't got the number of responsibilities that I have at the moment,' he told Arlott. He had never led England against South Africa and victory in that series would have been another impressive entry on his CV. In other interviews he looked forward to the defence of the Ashes in 1956 and, beyond that, the tour to South Africa in the winter of 1956–57.

Trevor Bailey believed Hutton was aggrieved not to have been offered the captaincy of Yorkshire. 'I sometimes feel that if Yorkshire had followed England's example and made him captain he might have been tempted to carry on longer,' Bailey said. Hutton denied this in the 1980s. Yardley remained in charge until 1956, when he was succeeded by Billy Sutcliffe, but had been open to the idea of retiring earlier if the committee were minded to promote Hutton. They were not: Yorkshire committeemen were in no hurry to end the tradition of amateur captaincy. It is not just at the distance of nearly 70 years that this feels like a considerable snub to the man who had just masterminded back-to-back Ashes victories. Hutton's close friend Vic Wilson became the first professional Yorkshire captain in 1960.

Others felt Hutton had simply had enough of cricket. 'I don't think he ever intended to go on after the 1954–55 tour,' Geoffrey Howard, MCC's manager in Australia, told his biographer Stephen Chalke. 'He'd been in touch with the *Evening News*. They were making him an offer to write for them with an amanuensis. For Len it would have seemed like an easier living with more money. And a motor car. "Is there a tank full of petrol?" he asked when they delivered it. There were only three things in Len's life: cricket, family and money. After he retired he was much more relaxed, much more communicative. I might even venture the possibility that he was happier.'

When Hutton's retirement announcement finally came on 17 January, 1956 it was a major news item. There was a short leading article in the *Daily Telegraph* and Swanton contributed an extended tribute on the sports page. 'To those who knew Hutton well, who were aware how the game monopolised his thoughts, and who realised the nervous effort involved in all he did, both as a player and a captain, it seemed clear two years ago that he was being taxed beyond his strength,' he wrote. The leader writers at the *Manchester Guardian* also offered an opinion: 'His own integrity and personal modesty and Yorkshire humour shone through the chain mail which he put on for the battle, and won him friends as well as matches.'

In *The Times*, the tribute was left to cricket correspondent John Woodcock: 'His defence was as an iron curtain; his cover drive was the game's most classic stroke; the way he touched the peak of his cap between each ball was cricket's most famous mannerism.' Compton, Bailey, Yardley, Brian Statham and Cyril Washbrook all added their farewells, and Dorothy Hutton was also asked for a comment: 'I feel a little sad, but we have been more or less prepared for it.'

Once again the BBC rearranged its schedules to salute Hutton. After the early-evening news bulletin, the airwaves were given over to MCC treasurer Harry Altham, not just a former chairman of selectors, but one of cricket's most distinguished historians. 'Tonight we realise that a great chapter in the history of cricket is closed,' he said. He then returned to the subject of Hutton's finest hour – the Ashes triumph 12 months earlier. 'On that tour I know he was often fighting physical disability and pain. But his courage carried him through, and his team and every cricketer in England will always be grateful to him.'

RECORDS AND STATISTICS

MCC TOUR OF AUSTRALIA AND NEW ZEALAND 1954–55

SUMMARY OF RESULTS

Tests: played 7, won 5, drawn 1, lost 1
All first-class: played 21, won 12, lost 2, drawn 7
All matches: played 28, won 17, lost 2, drawn 9
†Indicates non-first-class match

†30 September   Ceylon v MCC   Colombo Oval
MCC 178–8 dec (M.C. Cowdrey 66*); Ceylon 101–4 (F.C. de Saram 43)
Drawn

---

†11, 12 October   Western Australia Country XI v MCC   Bunbury
MCC 344–5 dec (W.J. Edrich 129, L. Hutton 59, T.W. Graveney 58); Western
Australia Country XI 116 (J.E. McConnon 5–30, P.J. Loader 4–35) & 128–6
Drawn

15, 16, 18, 19 October   Western Australia v MCC   Perth
Western Australia 103 (J.B. Statham 6–23) & 255 (K.D. Meuleman 109,
D.K. Carmody 75); MCC 321 (L. Hutton 145; H.R. Gorringe 4–102) & 40–3
MCC won by seven wickets
Combined attendance: 16,391

22, 23, 25 October   Western Australia Combined XI v MCC   Perth
Western Australia Combined XI 86 & 163 (J.H. Wardle 4–34); MCC 311
(P.B.H. May 129, J.V. Wilson 72)
MCC won by an innings and 62 runs
Combined attendance: 25,783

29, 30 Oct, 1, 2 November   South Australia v MCC   Adelaide

MCC 246 (D.C.S. Compton 113; J.W. Wilson 5–81) & 181 (L. Hutton 98;
J.W. Wilson 4–32); South Australia 254 (L.E. Favell 84; F.H. Tyson 5–62) & 152
(R. Appleyard 5–46)

MCC won by 21 runs

Combined attendance: 43,579

5, 6, 8, 9 November   Australian XI v MCC   Melbourne

MCC 205 (R.T. Simpson 74; I.W. Johnson 6–66); Australian XI 167–7 (R.E. Briggs
48, R. Benaud 47; T.E. Bailey 4–53)

Match drawn

Combined attendance: 50,285

12, 13, 15, 16 November   New South Wales v MCC   Sydney

MCC 252 (L. Hutton 102, M.C. Cowdrey 110) & 327 (M.C. Cowdrey 103,
L. Hutton 87; W.P.A. Crawford 4–86, J.C. Treanor 4–96); New South Wales 382
(W.J. Watson 155, K.R. Miller 86; A.V. Bedser 4–117, F.H. Tyson 4–98) & 78–2

Match drawn

Combined attendance: 59,290

19, 20, 22, 23 November   Queensland v MCC   Brisbane

MCC 304 (R.T. Simpson 136, D.C.S. Compton 110; R.R. Lindwall 4–66) & 288
(P.B.H. May 77, D.C.S. Compton 69, T.E. Bailey 51); Queensland 288 & 25–1

Match drawn

Combined attendance: 20,834

First Test

26, 27, 29, 30 November, 1 December   **Australia v England**   Brisbane

Australia 601–8 dec (A.R. Morris 153, R.N. Harvey 162, G.B. Hole 57,
R.R. Lindwall 64); England 190 (T.E. Bailey 88) & 257 (W.J. Edrich 88)

Australia won by an innings and 154 runs

Combined attendance: 77,008

Australia lead series 1–0

---

†4, 6 December   Queensland Country XI v MCC   Rockhampton

MCC 317 (W.J. Edrich 74, P.B.H. May 69, J.V. Wilson 61; D. Watt 5–56); Queensland
Country XI 95 & 210 (W.M. Brown 78; R. Appleyard 7–51)

MCC won by an innings and 12 runs

---

†8 December   Prime Minister's XI v MCC   Canberra

MCC 278–7 dec (P.B.H. May 101, T.W. Graveney 56); Prime Minister's XI 247 (R. Benaud 113, S.J.E. Loxton 47; J.H. Wardle 4–73)

MCC won by 31 runs

10, 11, 13, 14 December   Victoria v MCC   Melbourne

MCC 312 (T.E. Bailey 60, T.W. Graveney 48, M.C. Cowdrey 79) & 236–5 dec (P.B.H. May 105*, M.C. Cowdrey 54); Victoria 277 (R.N. Harvey 59; F.H. Tyson 6–68) & 88–3

Match drawn

Combined attendance: 42,857

Second Test

17, 18, 20, 21, 22 December   **Australia v England**   Sydney

England 154 (L. Hutton 30, J.H. Wardle 35; R.G. Archer 3–12, W.A. Johnston 3–56) & 296 (P.B.H. May 104, M.C. Cowdrey 54; R.R. Lindwall 3–69, R.G. Archer 3–53, W.A. Johnston 3–70); Australia 228 (J.W. Burke 44, R.G. Archer 49; T.E. Bailey 4–59, F.H. Tyson 4–45) & 184 (R.N. Harvey 92; J.B. Statham 3–45, F.H. Tyson 6–85)

England won by 38 runs

Combined attendance: 135,354

Series tied 1–1

---

†27, 28, 29 December   Northern New South Wales v MCC   Newcastle

Northern New South Wales 211 (R.M. Harvey 41, R. McDonald 63; J.H. Wardle 6–36) & 246 (R.C.A. Wotton 52; R. Appleyard 5–59); MCC 438 (D.C.S. Compton 60, P.B.H. May 157, T.G. Evans 69; J. Bull 5–80, B. O'Sullivan 4–107) & 20–1

MCC won by 9 wickets

Third Test

31 December, 1, 3, 4, 5 January   **Australia v England**   Melbourne

England 191 (M.C. Cowdrey 102; R.G. Archer 4–33) & 279 (P.B.H. May 91; W.A. Johnston 5–85); Australia 231 (L.V. Maddocks 47; J.B. Statham 5–60) & 111 (L.E. Favell 30; F.H. Tyson 7–27)

England won by 128 runs

Combined attendance: 300,270

England lead series 2–1

8, 10, 11 January　　　　　Tasmania Combined XI v MCC　　　　Hobart

Tasmania Combined XI 221 (R.N. Harvey 82, E.E. Rodwell 70; P.J. Loader 4–81) & 184–6 dec (R.N. Harvey 47, R. Benaud 68★); MCC 242 (D.C.S. Compton 46, T.E. Bailey 53; A.K. Davidson 4–45) & 99–2

Match drawn

Combined attendance: 20,783

13, 14, 15 January　　　　　Tasmania v MCC　　　　Launceston

MCC 427–7 dec (L. Hutton 61, T.W. Graveney 134, D.C.S. Compton 50, J.V. Wilson 62★, J.H. Wardle 63; N.V. Diprose 4–107) & 133–6 dec (T.J. Cowley 4–53); Tasmania 117 (P.J. Loader 6–22) & 200 (B.J. Hyland 49, J.M. Maddox 62★; J.H. Wardle 4–37)

MCC won by 243 runs

Combined attendance: 12,212

---

†18, 19 January　　　　South Australia Country XI v MCC　　　Mount Gambier

MCC 328 (R.T. Simpson 68, P.B.H. May 62, D.C.S. Compton 53); South Australia Country XI 106 (R. Appleyard 6–26) & 45 (J.B. Statham 6–3)

MCC won by an innings and 177 runs

21, 22, 24 January　　　　　South Australia v MCC　　　　Adelaide

South Australia 185 (P.L. Ridings 40, G.R.A. Langley 53) & 123 (P.L. Ridings 40★; P.J. Loader 4–32); MCC 451 (M.C. Cowdrey 64, D.C.S. Compton 182, P.B.H. May 114; D.M. Gregg 4–117)

MCC won by an innings and 143 runs

Combined attendance: 22,505

Fourth Test

28, 29, 31 January, 1, 2, February　　　　**Australia v England**　　Adelaide

Australia 323 (C.C. McDonald 48, K.R. Miller 44, L.V. Maddocks 69) & 111; England 341 (L. Hutton 80, M.C. Cowdrey 79; R. Benaud 4–120) & 97–5

England won by 5 wickets

Combined attendance: 162,499

England lead series 3–1

---

†5, 7 February　　　　Victoria Country XI v MCC　　　　Yallourn

Victoria Country XI 182 (W. Young 56; J.H. Wardle 5–46, P.J. Loader 4–29) & 99 (J.H. Wardle 7–45); MCC 307–8 dec (L. Hutton 75, R.T. Simpson 59, T.W. Graveney 50)

MCC won by an innings and 26 runs

369

11, 12, 14, 15 February   Victoria v MCC   Melbourne
Victoria 113; MCC 90–1

Match drawn

18, 19, 21, 22 February   New South Wales v MCC   Sydney
New South Wales 172 (B.C. Booth 74★; A.V. Bedser 5–57) & 314–8 dec (J.W. Burke
62, R.B. Simpson 98, R. Benaud 57, K.R. Miller 71); MCC 172 (L. Hutton 48; A.K.
Davidson 4–25) & 269 (L. Hutton 59)

New South Wales won by 45 runs

Combined attendance: 34,198

Fifth Test

25, 26, 28 February, 1, 2, 3 March   **Australia v England**   Sydney
England 371–7 dec (T.W. Graveney 111, P.B.H. May 79, D.C.S. Compton 84,
T.E. Bailey 72); Australia 221 (C.C. McDonald 72; J.H. Wardle 5–79) & 118–6

Match drawn

Combined attendance: 29,844

England win series 3–1

5, 7, 8 March   Canterbury v MCC   Christchurch
Canterbury 140 (J.H. Wardle 4–46) & 206 (J.G. Leggat 99); MCC 302
(T.W. Graveney 101, F.H. Tyson 62★; T.B. Burtt 4–74) & 45–3

MCC won by 7 wickets

First Test

11, 12, 14, 15, 16 March   **New Zealand v England**   Dunedin
New Zealand 125 (B. Sutcliffe 74; J.B. Statham 4–24) & 132 (F.H. Tyson 4–16);
England 209–8 dec (M.C. Cowdrey 42; J.R. Reid 4–36) & 49–2

England won by 8 wickets

England lead series 1–0

19, 21, 22 March   Wellington v MCC   Wellington
MCC 207 (T.W. Graveney 102; R.W. Blair 4–50) & 201 (P.B.H. May 41; J.R. Reid
5–65); Wellington 127 (J.H. Wardle 5–42) & 94 (R. Appleyard 6–21, J.H. Wardle 4–46)

MCC won by 187 runs

Second Test

25, 26, 28 March   **New Zealand v England**   Auckland

New Zealand 200 (B Sutcliffe 49, J.R. Reid 73; J.B. Statham 4–28) & 26
(R. Appleyard 4–7); England 246 (P.B.H. May 48, L. Hutton 53; A.M. Moir 5–62)

England won by an innings and 20 runs

England win series 2–0

LEADING ASHES RUN-SCORERS

		Matches	Innings	Not outs	Highest score	Average	Runs
R.N. Harvey	Aus	5	9	1	162	44.25	354
P.B.H. May	Eng	5	9	0	104	39	351
M.C. Cowdrey	Eng	5	9	0	102	35.44	319
T.E. Bailey	Eng	5	9	1	88	37	296
A.R. Morris	Aus	4	7	0	153	31.85	223
L. Hutton	Eng	5	9	0	80	24.44	220
D.C.S. Compton	Eng	4	7	2	84	38.20	191
C.C. McDonald	Aus	2	4	0	72	46.50	186
W.J. Edrich	Eng	4	8	0	88	22.50	180
K.R. Miller	Aus	4	7	0	49	23.85	167

Also scored more than 100 runs: L.V. Maddocks (Aus) 150, R. Benaud (Aus) 148,
T.W. Graveney (Eng) 132, L.E. Favell (Aus) 130, R.G. Archer (Aus) 117, I.W. Johnson (Aus)
116, J.H. Wardle (Eng) 109, R.R. Lindwall (Aus) 106, T.G. Evans (Eng) 102.

LEADING ASHES WICKET-TAKERS

		Matches	Overs	Maidens	Runs	Average	Wickets
F.H. Tyson	Eng	5	151	16	583	20.82	28
W.A. Johnston	Aus	4	141.4	37	423	22.26	19
J.B. Statham	Eng	5	143.3	16	499	27.72	18
R.R. Lindwall	Aus	4	130.6	28	381	27.21	14
R.G. Archer	Aus	4	97.6	32	215	16.53	13
I.W. Johnson	Aus	4	111	37	243	20.25	12
R. Appleyard	Eng	4	79	22	224	20.36	11
J.H. Wardle	Eng	4	70.6	15	229	22.90	10
K.R. Miller	Aus	4	88.4	28	243	24.30	10
T.E. Bailey	Eng	5	73.4	8	306	30.60	10
R. Benaud	Aus	5	116.7	23	377	37.70	10

Other wicket-takers: A.K. Davidson (Aus) 3—220, L. Hutton (Eng) 1—2, T.W. Graveney (Eng) 1—34, A.V. Bedser (Eng) 1—131.

LEADING ENGLAND TOUR RUN-SCORERS

	Matches	Innings	Not outs	Highest score	Average	Runs
P.B.H. May	18	29	3	129	42.15	1096
L. Hutton	15	25	2	145★	46.04	1059
M.C. Cowdrey	17	31	1	110	33.96	1019
T.W. Graveney	15	22	3	134	45	855
D.C.S. Compton	11	16	2	182	57.07	799
R.T. Simpson	16	27	3	136	26.83	644
T.E. Bailey	15	21	2	88	29	551
J.H. Wardle	18	23	3	63	17.05	341
J.V. Wilson	11	19	2	72	17.71	301
W.J. Edrich	11	18	0	88	16.28	293

Other run-scorers: F.H. Tyson 286, T.G. Evans 244, J.B. Statham 132, P.J. Loader 90, J.E. McConnon 85, A.V. Bedser 85, R. Appleyard 82, K.V. Andrew 71
Includes first-class matches in Australia and New Zealand.

LEADING ENGLAND TOUR WICKET-TAKERS

	Matches	Balls	Maidens	Runs	Average	Wickets
F.H. Tyson	14	2764	65	1140	17.81	64
J.H. Wardle	18	3153	135	1666	20.46	57
J.B. Statham	13	2445	69	916	16.96	54
R. Appleyard	13	1962	82	656	14.91	44
P.J. Loader	11	1902	42	817	19.93	41
T.E. Bailey	15	1898	49	769	21.36	36
A.V. Bedser	7	1655	33	659	27.46	24

Other wicket-takers: J.E. McConnon 8, J.V. Wilson 5, D.C.S. Compton 2, R.T. Simpson 2, T.W. Graveney 1, M.C. Cowdrey 1, L. Hutton 1
Includes first-class matches in Australia and New Zealand.

ASHES WICKETKEEPING RECORDS

		Matches	Catches	Stumpings	Total
T.G. Evans	Eng	4	13	—	13
G.R.A. Langley	Aus	2	9	—	9
L.V. Maddocks	Aus	3	6	—	6
K.V. Andrew	Eng	1	—	—	1

ASHES OUTFIELD CATCHES

		Catches
P.B.H. May	Eng	6
R. Appleyard	Eng	4
R.G. Archer	Aus	4
M.C. Cowdrey	Eng	4
A.K. Davidson	Aus	4
T.W. Graveney	Eng	4
R. Benaud	Aus	3
W.J. Edrich	Eng	3
R.N. Harvey	Aus	3
G.B. Hole	Eng	3

ASHES CENTURIES

R.N. Harvey	Aus	162	First Test, Brisbane
A.R. Morris	Aus	153	First Test, Brisbane
T.W. Graveney	Eng	111	Fifth Test, Sydney
P.B.H. May	Eng	104	Second Test, Sydney
M.C. Cowdrey	Eng	102	Third Test, Melbourne

ASHES CENTURY PARTNERSHIPS

		Score	Wicket	Test/Venue
R.N. Harvey & A.R. Morris	Aus	202	3rd	First Test, Brisbane
T.W. Graveney & P.B.H. May	Eng	182	2nd	Fifth Test, Sydney
D.C.S. Compton & T.E. Bailey	Eng	134	5th	Fifth Test, Sydney
R.N. Harvey & G.B. Hole	Aus	131	4th	First Test, Brisbane
W.J. Edrich & P.B.H. May	Eng	124	3rd	First Test, Brisbane
P.B.H. May & M.C. Cowdrey	Eng	116	4th	Second Test, Sydney

HIGHEST ENGLAND SCORES ON TOUR

D.C.S. Compton	182	v South Australia at Adelaide
P.B.H. May	157	v Northern New South Wales at Newcastle†
L. Hutton	145*	v Western Australia at Perth
R.T. Simpson	136	v Queensland at Brisbane
T.W. Graveney	134	v Tasmania at Launceston
W.J. Edrich	129	v Western Australia Country XI at Bunbury†
P.B.H. May	129	v Combined XI at Perth
P.B.H. May	114	v South Australia at Adelaide
D.C.S. Compton	113	v South Australia at Adelaide
T.W. Graveney	111	v Australia at Sydney (fifth Test)
M.C. Cowdrey	110	v New South Wales at Sydney (first innings)
D.C.S. Compton	110	v Queensland at Brisbane
P.B.H. May	105*	v Victoria at Melbourne
P.B.H. May	104	v Australia at Sydney (second Test)

M.C. Cowdrey	103	v New South Wales at Sydney (second innings)
M.C. Cowdrey	102	v Australia at Melbourne (third Test)
T.W. Graveney	102	v Wellington at Wellington
L. Hutton	102	v New South Wales at Sydney
T.W. Graveney	101	v Canterbury at Christchurch
P.B.H. May	101	v Prime Minister's XI at Canberra†

†Not first class

BEST ENGLAND BOWLING ON TOUR

F.H. Tyson	7—27	v Australia at Melbourne (third Test)
P.J. Loader	6—22	v Tasmania at Launceston
J.B. Statham	6—23	v Western Australia at Perth
F.H. Tyson	6—68	v Victoria at Melbourne
F.H. Tyson	6—85	v Australia at Sydney (second Test)
R. Appleyard	5—46	v South Australia at Adelaide
A.V. Bedser	5—57	v New South Wales at Sydney
J.B. Statham	5—60	v Australia at Melbourne (third Test)
F.H. Tyson	5—62	v South Australia at Adelaide
J.H. Wardle	5—79	v Australia at Sydney (fifth Test)
J.H. Wardle	5—118	v New South Wales at Sydney

BIBLIOGRAPHY

CONTEMPORARY TOUR BOOKS

Arlott, J., *John Arlott's Australian Test Journal: Australia v. England 1954–55* (Phoenix Sports Books, 1955)

Barnes, S., *The Ashes Ablaze: The MCC Australian Tour 1954–55* (William Kimber, 1955)

Batchelor, D., *The Picture Post Book of the Tests 1954–5* (Hulton Press, 1955)

Gilligan, A.E.R, *The Urn Returns: a Diary of the 1954–55 MCC Tour of Australia* (André Deutsch, 1955)

Harris, B., *Ashes Triumphant: Australia versus England 1954–5* (Hutchinson's Library of Sports & Pastimes, 1955)

Hughes, M., *The Long Hop* (Stanley Paul, 1955)

Miller, K. & Whitington, R.S., *Cricket Typhoon* (Macdonald, 1955)

Moyes, A.G., *The Fight for the Ashes 1954–1955: a critical account of the English tour in Australia* (George G. Harrap, 1955)

Peebles, I., *On the Ashes 1954-1955* (Hodder & Stoughton, 1955)

Ross, A., *Australia 55: A Journal of the MCC Tour* (Michael Joseph, 1955)

Swanton, E.W., *Victory in Australia: The Test Matches of 1954/55* (The Daily Telegraph, 1955)

Wellings, E.M., *The Ashes Retained* (Evans Brothers, 1955)

RETROSPECTIVES

Hill, A., *Daring Young Men: the story of England's Victorious Tour of Australia and New Zealand, 1954-55* (Methuen, 2005)

Swanton, E.W., *Swanton in Australia: With MCC 1946–1975* (William Collins & Sons, 1975)

Tyson, F., *In the Eye of the Typhoon: Recollections of the Marylebone Cricket Club Tour of Australia 1954/55* (The Parrs Wood Press, 2004)

Valentine, B., *When England Beat Australia: Two Books in One on the Fight for the Ashes* (TSO Ireland, 2005)

BOOKS ON OTHER TOURS

Compton, D., *In Sun and Shadow* (Stanley Paul, 1952)

Frith, D., *Bodyline Autopsy: The Full Story of the Most Sensational Test Cricket Series: Australia v England 1932–33* (Aurum, 2002)

Wellings, E.M., *Dexter v Benaud: M.C.C. Tour of Australia 1962–3* (A.H. & A.W. Reed, 1963)

Woodhouse, D., *Who Only Cricket Know: Hutton's Men in the West Indies 1953/54* (Fairfield Books, 2021)

AUTOBIOGRAPHIES

Arlott, J., *Basingstoke Boy: The Autobiography* (Collins Willow, 1990)

Bailey, T., *Wickets, Catches and the Odd Run* (Willow Books, 1986)

Bedser, A., *Twin Ambitions: An Autobiography* (Stanley Paul, 1986)

Bedser, A. & E., *Following On* (Evans Brothers, 1954)

Bowes, B., *Express Deliveries* (Stanley Paul, 1950)

Brown, F., *Cricket Musketeer* (Nicholas Kaye, 1954)

Compton, D., *End of an Innings* (Oldbourne Book Co, 1958)

Cowdrey, C., *Time for Reflection* (Frederick Muller, 1962)

Cowdrey, C., *M.C.C: the Autobiography of a Cricketer* (Hodder & Stoughton, 1976)

Davidson, A., *Fifteen Paces* (Souvenir Press, 1963)

Edrich, W.J., *Round the Wicket* (Frederick Muller, 1959)

Evans, G., *Action in Cricket* (Hodder & Stoughton, 1956)

Evans, G., *The Gloves Are Off: a Close-Up of Cricket* (Hodder & Stoughton, 1960)

Ferguson, W.H., *Mr Cricket: the autobiography of Fergie* (Nicholas Kaye, 1957)

Favell, L., *By Hook or By Cut* (Investigator Press, 1970)

Frith, D., *Paddington Boy* (CricketMASH, 2021)

Gover, A., *The Long Run: An Autobiography* (Pelham Books, 1991)

Graveney, T., *Cricket Through the Covers* (Frederick Muller, 1958)

Harvey, N., *My World of Cricket* (Hodder & Stoughton, 1963)

Hutton, L., *Cricket is My Life* (Hutchinson, 1952)

Hutton, L., *Just My Story* (Hutchinson, 1956)

Hutton, L., *Fifty Years in Cricket* (Stanley Paul, 1984)

Kilburn, J.M., *In Search of Cricket* (The Pavilion Library, 1990)

Laker, J., *Spinning Round the World* (Frederick Muller, 1957)

Laker, J., *Over To Me* (Frederick Muller, 1960)

Lock, T., *For Surrey and England* (Hodder & Stoughton, 1957)

May, P., *A Game Enjoyed: An Autobiography* (Stanley Paul, 1985)

Miller, K., *Cricket Crossfire* (Oldbourne Press, 1956)

Sayen, H., *A Yankee Looks at Cricket* (Putnam, 1954)

Sheppard, D., *Parson's Pitch* (Hodder & Stoughton, 1964)

Statham, B., *Flying Bails* (Stanley Paul, 1961)

Tasker, N., *McGilvray: The Game is Not the Same…* (David & Charles, 1985)

Trueman, F., *Ball of Fire: An Autobiography* (J.M. Dent & Sons, 1976)

Trueman, F., *As It Was: The Memoirs of Fred Trueman* (Macmillan, 2004)

Tyson, F., *A Typhoon Called Tyson* (Sportspages/Simon & Schuster, 1990)

Wardle, J., *Happy Go Johnny* (Robert Hale, 1957)

BIOGRAPHIES

Arlott, T., *John Arlott: A Memoir* (André Deutsch, 1994)

Bailey, J., *Trevor Bailey: A Life in Cricket* (Methuen, 1993)

Bradstock, A., *David Sheppard Batting for the Poor: The Authorized Biography of the Celebrated Cricketer and Bishop* (SPCK, 2019)

Chalke, S., *At the Heart of English Cricket: The Life and Memories of Geoffrey Howard* (Fairfield Books, 2001)

Chalke, S., *Guess My Story: The Life and Opinions of Keith Andrew, Cricketer* (Fairfield Books, 2003)

Chalke, S. & Hodgson, D., *No Coward Soul: The Remarkable Story of Bob Appleyard* (Fairfield Books, 2003)

Fay, S. & Kynaston, D., *Arlott, Swanton and the Soul of English Cricket* (Bloomsbury, 2018)

Hamilton, D., *Harold Larwood: The Authorised Biography of the World's Fastest Bowler* (Quercus, 2009)

Hamilton, D., *The Great Romantic: Cricket and the Golden Age of Neville Cardus* (Hodder & Stoughton, 2019)

Hill, A., *Bill Edrich: A Biography* (André Deutsch, 1994)

Hill, A., *Jim Laker: A Biography* (André Deutsch, 1998)

Hill, A., *The Bedsers: Twinning Triumphs* (Mainstream, 2001)

Howat, G., *Len Hutton: The Biography* (Heinemann Kingswood, 1988)

Jones, T., *Don Kenyon: His Own Man* (Amberley Publishing, 2015)

McKinstry, L., *Jack Hobbs: England's Greatest Cricketer* (Yellow Jersey Press, 2011)

McKinstry, L., *Bill Edrich: The Many Lives of England's Cricket Great* (Bloomsbury, 2024)

Midwinter, E., *George Duckworth: Warrington's Ambassador at Large* (ACS Publications, 2007)

Miller, D., *Charles Palmer: More Than Just a Gentleman* (Fairfield Books, 2005)

Murtagh, A., *Touched by Greatness: The Story of Tom Graveney, England's Much-Loved Cricketer* (Pitch Publishing, 2014)

Parkinson, J., *Then Came Massacre: The Story of Maurice Tate, Cricket's Smiling Destroyer* (Pitch Publishing, 2013)

Peebles, I., *Denis Compton* (Macmillan, 1971)

Peel, M., *The Last Roman: A Biography of Colin Cowdrey* (André Deutsch, 1999)

Rayvern Allen, D., *Arlott: The Authorised Biography* (HarperCollins, 1994)

Ringwood, J., *Ray Lindwall, Cricket Legend* (Robert Hale, 1996)

Sandford, C., *Godfrey Evans: A Biography* (Simon & Schuster, 1989)

Thomson, A.A., *Hutton & Washbrook* (The Epworth Press, 1963)

Waters, C., *Fred Trueman: The Authorised Biography* (Aurum, 2011)

Whitington, R.S., *Keith Miller: The Golden Nugget* (Rigby, 1981)

CRICKET HISTORY

Arlott, J., *John Arlott's 100 Greatest Batsmen* (Queen Anne Press, 1986)

Bailey, T., *The Greatest of My Time* (Eyre & Spottiswoode, 1968)

Barker, R., *Innings of a Lifetime* (Collins, 1982)

Birley, D., *A Social History of English Cricket* (Aurum, 1999)

Brodhurst, R., ed, *The Bradman-Altham Letters* (Christopher Saunders Publishing, 2020)

Cardus, N., *Close of Play* (Collins, 1956)

Chalke, S., *Caught in the Memory: County Cricket in the 1960s* (Fairfield Books, 1999)

Chalke, S., *The Way it Was: Glimpses of English Cricket's Past* (Fairfield Books, 2008)

Cotter, G., *The Ashes Captains* (The Crowood Press, 1989)

Diehm, I., *Green Hills to the Gabba: The Story of Queensland Cricket* (Playright Publishing, 2000)

Eason, A., *The A-Z of Bradman* (Alan Eason, 2002)

Fingleton, J., *Fingleton on Cricket* (Collins, 1972)

Frith, D., *By His Own Hand: A Study of Cricket Suicides* (Stanley Paul, 1990)

Frith, D., *The Fast Men: A 200-Year Cavalcade of Speed Bowlers* (Allen & Unwin, 1975)

Frith, D., *The Slow Men* (Allen & Unwin, 1984)

Gibson, A., *The Cricket Captains of England* (The Pavilion Library, 1989)

Haigh, G., *On the Ashes* (Allen & Unwin, 2023)

Haigh, G., *The Summer Game* (The Text Publishing Company, 1999)

Hamilton, D., ed, *Sweet Summers: The Classic Cricket Writing of J.M. Kilburn* (Great Northern Books, 2008)

Lewis, T., *Double Century: The Story of MCC and Cricket* (Guild Publishing, 1987)

Marshall, M., *Gentlemen and Players: Conversations with Cricketers* (Grafton, 1987)

Pollard, J., *Australian Cricket: The Game and the Players* (Angus & Robertson, 1988)

Roberts, R., ed, *The Cricketer's Bedside Book* (B.T. Batsford, 1966)

Robinson, R. & Haigh, G., *On Top Down Under: Australia's Cricket Captains* (André Deutsch, 1997)

Ross, G., *The Testing Years: The Story of England's Rise to the Top in Post-war Cricket* (Stanley Paul, 1958)

Synge, A., *Sins of Omission: The Story of the Test Selectors 1899–1900* (Pelham Books, 1990)

Turbervill, H., *The Toughest Tour: The Ashes Away Series Since the War* (Aurum, 2010)

Whimpress, B. & Hart, N., *Adelaide Oval: Test Cricket 1884–1984* (Wakefield Press and the South Australian Cricket Association, 1984)

Whitehead, R., ed, *The Times on the Ashes* (The History Press, 2015)

Wilde, S., *The Tour: The Story of the England Cricket Team Overseas 1877–2023* (Simon & Schuster, 2023)

Williams, C., *Gentlemen & Players: The Death of Amateurism in Cricket* (Weidenfeld & Nicholson, 2012)

GENERAL HISTORY

Hennessey, P., *Having It So Good: Britain in the Fifties* (Allen Lane, 2006)
Kynaston, D., *Family Britain 1951 – 57* (Bloomsbury, 2009)
Todman, D., *Britain's War: Into Battle 1937 – 1941* (Penguin, 2017)

REFERENCE

Dexter, T., ed, *The Rothmans Book of Test Matches: England v Australia, 1946–63* (Arthur Barker, 1964)
Frindall, Bill, ed, *The Wisden Book of Test Cricket 1877-1977, sixth edition, volume one,* (John Wisden & Co, 2010)
Wisden Cricketers' Almanack, various editions

NEWSPAPERS AND MAGAZINES

Adelaide Advertiser, Birmingham Post, Brisbane Courier-Mail, Bristol Evening Post, Country Life, Daily Express, Daily Herald, Daily Mail, Daily Mirror, Daily Telegraph, Evening News, Evening Standard, Manchester Guardian, Mirror (Perth), Newcastle Sun, News Chronicle & Daily News, News of the World, People, Sun (Sydney), Sunday Pictorial, Sunday Times, Sydney Morning Herald, Sydney Sun-Herald, The Age, The Cricketer, The Times, Western Australian, Western Mail, Yorkshire Post

WEBSITES AND DATABASES

adb.anu.edu.au
amsr.contentdm.oclc.org
britishpathe.com
cricketarchive.com
cricketweb.net
oldebor.wordpress.com
oxforddnb.com
sportstats.com.au/bloghome
test-cricket-tours.co.uk
trove.nla.gov.au
who-only-cricket-know.uk
wikipedia.org
youtube.com

DVDS, VIDEOS AND RADIO PROGRAMMES

Captain of England: Len Hutton (BBC Radio programme)
Cricket Society online interview with Robin Brodhurst
England's Finest: On Tour With Hutton's Men (MCC, 2009)
The Poms Down Under 1954-5 (*Test Match Special* documentary)

ACKNOWLEDGEMENTS

In writing and researching *Victory in Australia*, I was blessed to have the assistance of a number of wonderful writers and editors, all of whom gave their time freely and generously. It was not just that their comments and opinions were extremely helpful, I was touched that they came to share my enthusiasm for exploring the adventures of Len Hutton and his players in the winter of 1954–55.

Stephen Chalke is rightly celebrated as the indefatigable writer and publisher of many of the best cricket books of the past 25 years. He made a key early contribution to the structure of this book, and from that moment proved to be the wisest of sounding boards and a never-ending source of good advice. He also loaned a boxful of relevant books from his own library, and photographs from his own books. The writer and editor John Stern, who gave me my first break as a cricket writer during his brilliant stewardship of *Wisden Cricket Monthly* magazine, was my other 'first-responder', and also made a number of invaluable suggestions and important edits.

Tim Hallissey offered the same shrewd and cool judgment he brought on a daily basis to his 15 years as sports editor of *The Times*. Steven Lynch, my colleague in compiling the obituaries section of *Wisden*, was once described to me as having the best knowledge of cricket in the world: I've never seen any reason to doubt that view. Steven was predictably eagle-eyed and saved me from a few blush-making errors. A vital perspective from outside cricket was provided by Mark Hodkinson, a friend for many years, and a writer I have always hugely admired. David Woodhouse, author of a brilliant book on Hutton's 1953–54 tour of the West Indies, read the manuscript in its entirety and raised some points others had missed, while offering some thoughtful suggestions. He also loaned me the scrapbook lovingly compiled by masseur Harold Dalton during the tour. Although he was busily engaged on an epic round-the-world trip, Walter Gammie, one of my oldest and dearest friends, also read sections of the book and offered his customary wisdom. Dean Rockett proved an inspired choice as fact-checker, and Lisa Hughes performed an exacting copy-edit.

This book would not have come to fruition without the expert guidance of my editor at Bloomsbury, Matt Lowing. My heartfelt thanks to him for running with the idea and also for suggesting borrowing the title of E. W. Swanton's booklet on the tour. Caroline Guillet at Bloomsbury worked tremendously hard at the production stage. Bloomsbury's design department are also deserving of praise for their work on the fabulous cover. Thanks also to my agent David Luxton and his team for their work in negotiating the contract.

'Follow the documents,' is the advice of the Beatles author and historian Mark Lewisohn, and I was incredibly fortunate that the MCC archive at Lord's contains a remarkable wealth of material on the 1954–55 tour. I spent many happy hours in the library at Lord's, combing through committee minutes, relishing the sometimes furious letters from members of the public and, perhaps best of all, reading the huge volume of correspondence between tour manager Geoffrey Howard and MCC officials at Lord's. Neil Robinson, head of heritage and collections, introduced me to the archive and I was wonderfully well looked after by the genial archive and library manager Alan Rees.

In trying to recreate a Test match that happened before extended TV coverage, it is vital to have detailed and reliable information on the granular detail on the progress of the game. Barry Valentine, who re-scored the 1953 and the 1954–55 Ashes for his book *When England Beat Australia*, generously shared his scoresheets. I also regularly consulted and cross-checked with the awesome sport stats website created by Charles Davis. Thanks to both these remarkable statisticians.

A number of others deserve my gratitude. Peter Baxter, former producer of *Test Match Special*, unearthed a documentary he had made about the tour in which some of the participants were interviewed. It also provided some precious nuggets of original commentary from the Australian Broadcasting Commission team. The Australian journalist Ashley Gray tried very hard to persuade Neil Harvey, the sole surviving participant in the series, to be interviewed, but in the end, sadly, his efforts were in vain.

Gideon Haigh, the greatest of cricket writers and a constant inspiration, pointed me in the direction of the photographic archive at the Bradman Museum in Bowral. The museum's Corydon Unwin helped me to source the pictures. Also in Australia, the writer and broadcaster Barry Nicholls provided background on Aboriginal communities in the 1950s. I would also like to thank the writer and historian David Frith for sharing his memories of watching the second Test at Sydney, to Micky Stewart for recalling what it was like to face Frank Tyson, to Daniel Lightman for sharing his interview with the Queensland player Ken Archer, and to Steve Fleming for unearthing Lord Kitchener's celebratory calypso.

Further thanks should be extended to Jonathan Colls of the Audit Bureau of Circulations, to Gavin Fuller, archivist at the *Daily Telegraph*, and to Nick Mays, who has the same role at *The Times*. Many other people performed small acts of kindness, among them Lawrence Booth, Nicholas Brookes, David Brown, Michael Bullen, Matthew Engel, Peter Hayter, Richard Hobson, Simon Lister, the Rev. Malcolm Lorimer, Leo McKinstry, Graham Morris, David Tossell and Kevin Wheeler.

Finally, but most importantly, this book would not have been possible without the love and support of my family. To my son Alex and my wife Marion, my heartfelt thanks.

INDEX